3rd edition

License Your Invention

by Attorney Richard Stim

Keeping Up-to-Date

To keep its books up-to-date, Nolo issues new printings and new editions periodically. New printings reflect minor legal changes and technical corrections. New editions contain major legal changes, major text additions or major reorganizations. To find out if a later printing or edition of any Nolo book is available, call Nolo at 510-549-1976 or check our website at www.nolo.com.

To stay current, follow the "Update" service at our website at www.nolo.com/lawstore/update/list.cfm. In another effort to help you use Nolo's latest materials, we offer a 35% discount off the purchase of the new edition of your Nolo book when you turn in the cover of an earlier edition. This book was last revised in July 2002.

Third Edition	JULY 2002
Editor	RICHARD STIM
Cover Design	SUSAN PUTNEY
Book Design	TERRI HEARSH
Proofreading	JOE SADUSKY
Index	NANCY BALL
Printing	BERTELSMANN PRINTERS, INC.

Stim, Richard
    License your invention / by Richard Stim.-- 3rd ed.
       p. cm.
    Includes index.
    ISBN 0-87337-857-1
    1. License agreements--United States--Popular Works. 2. Patent laws and legislation--United States--Popular Works. I. Title.

KF3145.Z9 S75 2002
346.7304'86--dc21
                                 2002029398

For information on bulk purchases or corporate premium sales, please contact the Special Sales Department. For academic sales or textbook adoptions, ask for Academic Sales. Call 800-955-4775 or write to Nolo at 950 Parker Street, Berkeley, CA 94710.

Dedication

This book is dedicated to A.I.B. (keep ideating, brother!).

About the Author

Rich Stim is a graduate of the University of San Francisco School of Law where he studied intellectual property law under J. Thomas McCarthy. He practices law in San Francisco, specializing in intellectual property and licensing, and is an adjunct professor at San Francisco State University. He is also the author of several books including *Music Law: How to Run Your Band's Business* (Nolo), *Intellectual Property: Patents, Trademarks & Copyrights* (West) and *Getting Permission: How to License and Clear Copyrighted Materials Online and Off* (Nolo).

Table of Contents

3 Ownership Issues for Inventor Employees

4 Joint Ownership of Your Invention

5 Licensing Agents and Representatives

6 Soliciting Potential Licensees

7 Protecting Confidential Information

8 The Key Elements of Your Agreement

9 Money: It Matters

10 Negotiating Your Agreement

11 Sample Agreement

12 Warranties, Indemnification and Proprietary Rights Provisions

13 Termination and Post-Termination

14 Boilerplate and Standard Provisions

15 Service Provisions

16 Handling the Licensee's Agreement

17 After You've Signed the Agreement

18 Help Beyond This Book

Appendices

A How to Use the CD-ROM

B Forms

Index

Introduction

How to Use This Book

A. What Is a License?

A license is an agreement that allows someone else to use or sell your invention for a limited period of time. In return you receive a one-time payment or continuing payments called royalties.

B. Who This Book Is For

This book is for inventors who want to license their inventions ("licensors"). Our primary goals in writing this book are to protect your invention, reduce your risks and save you money. By streamlining the licensing process and offering a layperson's guide to licensing deals, we hope you will be able to make a smooth transition from inventor to licensor.

C. Who This Book Is Not For

This book is not for people who wish to manufacture and market their inventions themselves (sometimes known as *venturers*). For example, if you invented a new mousetrap and created a company to make and sell your product, then this would not be the proper book for you.

D. How This Book Is Organized

This book is designed to guide you through the licensing process. There are basically four parts:

- **Ownership Rights.** Chapters 1 through 4 are geared at sorting out your ownership rights. You will learn how to determine your legal rights and how to protect your rights under patent, trade secret or copyright laws.
- **Soliciting Licensees.** Chapters 5 through 7 explain how to deal with licensing agents, how to find and solicit prospective licensees (those who wish to license your invention from you) and how to protect your trade secrets during this process.
- **The License Agreement.** Chapters 8 through 15 provide information about every aspect of the license agreement, from the key elements (including royalties, geographic boundaries

and length) to the boilerplate (or more secondary terms). These chapters further discuss how to keep information confidential, the negotiating process and drafting the licensing agreement yourself.

- **Dealing With Licensees.** Chapter 16 shows you how to deal with licensee changes to your agreement (or how to deal with the licensee's proposed agreement). Chapter 17 discusses issues that may arise after you sign the license agreement.

The following icon appears throughout this book:

 A legal or commonsense tip to help you understand or comply with legal requirements.

 An indication that you may be able to skip some material.

 A cross-reference to another section of this book, or a suggestion to consult another book or resource.

 This cautions you to slow down and consider potential problems.

E. Readers With a Specific Question

It's possible that you chose this book because you have a specific question. For example, you're unsure whether you or your employer has the right to license your invention. If you have a specific question, look for a chapter title that is relevant to your question and review the section headings in that chapter, or use the index in the back of the book for words or terms that are related to your question.

F. Sample Agreements and the CD-ROM

You will find sample agreements with detailed explanations throughout this book. Selected full-length agreements are located in the Appendix in the back of the book and on the attached CD-ROM. Instructions on how to use the CD-ROM are also located in the Appendix and in a read me file on the CD-ROM. ∎

1

Gearing Up to License Your Invention

Eureka! You've developed an invention and believe it has commercial potential. What's next? For many inventors, the best way to profit from an invention is to have someone else—usually a company that already specializes in similar products—develop, manufacture or market the invention. However, since an inventor holds ownership rights (sometimes called title) in an invention, another company cannot do these things unless the inventor gives permission. Broadly speaking, this permission is called a license.

This chapter will give you an overview of the licensing process and help you screen out potential problems that could hinder your ability to license your invention. Review this chapter if you answer "yes" to any of the following questions:

- Would you like an explanation of the difference between a license and an assignment?
- Do you want a brief description of the legal rights related to your invention?
- Have you signed any documents regarding your invention?
- Would you like a clearer understanding of who might own your invention besides yourself?
- Have you shown your invention to—or discussed it with—anyone?
- Do you want some help in keeping track of your business transactions?
- Would you like more information about how to assess what your invention may be worth in the marketplace?

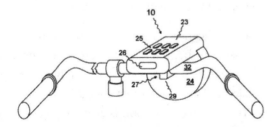

Voice Alert System for Use on Bicycles
NO. 6,317,036

What We Mean By an Invention

The term "invention" as used throughout this book refers to any innovation, device or process that can be commercially used or developed. Although the strongest form of protection for your invention is a patent, this book does not deal solely with patented or patentable inventions. Many inventions may not qualify for patent protection but can be protected under some other legal principle such as trade secret or copyright. If your invention has commercial potential and is protectible under some form of intellectual property law, you can use this book to help you license it to others. See Chapter 2 for an overview of the different ways your invention may be protected.

A. Licenses

A license is an agreement in which you let someone else commercially use or develop your invention for a period of time. In return, you receive money—either a one-time payment or continuing payments called royalties. Your power to make this kind of agreement is based on the premise that you control the right to make and sell your invention. Your right to make and sell your invention depends upon whether your invention is protected under intellectual property laws (see Chapter 2). If your invention cannot be protected under intellectual property laws, it is unlikely you will license your invention. Why? Because if your invention is not protected, anyone can make and sell it. Therefore, why should they pay you?

If your invention is protectible, you can stop others from making or selling it. In other words, a company can only make and sell a "protected" invention if you give them permission. By negotiating a license, a company can make, sell or use your invention without fear of a lawsuit. In other words, a license gives the company a right to do something it would otherwise be prohibited from doing.

You Are the Licensor, They Are the Licensee

For purposes of this book, you, as owner of the invention, will always be the *licensor* and the party receiving the license for your invention is called the *licensee*. In law, the person who is the source of the activity gets an "er" or "or" suffix (such as employer, lessor, discloser). The person who is the recipient of the activity gets an "ee." So, an employer provides employment, while a person who is employed is called an employee. Similarly a lessor leases property to a lessee and a discloser discloses information to a disclosee. Since you're licensing your invention, you're the licensor and the party receiving the license is the licensee.

---

1. When You License, You Are Leasing Your Legal Rights

A license for an invention is similar to a lease for a house or apartment. A tenant makes periodic payments to an owner of property for the right to use it. If the tenant fails to honor the terms of the lease or rental agreement, the owner can reclaim possession and make the tenant leave. Similarly, a licensee pays you royalties (similar to rent) for the right to manufacture, sell or use your invention for a period of time. If the licensee fails to pay you or otherwise breaches your agreement, the agreement may terminate and you can license your invention to someone else (provided the license is drafted properly).

It is also important to realize that you do not license your invention, per se. Rather, you license your legal rights to the invention. This distinction causes confusion for some inventors. Legal rights—patent, copyright, trademark, or trade secret rights—are what give you title or ownership of the invention, much like a deed to a house gives you title to the property. When you license your invention, what you are really transferring to the licensee are your legal rights such as your rights to manufacture, sell and use the invention. These legal rights will be explained in more detail in Chapter 2. However, it is beyond the scope of this book to assist you in securing intellectual property protection. In Chapter 18, Help Beyond This Book, we refer you to other resources for protecting intellectual property.

For now, keep in mind that the primary goals in licensing are to determine what legal rights you have, acquire the appropriate protection for those right and license those rights to others who can make you money.

2. Licenses Can Be Flexible

A license agreement can be drafted according to the specific needs of the licensor or licensee. For example, you can limit the license of your invention for a period of time, such as one year. You can limit the license to a certain area, such as Canada. You can even license your invention to more than one manufacturer at one time.

> **Example:** Joe invented a patented flotation device. Two companies are interested in it: a toy company and a company that makes boating products. Joe can sign two license agreements and earn royalties for both uses.

Because a license can be as flexible as the parties wish it to be, the task of drafting a license typically involves much more than simply agreeing to standardized language often found in legal agreements. That is what this book is all about—teaching you how to draft a license agreement that is just right for you. Drafting a license agreement is covered thoroughly in Chapter 8.

Forms of Intellectual Property

Since licensing basically involves lending your legal rights to someone else, it's crucial that you know precisely which legal rights are associated with your invention. These rights are sometimes referred to as proprietary rights or intellectual property rights. Below are examples of the common forms of intellectual property rights associated with inventions. Chapter 2 provides more information on intellectual property.

Utility patents protect inventions that are new and unique. When you have a utility patent, you can stop others from making, selling or using your invention. You must apply for and receive a patent from the federal government before you have patent rights in the United States.

Design patents protect decorative designs that are used on inventions. You must acquire a design patent from the federal government before you have design patent rights. As with utility patents, you can't stop illegal copying of your design until your design patent has been issued.

Trade secret law protects confidential information that gives you an advantage over competitors. You must treat the information with secrecy and disclose it only to those who agree to keep it secret. No registration is necessary, as registration would defeat the confidentiality requirement. A trade secret is sometimes an alternative or complement to patent protection, particularly for inventors who don't wish to make their methods or processes public. Trade secrets are also used as a form of protection during the period after an inventor has applied for a patent but before the patent is issued.

Copyright protects the artistic expression contained in writing, software, art, music and movies. Copyright does not protect functional objects such as clothing or furniture, only the artistic elements such as fabric designs or ornamental furniture legs. You get a copyright as soon as you create the work. You don't have to register your work to get copyright protection, but we advise doing so to strengthen your rights.

Trademark law is in a family of laws known as "unfair competition" (see below) and protects your right to exclusively use a name or symbol to signify your goods or services. Trademark law also protects certain designs or features of your goods, such as the uniquely shaped Absolut vodka bottle. You get trademark rights once you use the trademark in commerce (that is, once you sell the goods to consumers). You don't have to register your work to get trademark protection, but we advise doing so to strengthen your rights.

Unfair competition law protects the way you sell your product. There are a number of state and federal laws prohibiting business practices that unfairly hinder marketplace rivalries, such as making fraudulent (false) claims about a competitor's invention. Generally, however, with the exception of rules about trademarks, unfair competition does not pertain to the rights that you are licensing.

More information on the different forms of intellectual property protection is provided in Chapter 2.

3. Licenses Can Be Written or Oral

Most licenses involving technology are written. However, a license doesn't have to be written to be valid. An oral license may also be enforceable as long as it qualifies as a contract under general contract law principles. However, there are limits on oral agreements. For example, in most states, an oral agreement is only valid for one year. Because of these limitations and because it is usually more difficult to prove an oral agreement than one set out in writing, we strongly recommend against relying on an oral licensing agreement.

B. Assignments

Unlike a license, an assignment is a permanent transfer of ownership rights. When you assign your invention, you are the assignor and whoever purchases the rights is the assignee. An assignment is like the sale of a house, after which the seller no longer has any rights over the property. As the assignor, you may receive a lump sum payment or periodic royalty payments.

Even though they have different legal meanings, the terms assignment and license are sometimes used interchangeably. Indeed, these two types of agreements sometimes seem to have the exact same effect. This is true in the case of an unlimited exclusive license, in which a licensee obtains the sole right to market the invention for an unlimited period of time. Since in this situation the licensee is not keeping any rights that could be made the subject of another license, the license really has the same effect as an assignment. For more information on assignments, see Chapter 4.

Because the two terms may overlap, it's important to examine the specific conditions and obligations of each agreement rather than simply to rely on terms such as assignment and license.

C. The Licensing Process

Licensing is a union between the inventor (the licensor) and the company that licenses the right to manufacture or distribute your invention (the licensee). It begins with a meeting and disclosure period followed by a proposal and negotiation stage. If you agree on the major principles, a formal relationship is created. After entering into the agreement (often called executing the agreement), there is a continuing review by both parties called monitoring. If either party breaches (fails to honor) the agreement, the agreement may be terminated.

The following sections describe the various stages in the licensing process.

Should You Manufacture and Market Your Invention Instead of Licensing It?

Before considering licensing, it's important for an inventor to consider the two other basic options to licensing—assigning your rights or manufacturing and selling the invention by yourself. Although a license allows you to retain ownership of the invention, some inventors prefer to assign all rights in return for a large one-time payment. As for manufacturing and selling the invention yourself (referred to as a venture), most inventors do not have the funds or experience to create ventures or to market their own products. Manufacturing and marketing requires money, knowledge about the industry, connections with distributors and a lot of hard, hard work. In addition, many inventors cannot afford the significant expense of pursuing infringers. For this reason, most inventors choose licensing instead of ventures. However, if you are inclined to sell your invention on your own, we provide some resources for ventures in Chapter 18, Help Beyond This Book.

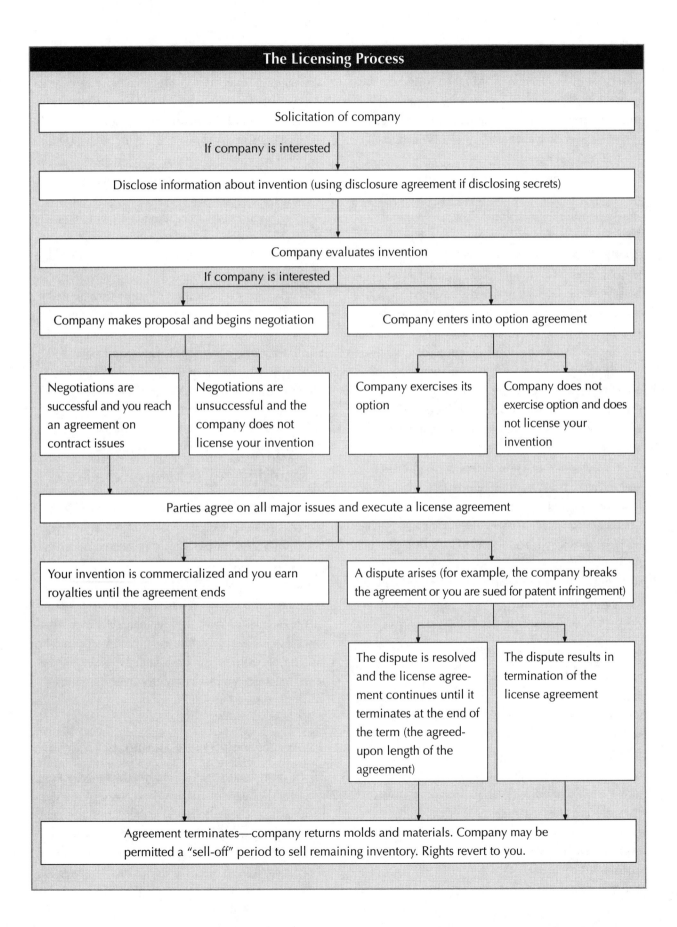

The Licensing Process

Solicitation of company

If company is interested

Disclose information about invention (using disclosure agreement if disclosing secrets)

Company evaluates invention

If company is interested

Company makes proposal and begins negotiation

Company enters into option agreement

Negotiations are successful and you reach an agreement on contract issues

Negotiations are unsuccessful and the company does not license your invention

Company exercises its option

Company does not exercise option and does not license your invention

Parties agree on all major issues and execute a license agreement

Your invention is commercialized and you earn royalties until the agreement ends

A dispute arises (for example, the company breaks the agreement or you are sued for patent infringement)

The dispute is resolved and the license agreement continues until it terminates at the end of the term (the agreed-upon length of the agreement)

The dispute results in termination of the license agreement

Agreement terminates—company returns molds and materials. Company may be permitted a "sell-off" period to sell remaining inventory. Rights revert to you.

1. Meet & Greet the Potential Licensee

The most difficult step you will face is finding a company to license your invention. For a shy, introverted inventor, meeting marketing people and displaying work at trade shows can be a jolting and frustrating experience.

Sometimes an inventor is so relieved to find a receptive company that she fails to properly evaluate the opportunity. Once you find a prospective licensee, you should thoroughly research it; this book will explain how. Every business opportunity is not a great opportunity. Sad as it may seem, you may be better off with no license at all than a license with a company that has a reputation for acting unethically. In addition, you must be careful during the disclosure process to properly protect confidential information. Disclosing your invention requires a balancing act: presenting the best aspects of your invention while protecting the confidential aspects of your work. We'll discuss confidentiality and disclosure in further detail in Chapter 7.

It is beyond the scope of this book to inspire you to make great sales pitches or presentations, although we will offer some tips and guidelines in Chapter 6. We will also help you locate appropriate trade magazines and trade shows at which you may find prospective licensees (see Chapter 6). And we'll help you identify and avoid scam marketing companies that will rip you off.

2. Negotiating the License

Negotiation skills are learned, not inherited. The simple rule is that the best approach to negotiating your licensing contract is to educate yourself and to set goals. Good negotiators are well-prepared and have a realistic knowledge of the marketplace. Chapter 6 provides information about researching industries and markets. Also important in any negotiation is flexibility, being willing to adapt your goals to match the situation. We will provide an overview of common negotiating strategies in Chapter 10.

3. Execution and Monitoring

The signing (execution) of the licensing agreement is usually accompanied by an advance payment and an exchange of information or technology. For example, upon executing a licensing agreement, an inventor may receive an advance payment and have to provide the specific methods of efficiently manufacturing the invention.

The execution of a licensing agreement is the climax, but not the end of the licensing process. It may also be the beginning of a services or consulting agreement between you and the licensee. For example, you may be hired to supervise the making of the initial molds or manufacturing prototypes. Service agreements are covered in Chapter 15. Plus, as a licensor you have to monitor your payments and the performance of the licensee. Chapter 17 offers information on post-signing activities.

D. Avoiding Conflicts Among Multiple Agreements

As an inventor, you may enter into various agreements, each of which may have an impact on your ability to license in the future. Before you license your invention, review your current signed commitments to make sure that none of them conflict with your ability to license. The easiest way to manage this review is to create and maintain a record of all signed documents. For the most part, you should be concerned with documents that affect your ownership, financial interest or control over the rights to your invention.

1. Agreements That Can Impact Licensing

When examining other agreements, first determine what kind of agreement it is. The name of the document will probably help you classify it (although titles are not always conclusive proof). If you are not sure of the type of document, the first or second paragraph often describes the document's purpose. If you are still not sure, try comparing the document's provisions with the provisions of the sample agreements in this book.

Below is a brief description of some common documents an inventor may execute and the effect they may have on the inventor's ability to license an invention.

a. Co-ownership or Joint Inventor Agreements

These agreements are executed between the owners —usually the creators—of an invention. They establish the rights and obligations of each party in respect to the invention.

Impact on Licensing: A co-ownership agreement may establish which owner has the right to enter into licensing agreements and may require a mutual decision when it's time to decide upon a licensee. See Chapter 4 for more information.

b. Corporate and Stock Agreements

Have you created a corporation to exploit your invention? Corporate agreements are executed as part of the state incorporation process. Stock agreements formalize sales of corporate stock to investors.

Impact on Licensing: Corporate and stock agreements establish who makes decisions about licensing or whether such decisions require a vote of the board of directors (the group that is elected by stockholders to make the important corporate decisions). See Chapter 4 for more information.

c. Employment Agreements

Employment agreements define your employment obligations and responsibilities.

Impact on Licensing: An employment agreement may limit your rights to inventions created during your employment. See Chapter 3 for more information.

d. Loan Agreements

A loan agreement is an agreement to lend money, services or supplies in exchange for a promise of repayment, usually with interest.

Impact on Licensing: If a loan agreement uses your legal rights to an invention as collateral to secure repayment of the loan, it may prevent you from licensing the invention. See Chapter 4 for more information.

e. Nondisclosure Agreements

A nondisclosure agreement is an agreement to keep confidential certain information identified in the agreement.

Impact on Licensing: An improperly drafted nondisclosure agreement may mean that you have lost the right to consider your invention a trade secret— which could, in turn, impact your ability to license the invention if the licensee considers trade secret protection an important part of the transaction. See Chapter 7 for more information.

f. Option Agreements

An option agreement gives one party the right to enter into a license (or other type of agreement) at a later date.

Impact on Licensing: An option agreement may establish terms to be used in a license, and may prevent you from licensing to anyone other than the option owner. See Chapter 10 for more information.

g. Evaluation Agreements

An evaluation agreement is a mixture of a nondisclosure and an option agreement. With an evaluation agreement, a company acquires the right to evaluate an invention and then, if they desire, to enter into a license agreement.

Impact on Licensing: An evaluation agreement with one company may prevent you from signing a licensing agreement with a different company. See Chapter 10 for more information.

h. Outsourcing or Manufacturing Agreements

An outsourcing or manufacturing agreement authorizes a company to manufacture—but not necessarily sell—goods embodying your invention.

Impact on Licensing: Your failure to include a confidentiality provision in an outsourcing or manufacturing agreement may result in the loss of trade secret rights which could have an impact on your ability to license. See Chapter 7 for more information.

i. Partnership Agreements

A partnership agreement is an agreement in which two or more persons join together in an enterprise. The partnership agreement establishes the contributions, liabilities and shares of profit for each contributing partner.

Impact on Licensing: Your partnership agreement may define which partner can execute a license, and it may require participation by all partners in the negotiation process. See Chapter 4.

j. Representation Agreements

A representation agreement (sometimes referred to as a rep agreement or an agency agreement) is an arrangement with an agent or representative who will attempt to license your invention for you. In return, an agent usually seeks a portion of the profits or royalties.

Impact on Licensing: A rep agreement may require you to pay the rep percentages for a license which the rep did not even negotiate. See Chapter 5 for more information.

2. Keeping Track of Agreements

After you identify your agreements, make sure you have copies for your records. Then list each agreement along with any appropriate dates for activity (for example, due dates for loan payments) on a worksheet (we provide a sample below). If you believe that one of these agreements will have an impact on your ability to license, it is important to identify these potential obstacles now, before the licensing process begins.

We suggest you use the following worksheet to keep track of each agreement. Some agreements terminate by a certain event or date. Some agreements can be renewed on a specific date. You should review your agreements for the relevant information and plug it in your worksheet. You should keep your worksheets and other important documents—including the copies of the agreements themselves—in a special notebook. We discuss recordkeeping in Section G below.

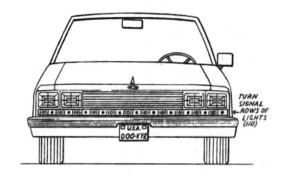

**Vehicle Direction Signal
No. 4,556,862**

Agreement Worksheet

Title of Agreement:_____

Category (circle one):

    co-ownership   corporate   employment   nondisclosure   evaluation

    option   outsourcing   loan or financial   representation   partnership

    other: _____

Date of Agreement: _____

Parties to Agreement: _____

_____

Is there a Termination Date?   Yes _____   No _____   If yes, list date: _____

Is there a Renewal Date?   Yes _____   No _____   If yes, list date: _____

Where is the agreement located or filed? _____

Ownership Notes: _____

_____

_____

_____

_____

_____

_____

_____

_____

_____

_____

_____

_____

_____

E. Challenges to Your Ownership

Is anyone likely to challenge your claim to ownership of your invention? Of course if someone has already asserted an ownership claim, then the answer to this question is yes. But even if there has been no actual assertion, an informal conversation may have alerted you to this possibility. The ownership issue may have been raised in several different contexts:

1. Someone you worked with believes that he or she is entitled to be considered one of the inventors.
2. Another inventor has already alerted you to his or her belief that your invention infringes a previous invention that is protected by a patent or some other intellectual property device.
3. You know about an active (in-force) patent which describes an invention very similar to yours.

1. Types of Ownership Challenges

The first type of claim ("I worked for/with you, or you worked for/with me, and I own part or all of that invention") usually occurs when a former employer, employee or co-worker claims rights to your invention. If you are not familiar with principles such as joint ownership, joint authorship, work for hire or shop right rules, then you should read Chapters 3 and 4.

The second and third types of potential challenges to your rights are based on a doctrine known as patent infringement. Patent infringement claims are usually brought by an inventor who believes your invention is the same as his (that is, "I created this invention first and you ripped me off"). Under patent law, an infringement may be exactly the same invention or it may be a similar or "equivalent" invention.

2. Dealing with Ownership Challenges

You may have difficulty licensing your invention in any of these situations. Since a potential licensee will want to make sure that you own the rights you are licensing, the agreement will inevitably contain a warranty clause which guarantees that you do, in fact, have the right to license. Many licensees will also insist on an indemnity clause, which basically holds you financially responsible for damages suffered by the licensee if your warranty proves false. If you don't have ownership rights or if those rights are challenged in a lawsuit, you may have to pay to defend yourself and the licensee.

What do you do if there is an ownership issue? You'll need to determine if the challenge is valid. Do you really own your invention to the extent you thought you did? If you don't, you will have to settle the dispute. If the challenge is bogus, you can disregard it. Either way, you should consult with an intellectual property attorney experienced in your type of intellectual property, because you will most likely need an expert legal opinion regarding the validity of the challenge. See Chapter 2 for more information about types of intellectual property.

When Others Infringe Your Invention

If you think that someone may have ripped off your invention, review your rights under intellectual property laws. You may not have been "ripped off" in a legal sense. If you are unsure, you will need to consult with an intellectual property attorney (see Chapter 18, Help Beyond This Book). If you have been ripped off, you must determine whether you can handle the dispute yourself or whether you need an attorney. Dealing with infringers is especially important if your licensing agreement requires you to defend the invention against thieves. See Chapter 2 for more information about intellectual property laws.

F. Disclosing Information About Your Invention

If you invented something new and exciting, then you have a natural desire to share your discovery. Unfortunately, sharing your invention without proper precautions may cost you your legal rights. That's because one method of protecting your invention is trade secret law. A trade secret is confidential information which gives you a competitive advantage over other inventors or their licensees. Trade secrets are valuable because they are not known to the public. Trade secret laws will protect your invention so long as you do not disclose information about it indiscriminately. Unrestricted disclosures about an invention protected by trade secret will usually terminate the protection.

Trade secret protection isn't a concern for all inventions, however. An invention that has received a patent does not need trade secret protection. Disclosures about a patented invention will not affect your patent rights. However, as explained below, if you have applied for a patent that has not yet been issued, the only protection you might have is trade secret protection. In that situation, you should not disclose confidential information about your invention. Finally, if you have trade secrets that complement the patent but are not part of the patent (for example, an efficient way to construct the invention), you must treat these with confidentiality, as well.

Summing up, there are four major concerns regarding disclosing information about your invention:

1. If you have not applied for a patent, the disclosure may trigger the time period in which a patent application can be filed (see Chapter 2);
2. A disclosure may affect your claim of trade secret rights;
3. A disclosure may affect your ability to compete because the information could become available to makers of similar or related inventions; and
4. A disclosure may affect your ability to contract because a company may not want to enter into an agreement if the information is available to competitors.

If you have made disclosures regarding your invention to anyone, you should determine how trade secret law might affect your situation. If you disclosed information about your invention in printed materials such as journals, financial agreements (such as loan documents) or advertisements, you will also need to determine if the timing or disclosure will impact your ability to obtain patent protection (see Chapter 2). If you entered into a disclosure or confidentiality agreement, you should compare its provisions with those in the sample agreements in Chapter 7.

Beware that your patent rights will be lost if you file your application more than one year after public disclosure of the invention. This may include publications in journals or even on the World Wide Web.

G. Keeping Your Records

There is a Chinese proverb that says the palest ink is better than the best memory. This is certainly true in law and science, where a written document is the best way to authenticate facts. Although agreements and scientific claims can be based upon oral conversations or implied by the actions of the parties, as a general rule: GET IT IN WRITING! The best legal and scientific protection is documentation. This rule is repeated throughout this book and should be immediately applied in the following ways.

1. Keep an Inventor's Notebook

Every inventor should keep a notebook documenting the creative process. This notebook is necessary to record the steps involved in creating the work and to deflect claims by others that they are the true inventors. If you seek a patent, or are sued by a patent holder, the notebook may assist you in proving the dates of your invention. It may also assist in your claims for tax deductions. To help you start and maintain your notebook, Nolo offers a guide for inventors, *The Inventor's Notebook,* by Fred Grissom and attorney David Pressman (see Chapter 18, Help Beyond This Book).

2. Use Disclosure Agreements

If someone wants to learn technical details about your invention, review Chapter 7 to determine if a written disclosure agreement or similar document is necessary. It probably is. Information about your invention should be disclosed only on a need-to-know basis and under a guarantee of secrecy. This includes disclosures to co-workers, contractors, suppliers and persons who evaluate your work.

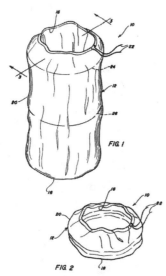

Disposable Standing Trash Bin
No. 6,315,143

3. Maintain a Business Notebook and Files

Poor recordkeeping is a roadblock to success. You must maintain a central depository such as a notebook or binder of files for all paperwork. Besides maintaining your signed agreements and other records, you should document business discussions, including phone calls and business-related conversations. Your file should have a section for contacts, a log of meetings and phone calls, a method of tracking money and a listing of business documents.

This is also a good place to store registration certificates or any proofs of ownership.

⚠️ For purposes of documenting phone conversations, it is not legal in some states (such as California) to record a telephone conversation without the consent of all parties to the conversation.

4. Insist on Written Agreements

If you are in a discussion regarding licensing, even if you are positive about the deal, you should preface your comments with a disclaimer such as, "This sounds fine, but I can't commit until I see a written agreement." Make it a part of your business vocabulary, and avoid taking actions that are contrary. For example, don't claim you need a written agreement and then subsequently permit someone to invest money or begin production of your invention without something in writing. Similarly, don't contract for design of a prototype or model without a signed contractor's or outsourcing agreement. Even a one-page signed summary of the contract terms is better than nothing at all. See Chapter 10 for information about Letters of Intent and contract summary sheets.

H. No False Hopes! Reviewing Your Invention's Commercial Potential

For many inventors, the process of pitching an invention is heartbreaking and fruitless. After thousands of hours of invention and hundreds more attempting to license it, an inventor may sadly conclude that there is no market for this product.

One way to avoid this problem is to make an effort to determine how marketable your product is before attempting licensing or even beginning the patent process. Two or three out of every 100 new inventions succeed in the marketplace. What good is investing thousands of dollars and weeks of work into the patent or licensing process without some expectation of a return? Although there is no foolproof method of determining commercial potential, there are a few ways to figure your odds of success and to act accordingly.

1. The SBA's Four Tests for Commercial Potential

The U.S. Small Business Administration (SBA) poses four tests for an invention to pass to show that it will have commercial potential. These are:

- **Is it original, or has someone else already come up with it?** You may be surprised to learn that someone else has already thought up something similar to your invention and that the invention has already been rejected in the marketplace. You can get a rough notion of whether your invention has already been tried by checking trade directories or Internet services, or by performing an abstract search of the Patent and Trademark Office at its website—all of which are free and explained in Chapter 18.
- **Is there a likely distributor?** As you will learn (or may have already learned), very large companies are generally not interested in unsolicited ideas from outsiders. It is difficult to penetrate these companies and convince them to take a chance on manufacturing and distributing your product. Smaller or mid-sized companies may be more receptive, but they will still view your invention from a bottom-line mentality. Their approach will be, "What's the cost to make it, and what is the likely return?" If the profit margin is small, it will be difficult to convince anyone to take a chance. As an alternative, you may consider forming your own company and manufacturing your invention yourself. This tactic—known as creating a venture—is risky (see sidebar in Section C).
- **Is it a money maker?** This is the question that is most difficult to answer. Below we suggest some methods of testing the marketability of your invention.

- **Does your invention qualify for legal protection?** Unless you have some legally protectible invention, you won't be able to stop others from copying it. Without legal protection you can rely only on the forces of strong marketing to gain a position in the marketplace.

2. The Innovation Center Factors for Commercial Potential

In the 1970s, the University of Oregon's Innovation Center developed a list of 33 areas and factors that should be considered when determining the commercial potential of an invention. These factors are:

- **Legality:** will there be legal problems commercializing your invention?
- **Safety:** are there safety issues (for example, a potential for consumer injuries) that may scare away licensing companies?
- **Environmental impact:** will your invention have a positive or negative effect on the environment, and how will this affect the commercial potential?
- **Societal impact:** will your invention have a positive or negative effect on society, and how will this affect the commercial potential?
- **Potential market:** who will buy your invention?
- **Product life cycle:** does your invention's usefulness diminish over time?
- **Usage learning:** how long does it take to learn how to use your invention?
- **Product visibility:** will your product have a distinctiveness so as to stand out in the marketplace?
- **Service:** will your product provide a valuable service?
- **Durability:** how sturdy is your invention? Will it require frequent maintenance?
- **New competition:** what is the likelihood of new competitors appearing once your invention is commercialized?
- **Functional feasibility:** how workable are the functional aspects of your invention?

- **Production feasibility:** how practicable is it to produce your invention for sale?
- **Stability of demand:** will the demand for your invention die off?
- **Consumer/user compatibility:** will consumers find that your invention is compatible with their needs or lifestyle?
- **Marketing research:** what does marketing research indicate?
- **Distribution:** how can your invention reach consumers? What types of distribution are available?
- **Perceived function:** what do you perceive as the invention's primary function? Will consumers perceive this as its function as well?
- **Existing competition:** what competition exists now?
- **Potential sales:** have you any way of estimating the potential sales?
- **Development status:** in what stage of development is your invention?
- **Investment costs:** what type of startup expenses do you anticipate in order to manufacture the device?
- **Trend of demand:** what do consumer trends indicate for the demand for your invention?
- **Product line potential:** is there a potential to expand your invention into a line of products?
- **Need:** is there a need for your invention?
- **Promotion:** what type of promotion is needed to sell your invention?
- **Appearance:** does your invention's appearance add to its commercial appeal?
- **Price:** is your invention affordable to the relevant market?
- **Protection:** what forms of legal protection are available for your invention?
- **Payback period:** how long will it take to receive a payback on your invention?
- **Profitability:** what is the margin between the cost and the sale price?

- **Product interdependence:** is your invention dependent on or related to another device or product?
- **Research and development:** is further research and development necessary before you sell the invention?

It may be difficult for you to assess each factor, particularly at the beginning of the invention process. In addition, the importance of each factor may vary. However, it becomes obvious when you view all of the factors cumulatively that the brilliance of your invention may pale under the light of commercial scrutiny. For example, an invention that has fluctuating demand, an unfeasible production system and a slow payback period will be very difficult to license.

3. The Pressman Factors for Commercial Potential

In his book *Patent It Yourself* (Nolo), attorney David Pressman provides excellent explanations for 55 positive and negative factors which can help you determine whether your invention has commercial potential—in other words, whether someone will be interested in licensing or buying your invention.

One factor is an easy starting point: cost. How much will it cost to make your invention? How much will the parts cost? How much will the assembly of the parts cost? How much will the packaging cost?

Other factors that may be equally important include:

- **Competition:** are opposing products firmly entrenched? Is the field crowded with competition? Is the market too small to merit the promotional effort?
- **Ease of use:** how easy is it to obtain results from your device?
- **Demand:** is there a need for your device?

As to the final factor—demand—you may wish to pursue your own research with family and friends, as described below.

The Bag of Parts Analysis

One successful toy representative explained that when presented with a prospective toy idea, the first thing he does is isolate the parts and imagine the parts were in a bag. How much would this bag of parts cost? He then multiplies the cost of the parts by five to get an idea of the retail price (referred to as the "price point"). Finally he compares the potential retail price with the competition. If the price point is above the range of competing toy items, the rep will not handle the toy. No matter how brilliant the toy idea, the rep believes that it will be too difficult to convince companies and stores to handle an item that is not priced competitively. The same is true for most industries. The buying public is price conscious and will forego a brilliant invention if its price is prohibitive.

4. Testing the Waters Yourself

One of the simplest methods of determining marketability is to conduct your own personal market research. In his book *Patent It Yourself,* Mr. Pressman provides a methodology for performing focus group research. This is a system in which you present your invention to groups of people and get their responses. Conducting such a market survey may reveal whether potential consumers will have any interest in the device.

This type of research requires organization. You will need to prepare your presentation. If you don't have a prototype, you'll need to find some way of showing or describing your creation so that the viewers can evaluate it. You will also need to pinpoint the right questions to ask (for example, Would you buy it? What is the most you would pay?) and to be able to compile the responses. Even if the research convinces you not to proceed, this method is excellent practice for making presentations to licensees or potential business partners.

Since you might be disclosing certain information that should be maintained as a trade secret, you may need to take precautions. Rather than have each guest sign a nondisclosure agreement (an unfriendly method of getting opinions), Mr. Pressman suggests a log book or a page in the inventor's notebook that evaluators can sign which states something such as:

The undersigned have seen and understood Joan Smith's confidential invention known as [insert the name of your invention— for example, "the Purple Plunger"] *on the dates indicated below.*

Although this is not as protective as a disclosure agreement, it puts the evaluator on notice that the invention is confidential.

Testing Your Idea on Friends or Family. Using friends or family for opinions can create uncomfortable situations. You may be offended by their comments. They may be hesitant to tell you the truth. Here are four tips to help deal with this issue:

- Create an atmosphere where your viewers are comfortable expressing their opinions.
- Avoid taking criticism personally. It's hard, but it will help you in business.
- Do not interrupt or argue when others are making criticisms.
- Don't disclose your invention to someone if you don't trust them.

5. Getting an Expert Opinion

The opinions of a test group may be helpful, but they may not be sufficient. Perhaps they are not the intended consumers of the item, or perhaps they lack the proper industry perspective to determine potential success. You may need an expert opinion.

Who counts as an expert? Generally, anyone involved in the chain of distribution is an expert to a certain degree, from inventor to manufacturer to supplier to distributor to salesperson to consumer. If you have an auto accessories product, for example, you might solicit the opinion of a mechanic, a driver, the owner of an accessories store or even a gas station attendant. Being an expert doesn't require a college education, only experience, knowledge or expertise in the appropriate marketplace.

Local inventor groups may provide expert assistance for evaluation, or they may lead you to organizations that assess marketability. Objective evaluations are performed by some companies, often for a fee. For more information, check the resources in Chapter 18, Help Beyond This Book.

Note: You will need a prototype (or some model or mock-up) of your invention in order to obtain an expert evaluation. For information about prototypes and presentations, see Chapter 6.

⚠ Beware of Scam Invention Marketing Firms!

If you have contacted an invention marketing firm and their so-called experts told you that your invention will be a success and sell millions, then you're in trouble! Hopefully you haven't paid any money for this opinion. If you have, you should not pay any more. Although there are legitimate companies that will evaluate your product's commercial potential, the majority of the invention marketing firms are scam operations. If you are not sure what an invention marketing firm is, or if you are considering making a payment to a company that proposes to help you patent your invention or get you a licensing deal, review Chapter 5 before proceeding.

6. What If There Is No Commercial Potential?

Trying to market a new product is like gambling, and as in any game of chance, you have to know when to quit. This may be the most difficult decision for an inventor to face. Because of this, you must have a realistic view and avoid the false hopes that come with the excitement of inventing. It is important to remember that the invention only embodies one aspect of your creative ability and if you were able to create one invention, there is more intellectual property in your brain waiting to be mined. Don't be discouraged! You can still achieve your goal of commercial success, but perhaps with a different invention. Remember: It is the ability to invent, not the invention itself, that is rewarded. ■

Intellectual Property Protection

ntellectual property includes the legal rights associated with patents, trade secrets, trademarks and copyrights. Each type of intellectual property gives you certain rights. For example, if a patent is issued for your invention, you have the exclusive right to make, use and sell the invention. If the name of your invention qualifies as a trademark, you have the exclusive right to use the name on certain products. It is these rights that are the subject of a license: When you license your invention, you are actually licensing your rights to it under intellectual property laws.

Since licensing your invention basically involves a transfer of your rights to someone else, it should be clear that you cannot license your invention until you know what intellectual property rights you have. Ideally, by now you already know what type of intellectual property protection your invention has or can get. If you haven't already figured this out, you'll need to do so before proceeding with the licensing process.

➡️ If you already own a patent for your invention or if you understand the type of intellectual property that you own in your invention, you can skip this chapter and go to Chapter 3, which discusses ownership rights.

It's beyond the scope of this book to cover all the aspects of obtaining intellectual property protection for your invention, but this chapter will point you in the right direction. We'll give you the basics of what types of intellectual property are available and what they provide. For more information on intellectual property protection, including other books on intellectual property and contact information for the U.S. Patent and Trademark Office and the Copyright Office, read Chapter 18, Help Beyond This Book.

Unfortunately, obtaining intellectual property protection is a little like getting a bank loan: some inventions qualify and some don't. Since legal protection can enhance the value of your invention, we suggest you evaluate every aspect of your creation in order to acquire the broadest possible protection.

The Public Domain

When an invention, artwork or a symbol used on a product is not protected by intellectual property law, it is considered to be in the public domain. A work that is in the public domain is free for all to use and may be copied. Inventions that are not protected by intellectual property laws are in the public domain.

A. General Rules for Legal Protection of Inventions

A basic rule of intellectual property law is that various features of the same invention may be protected by different types of intellectual property. In general:

- The *functional* features of your invention (how it works and what it does) may be protectible under:
  - utility patent laws
  - trade secret laws.
- The *nonfunctional* features (the decorative appearance or packaging) may be protectible under:
  - trademark laws
  - design patent laws
  - copyright laws.

1. Functional vs. Nonfunctional

Intellectual property rights are often divided between functional elements (protected by utility patents and trade secrets) and nonfunctional elements (protected by trademarks, copyrights and design patents). How can you determine if a feature is functional or nonfunctional? Ask the question: "Does this feature make the invention work better or is it done primarily for aesthetic reasons?"

For example, a unique V-shape of an electric guitar is not necessary for the guitar to function. It is primarily a decorative or nonfunctional element. Similarly, the unique shape of a maple syrup bottle is not necessary for the bottle to hold liquid; it is primarily aesthetic and nonfunctional because it serves to distinguish the product's appearance. On the other hand, a uniquely shaped hook used on a hanger could be primarily functional if it prevented the hanger from snagging on clothing.

2. The Component Approach

Since intellectual property protection overlaps, it can be tricky to determine the type of intellectual property that is suitable for your invention. We suggest taking the approach of viewing your product in terms of its components. One way to do this is to separate the functional and nonfunctional features of your invention.

> EXAMPLE: The "Buz" device from the Iomega corporation allows Macintosh computer owners to plug many devices (such as camcorders, VCRs and CD players) into a computer and record sounds and pictures. The device has two parts, an internal board with chips that is installed in the computer and an external device nicknamed "BOB" (for "break out box") into which the user inserts cords. BOB is purple and has a playful shape, a little like a clam shell. Imprinted on the shell is the Iomega logo (an eye with eyelashes) and the word "buz." The functional components of "Buz" are the chip board and the mechanism that holds cords inside the external device. The nonfunctional components are the name, "Buz," the Iomega logo and BOB's distinctive shape and color.

Once you've broken down your invention into components, categorize which laws protect which components. For example, is your product shape protectible under design patent law? Once you've determined which types of intellectual property apply to the various components of your invention, pursue the legal protection for each component.

> EXAMPLE: Jay Sorensen was a real estate broker when he was accidentally burned by a cup of takeout coffee. Instead of suing the store for the coffee burn, Mr. Sorensen invented the Java Jacket: a cup holder assembled from pressed paper pulp. Unlike other coffee cup holders, the Java Jacket is manufactured in a flat sheet and the user assembles it by interlocking the ends and slipping the coffee cup into it. The Java Jacket is a functional device that prevents coffee drinkers from being burned. Since the device is functional, Mr. Sorensen applied for and received a utility patent (5,425,497) for his creation. One nonfunctional feature of the Java Jacket is also protectible—its name. The term "Java Jacket" meets the standards for federal trademark registration. Mr. Sorenson registered it as a federal trademark in 1995 (serial #74-553168).

B. Utility Patents

For purposes of invention licensing, a utility patent is the *strongest* protection available. If you can obtain a patent for your invention *and* your invention has commercial potential, then you will be in the best position for licensing it.

A utility patent is a federal grant to an inventor who has created a new and useful invention. It allows the inventor the exclusive right to make, use and sell his invention—and the right to prevent others from doing so with a similar (or infringing) invention. Attorney David Pressman, in his book *Patent It Yourself*, refers to the utility patent as a "hunting license." It gives the inventor the right to hunt infringers and obtain damages and other legal remedies.

A utility patent is obtained by filing a patent application with the U.S. Patent and Trademark Office (PTO), meeting the standards of that agency's examiners and paying the appropriate filing, issuance and maintenance fees. The types of inventions that may qualify for a utility patent, the standards by which they are judged and other details on the utility patent process are discussed below.

1. Types of Inventions Qualifying for a Utility Patent

A utility patent can be issued for any new and useful:

- process—a method of accomplishing a result through a series of steps, for example, a process for sterilizing surgical equipment.
- machine—a device that accomplishes a result by the interaction of its parts, for example, a gear shift in a rowing machine.
- article of manufacture—a single object without movable parts such as a pencil or a garden rake, or an object with movable parts that are incidental such as a folding chair or an ironing board.
- composition of matter—any combination of chemical or other materials, for example, Teflon or WD-40.
- improvement on an already-existing invention —for example, an improvement upon a household plunger. Note, however, if the underlying invention is still protected under patent law you will not be able to make, sell or use it unless you have authorization from the patent owner.

These categories are interpreted very broadly, and it is possible that your invention may overlap various classes.

2. Useful, Novel and Nonobvious

In order to qualify for a utility patent, your invention must also be: 1) useful, 2) novel and 3) nonobvious. These three standards are the basis of utility patent protection.

a. Usefulness

An invention must have a use or purpose and it must work (that is, be capable of performing its intended purpose). The Patent and Trademark Office may reject an application if the use has not been established or if the only use would be illegal or deceptive. For example, an invention to counterfeit one-hundred-dollar bills would not be eligible for patent protection unless the inventor could demonstrate some alternative legal use of the device.

b. Novelty

To be novel, an invention must differ in some way from the publicly known or existing knowledge in the field of the invention. The existing knowledge in the field is referred to as *prior art* (see sidebar, What is Prior Art?, below). A patent will not be issued if the invention was known or used by others in this country, or patented or described in a printed publication in this or a foreign country, before the date of invention. In addition, the Patent and Trademark Office will not consider an invention to be novel if the application for the patent is made more

---

Myth of Intellectual Property: The First Person to Create Something Always Acquires Protection

Being the first to create something does not always entitle you to protection. Only in patent law (and only in the United States) is the first to invent entitled to superior rights. Furthermore, these rights can be lost to a later inventor if the first inventor fails to be diligent in pursuing a patent or to build and test the invention (called reducing the invention to practice). Don't presume that because you were the first to create something that you automatically have priority over other inventors.

than one year after sale, public disclosure, use or offer of sale in the United States, or if it is patented anywhere in the world. *In other words, you have one year from the first sale or public disclosure to file your patent application!* This is known as the one-year rule or on-sale bar.

What is Prior Art?

Prior art is the existing technical information against which your invention is judged. That is, in order to determine if your invention is novel and nonobvious enough to acquire patent protection, the patent examiner looks at the existing information related to your invention. If the prior art demonstrates that your invention was not novel or that your invention was obvious, the patent will not be issued. The patent examiner (or federal courts) will consider the following types of information as prior art:

- anything in public use or on sale in the U.S. more than one year before the filing date of the patent application at issue
- anything that was publicly known or used by others in this country before the invention at hand was conceived
- anything that was made or built in this country by another person before the invention at hand was conceived
- prior patents that issued more than one year before the filing date of the patent or anytime before the date the inventor conceived of the invention at hand
- prior publications having a publication date more than one year before the filing date of the patent or anytime before the inventor conceived of the invention at hand, or
- U.S. patents that have a filing date prior to the date when the invention at hand was conceived.

c. Nonobviousness

All inventions must meet a standard of nonobviousness, which is an inquiry into whether persons working in the field of the invention would consider the invention unexpected and surprising (nonobvious), rather than evident or apparent (that is, obvious). So many inventions—the safety pin, the ironing board, the sewing machine, the collapsible tube and the cylinder lock—all seem obvious now, but they weren't when they were invented. This is one of the paradoxes of great inventions: once created they seem obvious.

In addition to being unexpected, other factors that bear on whether an invention is nonobvious are: 1) whether the invention has enjoyed commercial success; 2) whether there has been a need in the industry for the invention; 3) whether others have tried but failed to achieve the same result; 4) whether the inventor did what others said could not be done; 5) whether others have copied the invention; and 6) whether the invention has been praised by others in the field.

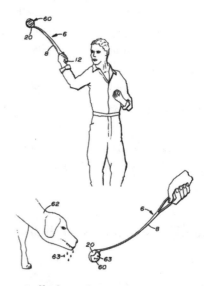

Ball ThrowingApparatus
No. 6,076,829

What Are Patent Claims?

As mentioned above, a utility patent grants you the right to stop others from making, selling or using your invention during the term of the patent. The extent of these rights depends largely upon the scope and boundaries of your invention. Patent claims—which essentially define the scope of your invention—are the heart of your invention and what makes it attractive to licensees. These claims are located in your patent application. The claims define the boundaries of the invention in the same way that a deed establishes the boundaries of real property. Drafting patent claims is a specialized skill (as you will no doubt see from the example claim for a Toy Glider Airplane below). It often, but not always, requires the expertise of a patent attorney. For more information about drafting patent claims, see the patent resources in Chapter 18, Help Beyond This Book.

EXAMPLE: Patent claims for a toy glider airplane: a model airplane or toy glider having a wing adapted to be assembled with a complex three-dimensional folded fuselage constructed of semi-rigid scorable and foldable material, said fuselage having generally symmetrical left and right half portions joined along less than the length of said fuselage, said fuselage in unassembled unfolded condition being generally V-shaped, said folded fuselage being attached to said wing via elastic band.

3. Deadlines and Length of Patent Protection (Patent Term)

Under U.S. patent law, the "first to invent" is entitled to superior rights, whereas throughout the rest of the world, the first inventor to file a patent application (or "first to file") is granted protection, regardless of who was first to create the invention.

For U.S. patents filed before or on June 7, 1995, the patent lasts for 17 years from the date the patent is issued, provided that fees necessary to keep the patent in force (maintenance fees) are paid. For patent applications filed after June 7, 1995, the patent lasts 20 years from the date of filing.

Under certain circumstances, the patent period may be extended if the commercial marketing of the product is delayed by government regulations or review. For example, the patent term for certain human and animal drugs may be extended for up to five years to compensate for lengthy government safety tests. In an attempt to guarantee at least 17 years of patent protection, Congress amended the patent laws in 1999 requiring the PTO to issue a patent within three years after its actual filing date. Under this law, the term of a patent will be extended if the PTO failed to issue a patent within three years from filing due to its own delays. The term of the patent will not be extended, however, if the delay was due to the applicant filing a continuation application or "buying" a delay.

After the patent expires, the invention falls into the public domain (see sidebar on page 2/3).

4. Patent Pending

Regardless of the length of the patent term, patent rights do not actually begin until the patent is actually issued. Quite some time may pass between a patent application and the issuance of the patent. This period of time is known as the *pendency* or *patent pending* period. The owner of a patent cannot prevent any infringing activity that occurs during the pendency period unless it continues after the patent is issued.

EXAMPLE: A Utah inventor developed a can capable of dispensing food. The invention permitted snack foods to be sold in machines originally manufactured to sell only beverages. During the period when the patent was pending, a snack food company test marketed the same idea. The inventor was awarded a patent on

Dec. 28, 2002 and filed an infringement lawsuit against the snack food company on the same day. If the inventor's patent was infringed, he can prohibit future sales of the snack food company's device and retain profits resulting from any infringements after December 28, 2002.

There is one exception to this rule. Unless the inventor files a Nonpublication Request with the USPTO, a pending application will be published for the public to view 18 months after its earliest effective filing date. An applicant whose application is published may seek damages from the application's publication date, provided that a patent is later issued and provided that the infringer had actual notice of the published application. Note: A Nonpublication Request should only be filed if the inventor does not intend to seek foreign patent rights.

> EXAMPLE: Sally applied for a patent for a new type of fogless night-vision swimming goggles on January 1, 2001. Swimco, a swimming products company, manufactured an identical pair of goggles starting in January 2002. Sally sent Swimco a copy of the patent application after it was published in June 2002. The PTO issues Sally's patent in December 2002. Once the patent issues, Sally can sue to stop Swimco from further manufacturing its goggles and can claim Swimco's profits for sales after June 2002 (the date Swimco had constructive notice of Sally's published application).

5. The Patent Application Process

The process of procuring a patent is often referred to as "prosecution of the patent application." The patent prosecution process is beyond the scope of this book. However, if you wish to pursue a patent, *Patent It Yourself* by attorney David Pressman (available in print and software formats) is recommended for inventors. If you are not comfortable preparing your own application, you should contact a patent attorney. You can locate a patent attorney through your local bar association or in the Yellow Pages. (Chapter 18, Help Beyond This Book, offers information on finding and working with attorneys.) If you don't handle your own patent application, the entire process—including fees for searching the patent database, attorneys and filing—can cost thousands of dollars. The application process can last 18 months to three years (or longer). There are legal deadlines for filing patent applications. Failure to meet these deadlines may prevent you from obtaining patent protection.

Myth of Intellectual Property: The Government Will Enforce Intellectual Property Rights

Although some intellectual property laws provide for government enforcement, that type of government action is rarely taken. When it is, it is because a business has already investigated the claim on its own and has the political clout to convince the local U.S. Attorney or Customs Office to go after the infringers. In other words, the government will not pursue infringers on its own.

6. Conception and Reduction to Practice

Although it's beyond the scope of this book to explain patent procedure in depth, you should be aware of the principles known as conception and reduction to practice. When the U.S. government issues a patent, it is certifying that the inventor is the first person to 1) conceive of and 2) reduce to practice the invention. (See Section B3 above on the difference between the first-to-invent and the first-to-file rules.)

a. Conception

Conception of an invention is a mental process—you formulate and perceive a method of solving a problem or carrying out a result. It will take more than just saying so to prove that you conceived of the invention. Your conception must be proven by other means, such as inventor's notebooks that show your mental processes, that are dated and that are properly witnessed, as explained below.

b. Reduction to Practice

Reducing to practice means that you can demonstrate, either through your patent application, provisional patent application or a prototype, that your invention works for its intended purpose. In other words, conception is the mental part of inventing and reducing to practice is the physical embodiment—a sufficient demonstration that the invention works.

> EXAMPLE: You are bothered by the straps on your knapsack so you conceive of a method of inflating the straps—inserting a specially devised hand pump in each strap so that the user can easily pump up and deflate them. This is the conception. Reduction to practice occurs when you create a prototype or prepare a patent application or provisional patent application with drawings, diagrams or a detailed description that demonstrates that the inflatable straps work for the purpose you intended—reducing the stress on your shoulders.

c. Documenting Conception

To fully protect and secure your patent rights, conception of your invention should be documented. This can be done simply by preparing an inventor's notebook and having two witnesses sign that they have observed your statements and sketches. Information on keeping an inventor's notebook is provided in *The Inventor's Notebook,* by Fred Grissom and attorney David Pressman, available from Nolo.

7. The Disclosure Document Program

Conception of your invention can also be documented by filing an Invention Disclosure with the PTO. This filing under the Disclosure Document Program (DDP) is not a patent application and does not guarantee any patent rights. It serves to verify the conception (in the event that you have no witnesses).

A fee is required, and as a general rule, it is cheaper and just as reliable to avoid the Disclosure Document Program and rely instead on your inventor's notebook. In addition, the document disclosure is destroyed by the PTO two years after you file it. Therefore, if you intend to reference it in your patent application, you must file your patent application within two years of the document disclosure.

Do not be confused by this two-year period. It does not extend the one-year bar (discussed above). In other words, if you sell or disclose your invention to the public after filing under the DDP, you still only have *one* year from the date of sale or disclosure to file your patent application. Using the DDP is not considered a public disclosure. In the event that you wish to use the PTO's Disclosure Document Program, you can obtain the required forms and related information from the PTO (see Chapter 18 on Help Beyond This Book). Note: You cannot claim patent pending status solely on the basis of a DDP filing.

8. The Provisional Patent Application: Shortcut or Detour?

Before 1995, there were two ways to document reduction to practice: using a lab notebook to record the building and testing of the invention, or filing a patent application. On June 8, 1995 a new system went into effect that permits an inventor to file a Provisional Patent Application (PPA), an abbreviated patent application that can be used to establish a filing date. If a regular patent application is filed within one year of filing the PPA, the inventor can use the PPA's filing date for the purpose of deciding whether prior art is relevant and, in the event an interference exists, who is entitled to the patent. (Note: the PPA is not available for design patents.)

The PPA must contain a description of the invention and drawings if necessary to understand the description. The description of the invention must clearly explain how to make and use the invention. If there are several versions or modes of operation for the invention, the best mode or version must be disclosed. If the inventor wishes, claims, formal drawings and other elements of the regular patent application may be included but are not required.

The advantages of the PPA are that it costs hundreds of dollars less than filing a patent application, doesn't require witnesses, saves the expense of building and testing and the application is much simpler to complete. Also, if a PPA is filed, the inventor can publish, sell or show the invention to others without fear of theft or loss of any U.S. patent rights. That's because anyone who sees and steals the invention would have a later filing date, and the inventor would almost certainly be able to win any interference with the thief.

However, if the inventor doesn't file a regular patent application within a year of the PPA, the PPA is abandoned and will no longer provide a filing date for purposes of prior art or interferences. The PPA is also worthless if the inventor changes the invention so that it no longer fits its own description. The filing of a PPA can affect an inventor's foreign rights. As with a regular U.S. application, an inventor must pursue foreign patent applications within one year of the PPA's filing date.

> **EXAMPLE:** Sam has invented an expandable picture frame, a device made from a flexible plastic that can adjust to fit different sized snapshots. He files a PPA on July 1, 2000. On May 1, 2001, he files a regular patent application. His patent issues on January 10, 2002. If anyone

contests Sam's right to his invention, Sam will have proof that his invention predated any similar invention as of July 1, 2000. If Sam had waited more than a year after filing his PPA to file his regular patent application, he would not be able to claim the 2000 filing date.

A filing under the Disclosure Document Program is often used by scam marketing invention companies to mislead an inventor into believing that the company has filed a patent application. Neither the Disclosure Document Program nor the Provisional Patent Application will, by itself, result in the issuance of a U.S. patent. For more details on scam marketing, see Chapter 5.

9. The U.S. Patent and Trademark Office

The United States Patent and Trademark Office (PTO) is responsible for the federal registration of patents. The PTO is a division of the Department of Commerce, and correspondence should be mailed to the Commissioner of Patents, Washington, DC 20231. Rules and regulations for PTO activities are established in the Code of Federal Regulations (known as the CFR) and in special Patent and Trademark Office publications such as the *Manual of Patent Examining Procedure* (MPEP). For more information about the PTO, see Chapter 18, Help Beyond This Book.

10. What Should You Do If You Think You Have Something Patentable?

- Act promptly, especially if you have disclosed your invention or offered it for sale. Unlike other forms of intellectual property, there are time limits for filing for a patent after sale or disclosure. You will lose all rights if the application is not filed on time.

You Can License Before Receiving a Patent

If you proceed with the patent application process, you can license your invention before the patent is issued. Sometimes a licensee may condition the license upon the granting of the patent. That is, if the patent does not issue, the license is canceled or the royalties are reduced to reflect only the nonpatentable aspects that have been licensed. Some inventors prefer to wait for the issuance of the patent because they feel more secure with patent protection when disclosing and licensing the invention.

- Determine if the invention is novel. This usually entails a patent search. The search can be performed by the inventor, by a patent attorney or by a company or individual patent searcher who specializes in patent searching. Online patent searches can be done in a Patent and Trademark Depository Library (PTDL) as listed in the Appendix or by visiting websites such as www.uspto.gov or www.delphion.com that provide free information on patents issued since the mid-1970s. More information regarding patents can be located in the patent resources section in Chapter 18, Help Beyond This Book.
- If your invention is patentable and you are convinced that it has commercial potential (see Chapter 1), review the trade secret section below to determine if you would prefer to rely on trade secret protection.

C. Trade Secrets

A trade secret is any information which is used in your business and which gives you an advantage over competitors who do not know it or use it. In order to maintain ownership rights over a trade secret, you must treat the information with secrecy.

Any public disclosure will end trade secrecy status for the information, and anyone will be free to use it.

One test for determining if material may qualify as a trade secret is to ask whether your business would be damaged if a competitor acquired the information. For example, if you have devised a new method of testing the life of a light bulb, you would want to keep that information secret in order to have an edge on your competitors. Information that appears to give your business an advantage over competitors should be kept secret until you have determined how to protect it (by either trade secret or patent protection).

As the owner of a trade secret, you can prevent anyone who has obtained the secret by improper means from using it. "Improper means" refers to misappropriation, and generally occurs through theft by former employees, bribery (the thief pays someone in your company in order to get the secret), misrepresentation (the thief poses as someone else to get the secret) or breach of a promise not to disclose the information (someone such as an ex-employee promises not to disclose it but tells the secret anyway).

However, you cannot prevent someone from using the secret if they have acquired it by legitimate means such as reverse engineering or independent invention (see below).

1. Protection for Functional and Nonfunctional Features

We indicated in our rules of intellectual property above that trade secrets generally protect functional features of your invention. In other words, trade secrets usually protect secret features of your invention that make it perform unlike other inventions. For example, the secret lubricant that your company uses may make your gear shift superior to other gear shift inventions. It is this valuable trade secret aspect of your invention that may make it licensable.

However, trade secrets may also protect information that is nonfunctional. For example, if you have designed a new logo or name for your invention, that would be a trade secret. Once this new name or logo is used in commerce, however, or once your new design is shown to the public, it will lose its trade secrecy status.

2. Protection of Know-How

In addition to a patented invention, a licensee may also want to license your "know-how." Sometimes the term "know-how" is used as a synonym to refer to trade secrets. That is, the licensee may want to license both your patent and any related trade secrets.

However, know-how does not always refer to secret information. Know-how sometimes refers to a particular kind of technical knowledge that is needed to accomplish some task. For example, your know-how may be necessary to train the licensee's employees how to make or use your invention. Think of know-how as a combination of secret and non-secret information that has value because it is needed to commercialize your invention. Know-how can also be the subject of a separate services agreement. For example, the licensor wants you to train employees using your knowledge of the invention and the industry. As a general rule, you should assume know-how is protectable as a trade secret and treat it as such. To that extent, if you are disclosing know-how to a licensee's employees or contractors, use a disclosure agreement. See Chapter 7 for more information about disclosure agreements.

3. Patents and Trade Secrets: A Comparison

Some inventors choose to protect their inventions under trade secret law rather than under patent law. The cost of trade secret protection is minimal, and it does not involve a public disclosure program (such as used by the U.S. Patent Office). But there is a downside to choosing trade secret protection in that

you risk losing the secret through reverse engineering (see below). Therefore, inventors must carefully weigh the methods of protection they choose. Below, some of the differences between trade secrets and patents are outlined.

a. Stopping Infringers

In general, the protection afforded by a patent makes it easier to stop an infringer, because all that has to be proven is that the person or company is making, using or selling your invention or an equivalent invention. It is not necessary to prove the intent to infringe (although that may influence the amount of damages), and it is not necessary to prove how the person acquired the information. Many patent owners use their patents to earn more money stopping infringers than from selling the invention.

To stop an infringer of your trade secret, you must be able to demonstrate a) that you have treated the secret with confidentiality and b) that the infringer acquired the secret through improper means. If it can be proven that you disclosed the information without confidentiality—even to someone other than the infringer—or that the information was legitimately reverse engineered or independently developed, then you will not able to stop a competitor.

b. Length of Protection

Trade secret protection will last as long as the secret is kept confidential. Patent protection lasts a) for 17 years from the date the patent is issued, if the application was filed before or on June 7, 1995, and provided that maintenance fees are paid, or b) for 20 years from the date of filing if the application was filed after June 7, 1995, and the maintenance fees are paid.

c. Reverse Engineering and Independent Invention

For some inventors, the downside of trade secrets is that any competitor is free to use a trade secret if the secret has been obtained legitimately. In other words, if your competitor obtains your secret through a legitimate means as described below, then you will not be able to prevent the use of the information.

This principle is not true for patents. No matter how the competitor obtained information about your invention, the competitor is prohibited under patent law from making, using or selling your invention.

How can a competitor obtain your trade secret legitimately? The two most common methods of obtaining a secret legitimately are by a) reverse engineering and b) independent development of the technology.

i. Reverse Engineering

It is not a violation of trade secret law to disassemble and examine a product which is available to the public. For example, you may purchase Coca-Cola and analyze the chemical formula, which is protected by trade secret. You are free to manufacture a similar cola based on your analysis of ingredients (although trademark laws prohibit you from calling it a name similar to Coca-Cola).

Reverse engineering must be done legitimately. That is, the person doing the reverse engineering must obtain the invention rightfully. For example, you cannot reverse engineer from a stolen computer program. When defending against a claim of trade secret protection, it is not enough for an infringer to claim he could have reverse engineered the invention and obtained the same information. The infringer must have actually reverse engineered it.

ii. Independent Development—The Clean Room

If you independently develop an invention, you can use or sell it even if it is similar or identical to some-

one else's trade secret. For example, if you invent a unique method of sorting coins, you can use it even if it is identical to a method protected under trade secret law. This is not true for patented inventions (see above).

In order to demonstrate that you independently developed an invention or method, you should keep an inventor's notebook or similar documentation. For independent inventors or small companies, this method should work fine.

Larger companies, however, should take additional precautions. The most reliable means of demonstrating independent development is the use of a clean room technique. There are various forms of clean rooms, but all of them involve isolating certain engineers or designers and filtering information to them. These engineers or designers are usually given an objective (such as to create a software program which connects a telephone to a computer) and are then presented with publicly available materials, tools and documents. The progress of the development team is carefully monitored and documented and any requests for further information by the team are reviewed by a technical expert or legal monitor.

Myth of Intellectual Property: You Have to Be an Intellectual to Understand Intellectual Property Law

Don't be fooled by the term "intellectual property." Although some aspects of copyrights, trademarks, trade secrets and patents are complex, you don't need to be a lawyer or techie to understand the basic principles. Common sense and a rudimentary knowledge of the law, as explained in this chapter, will help you grasp the major concepts and determine whether you possess or should pursue patent rights, copyrights, trademark rights, trade secrets or a mix of the above.

⚠️ **The Effect of a Patent Application on Trade Secrecy.** Filing a patent application does not end trade secrecy protection. However, trade secrecy protection will be lost when the PTO publishes the application 18 months after the filing date. If the application is not published and the patent issues, trade secrecy protection will be lost because the patent will be published. If your patent application is rejected and has not been published, then you can still claim the protection of trade secret laws. Publication, not filing the patent, is what ends the trade secret protection.

Starting in December 2000, every pending application will be published for the public to view 18 months after its earliest effective filing date (or earlier if requested by the applicant). The application will not be published however, if, at the time of filing, the applicant files a Nonpublication Request stating that the application will not be filed abroad. If the applicant later files the application abroad, the applicant must notify the PTO within 45 days.

There is one advantage to early publication. An applicant whose application is published may obtain royalties from an infringer from the date of publication provided: (1) that a patent later issues; and (2) the infringer had actual notice of the published application. If an applicant is concerned that a patent will not issue and wishes to preserve trade secrecy rights in the invention, the applicant must withdraw the application in order to prevent publication within 18 months of the filing.

Electric Lamp
No. 223,898

Keeping Trade Secrecy for a Patented Invention

Although the issuance of a patent usually ends trade secret protection for an invention, there may be features of the invention that are not described in the application and could therefore still be trade secrets. For example, say Sam has developed a peanut butter dispenser. The dispenser uses a unique combination of a tube and pump technology. The pump technology is patentable. However, Sam has also devised a method of speeding the peanut butter flow by using a combination of vegetable oils in the peanut butter. This is a trade secret. Sam can license both the patent and the trade secret.

4. Managing Your Trade Secrets

As a rule, you cannot be passive as a trade secret owner. You must actively protect your secrets by taking reasonable steps to maintain secrecy.

a. Smaller Businesses/Independent Inventors

Smaller businesses or independent inventors need not be concerned with issues such as building security (see below) and should focus primarily on maintaining information in a secure location, stamping it with appropriate legends (that is, "Confidential" or "Secret") and using disclosure agreements, as described in Chapter 7. A disclosure agreement preserves secret information during disclosure.

b. Larger Businesses

The following precautions should be considered by larger businesses:

- Control access to the building. The entrance to the building should be secure and visitors or after-hours employees should sign in. The building should have a fence, an alarm or a guard system. Employees' access should be restricted in areas where confidential material is located. Employees should be reminded about dealing with trade secrets. File cabinets and desks with confidential information must be locked, and the business should implement a document control policy.

- Secure computers, copying devices and other devices should be in secure areas and users of machines should log their usage. A machine (such as a paper shredder) should be used to destroy confidential material.

- Use security systems for computer and telephone networks. Passwords should be required for access, and the passwords should be changed frequently.

- Use stamps and signs. The company should use stamps such as "Confidential Material" or "Restricted" on relevant documents, and signs should be posted at restricted access areas.

- Secure documents. All notebooks or other materials used in the development or maintenance of trade secrets should be properly documented, labeled and filed in the restricted access area and treated with confidentiality and secrecy.

D. Trademarks

Trademark law protects your right to exclusively use a name, logo or any device that identifies and distinguishes your invention. In addition to names and logos, trademark law can be used to protect trade dress and product configuration. Trade dress is the product's packaging—all the elements that give your invention's appearance an identifiable quality, such as the combination of color, geometric shapes, imagery and lettering on a pain reliever bottle. Product configuration refers to the shape or design of your invention, for example, a distinctive oval-shaped stapler. To acquire protection for trade dress or product configurations, you must demonstrate that your product design is nonfunctional (see

Section A1) and distinctive. Functional designs will not be protected under trademark.

1. You Must Have "Trade" to Have a Trademark

Trademark law is different from copyrights, patents and trade secrets because trademark protection is not based upon creating something. It is based on selling something that features your trademark. In other words, trademark rights do not occur until the public has been exposed to your invention and its trademark. If you never sell or advertise your invention, you will not have any trademark rights. The first day that you use your trademark in commerce is referred to as the "date of first use," and you acquire superior rights over later users.

2. Length of Protection

Generally, trademark protection begins once you use the mark in commerce (that is, when you begin selling or advertising your invention). You do not have to register your trademark to acquire this

Myth of Intellectual Property: Intellectual Property Rights Will Prevent Others From Copying

Intellectual property law is like a STOP sign on the street. People are supposed to stop, but not everybody does. One of the measures of a successful inventor is the inventor's ability to enforce his or her rights, a burdensome and expensive task. This is a brutal fact about intellectual property law: acquiring legal protection is meaningless if you can't afford to enforce your rights. This is also one of the reasons that some inventors prefer licensing, because the licensee usually has the bankroll to pursue infringers.

2/16   LICENSE YOUR INVENTION

trademark protection (although registration has many advantages, as explained below). Trademark protection lasts for as long as you continually use the mark in commerce. Many trademarks have survived for over a century (Coca-Cola and Kellogg's, for example). If you register your trademark, you must periodically renew the registration.

3. Federal Registration

If you use your mark in federally regulated commerce (for example, across state lines or foreign exports) you can register your mark with the federal government. Owners of registered marks can use the federal registration symbol—®—and the use of the symbol serves as notice of your claim to rights. Federal registration can also serve as the basis for filing a trademark application in certain foreign countries, and it creates a presumption that you have a right to national ownership of the mark.

However, federal registration will not always give you superior rights. In some cases a person who has not registered a mark may have superior rights in a geographic area over a person who later uses a similar mark and registers it. This is because trademark rights in the U.S. are based on first use, and not registration. The first to use the mark in commerce has superior rights. For example, if you sell an antitheft device called The Perpetrator through a national home shopping cable channel and a large national company later registers and sells a similar device with the same name, you would be able to petition the government to cancel the registration or litigate in court to stop the company even though they had a registration and you did not.

4. Intent-to-Use Registrations

There is one way to protect your trademark before using it in commerce. You can reserve a mark, provided that you have a good faith intent to use the mark in interstate commerce (or other types of

commerce regulated by the federal government) within six months. You can extend that period to three years by filing extensions. In order to reserve your mark, you must file an intent-to-use trademark application with the Assistant Commissioner of Trademarks at the PTO. If the mark is not used within the required time period, then the intent-to-use application has no value.

5. The Application Process

The application for a federal trademark registration can be done without the assistance of an attorney. *Trademark: Legal Care for Your Business & Product Name,* by Stephen Elias (Nolo), explains how to evaluate the strength or weakness of your proposed trademark and provides the information and forms required for filing an application for federal trademark registration. Copies of federal trademark application forms are also located in the publication "Basic Facts About Trademarks," which is available from the U.S. Department of Commerce, Patent & Trademark Office, Washington, DC 20231. Registration requirements and forms are also posted at the PTO website at www.uspto.gov. For more information, see Chapter 18, Help Beyond This Book.

If you only use your trademark within your state, you can register it with your state government. The forms and filing information can be obtained from your Secretary of State. Keep in mind, however, that if you plan to use your trademark on a website, your use will necessarily be national because your site is accessible worldwide. Thus, federal registration would be your best option.

E. Design Patents

Design patents protect the ornamental features of inventions. A design patent doesn't protect the manner in which an invention functions (that's protected by utility patents and trade secret laws); it protects the aesthetic appearance, such as the shape of a lamp or a telephone. Design patents do not protect two-dimensional surface ornamentation such as photographs or drawings (they're protected by copyright law, covered below).

As the owner of a design patent you have the right to exclude others from making, selling or using the design for the term of the design patent. Your patent protection is limited to the category of invention in which you have designed. For example, if you obtained a design patent for a trumpet-shaped hanging lamp, that would not enable you to stop someone from making a trumpet-shaped clock.

1. Standard for Obtaining a Design Patent

The requirements for a design patent are that it be new, original and ornamental. The requirement of ornamentality means that the design is not utilitarian or functional (see Section A1 on functionality and nonfunctionality). For example, the unique shape of a tennis racquet may not be protectible because the shape may affect how the racquet functions—that is, how well it works in the game of tennis. On the other hand, a telephone shaped like a shark (for use in law offices) would be protectible by a design patent because the function of the device (the ability to use the telephone) is not affected by the fact that it's shaped like a shark.

Myth of Intellectual Property: Legal Rights Equate With Commercial Success

Acquiring patent or other intellectual property rights does not create value. It only enhances or preserves the inherent value, if any, of your invention. Intellectual property protection is like title to land. It guarantees your rights to the property, but it doesn't guarantee the value of the property.

2. Deadlines and Length of Protection

You must file your design patent within a year of when you first commercialize or publish your design. The design patent lasts 14 years from the date of issuance.

3. Registration

Compared to a utility patent application, the design patent application is relatively simple. For more information on pursuing a design patent, review the resources in Chapter 18, Help Beyond This Book.

F. Copyright Law

Copyright law protects writing, music, artwork, computer programs, photographs and other forms of artistic expression. Under copyright law, the creator of an original work (known as the author) is granted the exclusive right to make copies and to prevent others from copying the work or creating a derivative work (a work that is derived from or based on the artist's protected work).

There may be nonfunctional features (see Section A1) of your invention that are protectible under copyright, such as its packaging, the accompanying literature, software programs used in it, artwork included on the invention or advertisements for the invention.

1. What Copyright Won't Protect

Copyright protection doesn't extend to ideas, only the manner in which an idea is expressed. The key to separating an unprotectible idea from a copyrightable expression is to examine the amount of detail in the work. A soft doll with a big puffy face, for example, is an idea. There are very few unique details. However, the Cabbage Patch dolls with their unique face, name and "adoption papers" contain many specific details and are a copyrightable expression.

Copyright law will not protect the functional features of your invention and will not generally protect names, titles, short phrases, blank forms, facts and any works within the public domain.

Unlike patent law, it does not matter who is the first to create a work of art. All that matters is that the work is original to the author.

2. Length of Protection

For most copyrighted works, protection generally extends for the life of the author plus 70 years. In other words, if you have a copyrighted work, protection continues for 70 years after your death, allowing your family (or other beneficiaries of your will) to reap financial rewards from the work. For works that are created by companies, the term may be 95 years from date of first publication or 120 years from creation, whichever is longer. The length of copyright protection also depends upon when the work was first published. Different rules apply for works distributed before 1978. For more information, review the copyright resources in Chapter 18, Help Beyond This Book.

G. Sorting Out Nonfunctional Features: Design Patents, Product Configurations & Copyright

It may seem like there is a great deal of overlap when it comes to the protection of product designs and shapes. Copyright, trademark and design patent protection all seem to offer the same forms of protection for nonfunctional designs. How do you determine which form of protection can be used to enforce your nonfunctional features? Below is an explanation of some of the differences.

1. Not All Designs May Qualify for All Forms of Protection

Neither copyright, trademark or design patents protects functional works. They only protect the ornamentation or design of the object. However, not all designs qualify for copyright, trademark *and* design patent protection.

> **EXAMPLE:** Consider the external appearance of a computer monitor. Imagine that designers at Apple Computer created a monitor that was housed within an apple-shaped case. The concept of an apple shaped monitor may be protectible under a design patent if it is a novel, nonobvious and ornamental industrial design. The design shape of the apple may also be protectible under a product configuration trademark provided that it is unusual and memorable, conceptually separable from the monitor and likely to inform people that it is a product of the Apple Computer company. However, it would be difficult to protect the apple monitor design under copyright law because copyright protection generally does not extend to common shapes, colors or items found in nature. Unless the monitor had some unusual or trivial creative feature, it would probably not be protectible under copyright law.

2. Not All Forms of Design Protection Cost the Same

The cost and ease of acquiring protection may be an important factor in determining your method of protecting a product design. Consider the differences.

- Design patent protection requires a filing procedure often costing a few hundred dollars or more. Registration can take one or two years to acquire, and protection does not begin until the patent is issued. Protection lasts for 14 years.

- Trademark protection is inexpensive and begins once the item is sold to the public and achieves distinction (either by being very unique or through extensive sales and advertising). Protection is perpetual as long as the shape is continuously used in commerce. If you choose to file a federal trademark registration without a lawyer, the cost is relatively inexpensive (under $400).

- Copyright protection exists once you create a design. There is no registration requirement (unless you want to pursue infringers). Even if you choose to file a copyright registration, the application fee is only $30. In addition, the protection for copyright lasts the life of the author plus 70 years (or 95 to 120 years for a work made for hire).

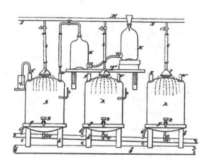

Brewing Beer and Ale
No. 135,245

3. Stopping Infringers: Trademarks, Copyrights and Design Patents

The different forms of protecting your product design also have different implications for stopping infringers.

- In order to stop an infringer under design patent law, you need only prove that you have a valid design patent and that the two works are equivalent. You wouldn't have to prove that the competitor saw your work and copied it.

- Under trademark law you must be able to demonstrate that your product design is distinctive and nonfunctional and that the competing company's mark is so similar to yours that is likely to confuse consumers.

- In order to stop someone from infringing a copyright, you must prove that they had access to your work and that they copied it. In other words, if they independently developed the work without first seeing your work, they would not be infringing your copyright.

What About Computer Chip Protection?

If your invention includes a semiconductor chip, you may need to review special rules regarding semiconductor chip protection. Semiconductor chips are tiny plastic and ceramic devices which transmit information inside computers and other machines. On each chip is encoded an integrated circuit pattern. These patterns are known as mask works and are governed by the Semiconductor Chip Act.

Mask works may be protected for a limited time (ten years) provided that the mask work is registered within two years after it is commercially exploited. The mask work is commercially exploited when the work is distributed to the public or when a written offer is made to sell it and the chip is fixed. Mask works are registered by using the Copyright Office's Form MW. Contact the Copyright Office for more information. See Chapter 18, Help Beyond This Book, for contact information.

Reference Collection of U.S. Patents Available for Public Use in Patent and Trademark Depository Libraries

The following are designated as Patent and Trademark Depository Libraries (PTDLs) and receive current issues of U.S. patents and maintain collections of earlier-issued patents. The scope of these collections varies from library to library, ranging from patents of only recent years to all or most of the patents issued since 1790. These patent collections, which are organized in patent number sequence, are available for use by the public free of charge. Each of the PTDLs, in addition, offers supplemental reference publications of the U.S. Patent Classification System, including the *Manual of Classification*, *Index to the U.S. Patent Classification* and *Classification Definitions*, and provides technical staff assistance in their use to aid the public in gaining effective access to information contained in patents. The PTO's CASSIS (Classification And Search Support Information System)— provides direct access to Patent and Trademark Office data, and is available at all PTDLs. Facilities for making paper copies of patents from either microfilm or paper collections are generally provided for a fee.

Since there are variations in the scope of patent collections among the PTDLs and in their hours of service to the public, anyone contemplating use of the patents at a particular library is urged to contact that library, in advance, about its collection and hours in order to avert possible inconvenience. Additional libraries are added from time to time, so check a recent edition of the *Official Gazette* to see if a library closer to you has opened. (This list is printed in every issue of the OG.)

Currently, 12 of these libraries have APS (Automated Patent System) search terminals which can search text of patents back to 1971. For the latest copy of this list, or for Web links to each PTDL, go to the PTO's *Official Gazette* site at www.uspto.gov.web/offices/com/sol/og. Then go to the latest *Official Gazette* and open "Patent and Trademark Deposititory Libraries."

State	Name of Library	Telephone
Alabama	Auburn University Libraries	334-844-1747
	Birmingham Public Library	205-226-3620
Alaska	Anchorage: Z.J. Loussac Public Library	907-562-7323
Arizona	Tempe: Noble Library, Arizona State Univ.	602-965-7010
Arkansas	Little Rock: Arkansas State Lib.	501-682-2053
California	Los Angeles Public Library	213-228-7220
	Sacramento: California State Library	916-654-0069
	San Diego Public Library	619-236-5813
	San Francisco Public Library	415-557-4500
	Santa Rosa: Bruce Sawyer Center (not a PTDL, but useful)	707-524-1773
	Sunnyvale Center for Innovation (has APS Image terminals	408-730-7290
Colorado	Denver Public Library	303-640-6220
Connecticut	Hartford Public Library	860-543-8628
	New Haven Free Public Library	203-946-8130
Delaware	Newark: Univ. of Delaware Lib.	302-831-2965
D.C.	Washington: Howard University Libraries	202-806-7252
Florida	Fort Lauderdale: Broward County Main Library	954-357-7444
	Miami: Dade Public Library	305-375-2665
	Orlando: Univ. of Central Florida Libraries	407-823-2562

State	Name of Library	Telephone
Florida	Tampa: Campus Library, University of South Florida	813-974-2726
Georgia	Atlanta: Price Gilbert Memorial Library, Georgia Institute of Technology	404-894-4508
Hawaii	Honolulu: Hawaii State Public Library System	808-586-3477
Idaho	Moscow: Univ. of Idaho Library	208-885-6235
Illinois	Chicago Public Library	312-747-4450
	Springfield: Illinois State Library	217-782-5659
Indiana	Indianapolis: Marion County Public Library	317-269-1741
	West Lafayette: Purdue University Libraries	765-494-2872
Iowa	Des Moines: State Lib. of Iowa	515-242-6541
Kansas	Wichita: Ablah Library, Wichita State Univ.	316-689-3155
Kentucky	Louisville Free Public Library	502-574-1611
Louisiana	Baton Rouge: Troy H. Middleton Library, Louisiana State Univ.	225-388-8875
Maine	Orono: Raymond H. Fogler Library, University of Maine	207-581-1678
Maryland	College Park: Engineering and Physical Sciences Library, University of Maryland	301-405-9157
Massachusetts	Amherst: Physical Sciences Lib., Univ. of Massachusetts	413-545-1370
	Boston Public Library	617-536-5400 Ext. 265

Reference Collection of U.S. Patents Available for Public Use in Patent and Trademark Depository Libraries (continued)

State	Name of Library	Telephone	State	Name of Library	Telephone
Michigan	Ann Arbor: Engineering Transportation Library, University of Michigan	734-647-5735	Ohio	Columbus: Ohio State Univ. Lib.	614-292-3022
	Big Rapids: Abigail S. Timme Library, Ferris State University	231-592-3602		Dayton: Paul Laurence Dunbar Library, Wright State Univ.	937-775-3521
				Toledo/Lucas County Public Lib.	419-259-5212
	Detroit Public Library (has APS Image Terminals)	313-833-3379	Oklahoma	Stillwater: Oklahoma State University Library	405-744-7086
Minnesota	Minneapolis Public Library and Information Center	612-630-6120	Oregon	Portland: Paul L. Boley Law Library, Lewis & Clark College	503-768-6786
Mississippi	Jackson: Mississippi Library Commission	601-961-4111	Pennsylvania	Philadelphia, The Free Library of	215-686-5331
				Pittsburgh, Carnegie Library of	412-622-3138
Missouri	Kansas City: Linda Hall Library	816-363-4600		University Park: Pattee Library, Pennsylvania State University	814-865-6369
	St. Louis Public Library	314-241-2288 Ext. 390	Puerto Rico	Bayamón: Univ. of Puerto Rico	787-786-5225
Montana	Butte: Montana College of Mineral Science & Technology Library	406-496-4281		Mayaguez General Library, University of Puerto Rico	787-832-4040 Ext. 2022
			Rhode Island	Providence Public Library	401-455-8027
Nebraska	Lincoln: Engineering Library, University of Nebraska	402-472-3411	South Carolina	Clemson University Libraries	864-656-3024
Nevada	Las Vegas: Clark County Library	not yet operational	South Dakota	Rapid City: Devereaux Library, S.D. School of Mines and Technology	605-394-1275
	Reno: University of Nevada-Reno Library	702-784-6500 Ext. 257	Tennessee	Nashville: Stevenson Science Library, Vanderbilt University	615-322-2717
New Hampshire	Concord: New Hampshire State Library	603-271-2239	Texas	Austin: McKinney Engineering Lib. Univ. of Texas at Austin	512-495-4500
New Jersey	Newark Public Library	973-733-7782		College Station: Sterling C. Evans Library, Texas A & M Univ.	979-845-5745
	Piscataway: Lib. of Science & Medicine, Rutgers University	732-445-2895		Dallas Public Library	214-670-1468
New Mexico	Albuquerque: University of New Mexico General Library	505-277-4412		Houston: The Fondren Library, Rice University	713-348-5483
New York	Albany: New York State Library	518-474-5355		Lubbock: Texas Tech University	806-742-2282
	Buffalo and Erie County Public Library	716-858-7101		San Antonio Public Library	210-207-2500
	New York Public Library (The Research Libraries)	212-592-7000	Utah	Salt Lake City: Marriott Library, University of Utah	801-581-8394
	Rochester Public Library	716-428-8110	Vermont	Burlington: Bailey/Howe Library, University of Vermont	802-656-2542
	Stony Brook: Engineering Library, State University of New York	631-632-7148	Virginia	Richmond: James Branch Cabell Library, Virginia Commonwealth University	804-828-1104
North Carolina	Raleigh: D.H. Hill Library, N.C. State University	919-515-3280			
North Dakota	Grand Forks: Chester Fritz Lib., University of North Dakota	701-777-4888	Washington	Seattle: Engineering Library, University of Washington	206-543-0740
			West Virginia	Morgantown: Evansdale Library, West Virginia University	304-293-4695 Ext. 5113
Ohio	Akron: Summit County Public Library	330-643-9075	Wisconsin	Madison: Kurt F. Wendt Library, University of Wisconsin	608-262-6845
	Cincinnati and Hamilton County, Public Library of	513-369-6971		Milwaukee Public Library	414-286-3051
	Cleveland Public Library	216-623-2870	Wyoming	Cheyenne: Wyo. State Lib.	not yet operational

Ownership Issues for Inventor Employees

I n order to license your invention, you must actually own the legal rights to the invention. Sometimes, however, it's not entirely clear who owns the rights to an invention, especially in an employee-employer context. In this chapter, we review how ownership of your invention is affected by employment relationships. You should review this chapter if:

- you created your invention while working for someone, or
- your current employer is interested in licensing the invention from you.

The ownership and employment issues discussed in this chapter deal with situations when an inventor is an employee, not a business owner. Ownership of your invention will be affected differently when you're working for yourself—for example, when you work for your own corporation or partnership. In the next chapter, we will review how your business form (such as a corporation, partnership or limited liability company) affects ownership, and we will also discuss joint ownership.

A. What Type of Intellectual Property Is Involved?

Each form of intellectual property—patent, trade secret, copyright and trademark—has different rules regarding ownership. For this reason, every ownership discussion must begin with an analysis of the legal rights associated with your particular invention. Before addressing the question of whether your employer has any legal rights to your invention, you need to have a clear idea of what area of intellectual property is associated with it. If you are not clear what intellectual property rights are associated with your type of invention, review Chapter 2.

Once you know what type of intellectual property your invention will involve, you can address the ownership issues that arise when that type of invention is created in a workplace environment. The sections below will discuss the rules governing ownership of your invention, which you'll see vary

considerably depending on the invention. In very broad strokes, here are some general rules regarding employment and invention ownership:

1. If you have created a patentable invention or a trade secret at work, your employer owns the invention or trade secret if:
   - you signed an employment agreement assigning invention rights; or
   - you were specifically hired (even without a written agreement) for your inventing skills or to create the invention.

   Note: Even if the employer does not acquire ownership under one of these two methods, the employer may still acquire a limited right to use your patent or trade secret (called a shop right) without paying you. Shop rights are discussed below in Section B3.

2. If you have created something copyrightable at work, your employer will own the copyright if the work was within the scope of your employment duties. (The rules regarding independent contractors are more complex.)

3. If you created a name or distinctive appearance for your employer's products, your employer is probably entitled to the trademark rights because these rights are owned by whoever first uses the mark in conjunction with the sale of goods (although there are exceptions to this rule, as discussed in Chapter 2). Trademark rights are usually not an issue in employer-employee disputes.

At the end of the chapter, we'll look at special rules for employees of the government or universities, and how to handle disputes between you and your employer.

B. Employer/Employee: Patent and Trade Secret Ownership

The rules regarding employer-employee ownership of trade secrets are essentially the same as for patents, despite the differences between these two types of intellectual property. (See Chapter 2 for details on how to obtain trade secret and patent protection and what each type of protection provides.) The general rule is that your rights to an invention can be acquired by your employer either through a written agreement (such as an employment contract) or if you were originally hired to create an invention. Writing agreements and hiring employees for the purpose of inventing are the two most common ways that employers obtain the rights to employee-created patents and trade secrets. Employers may also obtain more limited rights to employees' inventions in certain circumstances. These limited rights are called shop rights.

1. Written Employment Agreements and Pre-Invention Assignments

Some employment agreements have a provision requiring the employee to assign any inventions to the employer. Because these employment agreements are signed before the employee creates the invention, they are sometimes referred to as pre-invention assignments. You should examine your employment agreement (or other agreements you have with your employer) to determine if there are any pre-invention assignment provisions. These provisions might also be located in your employee manual or in other employee guidelines—which are often considered as legally binding terms of your employment agreement. A pre-invention assignment often includes three parts:

- an assignment provision which guarantees the employer the ownership of the invention. This is the most important (and the only necessary) requirement for the employer's total ownership of the patent.
- a power of attorney provision which guarantees that the employer can register and administer the ownership rights without the employee, even if she is willing and able to assist.

- a disclosure provision which requires the employee to report any discoveries to the employer. Advice regarding disclosures is provided below in Section (a).

If your employment agreement contains provisions such as these, you will not own inventions created for your employer. If you disregard the agreement and attempt to license your invention, the employer will be able to sue you for breach of the employment agreement. If your employment agreement is found valid and your employer wins the lawsuit, you may have to pay monetary damages.

Sample provisions from a pre-employment agreement appear below. As with any provision or restriction, the language may vary from agreement to agreement and may even be set out under a separate title or heading. Generally, you should be looking for key phrases such as "shall be the sole and exclusive property" or "assignment of all rights of employee."

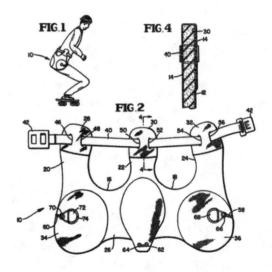

Protective Device for the Buttocks and Hips
No. 4,151,613

Sample Employer Ownership Provisions of an Employment Agreement

Assignment of Innovations. Employee agrees that any invention, process, system or patentable creation (Innovations) conceived, originated, discovered or developed in whole or in part by Employee: (1) as a result of any work performed by Employee with Company's equipment, supplies, facilities, trade secret information or other Company resources; or (2) on Company's time, shall be the sole and exclusive property of Company, provided that the Innovation relates either to Company's business or anticipated research. Employee agrees to sign and deliver to Company (either during or subsequent to his employment) such documents as Company considers desirable to evidence: (1) the assignment to Company of all rights of Employee, if any, in any such Innovation, and (2) Company's ownership of such Innovations.

Power of Attorney. In the event Company is unable to secure Employee's signature on any document necessary to apply for, prosecute, obtain or enforce any legal right or protection relating to any Innovation or copyrightable work referred to above, Employee irrevocably designates and appoints Company (and each of its duly authorized officers and agents) as his agent and attorney-in-fact, to act for and in his behalf and to execute and file any such document and to do all other lawfully permitted acts to further the prosecution, issuance and enforcement of patents, copyrights or other rights.

Disclosure. Employee agrees to promptly disclose in writing to Company all discoveries, developments, designs, programs, code, ideas, innovations, improvements, inventions, formulas, processes, techniques, know-how and data (whether or not patentable or registrable under copyright or similar statutes) made, written, conceived, reduced to practice or learned by Employee (either alone or jointly with others) during the period of his employment, that are related to or useful in Company's business, or that result from tasks assigned to Employee by Company, or from the use of facilities owned, leased or otherwise acquired by Company.

---

a. Disclosure of Inventions to Employers

Disclosure provisions require that you report to your employer all inventions made by you during your period of employment that relate to the company's business, result from tasks assigned to you by the company or are created using the company's resources. The purpose of the provision is to allow the employer to evaluate your inventions and determine if the company has any rights (either by assignment or under shop right rules).

If an invention is created with your own resources and is outside the scope of the employer's business, you will not need to disclose the invention under the terms of the sample provision above. However, each provision may be different. For example, some employers may ask for a list of all inventions you create or may ask for a list of inventions created before your employment. If you have any doubts about making a disclosure to your employer, you should consult with a patent attorney before making the disclosure. Generally, however, it is a good idea to furnish the employer with a list of inventions you created before your employment. This list can help to avoid any claims of employer ownership for these inventions.

b. Limitations on Pre-Invention Assignments

Five states (California, Illinois, Minnesota, North Carolina and Washington) have laws that limit pre-invention assignments to employers (Cal. Lab. Code §§ 2870-2872; Ill. Rev. Stat. ch. 140, para. 302; Minn. Stat. § 181.78; N.C. Gen. Stat. §§ 66-57.1, .2; Wash. Rev. Code Ann. §§ 49.44.140, .150). These laws prevent an employer from claiming ownership of an invention if the invention:

- is created with the employee's resources
- does not result from work performed for an employer, and
- does not relate to the employer's business.

For example, if you are employed as a computer programmer and you invent a new method of book-binding at home with your own resources, then your employer could not claim ownership of your bookbinding invention in these five states. The California statute also requires employers to inform employees about the law. This is usually done by adding a statement to the employment agreement:

> Employee assigns to Company all right, title and interest Employee may have or acquire in and to all such Innovations created by Employee. Innovations that qualify fully under the provisions of California Labor Code § 2870 et seq. shall not be subject to this provision.

If an employer in one of these five states required you to sign an agreement violating the law, the agreement would be invalid. It may seem odd that a signed agreement can be invalid. After all, if both parties agreed, how can it be void? The reason is that certain laws are considered to be public policy laws and you cannot "contract around" those laws. In other words, you cannot agree to violate a policy that is for the public benefit.

2. Employed to Invent

It is possible that even without a written employment agreement, an employer may own rights to your patent or trade secret under the "employed to invent" doctrine. How might this rule apply to you? If you were employed—even without a written employment agreement—for your inventing or designing skills, or you were hired or directed to create an invention, your employer would own all rights to your subsequent invention. This doctrine is derived from a Supreme Court ruling that stated, "One employed to make an invention, who succeeds, during his term of service, in accomplishing that task, is bound to assign to his employer any patent obtained."

Generally, most companies prefer to use a written agreement, which is more reliable and easier to enforce than this implied agreement. However, the issue of "employed to invent" still arises.

EXAMPLE: An engineer had no written employment agreement with his employer. He was assigned as the chief engineer on a project to devise a method of welding a "leading edge" for turbine engines. The engineer spent at least 70% of his time on the project. He developed a hot forming process (HFP) for welding a leading edge and built the invention on his employer's time and using his employer's employees, tools and materials.

The engineer claimed that he was the sole owner of patent rights. A court held that the company owned the patent rights because the engineer was hired for the express purpose of creating the HFP process. That fact, combined with the use of the employer's supplies, payment for the work and the payment by the employer for the patent registration, demonstrated that there was an implied contract to assign the patent rights to the employer. Therefore, even without a written employment agreement, the employer acquired ownership.

3. Shop Rights

The previous two situations (written employment agreements and the "employed to invent" rule) allow the employer to become the owner of all patent and trade secret rights. There is another situation in which the employer may not acquire ownership of your patent or trade secret, but may acquire a limited right to use these innovations, known as a shop right. Under a shop right, you retain ownership of the patent or trade secret, but the employer has a right to use the invention without paying you.

A shop right can only occur if you use the employer's resources (materials, supplies, time) to create an invention. Other circumstances may be relevant, but use of employer resources is the most important criterion. Shop right principles are derived from state laws and precedents in court cases. Generally, the shop right claim arises when an inventor sues a former employer for patent infringement. The employer defends itself by claiming a shop right.

> EXAMPLE: In 1982, an inventor was a consultant for a power company and conceived of a device for detecting the levels of fly ash (fine particles of ash sent up by the combustion of a fuel) at steam electric stations. In 1983 the inventor applied for a patent on his device, and it was issued in 1985. That same year, the power company contracted to have the fly ash invention installed (without the inventor's authorization) at several of its stations. The inventor sued for patent infringement claiming the power company had no right to use or install his invention without his permission. The power company defended itself claiming it had a shop right. The federal court agreed with the power company, since the inventor had developed the invention while working at the power company.

If you do not have a written employment agreement assigning patents and were not hired to create the invention, you may be able to prevent the creation of a shop right by making a statement to the employer at the time you create the invention that you do not consent to a shop right or any royalty-free use of the invention. This method was effective in one federal court case. However, it is also possible that an employer may balk at your claim and initiate a dispute over the invention.

You should only be concerned about shop rights if the invention was created on the employer's time or using the employer's resources (materials, supplies or trade secrets). If it wasn't, the shop right rule is irrelevant.

C. Inventions Covered by Copyright

The rules for employer ownership are different if the invention (or some part of it) is subject to protection under copyright law. When a copyrightable work is created while the inventor is employed, it is said to be a "work made for hire" or "work for hire" and the employer, rather than the inventor, owns it. For example, if you work for a toy company and create a copyrightable design for a new toy rocket, your employer will own all copyright in the design. Under copyright law, an employer *always* owns copyrights created by an employee which are within the scope of the employment, even without a written agreement. If it is not within the scope of your employment (for example, you are employed as a bike messenger but create a copyrightable computer program), then you would retain ownership.

If you are an independent contractor, however, the rules are much different for copyright ownership. The hiring party will own the work only if there is a written agreement that specifies it is a work made for hire and the work fits within one of the categories listed in the copyright act (see sidebar, below). For more information on independent contractors and works made for hire, read *The Copyright Handbook* and *Working for Yourself*, both by attorney Stephen Fishman (Nolo).

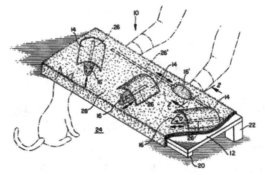

**Recreational Device
No. 4,327,668**

Copyright and Independent Contractors

If you are an independent contractor, the person hiring you will own the work only if your work belongs in one of the following categories listed in the copyright act:

1. a contribution to a collective work;
2. as a part of a motion picture or other audio-visual work;
3. as a translation;
4. as a supplementary work (for example, a work prepared for publication as a supplement to a work by another author for the purpose of introducing, concluding, illustrating, explaining, revising, commenting upon or assisting in the use of the other work, such as forewords, afterwords, pictorial illustrations, maps, charts, tables, editorial notes, musical arrangements, answer material for tests, bibliographies, appendixes and indexes);
5. as a compilation;
6. as an instructional text. (An instructional text is a literary, pictorial or graphic work prepared for use in day-to-day instructional activities. For example, a textbook would be an instructional text, but a novel used in a literature class would not be an instructional text.);
7. as a test or as answer material for a test;
8. as an atlas; or
9. as a sound recording.

These categories only apply to independent contractors. Any work created by an employee within the course of employment will be owned by the employer regardless of the category.

D. Special Employment Situations

If you work for a government agency or for a university, there are special rules for ownership of inventions.

1. Government Employees

According to a federal policy implemented in 1983, federal agencies may waive or omit patent rights when awarding government contracts (although there are some exceptions for space research, nuclear energy or defense). If you are contracting directly with the federal government (that is, you are not working for the federal government through a private company), then you should ask about patent ownership at the time of contracting. You may be able to retain patent rights to a government-sponsored invention. If you are working for an employer who has contracted with the federal government and you want to assert patent rights: (1) your employer would have to retain patent rights from the federal government; and (2) you would have to have some basis to assert your claim to patent rights, as discussed in the previous sections.

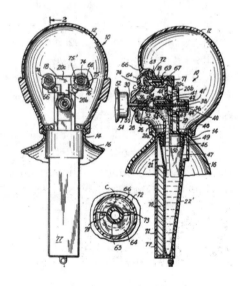

Doll Tearing Mechanism
No. 3,789,539

University Licensing: The Bayh-Dole Act

The Bayh-Dole Act, enacted in 1980, permits universities to claim patent rights in inventions created at the university with federal funding. The university may then license these discoveries to private industry—a practice some critics have likened to corporate welfare.

As a result of Bayh-Dole, university patent acquisition and licensing has expanded dramatically in the last two decades. Before 1980, the total of all U.S. university patents was less than 150 per year. In 2000, the University of California alone obtained 324 patents (and earned 261 million dollars in licensing revenue). Regulations for the Bayh-Dole law (35 USC § 200-212) can be found at 37 CFR Part 401. The key regulations are:

- The university must have written agreements with its faculty and technical staff requiring disclosure and assignment of inventions.
- The university has an obligation to disclose each new invention to the federal funding agency within two months after the inventor discloses it in writing to the university.
- The decision whether or not to retain title to the invention must be made within two years after disclosing the invention to the agency.
- The university must file a patent application within one year, or prior to the end of any statutory period in which valid patent protection can be obtained in the United States.

- Any company holding an exclusive license to a patent that involves sales of a product in the United States must substantially manufacture the product in the U.S.
- In their marketing of an invention, universities must give preference to small business firms (fewer than 500 employees), provided such firms have the resources and capability for bringing the invention to practical application.

However, if a large company has also provided research support that led to the invention, that company may be awarded the license.

- Universities may not assign their ownership of inventions to third parties, except to patent management organizations.
- Universities must share with the inventor(s) a portion of any revenue received from licensing the invention. Any remaining revenue, after expenses, must be used to support scientific research or education.
- Under certain circumstances, the government can require the university to grant a license to a third party, or the government may take title and grant licenses itself (these are called "march-in rights").

For an example of how the government avoids "march-in rights," see *Patient Number One* by Rick Murdock and David Fisher (Crown), pages 250-255.

2. University Employees

If you work for a university, you should look first to your employment agreement to determine who owns any inventions you create. Most colleges and universities require that faculty execute formal agreements which grant the university rights to all discoveries made by employees using its labs, equipment or other resources. Normally, when an invention or discovery is successful and results in a licensing deal, the school pays some portion of the revenues to the inventor. At one major university, for example, inventors get 50% of the first $100,000 of net revenue, 40% of the second $100,000 and 30% of any sums after that. But if there's no ownership agreement, the deal might be quite different (see sidebar, below).

The Battle for Gatorade

In the mid-sixties, a football coach at the University of Florida asked a team of school physiologists to create a high-energy drink that would provide fluid replacement for perspiring athletes. The physiologists created a potion which eventually came to be known as Gatorade. At the time, the University of Florida and the physiologists had no written arrangement regarding the ownership of employee-created inventions. On their own, the physiologists licensed Gatorade to a food company and started reaping huge revenues. The university felt it should own the rights to the drink and sued. After a long lawsuit, the university was awarded 20% of the money paid to the physiologists, far less than the school would have gotten under current employment agreements. But even at 20%, the university is still believed to earn over $4 million a year from licensing Gatorade, which now generates $1.2 billion in annual sales.

your attorney believes that you have rights to the invention, she will work with you to clear ownership so that you can license the invention freely. If the employer claims a shop right, your attorney may be able to reach an agreement as to the extent of this right.

If, for some reason, your employer owns rights to your invention and is willing to transfer those rights to you, then an agreement should be executed confirming the arrangement. It is rare that an employer is willing to transfer rights to an employee. However, it may occur in some situations; for example, if the company is in financial difficulty, if the company is attempting to settle a dispute with the employee or if the company does not believe the invention has any commercial potential.

The letter agreement shown below enables an employee to retain control over a specific invention. If the invention already has been patented by the company, you will also need the company to assign the patent to you and the assignment should be recorded with the PTO. See Chapter 2 for more information on patent procedures and Chapter 4 for more information on patent assignments.

E. Working Out Ownership Issues With Your Employer

What do you do if you and your employer dispute ownership? Your employment agreement, if there is one, may control how the dispute is resolved. For example, the agreement may call for mediation or arbitration in case of a dispute over the agreement's provisions. If not, you can always invite the employer to submit to arbitration or mediation in an effort to avoid a costly courtroom battle. And if all else fails, you could end up in court.

In any ownership dispute, you should seek the advice of an intellectual property attorney before proceeding (see Chapter 18, Help Beyond This Book). The attorney can assess your position in relation to the state law and explain your options. If

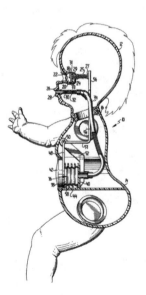

Toy Kissing Doll
No. 3,916,561

Confirming Employee's Ownership of Copyright

Dear _[insert name of company's representative]_ :

This confirms the agreement between ____ _[name of company]_ ____ and myself that I shall own exclusive rights to the invention known as _____ ____ _[name of invention]_ _____, which is more specifically described below.

Although I created ____ _[name of invention]_ _____ within the scope of my employment, _[name of company]_ ____ now agrees that I shall be the owner of all rights under patent, trademark, trade secret and copyright law to ____ _[name of invention]_ ____, as well as to any derivative versions under copyright law or improvements under patent law. You represent and warrant that you have the power to grant these rights on behalf of _[name of company]_ ____ and that if required, a representative of _[name of company]_ ____ will furnish any other necessary documents that are required to demonstrate my ownership.

Description of Invention:

[name of invention] _____

comprises _[Describe invention in detail. If there is a patent application, use_

the claims section to describe it. If a patent has already been issued to the

company, you will need a patent assignment and the assignment will have

to be recorded with the PTO.] _____

If this letter accurately reflects our agreement, please sign and return one copy to me.

Yours truly,

_____
Inventor

_____
Date

Acknowledged and Agreed to:

_____
Representative, Name of Company

_____
Date

Joint Ownership of Your Invention

In the last chapter we discussed how ownership of your invention may be affected by employment relationships. In this chapter, we discuss what happens when your invention is owned by two or more people. Joint ownership can occur in various ways: for example, two inventors co-create an invention; an inventor sells or assigns rights; or an inventor dies and a court awards ownership to two people. When there is more than one owner of your invention, it affects the ability to license, and it affects the revenue from the license. We will discuss the issues raised by joint ownership and will help you explore whether your ownership is affected by other factors such as gifts, loans or investments. We will also review how to transfer ownership of your invention to a partnership or other business in which you have an interest.

A. Joint Ownership

Joint owners (sometimes called co-owners) are two or more people who share in the ownership rights to an invention. Below are some examples of how joint ownership occurs.

> **EXAMPLE: Joint Ownership Created by Joint Invention.** Dr. Wilcox was stumped and unable to finish his modem invention until Fran, his daughter, showed him how to triple the telephone transfer rate. A patent was granted for the invention to Dr. Wilcox and Fran, as joint inventors. As joint inventors, they are also joint owners.

> **EXAMPLE: Joint Ownership Created by Assignment for Money.** Tom invents a metal detector that works underwater. He needs money to build a prototype and to promote the invention. Jerry agrees to give Tom $100,000 in return for an assignment of 50% ownership interest in the invention. Tom and Jerry become joint owners.

> **EXAMPLE: Joint Ownership Created by Will.** Sam patents a process for scrambling and cooking eggs within their shells. He dies, and in his will he leaves half ownership interest in the invention to his daughter, Carol, and the other half to Dartmouth College. Carol and Dartmouth become joint owners.

> **EXAMPLE: Joint Ownership Created by Assignment to a Partnership.** Jill invents a new style of camping stove. Ian wants to invest money to perfect the invention. Jim, a lawyer, wants to contribute his legal and licensing experience to help license the invention. Jill, Ian and Jim form a partnership, and Jill assigns the invention to the partnership. Each partner is a joint owner in the invention.

1. Patent Laws and the Effect of Joint Ownership

When there are joint owners, all of the owners must consent to an assignment of all rights to the invention. That is, none of the owners can give up *all* rights to the invention without obtaining agreement from the other owners. Generally, the joint owners decide amongst themselves how to split the revenue from sales and licensing (for example, a 65-35% split). If the joint owners cannot decide and a dispute results, a court will make the final determination.

However, in the case of joint owners of a *patented* invention, there are some special rules regarding joint ownership and division of income. Patent law provides that:

> *In the absence of any agreement to the contrary, each of the joint owners of a patent may make, use, offer to sell, or sell the patented invention within the United States, or import the patented invention into the United States, without the consent of and without accounting to the other owners. (Title 35 of the United States Code, § 262.)*

In other words, *any* joint owner of a patented invention can make, sell or use the invention without the consent of the other owners and without compensating the other owners. For example, one owner can enter into a non-exclusive license and keep all the revenue. Seem unfair? The only way for the joint owners of a patented invention to protect their interest is to enter into a joint ownership agreement, as provided below.

Exclusive Versus Non-Exclusive

A license is either exclusive or non-exclusive. If it is exclusive, only the licensee has the rights conveyed in the grant provision. If it is non-exclusive, you can convey the same rights to different licensees. For more information, see Chapter 8.

The Married Inventor

Many inventors acknowledge that without the support of a faithful spouse, their inventions would never have reached fruition. Alexander Graham Bell's wife, for example, testified on his behalf in a patent case and helped preserve his rights to the telephone. Being married while you create an invention has legal implications. Under state laws, when one spouse creates intellectual property (patents, trade secrets, copyrights) during the marriage, the other spouse is entitled to a share of the revenue. (How much of an interest depends upon state laws and the facts in your case). Because a spouse is entitled to the revenue, some attorneys require that a spouse sign any assignments in order to avoid a dispute in the event of divorce (for example, the spouse claims that the assignment was an improper transfer of her rights). A sample spouse signature provision is provided later in this chapter.

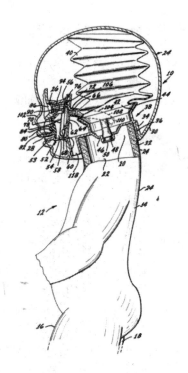

Animation Device for a Figure Toy
No. 3,855,729

2. Joint Ownership Agreement

We recommend that joint owners enter into a joint ownership agreement in order to avoid disputes over revenue and rights. If the sample agreement does not meet your requirements, you should consult with an intellectual property attorney.

a. Introduction

Insert the names of the joint owners. If any of the owners are corporations or partnerships, indicate the correct business form (for example, The Techno Consortium, a New Jersey general partnership). You should insert a description of your invention at the end of the introductory paragraph. Choose the correct option: patent, patent application or no patent. If you have two patents or a patent and a patent application, we recommend that you execute separate agreements for each invention.

b. Ownership Percentage Interests

This is a statement setting forth the percentage interest and proportionate share of revenues each owner is to receive and, likewise, the share of expenses and liabilities to be shared. The owners must agree on what percentage each of them will receive (for example, each partner receives one-half of the revenue). The total of all of the owner percentages must equal 100%.

c. Decision-making

The parties to a joint ownership agreement can decide which issues require unanimous (all parties must agree) or majority approval (or ⅔ approval if you wish). However, as mentioned above, entering into an assignment of all rights to the invention should be with the consent of all parties. In the sample, all other decisions are listed for majority vote. These decisions include the following:

- entering into agreements with other parties to make, license, use, distribute or sell the invention
- permitting any party to make, use, distribute or sell the invention
- filing foreign patent applications
- filing a lawsuit to stop infringement of the invention, or
- hiring someone to help prepare and file the patent application or help file an infringement lawsuit.

If you want any decisions to be made by unanimous vote (for example, entering into an exclusive license), you may list them as requiring a unanimous vote in this section.

The owners can establish any decision-making process that suits them and, if necessary, they may also may establish a method of breaking a tie. In the sample, we suggest the use of mediation and arbitration.

d. Rights to Manufacture and Sell

The agreement can specify who is authorized to negotiate deals and it can also permit an individual owner to make, use or sell the invention. The provision in the sample agreement, for example, permits any joint owner to sell the invention (provided the owner sells it on the same terms as non-owner licensees).

e. Improvements, Revisions

The provision in the sample agreement permits all co-owners to share in improvements of the invention, provided that the owners have made themselves available to assist in such improvements. For example, if the relationship between the owners becomes hostile and they can no longer work together to improve the invention, then the revenues from improvements will be divided according to the contributors. This can be a touchy subject. For example, what if the improvement is minor? Should the owners who made this improvement be entitled to all of the revenue from it? Some co-owners use a sliding system, such as splitting only one quarter of the first improvement among those who contributed to it, and dividing the rest according to the original agreement. The percentages can change as more improvements are made.

f. Disputes

The sample agreement below provides for discussion, mediation and then, arbitration. Some people, however, do not like arbitration (see Chapter 14), and you may need to take the sentences dealing with arbitration out of the agreement.

Joint Ownership Agreement

Introduction

This agreement is made between _____
_____ *[insert name, address and business form of owner #1]*
and _____
[insert name, address and business form of owner #2] (the "Parties") as of _____
[insert date agreement is to be effective]. The Parties wish to set forth their respective rights to and
obligations for the invention tentatively named _____
_____ *[insert the name of invention]* (the "Invention")
and more accurately described below. The ownership rights to the Invention include all patent rights,
copyrights, trade secrets and trademark rights comprising, associated with or derived from the
Invention.

Patent Issued

The Invention as described in the United States patent number _____, dated
_____.

Patent Application Pending

The Invention as described in the application for United States patent (U.S. Patent Office Application
Serial No. _____).

No Patent

Description of Invention: _____
_____
_____

Therefore, the Parties agree as follows:

Ownership Percentage Interests

The Parties to this agreement are the owners of all legal rights in the Invention described above. The
percentage ownership interests of the Parties are as set forth below. Unless otherwise agreed: (a) all
income derived from exploiting the Invention shall be apportioned according to the percentage
interests set forth below; and (b) any costs, expenses or liabilities relating to the Invention and agreed
to by the Parties under this agreement, shall also be apportioned by the same percentage interests. In
the event any Party is unable to contribute a proportionate share for any cost or expense, the other
Parties may contribute the non-contributing Party's share and shall be reimbursed from subsequent
revenues related to the cost or expense. Reimbursement shall include interest at 1.5% per month, or
the maximum rate permitted by law, whichever is less.

Name	Percentage Interest

Decision-Making

Each Party shall have the right to participate in the decisions regarding the Invention, including decisions regarding exploitation, protection and enforcement of legal rights associated with the Invention. All decisions require a majority vote except for an assignment of all rights to the Invention. In the event there are equal votes in a case where a majority decision is required, the issue shall be resolved through the procedures set forth in the Dispute Resolution section, below.

Decision-Making Process/Time Limits

All decisions shall be made promptly and with the cooperation of all Parties, acting fairly and in good faith. If a decision requires some time to contemplate (for example, an offer to license, a decision by one Party to manufacture), the Parties may agree to postpone a decision for a period of up to 30 days.

Rights to Manufacture and Sell

Any Party may make, sell or use any product embodying the Invention (or any portion of the Invention) providing that the Parties have approved such action by a vote required under this agreement. In the event that any Party desires and is approved to license, manufacture, sell or distribute the Invention, the terms of such arrangement shall be the same as those available to third parties in similar transactions. That is, a Party to this agreement will have to pay a competitive royalty to the joint owners after deduction of reasonable manufacturing and overhead expenses.

Improvements, Revisions

Each Party to this agreement shall share, according to the proportions set forth in this Agreement, in any revenue derived from improvements or revisions of this Invention provided that each Party shall have made a good faith attempt to consult, contribute or otherwise make themselves available for services on such improvements or revisions of the Invention. In the event that any Party refuses to participate in any work resulting in an improvement or revision of the Invention, revenues derived from such improvements or revisions shall be distributed on a pro rata basis among the contributing Parties.

Disputes

The Parties agree that every dispute or difference between them arising under this Agreement, including a failure to reach a decision as described in section 2 of this Agreement, shall be settled first by a meeting of the Parties attempting to confer and resolve the dispute in a good faith manner. If the Parties cannot resolve their dispute after conferring, any Party may require the other Parties to submit the matter to non-binding mediation, utilizing the services of an impartial professional mediator approved by all Parties. If the Parties cannot come to an agreement following mediation, the Parties agree to submit the matter to binding arbitration at a location mutually agreeable to the Parties. The arbitration shall be conducted on a confidential basis pursuant to the Commercial Arbitration Rules of the American Arbitration Association. Any decision or award as a result of any such arbitration proceeding shall include the assessment of costs, expenses and reasonable attorney's fees and shall include a written record of the proceedings and a written determination of the arbitrators. Absent an agreement to the contrary, any such arbitration shall be conducted by an arbitrator experienced in intellectual property law. The Parties reserve the right to object to any individual who shall be employed by or affiliated with a competing organization or entity. In the event of any such dispute or difference, either Party may give to the other notice requiring that the matter be settled by arbitration. An award of arbitration shall be final and binding on the Parties and may be confirmed in a court of competent jurisdiction.

Miscellaneous

Each Party shall act in good faith and not take any action which hinders the rights of the other parties. The provisions of this Agreement shall be binding upon the heirs, executors, administrators, successors and assigns of the Parties. If any term, provision, covenant or condition of this Agreement is held to be illegal or invalid for any reason whatsoever, such illegality or invalidity shall not affect the validity of the remainder of this Agreement. This Agreement constitutes the entire understanding between the Parties and can only be modified by written agreement. This Agreement shall be governed by the laws of the state of _____ *[insert choice of state law]*. In the event of any dispute arising under this agreement, the prevailing Party shall be entitled to its reasonable attorney's fees.

MY SIGNATURE BELOW INDICATES THAT I HAVE READ AND UNDERSTOOD THIS AGREEMENT.

_____   _____
Signature   Date

_____   _____
Signature   Date

_____   _____
Signature   Date

g. Miscellaneous

If you would like an explanation as to the meaning of the provisions in this "Miscellaneous" section, read Chapter 14. In the blank space, we recommend that you insert the name of your state of residence or the state agreed upon by the joint owners.

h. Signature

Most joint owners are individuals acting as sole proprietors and can simply sign the agreement. However, if any joint owner is signing as a general partner representing a partnership or on behalf of a corporation, that person must have the authority to sign the agreement. If you have any doubt about any joint owner's authority to sign the agreement, review the section on "signatures" in Chapter 7.

B. How Payments, Loans or Investments Can Create Joint Ownership

Generally, unless money is given to you as a gift (no strings attached—see Section 1 below), there is a legal obligation attached to every payment. Our concern in this section is to determine if your acceptance of money affects your ownership rights. Review your payments and income to determine if you have received money from anyone in relation to your invention, particularly for services, supplies, equipment or rent. Then determine if the money can be classified according to one of the categories below:

- salary or other payment for services
- loans
- investments, or
- advance payments.

If the money was paid as salary, you should review Chapter 3 on employer/employee ownership issues. If there is a written document referencing your receipt of the money and what it was for— such as a loan agreement, employment agreement or investment agreement—that document should explain your rights in relation to the invention. If not, you will need to review the materials below to guarantee that you own the rights to your invention.

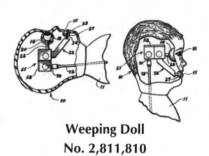

**Weeping Doll
No. 2,811,810**

1. Gifts

When you receive a gift, you have no legal obligations to the giver and the gift will not affect your ownership rights to your invention. This is true even if the gift is money, supplies or services. For example, if your Uncle Joe saw your invention, loved it and said, "I am so proud of you for inventing something, here is $2,000 to continue your work," the money he gave you would be a gift. However, if Uncle Joe puts some condition upon the money such as, "Here is $2,000 if you name it after me," or "Here is $2,000 and you can pay me back when you're successful," then the money is not a gift. If you accept it, a contractual obligation may be created and Uncle Joe may own a right to income from your invention.

Other examples of gifts are a friend giving you spare parts, or a neighbor allowing you to use her garage or workspace without demanding anything in return. As long as a payment to you is truly given as a gift, you will have no obligation, and you will not have lost any legal rights to your invention.

2. Loans

Did someone lend you money, services or supplies with the expectation of a return? A loan is a contract that is usually in writing. In some states, a loan of money *must* be documented by some form of writing. This doesn't necessarily mean a signed contract. It can simply be a notation above a check endorsement, such as "By cashing this check you acknowledge that you owe me $1,000."

Some loans are unsecured, and some are secured. A loan is secured when the borrower guarantees to hand over some item of property (sometimes referred to as collateral) if he defaults on the loan. As a general rule, a secured loan can only be created by a written agreement signed by the borrower, usually called a Security Agreement.

If you use the rights to your invention as collateral for your secured loan, you will most likely limit your ability to license the invention. Even if you do not default on your loan and pay it back in a timely manner, the fact that your invention is being used as property to secure the loan will often prevent you from licensing it. This is because secured loans usually forbid the license (or other transfer) of the invention until the loan is paid off.

> EXAMPLE: Jerry borrows $10,000 from a bank and secures the loan with his patent. His loan agreement prohibits him from writing or otherwise transferring his patent rights. He is then unable to license his invention to other companies because his patent rights are being used as collateral for his loan. He later defaults on the loan and the bank acquires the security—Jerry's patent rights.

3. Investments

An investment is a gamble because there is no guarantee that the investor will receive a return. For example, a loan may be a form of investment, if repayment is secured by profits from an invention. Since there is usually a written document that memorializes an investment, it is important to review that document with an attorney in order to determine the respective rights of the parties. A common form of investment occurs when you create a corporation to exploit your invention (see below) and someone buys shares in your corporation.

4. Advance Payments

Has someone given you money as an advance payment with the understanding that they will make, sell or distribute your invention? Such an advance payment arrangement (with or without a written agreement) may be a major obstacle in licensing your invention to someone else. As explained in Chapter 9, advance payments can be refundable (so that the inventor must pay it back if sales are not sufficient) or recoupable (the inventor does not have to pay it back, but it will be deducted against future royalties). Read Chapter 9 for more information on advances.

C. Transferring Ownership of Your Invention to Your Business

Every business has a structure (sometimes known as a "business form"). There are five common business forms:

- sole proprietorship
- general partnership
- limited partnership
- limited liability company, and
- corporation.

For legal or tax reasons, you may have formed a business to exploit your invention. For example, you and several investors formed a corporation to license your invention. Why form a corporation? Perhaps your accountant recognized a tax advantage, or perhaps the investors wanted a corporate business form to shield them from any personal liability.

Often, if you form a business to exploit your invention, you must share ownership of your invention (for example, in the case of a partnership, you may share it with your partners), or you must assign invention rights to the business (for example, you form a corporation and assign your rights to the corporation which then becomes the owner). If you assign all rights to your business, then that business, not you, will enter into the license agreement with the licensee.

Below are the common types of business forms.

Business Accounting

As a potential licensor, you should get into the habit of tracking payments and expenses of money for supplies or anything else of value. You should maintain two statements, one for income and one for expenses. If you use a computer and a financial accounting program, you probably already have this information sorted. If not, you should start with an expense ledger similar to the one below. At a minimum, your expense ledger should include outgoing payments for the following categories: Supplies, Services, Rent, Phone, Advertising, Postage, Utilities, Equipment (Depreciable) or Other (Miscellaneous).

Although a simple ledger book system can work quite effectively, you should consider using a computer spreadsheet or financial program for managing your business finances. Spreadsheet programs such as *Microsoft Excel* or any popular financial software programs such as *Quicken, Quickbooks, Managing Your Money* or *Money* can save time and effort. In addition, these programs will help you prepare budgets and "what if" calculations that can enable you to predict your product costs or revenues. Recordkeeping will also help when it comes time to prepare your business taxes.

Expense Ledger

Date	Payment Method or Check No.	Payment To	Amount	Supplies	Services (Contractors)	Rent	Phone	Postage/ Shipping	Equip. (Depreciable)
10/12/02	2417	Horace Jones	$254.00		$254.00				
10/14/02	VISA	Simco Inc.	1,007.58	$1,007.58					
10/31/02	2418	Fram Real Estate	1,500.00			$1,500.00			
11/6/02	VISA	USPS	321.00					$321.00	
TOTAL			$3,082.58	$1007.58	$254.00	$1,500.00		$321.00	

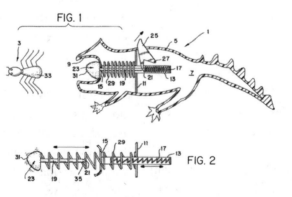

FIG. 1

FIG. 2

Tongue-Snatching Creature Toy
No. 6,017,262

1. Sole Proprietorships

If you are the sole inventor and owner of your invention, then you are probably a sole proprietor (explained below). A sole proprietorship is an unincorporated business owned by one person. You, as sole proprietor, make all business decisions.

The advantages of a sole proprietor are freedom to make decisions (no pesky partners to contradict you) and simplicity (no filings with the state government; no double taxation of income). The disadvantages are that sole proprietors are personally liable for all business debts. This means that if your business gets into financial hot water for reasons such as poor sales or an expensive lawsuit, your creditors can sue you and go after not only your business assets but your personal assets as well. If you have personal property that you want to protect from liability, you may want to incorporate. Unlike sole proprietors, owners of corporations are not personally liable for business obligations.

As a sole proprietor, you may create a name for your business and do business under that name. For example, if Joan Smith operates a sole proprietorship under the name SmittyCo, she would execute a license agreement as "Joan Smith, an individual *doing business as* SmittyCo."

Fictitious Business Names

If you operate your sole proprietorship under a fictitious name, you are required under most state laws to file a fictitious business name statement with your county government. This filing does not create your business, it only provides a public record of the names of the individuals who own the business. Many sole proprietors don't bother with this filing until they begin receiving revenue under the fictitious business name, at which point the bank will require the filing before cashing company checks.

For more information on sole proprietorships, visit the Nolo website at www.nolo.com or consult Nolo's *Legal Guide for Starting and Running a Small Business* or Bell Springs Press's *Small Time Operator* (available through Nolo).

2. General Partnerships

A general partnership is basically a sole proprietorship with more than one owner. If you're in business with one or more other people and haven't incorporated, you're engaged in a partnership. Each partner contributes something to the partnership, and each receives a percentage of the profits. You don't have to go through a formal procedure or even a written agreement to start a partnership. In fact, partnerships are often created by the actions of the parties. For example, say a friend of yours offers to help you promote the invention. You agree to give him a percentage of the profits, and in return he agrees to devote 20 hours a week to promoting your invention. He is contributing services and will be receiving a share of the profits. He is now your partner or joint venturer. (There is no difference between a partnership and a joint venture except that joint ventures are usually limited to two partners).

The advantage of a partnership is simplicity. It is not necessary to register with the state government, although your partnership must file a partnership tax form. The partnership's income is not taxed until it is distributed to the partners, who declare this income on their personal tax returns. The disadvantage of a partnership is that partners are personally liable for business debts. In addition, each individual partner can be liable for the entire debt of the business. That is, if a person sues the partnership, they can recover *all* of the damages from any one partner's personal property. This rule cannot be altered by the partnership agreement (although the agreement can obligate partners to repay such debts). To protect your personal assets from partnership debts, you should incorporate or form a limited liability company, discussed below.

Accepting money from someone does not necessarily create a partnership. As explained in this chapter, some payments may be characterized as loans, some as gifts and some as investments. However, if someone gives you cash or property with the understanding that they will share in the profits and ownership of the business, then you have formed a partnership. For example, you invented a fruit slicer and a friend agreed to contribute $25,000 to help manufacture prototypes, with the understanding that she would share in the profits. You and your friend are partners.

What Is Your Relationship With an Agent?

When you enter into an agreement with a product agent or anyone else who will represent you to a licensee, you are entering into an agency relationship, not a partnership. An agency relationship is similar to hiring an independent contractor to perform services for you. You are the principal and he is the agent, whose job it is to act on your behalf. In return for performing the services, you agree to pay the agent a percentage of the profits. For more information on product reps and agents, review Chapter 5.

3. Limited Partnerships

A limited partnership is a partnership with one or more general partners and one or more limited partners. The general partners manage the business, make contributions or perform services and share in the profits. Limited partners, however, do not participate in business management; they only invest money. In return for giving up any say in management, their liability is limited to the amount of their investment.

The advantage of a limited partnership is that limited partners are not personally liable for business debts. Using this system, you can obtain investment income from a limited partner who does not have to worry about being personally liable. The disadvantage is that you must abide by legal formalities such as filing with the state government and you must also have a written partnership agreement, as required by your state law. The other disadvantages are that limited partners cannot contribute to the business decisions and general partners can be personally liable for all business debts.

4. Corporations

A business corporation is a legal entity, created by law, which has an existence separate from its owners. Unlike other business forms, it can exist perpetually—that is, it does not end with the death of the investors or owners. In order to obtain capital (money) you sell shares in the corporation. Purchasers of these shares are called shareholders. These shares create an ownership interest for the shareholder. The shareholder invests in the hopes that the invention will become successful and the shares become more valuable. Shareholders generally acquire voting rights and use their votes to influence decisions about licensing. Those shareholders who maintain a controlling interest (that is, they have the most shares) will have control over what happens to the licensing of the invention.

Shareholders in a corporation are not personally liable for debts of the corporation. For example, if a corporation licensed an invention and that invention injured someone, the injured person could sue the corporation to the extent of the corporation's assets —but not the personal assets of the shareholders. There are a few exceptions to this rule, however, known as piercing the corporate veil, when shareholders may be held personally liable. This usually happens when the corporation is insufficiently capitalized or if the shareholders act in violation of the law.

The advantages of a corporation are its limited liability for shareholders. The disadvantage is the formality and expense. A corporation must file documents with the state government and receive a certificate of incorporation. Forming a corporation is a big step, particularly in states like California, where the formation fees can exceed $1,000. Certain legal formalities must be observed on a regular basis, such as creating a board of directors, establishing bylaws and issuing shares of stock.

5. Limited Liability Companies

A limited liability company (LLC) is a cross between a partnership and a corporation. The advantages of an LLC are that the owners receive the tax advantages of a partnership (that is, the income is only taxed as received by each investor) and have the limited liability of a corporation (that is, no personal liability). The aren't many disadvantages to an LLC except that you must file paperwork with your state government, usually the Secretary of State. The LLC is currently available in every state. LLCs are usually better suited for smaller businesses (that is, generally for a business with 35 or fewer investors), although this may depend upon your state law. With the exception of Massachusetts, you may form an LLC with one owner. In order to create an LLC, read *Form Your Own Limited Liability Company*, by Anthony Mancuso (Nolo).

Should You Be Concerned With Liability When Forming a Business?

Attorneys make their living attempting to predict, prevent or assess liability. But what is liability? Liability means that you are accountable for debts. What debts? That depends on the situation and the types of risks that the business might incur. Normally when inventions are involved, potential areas of liability are infringement claims, potential injuries resulting from acts of the business or its employees or contractual disputes. Although some people form corporations to limit individual liability, the same result can often be achieved by acquiring insurance.

Should You Be Concerned About Taxes When Forming a Business?

Each different business structure has its own rules for taxes, which you should understand before choosing which structure your business will have. In a sole proprietorship, the business does not itself pay taxes because all profits or losses are simply reported as part of the sole proprietor's personal income. Similarly, partnerships themselves do not pay taxes, but the profits or losses are counted as part of each partner's personal income. A corporation, on the other hand, is taxed as a separate entity from its owners. It must file its own state and federal income tax returns, plus the shareholders must declare profits or capital gains on their individual returns. These differences can have a huge impact on your business and its finances. Before making any decision about a business form, you should consult an accountant or tax expert to determine the financial effects.

6. How Do You Transfer Ownership of Your Invention to Your Business?

If you are the sole inventor and owner of your invention and you operate as a sole proprietor, you don't need to do anything. If you have formed a corporation, general partnership, limited partnership or limited liability company for the purposes of licensing, you will probably assign your invention rights to the business. In that case, the business—not you—owns the invention and any licenses are granted by the business (not you). *All assignments should be in writing*. If the invention is patented, any such assignment must be recorded with the U.S. Patent Office (PTO). In order to record it, you must send a copy of the signed assignment with a cover sheet and fee to the PTO. If you assign invention rights before filing a patent, you can record the assignment by sending it in with your patent application. (For more information on recording an assignment, visit the USPTO website or see the patent resources in Chapter 18, Help Beyond This Book).

Three sample assignments are provided below. The first is for the assignment of an invention for which a patent has been issued. The second assignment should be used if a patent application has been filed. The third assignment can be used if no patent application has been filed.

⚠️ Never assign your invention for the "promise" of future payments. Always get the money *before* signing the assignment. That's because if the assignee (the person who owes you the money) fails to pay you, you will be trapped in litigation, fighting to get your patent back. If the assignee insists on a series of payments, there are several solutions such as establishing an escrow account, transferring partial assignments per payment or setting up a license agreement that allows for ownership transfer after the final payment. You should consult with an attorney to best protect your interests.

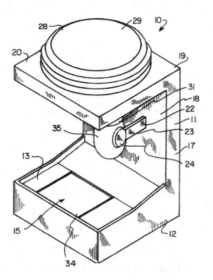

Hard-Boiled Egg Shelling Device
No. 6,314,872

Having a Spouse Sign an Assignment

As mentioned earlier, if you conceived of your invention at the time you were married, your spouse may claim a portion of your invention income. To make sure your assignment is complete and your spouse will not later dispute the assignment, you may want to include a provision in your assignment similar to the one below. This provision protects the assignee (person acquiring the rights to the invention) from later being sued by the spouse of the inventor. This provision is not required in license agreements. When used in assignments, it usually appears below the signature line for the inventor.

Sample Provision for Spousal Assignment

I am the spouse of Assignor and I acknowledge that I have read and understand this Assignment agreement. I am aware that my spouse agrees to assign his interest in the Invention, including any community property interest or other equitable property interest that I may have in it. I consent to the assignment, and agree that my interest, if any, in the Invention is subject to the provisions of this Agreement. I will take no action to hinder the Agreement or the underlying assignment of rights.

[Spouse signature]

Assignment of Rights: Patent

_____

[insert name of person or company assigning rights] ("Assignor") is owner of U.S. Patent Number: _____, dated _____, titled _____ _____ *[insert name of invention]* (the "Patent").

_____

[insert name of person or company to whom rights will be assigned] ("Assignee") desires to acquire rights in and to the Patent.

Therefore, for valuable consideration, the receipt of which is acknowledged, Assignor assigns to Assignee _____% *[insert percentage of interest that is being assigned—it can be less than 100%, but it cannot be more than 100%]* of his right, title and interest in the invention and Patent to Assignee for the entire term of the Patent and any reissues or extensions and for the entire terms of any patents, reissues or extensions that may issue from foreign applications, divisions, continuations in whole or part or substitute applications filed claiming the benefit of the Patent as well as any priority rights resulting from patent application filings. The right, title and interest conveyed in this Assignment is to be held and enjoyed by Assignee and Assignee's successors as fully and exclusively as it would have been held and enjoyed by Assignor had this assignment not been made.

Assignor further agrees to: (a) cooperate with Assignee in the protection of the patent rights and prosecution and protection of foreign counterparts; (b) execute, verify, acknowledge and deliver all such further papers, including patent applications and instruments of transfer; and (c) perform such other acts as Assignee lawfully may request to obtain or maintain the Patent and any and all applications and registrations for the invention in any and all countries.

_____   _____
Assignor   Date

[To be completed by notary public]

On this _____ day of _____, before me, _____ _____, the undersigned Notary Public, personally appeared _____, ASSIGNOR, personally known to me (or proved to me on the basis of satisfactory evidence) to be the person whose name is subscribed to the within instrument, and acknowledged to me that he executed the same. WITNESS my hand and official seal in _____ County of _____ on the date set forth in this certificate.

_____
Notary Public

Assignment of Rights: Patent Application

_____

[insert name of person or company assigning rights] ("Assignor") is owner of _____
_____ *[insert name of invention]*
as described in the U.S. Patent Application signed by Assignor on _____ *[insert date application was signed]*, U.S. Patent and Trademark office Serial Number:_____,
filed _____ *[insert filing date]*, (the "Patent Application"). _____
_____ *[insert name of person or company to whom rights will be assigned]* ("Assignee") desires to acquire all rights in and to the Patent Application and the patent (and any reissues or extensions) that may be granted.

Therefore, for valuable consideration, the receipt of which is acknowledged, Assignor assigns to Assignee _____% *[insert percentage of interest that is being assigned—it can be less than 100%, but it cannot be more than 100%]* of his right, title and interest in the invention and Patent Application (as well as such rights in any divisions, continuations in whole or part or substitute applications) to Assignee for the entire term of the issued Patent and any reissues or extensions that may be granted and for the entire terms of any and all foreign patents that may issue from foreign applications (as well as divisions, continuations in whole or part or substitute applications) filed claiming the benefit of the Patent Application and any priority rights resulting from the Patent Application.

Assignor authorizes the United States Patent and Trademark Office to issue any Patents resulting from the Patent Application to Assignee according to the percentage interest indicated in this assignment. The right, title and interest is to be held and enjoyed by Assignee and Assignee's successors and assigns as fully and exclusively as it would have been held and enjoyed by Assignor had this assignment not been made.

Assignor further agrees to: (a) cooperate with Assignee in the prosecution of the Application and foreign counterparts; (b) execute, verify, acknowledge and deliver all such further papers, including patent applications and instruments of transfer; and (c) perform such other acts as Assignee lawfully may request to obtain or maintain the Patent for the invention in any and all countries.

_____ _____
Assignor   Date

[To be completed by notary public]

On this _____ day of _____, before me, _____
_____, the undersigned Notary Public, personally appeared
_____, ASSIGNOR,
personally known to me (or proved to me on the basis of satisfactory evidence) to be the person whose name is subscribed to the within instrument, and acknowledged to me that he executed the same. WITNESS my hand and official seal in _____ County of
_____ on the date set forth in this certificate.

_____
Notary Public

Assignment of Rights:
No Patent Issued or Application Filed

[insert name of person or company assigning rights] ("Assignor") is the owner of all proprietary and intellectual property rights, including copyrights and patents, in the concepts and technologies known as _____ *[insert name of invention]* and more specifically described in Attachment A *[attach a description of the invention to the Assignment and label it "Attachment A"]* to this Assignment (and referred to collectively as the "Invention") and the right to registrations to the Invention; and

[insert name of person or company to whom rights will be assigned] ("Assignee") desires to acquire the ownership of all proprietary rights, including, but not limited to the copyrights, trade secrets, trademarks and associated good will and patent rights in the Invention and the registrations to the Invention;

Therefore, for valuable consideration, the receipt of which is acknowledged, Assignor hereby assigns to Assignee _____% *[insert percentage of interest that is being assigned—it can be less than 100%, but it cannot be more than 100%]* of all right, title and interest in the Invention, including:

(1) all copyrights, trade secrets, trademarks and associated good will and all patents which may be granted on the Invention;

(2) all applications for patents (including divisions, continuations in whole or part or substitute applications) in the United States or any foreign countries whose duty it is to issue such patents;

(3) any reissues and extensions of such patents; and

(4) all priority rights under the International Convention for the Protection of Industrial Property for every member country.

Assignor warrants that: (1) Assignor is the legal owner of all right, title and interest in the Invention; (2) that such rights have not been previously licensed, pledged, assigned or encumbered; and (3) that this assignment does not infringe on the rights of any person. Assignor agrees to cooperate with Assignee and to execute and deliver all papers, instruments and assignments as may be necessary to vest all right, title and interest in and to the intellectual property rights to the Invention in Assignee. Assignor further agrees to testify in any legal proceeding, sign all lawful papers and applications and make all rightful oaths and generally do everything possible to aid Assignee to obtain and enforce proper protection for the Invention in all countries.

_____   _____
Assignor   Date

[To be completed by notary public]

On this _____ day of _____, before me, _____ _____, the undersigned Notary Public, personally appeared _____, ASSIGNOR, personally known to me (or proved to me on the basis of satisfactory evidence) to be the person whose name is subscribed to the within instrument, and acknowledged to me that he executed the same. WITNESS my hand and official seal in _____ County of _____ on the date set forth in this certificate.

_____
Notary Public

Licensing Agents and Representatives

Some inventors use the services of agents to obtain licensing deals. In this chapter, we examine the relationship between inventors and agents and provide you with a sample agreement for agent representation. We also examine scam marketing firms, which are companies that pretend to assist inventors but actually prey on them. You should review this chapter if you answer "yes" to any of the following questions:

- Are you considering using the services of a company or an agent who will help market your invention?
- Are you looking for a sample agreement to use with an agent?
- Are you concerned about falling victim to an invention marketing scam?

A. Agents

A person or company that represents your invention is known as your agent (sometimes referred to as a product rep). The agent makes the sales pitches and negotiates licenses. In return, the agent is usually paid a commission which is a percentage of royalties. This fee is usually somewhere between 10% and 50% of gross revenues. Gross revenues include all income (including advances) received as a result of the license.

1. The Principal/Agent Relationship

When you authorize someone to act on your behalf, you create an agency relationship. You are the "principal" and the person who acts on your behalf is the "agent." The principal seeks a result such as a license agreement. The agent is paid to obtain the result.

An agent has a legal obligation to protect your interests and to fully disclose opportunities and dangers. This obligation exists because the law considers an agency relationship to be a fiduciary relationship. A "fiduciary," such as an agent, is a person who owes the highest degree of loyalty and honesty

to the principal (you). In other words, an agent is held to a higher standard of care towards the principal than a contractor or employee. For example, it would be a breach of the agent's fiduciary duty if she failed to tell you that she was representing an invention that was in direct competition with yours.

An agency relationship is *not* an employment relationship because you cannot control how the agent performs the work. You only control the end result—the license agreement that you are willing to sign. An agency relationship is also not a partnership because you and agent are not sharing the expenses and losses for your invention and the agent is not personally liable for your business debts. To ensure that a court does not interpret your relationship as either an employer-employee or partnership, your agreement with the agent should contain the disclaimer, "Nothing contained in this Agreement shall be deemed to constitute either agent or inventor a partner, joint venturer or employee of the other party for any purpose."

An agent cannot guarantee a licensing deal. Any attempt by an agent to do so should make you suspicious. Reputable agents don't offer guarantees; rather, they tell you they will assess the likelihood of obtaining a license for your invention and use their best efforts to obtain an acceptable deal.

2. The Benefits of Using an Agent

Why would you want to give up one-third or more of potential licensing revenues to an agent? The answer depends on two factors:

- your ability to license your invention on your own, and
- the industry within which you are attempting to license your invention.

If you cannot make an effective sales pitch or if you are intimidated by the prospect of hawking your invention, then you should consider using an agent. An agent understands how to sell a product and how to make a demonstration, and is thick-skinned enough to accept rejection without giving up.

Using an agent may also depend upon the industry within which you are attempting to license. Some industries simply don't want to hear from unknown inventors because these companies either develop their own products or deal with selected agents.

3. Finding a Knowledgeable Agent

Obtaining an agent can be as difficult as locating a licensee. Most agents are not looking for clients. They rely on word of mouth from friends or other inventors. The agents we spoke with when researching this book requested that their names not be included. Why? Because they already have sufficient client listings and attract business strictly from referrals.

How do you find an agent? There are four common methods:

- referrals from businesses
- referrals from inventors
- trade shows, and
- trade magazine advertisements.

a. Referrals From Businesses

If a company will not speak with you about your invention, ask if they deal with agents and if they can recommend any in particular. For example, when the author of this book approached a toy company about manufacturing a new toy, the company responded by providing a list of toy company agents with whom it would feel comfortable dealing.

b. Referrals From Other Inventors

If you know of other inventors who use agents, ask if they are satisfied, and if so, find out if they will refer you. A referral from a fellow inventor is the best method of obtaining an agent.

c. Trade Shows

Agents often appear at trade shows to make presentations to businesses. Each trade show or convention distributes a publication with advertisements and an index of attendees. Agents are often listed in this publication as agents, product reps or product developers. Occasionally an agent may have a booth at a convention or trade show. Other times, the agent may be roving the show looking for new products to represent.

d. Trade Magazine Advertisements

Industry trade publications often contain information about agents. These trade publications usually publish an annual index, and agents are included. Occasionally agents advertise in a magazine. Some inventors have found agents by placing an "Agent Wanted" ad in trade publications.

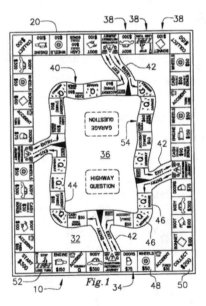

**Educational Board Game for
Learning to Drive Safely
No. 6,315,292**

Licensing Publications

Certain licensing publications also list licensing agents and service organizations that appraise new inventions. For example, *The Licensing Journal* often includes lists of technology agents. See Chapter 18, Help Beyond This Book.

4. Agents in Action

Most agents are industrious, type A individuals. Many started by developing their own products and then represented other inventors as an additional source of income. Most agents have a niche, specializing in a certain industry—for example, representing only designers of medical devices.

If an agent is interested in representing your product, you will have to enter into a representation agreement (a sample is provided below) and furnish a prototype that can be used to demonstrate your invention. Not only will you have to pay the costs of preparing the prototype, but you will have to absorb some other expenses such as shipping of the prototypes or reproduction of presentation materials.

Once the agent has a suitable prototype, he or she takes your invention to company offices, trade shows or conventions. An agent maintains a database which indicates when presentations were made, with whom and the date. Once an agent has made a presentation, that company is listed as a "solicited company" on the rep's database.

What happens if an agent exhausts all of his or her contacts and no one is interested? Depending on the terms of the agreement, the agent may retain the invention to try again in six months or a year, or the agent may return the invention to you and terminate the agreement. Some agreements provide that the agent will get royalties if, within a certain period of time after termination, a previously solicited company decides to license the invention.

For example, assume your agent shows the invention to DesignCo. They decide not to license

it. You terminate the agent agreement and five months later show your invention to another DesignCo executive who decides to license it. Depending on your agreement, you may have to pay royalties to the agent. This type of provision is not uncommon.

Executing a Nondisclosure Agreement With Your Agent

Before presenting your invention to an agent, you should enter into a nondisclosure agreement with the agent. An explanation of nondisclosure provisions and a sample nondisclosure agreement are provided in Chapter 7.

B. Completing the Agent Agreement

The sample agent agreement set out below is created in a letter format. Although a letter agreement is less formal, the agreement is as enforceable as a nonletter contract. If you don't want to use the letter format, simply remove the date and salutation.

Below is an explanation of the provisions in the agent agreement.

1. Introduction

Insert your name, business form (if any) and address (for example, "George Earth, a sole proprietor, with his address at 14 East 40th Street, New York, NY 10017.") If you are unsure of your business form, review Chapter 4. Insert the same information for your agent. You should attach a separate piece of paper to the agreement containing a detailed description of the invention. This description may only be a few paragraphs, but it will provide the basis for the agent to license your invention. If drafted properly, this description will probably also be used in any license agreement that is subsequently negotiated. If your invention is patented, you can attach a copy of the patent or make a

Agent Letter Agreement

Date: _____

Dear _____ *[insert name of agent]*

Introduction

This agreement sets forth the terms and conditions of this agreement (the "Agreement") between
_____ *[insert*
your name, business form and address] ("Inventor") and _____
_____
[insert Agent's name, business form and address ("Agent"). Inventor is the owner of licensing rights to
various processes and technologies, referred to in this Agreement as the "Properties" and described
more fully in Attachment A *[attach a description of the invention to the Assignment and label it*
"Attachment A"] to this Agreement. Inventor agrees to have Agent serve as an exclusive representative and agent for the Properties within the
_____ *[indicate the industry(ies) in which*
the agent will represent your invention] industry (the "Industry").

Obligations of Agent

Agent shall perform the following services:

- Evaluation and Consultation. Agent will identify potential licensees for the Properties within
  the Industry.
- Sales Representation. Agent shall serve as Inventor's exclusive agent for the exploitation of the
  Properties within the Industry. As Inventor's agent, Agent shall contact and solicit potential
  licensees or purchasers and present and communicate potential license information between
  the parties.
- Negotiation of Agreements. Agent shall work in association with Inventor in the negotiation of
  sales, licensing, option or other agreements transferring licensing rights to the Properties.

Obligations of Inventor

Inventor shall perform the following services:

- Technical Assistance and Support. Inventor will consult with licensees of the Properties and
  provide technical assistance and support for the Properties.

Payments

Inventor agrees that all income paid as a result of any agreement solicited or negotiated by Agent for
the Properties (the "Properties Income") shall be paid directly to Agent and that Agent shall issue
payments to Inventor within ten (10) days of Agent's receipt of any Properties Income along with any
client accountings as provided by the licensee. As compensation for the services provided above,
Agent shall receive _____% *[indicate percentage of income paid to Agent]* of any
Properties Income, including, but not limited to, any advances, guarantees or license fees. The
provisions of this Payments Section shall survive any termination of this Agreement.

reference to the patent (for example, "the invention and claims embodied in Patent No. _____"). If the invention is the subject of a patent or copyright application, refer to that application. Finally, insert the name of the industry in which the agent will represent your invention, for example, "the toy hobby and game" industry.

2. Obligations of Agent

This section establishes the agent's duties: evaluating, representing and negotiating. It also establishes that the agent is the exclusive representative for the Properties within the specified industry. This means that while the agreement is in force, only the agent (not you or another agent) can represent the properties within those industries. If the agency relationship is nonexclusive, then others (including yourself) could solicit potential licenses within the specified industry.

3. Obligations of Inventor

It is possible that more duties may be required of the inventor, for example, if the product presentation requires technical assistance. Additional duties, once agreed upon, can be inserted in the final agent agreement.

4. Payments

Insert the proper percentage payment for the agent. Under most agent agreements, the agent receives 25%–40% of all "Properties Income" (as defined), and the Properties Income is paid directly to the agent. After deducting the appropriate percentage, the agent pays the remaining sum to the inventor. Some agents may seek to deduct reasonable expenses before splitting the revenues. If the agent wants to deduct expenses, be sure these expenses (postage, telephone or travel) are spelled out. You can also request approval of any expenses over a certain amount (for example, over $500).

If you are uncomfortable with the agent receiving the licensing money directly, you can suggest providing for an escrow account to hold "Properties Income." For example, you can insert the statement below at the end of the payment section:

Separate Agent Escrow Account—Optional

Agent agrees to maintain a separate interest-bearing escrow account for all Properties Income. Inventor's rights to the account shall be established in a separate escrow agreement and Inventor's access shall be triggered by Agent's death, incapacity, bankruptcy or insolvency.

Many banks can assist you in the creation of an escrow account and will usually provide the escrow agreement. Maintaining an escrow account will incur special fees.

5. Proprietary Rights; Indemnity

The agent (like a potential licensee) will not want any surprises. For this reason, the agent will want your indemnification—a guarantee that you own the invention and that you have the right to license it. You should review the section on indemnity in Chapter 12. Also, review the material on ownership of inventions in Chapters 2 and 3.

6. Disclaimer

An agent almost always requests this provision and it reinforces what you already know—that the agent cannot guarantee a license deal.

7. Confidentiality

This is a standard nondisclosure provision. For more information on such provisions, see Chapter 7.

Proprietary Rights; Indemnity

Inventor represents and warrants that it has the power and authority to enter into this Agreement and that it is the owner of all proprietary rights, whether they are patent, copyright or otherwise and that the Properties are not in any way based upon any confidential or proprietary information derived from any source other than Inventor. Because Agent is relying on these representations, Inventor agrees to indemnify Agent and its assignees and hold them harmless from any losses or damages resulting from third party claims arising from a breach of these representations. Inventor's indemnification of Agent shall survive any termination of this Agreement.

Disclaimer

Nothing in this Agreement shall be interpreted by Inventor as a promise or guarantee as to the outcome of any solicitation or negotiation by Agent on behalf of Inventor or the Properties.

Confidentiality

The parties acknowledge that each may be furnished or may otherwise receive or have access to information that relates to each other's business and the affairs of the respective clients (the "Information"). The parties agree to preserve and protect the confidentiality of the Information and all physical forms. Information relating to the terms, provisions and substance of this Agreement shall remain within the strictest confidence of both parties, and neither party shall disclose such information to third parties without the prior written consent of the other.

Termination

This Agreement may be terminated at any time at the discretion of either Inventor or Agent, provided that written notice of such termination is furnished to the other party thirty (30) days prior to such termination. If this Agreement is terminated by Inventor, and within _____ *[number of months]* months of termination, Inventor enters into an agreement to option, license, sell or otherwise exploit the Properties with any company solicited or contacted by Agent on Inventor's behalf, Inventor agrees to pay the fees established in the Payments Section.

General

Nothing contained in this Agreement shall be deemed to constitute either Agent or Inventor a partner, joint venturer or employee of the other party for any purpose. Any material contained in an attachment, exhibit or addendum to this Agreement shall be incorporated in this Agreement. From time to time, the parties may revise the information specified in the attachments or exhibits. Such revisions, if executed by both parties shall be incorporated in this Agreement and shall be binding on the parties. This Agreement may not be amended except in writing signed by both parties. Each and all of the rights and remedies provided for in this Agreement shall be cumulative. No waiver by either party of any right shall be construed as a waiver of any other right. If a court finds any provision of this Agreement invalid or unenforceable as applied to any circumstance, the remainder of this Agreement shall be interpreted so as best to effect the intent of the parties. This Agreement shall be governed by and interpreted in accordance with the laws of the State of _____ *[insert state law that shall govern the agreement]*. Any controversy or claim arising out of or relating to this Agreement, or the breach of this Agreement shall be settled by arbitration in accordance with the rules of the American Arbitration Association and judgment upon the award rendered by the arbitrator(s) may be entered in any court having jurisdiction. The prevailing party shall have the right

8. Termination

What happens if you terminate (end) the agent agreement and enter into a licensing agreement with a company that had been solicited by the rep? Under this provision, if you enter into such an agreement within a certain number of months of termination, you will have to pay the agent a fee. The time period often ranges from six to 18 months. The amount of the rep's fee can also be altered. For example, you can establish that the agent will only get one-half of the fees if any agreement is entered into after three months but before six months.

In order to be sure that the agent has solicited the company, you should request that the agent furnish you a list of companies that were solicited (and the dates of solicitation and the name of the person contacted). This list can be furnished at the time of termination, or you can request that the agent notify you periodically (every six months) of all solicitations during that period.

9. General

These general provisions are explained in detail in Chapter 14. It is possible that either you or the agent would not like to participate in arbitration in order to settle disputes. Read Chapter 14 for more information on arbitration. In the blank space, we recommend that you insert the name of your state of residence or the state agreed upon by you and the agent.

10. Signatures

Each party must sign the agreement in relation to the business that is represented (for example, as a general partner representing a partnership), and each party must have the authority to sign the agreement. If you have any doubt about the agent's authority to sign the agreement, review the section on "signatures" in Chapter 7.

C. Attorneys as Agents

Sometimes, an attorney can act as an agent. The attorney may have connections within an industry and may be willing to represent you to potential licensees. For example, a patent attorney sees potential in your invention and agrees to represent it and waive attorney's fees in return for a percentage of the royalties.

> EXAMPLE: Phil has invented a drafting system by which an architect, using proprietary ink, can create notes or special instructions that can only be seen under a blue light. A patent attorney, Sam, offers to waive his attorney's fees and to represent Phil's invention in return for one-third of all revenue. Phil agrees and Sam licenses the invention to a large engineering company, DesignCo.

If an attorney offers to represent your product, you should take the same precautions you would with any agent. Find out if they have represented other clients and what their success rate was. Also, check with your state bar association to determine if the attorney has a record of disciplinary actions. When an attorney performs non-attorney services, such as acting as your agent, the attorney is mixing legal and nonlegal services. In some states, such as California, the law requires that an attorney entering into such a relationship advise the client in writing to seek the advice of another (independent) attorney. The terms of the business arrangement must be in writing and should be in a manner which "should reasonably have been understood" by the client. In other words, you should understand everything you sign and, if necessary, seek independent advice.

Obtain a written agreement from the attorney. If the attorney is representing your product or waiving fees, it should be stated in the agreement. Another concern about having an attorney as an agent is that there may be a conflict of interest. Lawyers are bound by ethical rules to disclose if there is a potential conflict of interest. A conflict of interest occurs whenever the lawyer represents adverse interests, for example, if your attorney also represents to collect from the other party its reasonable costs and attorney's fees incurred in enforcing this agreement. Any such arbitration hearing shall include a written transcript of the proceedings and a written explanation for any final determination. This Agreement expresses the complete understanding of the parties with respect to the subject matter and supersedes all prior proposals, agreements, representations and understandings.

If these terms and conditions are agreeable, please sign and execute both copies of this Agreement and return one copy to Agent.

INVENTOR: AGENT:

_____   _____
Signature   Signature

_____   _____
Name/Title   Name/Title

_____   _____
Company   Company

_____   _____
Date   Date

the licensee. When there is a conflict of interest, there is the potential that your attorney may not battle as forcefully for your position. Consider, in the example above, if Phil learns that DesignCo is a client of Sam's and that Sam earned money by advising the company as to the purchase. In other words, there was a conflict of interest and Sam failed to inform Phil about the conflict. This could create a problem for you because DesignCo may have been given more favorable terms than if Sam *only* represented your interests. (Although it is not common, attorneys do occasionally represent both inventors and licensors.)

What if the attorney does not want to represent your invention but is willing to waive fees for performing legal duties in exchange for a piece of the action? For example, maybe the attorney is willing to draft the patent application or assist in the negotiation of the license in exchange for royalties from the license. This is not uncommon in the business of software technology. The attorney is willing to take a gamble (possibly working for free) for the potential of a percentage of future sales. However, you should proceed carefully. Check the attorney's record. Find out if the attorney has done this with other clients and ask for a list of clients or if it is possible to speak with any clients. Some law firms will furnish lists of clients; others will not. Sometimes this information is available through legal directories such as the Martindale Hubbell guide, available at law libraries and at some public libraries. Becoming intertwined with an attorney in your business dealings can sometimes prove disastrous. It may be difficult to extricate yourself and may be very expensive. Proceed cautiously. For more information regarding attorneys, review Chapter 18, Help Beyond This Book.

D. Invention Marketing Scams

According to one industry insider, if you have to ask about invention marketing companies, your product is already doomed. Invention marketing companies prey on inventors and innovators. Inventors pay anywhere from $2,000 to $10,000 and (despite the promises) are left with no protection and no prospects. When consumers complain or attempt to sue under the contract, they rarely collect damages even if they win their lawsuit. The annual profits for these companies is estimated to be in the millions.

1. How They Operate

Most invention marketing scams operate in the same manner. They combine unrealistic promises with high-pressure sales techniques. They offer to evaluate your product, yet they never criticize or reject any products they consider. Some common methods employed by these firms include:

- advertising through television, radio and classified ads in newspapers and magazines.
- offering *free* information to help patent and market inventions.
- advertising a toll-free "800" number that inventors can call for written information (usually brochures about the promoters).
- sales calls asking for information about yourself, your ideas and a sketch of the invention.
- offering to do a free preliminary review of your invention.
- suggesting a market evaluation on your idea and charging anywhere from several hundred to several thousand dollars.
- supplying a marketing evaluation report that makes vague and general statements that could apply to *any* invention, not just yours ("You could make $2-3 million from your sprocket mirror invention."). The report provides no hard evidence that there is a consumer market for your invention.
- asking the inventor to pay a fee plus a percentage of future royalties. The "future royalties" portion of the payment is part of the scam, because the inventor is led to believe that the invention has commercial value when no actual research has been done to support this claim.

- seeking more money after the preliminary evaluation (from $2,000 to $8,000) to acquire adequate legal protection for your invention. Despite the promises of "government protection," the company merely files a Document Disclosure form or a Provisional Patent Application. Because the paperwork resulting from these efforts has U.S. Government letterhead and *looks* similar to a patent, inventors mistakenly believe they have obtained patent protection (see Chapter 2 for a more thorough explanation of these procedures). Sometimes the company may file a design patent, which will only protect the appearance of your invention, not its functions. In other words, the companies create a false sense of security and belief that the company is earning its fees.

- seeking more money to promote your invention. The scam marketer informs you that more money is necessary to take your product to the "right" companies. Instead of actually presenting your product, the marketer sends you a list of companies, most (or all) of which will have no relation to your invention.

Periodically the government cracks down on these organizations. The Raymond Lee Organization (RLO) was convicted for falsely alleging that it would obtain patent protection for inventors. A Colorado company, Allied Marketing, was shut down for fraud. The Federal Trade Commission brought an action against one invention marketer and a settlement was reached where the company was ordered to pay $1.2 million into a fund for defrauded inventors (a noble idea, but in reality one victim reportedly received less than $100 on his $5,000 investment). According to another report, an invention marketing company settled with the government and was required to follow certain guidelines to avoid fraud. The company used this settlement to their advantage, brazenly advertising they are the only invention promotion company "following government guidelines." Other companies close down but reopen under a new name.

2. Congress Steps In: Invention Promotion Laws

Congress finally provided some legal controls over scam marketing companies when it enacted the "Invention Developers" law in 1999. This amendment to the patent law provides some regulation of unscrupulous invention promotion services that charge substantial fees for marketing efforts that generally are unsuccessful.

There are four parts to the new law located at 35 USC § 297. Section 297(a) requires that an invention promoter provide a written disclosure that includes:

- the number of inventions evaluated by the invention promoter and stating the number of those evaluated positively and negatively

- the number of customers who have contracted for services with the invention promoter in the past five years

- the number of customers known by the invention promoter to have received a profit as a direct result of the invention promoter's services

- the number of customers known by the invention promoter to have received license agreements for their inventions as a direct result of the invention promoter's services, and

- the names and addresses of all previous invention promotion companies with which the invention promoter has been affiliated in the previous 10 years to enable the customer to evaluate the reputations of these companies.

Section 297 (b) permits a lawsuit against any invention promoter who causes an injury to a customer as a result of a false statement or omission or through failure of the invention promoter to make all the disclosures. The customer can recover the actual damages or statutory damages up to $5,000 as well as reasonable costs and attorney fees. A court can increase damages up to three times the amount awarded if the invention promoter intentionally misrepresented or omitted a material fact.

Section 297 (c) defines the terms used in the new law. Section 297 (d) requires that the PTO make publicly available all complaints submitted to the PTO regarding invention promoters, together with any responses by invention promoters to those complaints.

The Inventor's Awareness Group (IAG) is the most vocal lobby attempting to stop scam marketing firms (see Chapter 18, Help Beyond This Book).

3. How to Tell an Agent From a Scam Artist

Scam marketers act like agents. They offer to help protect your invention and to license it. However, real agents and marketing companies can be distinguished from scams because legitimate agents:

- are hard to find because they rarely advertise
- do not give a sales pitch to inventors
- will tell an inventor if the invention has flaws or risk factors, and
- provide a list of satisfied clients.

In other words, a real agent is realistic about your invention and is usually willing to take a risk for a percentage of the profits. Some qualified agents may offer to evaluate your product. The evaluations performed by legitimate reps usually cost several hundred dollars and result in a critique that is particular to your invention and the appropriate industry.

Although scam marketers may seek a percentage of profits, they actually make their money by exorbitant upfront fees that are unrelated to any service that they perform. As a general rule, a person or company that demands more than $1,000 in upfront fees *and* will not furnish you with a list of clients is probably a scam marketing venture.

4. When in Doubt About a Marketing Company

If you are in doubt, some of the following methods of checking on a marketing company are recommended:

- Ask for a written estimate of the total cost of services (if they are a scam they will hesitate or be unwilling to provide a firm estimate).
- Ask what specific standards are used to evaluate your commercial success.
- Ask for a disclosure of the company's success and rejection rates. Under 35 U.S. § 297, the company must disclose its track record. Success rates show the number of clients who make more money from their invention than they paid the firm. Rejection rates reflect the percentage of all ideas or inventions that were found unacceptable by the invention promotion company. As a general rule, a reputable marketing firm rejects most of the inventions.
- Ask for a list of satisfied clients.
- Investigate the company before making any commitments (see Chapter 18, Help Beyond This Book).

You may feel comfortable dealing with an invention marketing firm because the contract you sign provides for "refunds" or is a "money-back guarantee," or perhaps you believe that you can always sue the company in your local small claims court. Good Luck! Remember that these companies did not get where they are by furnishing refunds. Regardless of the contract that you sign, the practical reality is that once a dishonest company has your money, you will never get it back. When in doubt, don't send money. ■

CHAPTER

6

Soliciting Potential Licensees

"I had a dreadful experience. I went from my house in London up to Glasgow to see this hotshot who I thought might be interested in my radio. I had my first radio (which ran for 14 minutes), and I had my patent in my pocket and my tie was straight and my nails were clean. I went to his office and I was kept waiting for 20 minutes without even a cup of tea, and then this woman went into this office and I heard her say, 'There's a silly little man with a silly clockwork thing who's come to see you. Have you got time to see him?' And he said, 'Not now, give him an excuse.' And then I came all the way back from Glasgow thinking, 'I'm a silly little man.' It's so degrading. So hurtful. But what can you do? You've got to swallow all that stuff."

— **Trevor Bayliss (inventor of the Freeplay Radio), interview on Todd Mundt Radio Show, February 8, 2001**

This chapter explains how to seek out and approach potential licensees, a process we refer to as solicitation. Solicitation occurs in two steps. First, you find likely candidates. Then, once you've gathered the names of prospective licensees, you contact them in the hopes of getting an appointment to pitch your invention.

You should read this chapter if you answer "yes" to any of the following questions:

- Are you trying to locate potential licensees but are unsure what companies might be suitable?
- Are you looking for information about a particular industry?
- Are you undecided on how to approach a potential licensee?
- Are you unsure of how to present your invention?

If you are not interested in soliciting licensees directly and plan on having someone else such as an agent or product representative do this for you, be sure to review the previous chapter on dealing with agents and reps.

As the experience of inventor Trevor Bayliss indicates above, many inventors find the solicitation process to be far more difficult and frustrating than the invention process. We will help you locate potential licensees via trade publications, newsletters, trade associations and trade shows. We will also offer you some help in overcoming some of the hurdles of invention licensing.

To Prototype or Not to Prototype

Prototypes are working models of your invention. A prototype can be quite helpful in making a presentation since it allows a licensee to actually see the invention, not simply listen to your idea. If it is possible to create a prototype for several hundred dollars, it may be worth the expense. However, if the prototype will cost thousands of dollars, you may want to consider an alternative. One method of demonstrating an invention without using a prototype is by furnishing a copy of the Provisional Patent Application (see Chapter 2). Another method is to create a computer simulation.

For example, a musician/inventor conceived of a new type of carrying case for musical instruments but could not afford to build a prototype. Instead, at a much cheaper cost, he used graphics and animation facilities and created a three-minute computer presentation which included an accurate rendering of the device. He took this computer rendering to a music manufacturer to demonstrate the product and to solicit an opinion as to its commercial potential. The music manufacturer liked the product, but not enough to manufacture the device. Although this may not seem like a happy ending, it would have been more tragic if the inventor had spent thousands of dollars creating a prototype, only to learn that it could not be licensed.

If you decide you do want a prototype created, you should look into a company that specializes in building them. These companies often advertise in the back of scientific and inventor magazines. For more information, see the section on Licensing and Inventor Organizations, in Chapter 18, Help Beyond This Book.

A. Before You Begin Your Search

Before beginning your search for a licensee, consider the following suggestions:

- **Learn about the industry.** One of the worst mistakes you can make as an inventor is to solicit a company blindly, without knowledge of that company or the overall industry. According to one successful inventor/agent, a common mistake is for an inventor to be unfamiliar with a company's product line and to show a product that is similar to something already being marketed. Before pursuing any leads, you should research the product lines, understand the industry, learn the major players and, in particular, learn about the chains of distribution. You will soon learn that distributors and retailers exert incredible influence over the potential success of a new invention. For example, it is unlikely that a toy company will release a new product unless it is confident that retailers such as Toys 'R' Us, eToys.com or Wal-Mart will carry it. This type of background knowledge is essential if you want to establish credibility when soliciting a company.

- **Be realistic.** In the business world, it's not enough to be a creative genius. If you intend to profit from your creations, you must be able to deal with business realities. Your invention may be your baby, but to someone at a large company, it's just another unsolicited product. Remember that most business people are oriented towards the bottom line—that's how they keep their jobs. It is for this reason that we suggest you seriously review the costs and commercial potential of your invention using one of the methods suggested in Chapter 1.

- **If you can't pitch your invention, find someone who can.** If you are not an aggressive or persuasive salesperson, consider affiliating with a business person or an agent. Don't be afraid of working with an agent, provided they are ethical and that you feel comfortable in the working relationship. In Chapter 5, we provide agreements that can help you work with an agent.

- **No license is better than a bad license.** Some inventors assume that any license is better than no license at all. This is not true. Entering into a licensing agreement is like a marriage. A license agreement—no matter how well drafted—cannot shield you from the aggravation and expense of dealing with the wrong company. The goal is not simply to get licensed, but to find the right partner for the license. Generally, this proves to be a much harder proposition than inventing or patenting your invention.

B. How to Find Potential Licensees

In order to solicit prospective licensees you need to gather a list of the most likely choices. Below are some methods for gathering this information.

Working Within the Industry

Some of the best information and resources for selling your invention comes from working within an industry. If you have created an invention that is applicable to the trade in which you work, you have an advantage because you probably already have contacts, understand the economics of the industry, know the trade magazines and trade shows and are aware of the major players. You are also familiar with the technology available in the trade and may be able to find new uses for old inventions.

However, there is a drawback to inventing in the industry within which you work. As discussed in Chapter 3, there is the possibility that you may, depending upon state law and your employment contract, have to relinquish title of your invention to your employer. See Chapter 3 for more on ownership issues between employers and employees.

1. Trade Associations

A trade association is group comprising the various companies within an industry. For example, the American Fan Association (AFA) is a trade group composed of companies that manufacture fans. The AFA has annual meetings and publishes a bi-monthly publication and a handbook for its member companies. Almost every industry has a trade association. Once you locate such an organization, you can obtain literature from it as well as information about conventions, meetings and directories. All of these resources are helpful in soliciting licensees.

A complete listing of all trade associations is in the *Encyclopedia of Associations* (Gale Research, Inc.), which is available at many libraries. You can locate the appropriate association in the index or by searching through the first section of the book. For example, say you have invented an automotive diagnostic tool for determining spark plug life. Using the *Encyclopedia of Associations,* you could search automotive service associations and find the address for the Equipment and Tool Institute (ETI), which is the trade association for manufacturers of automotive service equipment and tools. The ETI publishes an annual directory of all manufacturers.

2. Newsletters

Newsletters, often distributed monthly, bi-weekly or weekly, offer inside information about an industry. Some newsletters are free, some cost hundreds per year and some can be obtained only through membership in a trade association (see above). However, most newsletters will furnish a sample upon request. Newsletters can be helpful because they provide backgrounds on major companies (and their executives) within an industry and information about industry trends.

Most newsletters are listed in *Newsletters in Print* (Gale Research), available in most libraries. This book lists the newsletters in various manufacturing, retail and service industries. For example, say you

have invented a new style of woodworking gloves. You could seek an industry newsletter for the woodworking industry such as *Bit 'n' Chips,* the newsletter for the Woodworking Machinery Distributors Association. *Bit 'n' Chips* is free to members of the Association and costs $25 per year for non-members.

You may also find some newsletters on the Internet. Use your search engine and type in keywords for the industry. Many trade newsletters are available through private online subscription services such as Lexis/Nexis or Dow Jones.

3. Trade Magazines

Trade magazines are similar to newsletters. They include information about major companies, sales charts, advertisements for products and general news about particular industries. For example, *Food Service Director* is a trade magazine for the fast food industry. *Automotive Industries* provides inside information on the car industry.

Trade magazines are subsidized by trade advertising, and for this reason, they are often inexpensive. You may find the trade advertising helpful in learning about the product lines of various companies. One advantage of a subscription is that it often places you on a mailing list for industry-related publications, books, lectures and other materials.

The *Gale Directory of Publications and Broadcast Media* (Gale Research) and the *Standard Periodical Directory* (Oxbridge Communications) both provide information about trade magazines. For example, say you have invented a method of dispensing hair gel at a hair salon. You could seek a trade magazine for the salon industry. Looking under either Hairstyling or Cosmetics and Toiletries, you could locate a trade magazine, *Salon Biz,* published in Santa Monica, California. Many trade magazines are also available online either on the Internet or on private subscription services such as Lexis/Nexis.

Internet License Exchanges

Several web-based businesses seek to bring patent owners and potential licensees together. Sites such as Yet2.com (www.yet2.com), the Patent and License Exchange (www.pl-x.com), 2XFR.com (www.2xfr.com) and NewIdeaTrade.com (www.newideatrade.com) offer—for a fee—the ability to post information about patented inventions for would-be licensees. To explore these and other patent exchanges, type "patent exchange" into your Internet search engine and review the resulting sites.

www.superpages.com. It enables you to search by business category, name, street address, state or zip code.

Database companies (sometimes known as mailing list or sales leads companies) also compile listings of millions of businesses. For a fee they will supply you with a listing of all the companies within a particular industry. For example, if you invented a device that improves air circulation in motor homes, a database company could supply you with a printed mailing list for 128 motor home manufacturers. You can find database companies in your local yellow pages, usually listed under "Mailing Lists." For an example of one such company located on the Internet, check out Donnelly Marketing at www.databaseamerica.com.

4. Business Directories

Business directories are like Yellow Pages. They contain names of companies, addresses, fax and phone numbers and e-mail addresses. There are two types of business directories: general business directories that list all businesses throughout the country, and trade directories that list specific companies within an industry. Both types of directories may be helpful.

a. General Business Directories

A general business directory includes thousands of businesses, usually separated by industry. These general business directories are available in various formats.

One of the best-known general business directories is the Thomas Register, available online (www.thomasregister.com) or in print format, *Thomas Register of American Manufacturers* (Thomas Register Publishing). The *Thomas Register* lists manufacturers by subject and provides profiles and phone numbers.

In addition, there are various general business directories on the Internet, and any Internet search engine can locate them. For example, one site that may be helpful is SuperPages.com at

SIC Codes

Most corporate directories utilize a system known as the Standard Industrial Classification Code (SIC). The SIC is a four-digit number created by the Department of Commerce and is used to classify a business by the type of work it does. For example, if you invented a product to be worn while handling explosives, you might review companies classified as 1795, which is the code for the Wrecking and Demolition Industry. If you invented a timer for video cameras, you would check companies classified as 3651 for Video Equipment and Household Audio. The SIC is helpful when searching, since most corporate directories, whether in print, digital or online form, include an index of SIC codes.

b. Trade Directories

Trade directories are usually more helpful than general business directories because they only list the companies in one specific industry. If a trade directory is available for the industry related to your invention, we recommend that you obtain it. Most trade directories are published by trade magazines (see above) or as part of a trade show (see below). For example, *Playthings*, a toy industry magazine, publishes an annual directory of toy companies.

5. Sorting Out Your Research

After you've finished researching your industry, you will probably have a list of companies suitable as licensees. In some industries you may be surprised to find there are only a small number of prospects. This is often the result of corporate takeovers—one or two companies have cornered the market by acquiring the smaller players.

If, however, you are faced with many prospects, you can do more research in order to sort your list and perhaps eliminate some listings. To help in this sorting process, you should search for economic news and reports for the companies on your list.

You can obtain financial statements and news articles about many companies on the Internet. For example, check Hoovers Online (www.hoovers.com), Dow Jones (www.dowjones.com) or Thomson's Intelligence Data (www.intelligencedata.com). If you are fortunate enough to have access to the expensive Lexis/Nexis database, you can obtain a wide range of corporate information, including whether a company has been in a lawsuit, a company's assets, any financial claims against a company as well as news articles, bankruptcy reports, financial statements and other information. This background information will be helpful before you make your pitch.

C. How to Overcome a Licensee's Bias Against Submissions

Once you locate prospective licensee companies, how do you convince them to review your product? This is the toughest hurdle you will face in the licensing process, and you will need tenacity and patience. As a general rule, most companies are not actively seeking outside ideas or inventions. In fact, many companies are biased against ideas that come from the outside world. This bias stems from three major factors:

- fear of outside solicitations
- misunderstanding of independent inventors, or
- the notion that the company is doing well enough with its own internally created products.

1. Hurdle #1: Fear of Outside Solicitations

Just as you may be paranoid about showing your idea to a company (you're afraid they will steal it), a company may be fearful of you and your idea. One reason may be that the company is concerned it could get sued if it rejects your idea but later comes out with something similar. Or, if it accepted your idea, the company could later find out the idea was taken from someone else (a former employer, another inventor) who might then sue the company.

For these reasons, the only way that some companies will respond to your solicitation phone call or letter is by sending you a legal document to sign before even looking at your invention. These preliminary review agreements may have different titles (Disclosure Agreement, Nondisclosure Agreement, Waiver Agreement, Evaluation Agreement, Confidentiality Agreement). Chapter 7, on confidentiality, provides explanations, samples and advice regarding these types of agreements.

In some companies, there may be no preliminary evaluation agreement because the company has a simple policy of refusing to see outside solicitations. This is not uncommon, especially among larger companies. Unfortunately, unless you play golf with the company's CEO, there is generally no way around this policy.

2. Hurdle #2: Presumptions Regarding Independent Inventors

Like it or not, independent inventors are perceived as eccentric, kooky loners who have little knowledge of the business world. This cliché is commonly portrayed in Hollywood films: The Absent-Minded Professor, The Nutty Professor, etc. For this reason, one of the first things you must do when pitching your invention is to establish your credibility and create a climate in which the company may be more receptive to your ideas. If you can demonstrate any of the following experiences or skills, they should help strengthen your credibility:

- Academic training, if appropriate. For example, "I've studied hydroponic gardening at Purdue University where I first began experimenting with the idea of a hydroponics starter kit for children."
- Previous business success or experience, even if in another industry. For example, "For 25 years I've managed a company that sells auto parts and that's given me a good perspective on the needs of automotive consumers."
- A link between yourself and the company's products, even as a consumer. For example, "I've been using your frying pans for 20 years and I think I've come up with an improvement on the design."
- Past inventing experience. For example, "I've been doing research and development at LapCo for ten years where I was part of the team that invented the LapLander all-terrain vehicle."
- Patent protection. For example, "I recently received a patent for a device that I think would fit in well with your current line of rototilling machines." If your patent is pending but hasn't yet been issued, mention the patent status either from a regular application filing or from a provisional patent application filing.

3. Hurdle #3: The "We're Doing Okay Without You" Syndrome

Another common reason a licensee may not want to consider your submission is that the company feels that it's doing well enough without you and your invention. For example, "We have plenty of products. We have a lot of in-house developers. Why do we need you?" This theory pervades many large businesses and is difficult to overcome since it's entwined with the company's internal vision of itself.

There really is only one method of cracking this type of company and that is to use someone with insider contacts, either a business rep/manager or a contact of yours within the company. Short of that, you may be better off seeking out a smaller or mid-sized company that is still competitive and not yet stifled with inertia.

What About Selling It Yourself?

Because many companies are hostile to outside ideas, some innovators prefer trying to get the attention of these companies by making their invention a success under their own venture. In Chapter 1, we discuss selling your invention.

D. What's the Best Way to Solicit a Potential Licensee?

There is no surefire guaranteed way to successfully solicit a licensee. Each industry is different. Generally, you will have the best chance of reaching an executive at a trade show, but you may also have good luck writing a letter or calling by phone. Probably some combination of these various approaches will be needed.

The goal of your solicitation is to obtain an appointment for you to make your formal presentation. If possible, avoid disclosing more than necessary about your invention during your initial contacts.

How Do the Big Guys Do It?

Some companies that own and manage large collections of patents or trade secrets (known as portfolios) solicit licensees by means of a licensing memorandum. This is a letter that introduces the property, describes the scope of legal protection (patents, trade secrets, trademarks, etc.) and includes the general business terms for a proposed agreement. The memorandum often also includes a nondisclosure agreement (see Chapter 7) and a sample license agreement. Basically, the memorandum is a licensing kit and if the prospective licensee is interested, then the owner can move rapidly towards a licensing deal.

We do not recommend this course for you because it is unlikely that you will have the contacts or the clout to receive a response to a licensing memorandum. Instead, we recommend that you make a contact by letter or phone, present your invention and then work out the business terms.

January 10, 2002

Mr. Robert Rysher
Chief Operations Officer
Cookies, Inc.
1234 Main Street
Lakewood, NJ 08701

Re: New Innovation—Improved Biscuit Package

Dear Mr. Rysher:

I am an inventor with considerable experience in the field of packaging and design. I'm a graduate of Rhode Island School of Design. I am also a consumer of your biscuit and cookie products. Several years ago, I began researching a better method of mass-market packaging of baked goods. Last year, I reduced to practice a novel method of packaging that I believe could be less expensive than your present method and can better protect your baked goods. I am presently applying for patent protection for this process. I would very much like to discuss this innovation with you as I believe Cookies, Inc. would find it to be a valuable method of preserving your product and reducing costs. I look forward to speaking with you.

Sincerely,

Frances Kimberly

Frances Kimberly, Inventor

---

1. Solicitation Letters

Based on our limited experience and that of other inventors, letters may work as a form of solicitation, but don't expect a deluge of responses. Below is a sample solicitation letter. Remember to do your best to combine one or more of the credibility factors listed above in Section C2.

Does Letter Writing Work?

As an experiment to determine if letters were an effective method of soliciting companies with product ideas, we sent out solicitation letters to approximately 25 companies in a variety of fields such as health, hosiery, luggage, electronic musical equipment, bottling, biscuits, toys and paints. Each letter indicated that we had an invention suitable in the relative fields and included a self-addressed and stamped envelope. We received two letters back and one phone call.

2. Phone Calls

Soliciting a company by phone requires a sales mentality. You need to reach the right person and, in a very short time, convince that person that you have something worth presenting to the company. Remember, as a general rule you need to befriend every person you speak with at the company. Therefore, it is foolish ever to speak curtly or act rudely.

How do you reach the right person? If it is a large company, the receptionist may be helpful. Ask if there is someone at the company who considers new product ideas. If the person with whom you wish to speak is not expecting your call, chances are very good that you will be put through to voice-mail. In this case, you have about one minute to make a brief pitch.

To get the most out of your message, we suggest that you have your major credibility points written down and handy during your call. For example, you: 1) are an inventor with two patents and a graduate of Pratt Institute, 2) are knowledgeable about the company's products such as Product X and Y and 3) have a patent pending on a device that is more cost efficient than the company's present device. Having a list of points to cover will help prevent you from forgetting them if you're nervous or flustered.

If you do reach a real person (and not voice-mail), you should follow the same approach. Also, you should:

- get the name of the person—always keep a record of every person you speak with.
- keep the conversation short—don't get sidetracked. You should be friendly, but remember, the person on the phone is at work and your call is the equivalent of a sales pitch.
- get a direct mailing address—you want to follow up the call with a letter.
- stick to the facts and stick to the truth—don't deceive the caller in the hopes of making a sale. Any pitch that is based upon deceptions will eventually fall apart.
- thank the person at the end of the call and indicate how you intend to follow up.

3. Trade Shows

In today's security-conscious atmosphere, many executives are wary of being approached personally. However, there is one place where this rule doesn't apply—a trade show. Trade shows are conventions in which companies gather to show new products and exchange information. Trade shows and other industry gatherings are logical choices for in-person solicitations because executives are prepared to do business and they are used to meeting many different types of individuals. Also, everyone is wearing a name tag, so you know whom you're talking to. You can locate information about industry trade shows through trade associations, magazines or newsletters or by researching the publications *Trade Shows Worldwide: An International Directory of Events, Facilities, and Supplies* (Gale Research) or *Directory of Conventions* (Successful Meetings).

On the down side, trade shows are often expensive to visit (airfare, hotel fare) and to attend as a participant (booth costs, employees, etc.). Admission fees for some conventions can sometimes run into the thousands of dollars.

If your goal is to make contacts and to begin the licensing process at a trade show, you should find one that focuses on your area of invention, write to the show organizers for information on the show and attempt to determine who will be exhibiting. If an exhibitor directory is not available, find out if you can obtain a directory from the last convention.

When you register for the show, you will be given a name tag that identifies you (for example, Joan Smith, Inventor). The show organizers may be able to direct you to appropriate booths. There are three ways to make contacts at a trade show, and all three methods require an assertive personality and self-confidence.

- **Read the name cards.** This is the most challenging method. You walk through the convention, introduce yourself at booths and ask to speak with representatives of companies who are exhibiting.

- **Attend with someone who is knowledgeable.** Attend the convention with someone who has been there before. This person can walk you through, introduce you and help you make contacts. It may be possible to find such a guide beforehand by corresponding with the organizers of the event or the trade organization. If necessary, offer to pay for someone's services on an hourly basis as a consultant. For example, talk to someone exhibiting at a booth and ask if, during their off-time, you can pay them to walk you through the convention. It will probably be worth the expense.

- **Set up your own booth.** Exhibiting may enhance your ability to license because agents and licensors walk the floor examining the booths. Ideally, your invention will attract attention. But exhibiting can also be costly. The average booth is 200 square feet and ranges from $5 to $42 per square foot. You may also be charged set-up and dismantling fees and premiums for location on the floor and for electricity and furniture. Plus, you may need extra people to attend the booth who may need to be paid. Because of these costs, most trade show veterans advise that you attend a show once before you exhibit. That way, you will determine if exhibiting is worthwhile, the layout of the booths and the quality and appearance of the exhibitors.

Your goal during a trade show solicitation is to make contacts that you can follow up with a letter, phone call or presentation. As a general rule, don't expect large or mid-sized companies to set up presentations with you during the trade show, as most of these executives are already booked up with appointments. Even so, according to one successful agent, in case an executive asks to see a presentation on the spot you should always carry a nondisclosure agreement with you. (Nondisclosure agreements are covered in Chapter 7.) On-the-spot presentations sometimes happen with executives from smaller companies, who are more likely to have time to meet with you during trade shows.

Personal Appearance Counts

Unlike letters and phone calls, an in-person solicitation may be affected by your appearance. Your grooming, clothes and personal hygiene should demonstrate that you are a credible business person. You should have business cards available, and you should obtain a business card from any individual that you speak with. And as with phone conversations, keep the discussion short and stick to the facts.

E. Product Presentations

If you manage to secure an appointment for a product presentation—Congratulations! You've already gotten farther than most inventors. Your next step is to prepare yourself for the presentation (or what is often referred to as "the dog and pony show").

Some suggestions for presentations are as follows:

- **Be clear, fast and concise.** This is a sales pitch, not a dissertation. Hit the high points (cost, effectiveness, product superiority, etc.) quickly.
- **Practice your presentation but don't memorize or read it.** Your talk should have a conversational quality which is most likely to engage your listeners.
- **Know your costs.** This will probably be the first area of concern for a potential licensee. What will it cost to manufacture and sell your invention? How much can be earned?
- **Stick to the facts; stick to business.** It's fine to be friendly, but focus on the purpose of your visit, which is to convince people at the meeting to license your invention.
- **Be prepared.** Give your presentation a trial run. If you will need electrical power or additional facilities, even just a desk or bulletin board, make sure you will have them. Every marketer has disaster stories about prototypes

that failed or facilities that were unsuitable for presentation. Have a contingency plan. For example, "I'm afraid my power supply has died. In any event, I have a video that shows how this device functions and I'd be happy to leave it with you so you can see a demonstration."

- **Be flexible.** Be open to ideas and suggested modifications that are offered. Always "take them under advisement," although you probably shouldn't make changes until you can determine the seriousness of the licensee's commitment.

- **Be positive, without being foolishly upbeat.** Nobody wants to hear from a sad sack. Walk a line between enthusiasm for your invention and a calm business demeanor.

- **Have written materials to supplement your demonstration.** Use simple written materials such as numbered lists of your product's strengths to make your point. Determine the right moment to hand out paperwork— before, during or after a presentation. Charts, graphs and tables have a powerful effect in presentations and can make your point better than a spreadsheet.

- **Get feedback.** Ask for opinions. Even if the current audience is not interested, they may have suggestions that can benefit you in your next presentation.

- **Don't take it personally.** Don't appear offended by rejection. You should never have to accept a solicitee's bad manners, but don't confuse rudeness with simple rejection. If you want to stay in the invention business, you may have to deal with the same people over and over. Curb your anger and resentment, as they will be interpreted as a sign of unprofessionalism and may affect your ability to license in the future.

Kissing Shield
No. 6,293,280

Inventors' Associations

Over the past decade, groups of inventors have banded together to help each other and to get their new ideas to the marketplace. Once fragmented, these groups are now becoming more effective thanks to national organizations like the United Inventors Association (www.viausa.com) and the National Congress of Inventor Organizations (NCIO)(www.inventionconvention.com). These inventors' associations and groups can be quite helpful. For example, an Illinois man devised a lap board for quadriplegics. Unsure of how to manufacture his invention, he spoke with a volunteer from the Chicago-based Inventor's Council. The Council helped to have the device manufactured by a group of Amish woodworkers. For more information on inventor organizations see Chapter 18, Help Beyond This Book.

7

Protecting Confidential Information

This chapter guides you through the process of disclosing confidential information. This confidential information may include secret information about your invention or about any of your intellectual property rights. Confidentiality can be an important issue for inventors. If an inventor describes or shows her invention to a prospective licensee, she runs the risk that her idea may be stolen or lose intellectual property protection. The best way to protect yourself is to have a nondisclosure agreement signed before you disclose any secrets to a prospective licensee. A nondisclosure agreement is a contract in which the parties promise to protect the confidentiality of secret information that is disclosed. If you have a nondisclosure agreement with someone and they use your secret without authorization, you can sue them for damages and can request a court to stop them from making any further disclosures. Sometimes, however, a prospective licensee is unwilling to sign a nondisclosure agreement and the inventor is placed in a predicament: whether to risk confiding secret information or lose a prospective business opportunity. In this chapter, we discuss the inventor's three choices when making a disclosure:

- provide a written nondisclosure agreement
- provide no agreement, or
- provide a waiver agreement.

Using a nondisclosure agreement, you can prohibit someone from disclosing your secret invention design or from disclosing the trade secrets in your copyrighted software program. We explain the nuances of the various provisions in a standard nondisclosure agreement, and we help you evaluate another company's nondisclosure agreement. We also review situations when a company refuses to sign a confidentiality agreement or when a company asks you to relinquish any claims of secrecy.

Nondisclosure agreements are often known by other names such as Disclosure Agreements and Confidentiality Agreements. However, the name of the agreement is not as important as the content. Some agreements are titled Disclosure or Confidentiality Agreements yet their terms have the *opposite* effect. Instead of agreeing to secrecy, the inventor effectively waives any claim of trade secret confidentiality. By signing one of these waiver agreements, you can lose rights that may affect your invention. For example, you may risk disclosing secret information about a pending patent. An explanation of waiver agreements is provided in Section C of this Chapter.

A. Confidential Information and Nondisclosure Agreements

In Chapter 2, we explained that confidential business information that is not known by your competitors can be protected under an area of intellectual property law known as trade secrets. In a sense, trade secrets relate to all forms of intellectual property. In the early stages of their development, a trademark, a copyrighted design or a patentable invention can be confidential business information. Once the patent is published, the trademark is printed or the copyright is distributed, the secret status will end. Until the information is made public, however, it has a value because it is your secret.

The best strategy to protect your secret information is to sign a written nondisclosure agreement—a contract in which both parties agree to maintain certain information in confidence. If the agreement is breached—if the information is disclosed without your authorization—you can sue for monetary damages.

1. Nondisclosure Agreements

The sample agreement provided below includes many provisions which are considered standard. This agreement is designed for a one-way disclosure. You (the disclosing party) are disclosing secrets and the person or company who receives the secrets (the receiving party) is obligated to maintain secrecy. If the company wants to give you confidential information such as sales information, then you use a mutual (two-way) nondisclosure agreement. Mutual disclosures are discussed in Section 2a, below. It is possible that prospective licensees may furnish you with their own version of a confidentiality agreement. We discuss how to review a nondisclosure agreement in the sidebar, Reviewing Their Nondisclosure Agreement, below.

You Must Protect Your Confidential Information

Although a nondisclosure agreement will assure your right to sue, it will not guarantee your success in court. You can never rely solely on an agreement as a basis for protection of confidential information. As explained in Chapter 2, you must also be able to prove that you took reasonable steps to protect your secret and that the secret has not become known to the public.

For more information about nondisclosure agreements and trade secrets, consult *Nondisclosure Agreements: Protect Your Trade Secrets and More,* by Richard Stim and Stephen Fishman.

2. One-Way Nondisclosure Agreement

The sample nondisclosure agreement below provides the minimum level of protection necessary for an inventor. It is possible to draft an agreement that provides stronger protection. Provisions can be inserted that will provide for legal remedies such as injunctions (the right to obtain a court order) or personal jurisdiction (the right to force someone to bring or defend against a lawsuit in your geographic area). However, these provisions often raise flags with prospective licensees, who routinely seek to have them removed. If you would like to use these provisions, they are provided in Section D.

Reviewing Their Nondisclosure Agreement

A company may want you to sign their written nondisclosure agreement or modify yours. Generally, it does not matter who furnishes the nondisclosure agreement. If a company is willing to enter into a nondisclosure agreement, you're already ahead of the game. If the nondisclosure agreement contains the basic elements to limit disclosure (described below) and your research indicates a sense of trust about the other party, sign the agreement rather than arguing about details. Save your serious negotiations for the licensing contract.

EXAMPLE: In the early 1980s, IBM was considering two different operating system programs for its first personal computer. Bill Gates owned one operating system and the other was owned by a rival of Mr. Gates. IBM first went to Gates's rival. What followed was a lengthy negotiation about the terms of the nondisclosure agreement involving lawyers for both sides. When the negotiations bogged down, IBM offered the same nondisclosure agreement to Gates, who read it once and signed it. IBM reviewed Gates's program and quickly licensed the DOS program. Out of this relationship Microsoft was created.

This is not to imply you should blindly sign any nondisclosure agreement. *You shouldn't!* But you *should* avoid lengthy negotiations over disclosure issues, particularly if the agreement contains the minimum elements of protection.

The nondisclosure agreement you will be furnished can vary in format. You should make a copy so that you can mark it up and then identify and label each of the basic elements. Generally there are five important elements to a nondisclosure agreement.
- definition of confidential information
- exclusions from confidential information
- obligations of receiving party
- time periods, and
- miscellaneous provisions.

One-Way Nondisclosure Agreement

Parties

This nondisclosure agreement (the "Agreement") is entered into by and between _____ _____ *[insert your name, business form and address]* ("disclosing party") and _____ _____ *[insert name, business form and address of person or company to whom you will disclose information]* ("receiving party") for the purpose of preventing the unauthorized disclosure of Confidential Information (as defined below).

Summary

Disclosing party may disclose confidential and proprietary trade secret information to receiving party. The parties mutually agree to enter into a confidential relationship with respect to the disclosure of certain proprietary and confidential information (the "Confidential Information").

Definition of Confidential Information (Written or Oral)

For purposes of this Agreement, "Confidential Information" shall include all information or material that has or could have commercial value or other utility in the business in which disclosing party is engaged. In the event that Confidential Information is in written form, the disclosing party shall label or stamp the materials with the word "Confidential" or some similar warning. In the event that Confidential Material is transmitted orally, the disclosing party shall promptly provide a writing indicating that such oral communication constituted Confidential Information.

Exclusions From Confidential Information

Receiving party's obligations under this Agreement shall not extend to information that is: (a) publicly known at the time of disclosure under this Agreement or subsequently becomes publicly known through no fault of the receiving party; (b) discovered or created by the receiving party prior to the time of disclosure by disclosing party; or (c) otherwise learned by the receiving party through legitimate means other than from the disclosing party or anyone connected with the disclosing party.

Obligations of Receiving Party

The receiving party shall hold and maintain the Confidential Information of the other party in strictest confidence for the sole and exclusive benefit of the disclosing party. The receiving party shall carefully restrict access to any such Confidential Information to persons bound by this Agreement, only on a need-to-know basis. The receiving party shall not, without prior written approval of the disclosing party, use for the receiving party's own benefit, publish, copy or otherwise disclose to others, or permit the use by others for their benefit or to the detriment of the disclosing party, any of the Confidential Information. The receiving party shall return to disclosing party any and all records, notes and other written, printed or tangible materials in its possession pertaining to the Confidential Information immediately on the written request of disclosing party.

Time Periods

The nondisclosure and confidentiality provisions of this Agreement shall survive the termination of any relationship between the disclosing party and the receiving party.

PROTECTING CONFIDENTIAL INFORMATION

Miscellaneous

Nothing contained in this Agreement shall be deemed to constitute either party a partner, joint venturer or employee of the other party for any purpose. This Agreement may not be amended except in a writing signed by both parties. If a court finds any provision of this Agreement invalid or unenforceable as applied to any circumstance, the remainder of this Agreement shall be interpreted so as best to effect the intent of the parties. This Agreement shall be governed by and interpreted in accordance with the laws of the State of _____ *[insert your state of residence]*. Any controversy or claim arising out of or relating to this Agreement, or the breach of this Agreement, shall be settled by arbitration in accordance with the rules of the American Arbitration Association and judgment upon the award rendered by the arbitrator(s) may be entered in any court having jurisdiction. The prevailing party shall have the right to collect from the other party its reasonable costs and attorney's fees incurred in enforcing this agreement. Any such arbitration hearing shall include a written transcript of the proceedings and a written explanation for any final determination. This Agreement expresses the complete understanding of the parties with respect to the subject matter and supersedes all prior proposals, agreements, representations and understandings. This Agreement and each party's obligations shall be binding on the representatives, assigns and successors of such party. Each party has signed this Agreement through its authorized representative.

DISCLOSING PARTY:

_____   _____
Disclosing Party's Name   Date

RECEIVING PARTY:

_____   _____
Receiving Party's Name/Title   Date

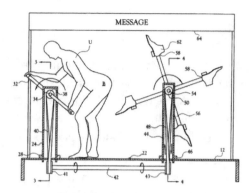

**User-Operated Amusement Apparatus
for Kicking the Users Buttocks
No. 6,293,874**

a. Parties and Summary

The introductory "Parties" paragraph defines the parties and indicates which party will disclose information and which will receive it. Some companies will want to give you confidential information, not just receive it. For example, they may want to disclose marketing or sales information in order to prepare a course of action with your invention. Or perhaps the company is unsure if it will disclose confidential information to you but wants to have the option available. In this case, a mutual non-disclosure agreement will be needed. In order to modify the sample agreement to be a mutual agreement, substitute the following title and introductory paragraphs.

Creating a Mutual Nondisclosure Agreement— Optional

Parties. This Nondisclosure agreement (the "Agreement") is entered into by and between

insert your name, business form and address insert

name, business form and address of and other person

or company with whom you are exchanging information

(collectively referred to as the "parties") for the purpose of preventing the unauthorized disclosure of Confidential Information (as defined below).

Summary. The parties may disclose confidential and proprietary trade secret information to each other for the purpose of exploring a possible business relationship. The parties mutually agree to enter into a confidential relationship with respect to the disclosure by one or each (the "disclosing party") to the other (the "receiving party") of certain proprietary and confidential information (the "Confidential Information").

b. Definition of Confidential Information

Every nondisclosure agreement provides a definition of confidential information or trade secrets. The purpose is to establish the boundaries or subject matter of the disclosure. You may be furnished a nondisclosure agreement that defines confidential information by listing the types of confidential information, such as: "Confidential Information includes programming code, financial information, materials or innovative processes, etc." You can safely sign this type of agreement, provided that you can find something on the list that will fit your type of disclosure.

Many nondisclosure agreements include an obligation to certify the confidentiality of the disclosure (for example, stamping it "confidential"). In some nondisclosure agreements, an oral disclosure will only be protected when confirmed with a follow up letter. For example:

Dear Sam:

Today at lunch, I disclosed information to you about my kaleidoscopic projection system (specifically, the manner in which I have configured and wired the bulbs in the device). That information is confidential (as described in our nondisclosure agreement) and this letter is intended to confirm the disclosure.

William Smith
William Smith

Notice that the actual trade secret is not disclosed in the letter. The inventor has described the disclosure without revealing anything proprietary. In some cases, the nondisclosure agreement may not permit oral disclosures.

⚠️ Whatever you disclose (or is disclosed to you) should be noted in your business file, along with the dates of disclosure and to whom the disclosure was made.

c. Exclusions From Confidential Information

Every nondisclosure agreement excludes some information from protection. That is, the receiving party has no obligation to protect certain information. These exceptions are based upon established principles of law—the most important one being that information is not protected if it was created or discovered by the licensee prior to (or independent of) any involvement with you. That is, if a prospective licensee develops an invention with similar trade secret information *before* being exposed to your secrets, then the company is still free to use its independently created invention.

This seems fair, but some companies go farther when excluding information. They request the right to exclude information that is independently developed *after* the disclosure. That is, a company does not want to be prohibited from independently developing similar trade secrets after learning your secrets.

If you can avoid this provision, great. But it's not quite as frightening as it may seem. The fact is that under most state laws, the prospective licensee has the right to independently develop a similar product after exposure to your trade secret. The prospective licensee only violates the law if your secret is improperly used to develop the company's product. It is possible, for instance, that one division of a large company could invent something without any contact with the division that has been exposed to your secret. However, if you disclosed your trade secret to a company and they soon came out with a competing product, it may well be hard for you to believe that the creation was independent. Common

sense (or a natural suspicion of business practices) would lead you to believe that your secret was stolen. How do you prove it?

That's the real issue with excluding information developed after the disclosure—proof of independent development. How do you prove your secret was (or was not) used improperly in a company's product? How does the company prove that the product was developed independently? The best you can do is to document your exchange of information and be able to prove that you have used reasonable standards to protect the information. The rest of it is in the hands of your attorney, who will apply legal standards of proof.

Nondisclosure agreements commonly exclude information that is in the public domain. This is based on the principle that no party should have a monopoly over publicly known information. However, this type of provision has a downside. A company may sign a nondisclosure agreement, take a submitted idea without permission and when sued, conduct an extensive prior art patent search to locate a patent that is similar to the idea. Even though the company did not rely on the prior art patent, the published patents qualified as public domain information. A defense such as this was successfully used by a toy company accused of violating a nondisclosure agreement. *Kublan v. Hasbro Toy Division,* 50 U.S.P.Q. 2d 1539 (S.D.N.Y. 1999). The only means of avoiding such a defense is for the inventor to conduct a prior art search, list any patents relating to the disclosure and modify the exclusion statement in section (a) regarding public domain material as follows (the added material is in bold type):

Exclusions from Confidential Information.
Receiving party's obligations under this Agreement shall not extend to information that is:
(a) publicly known at the time of disclosure under this Agreement or subsequently becomes publicly known through no fault of the receiving party, ***excluding information contained in pending or issued patents other than those patents listed in Exhibit A: [list of prior art patents would then be attached to the agreement in an Exhibit A]. (b) ...***

d. Obligations of the Receiving Party

The receiving party generally must hold and maintain the information in confidence and limit its use. Under most state laws, the receiving party cannot breach the confidential relationship, induce others to breach it or induce others to acquire the secret by improper means. Most companies will accept these contract obligations without discussion. If you enter into a mutual nondisclosure agreement, you should also feel comfortable with these requirements.

e. Time Periods

The sample agreement has no time limit for how long the secret must be kept confidential. Some agreements require that the receiving party maintain the secret information for a limited period of years. For example, the receiving party must not use or disclose the secret for a period of five years from the date the agreement was executed. The time period is often an issue of negotiation. Disclosing parties want an open period with no limits; receiving parties want a short period. Five years is a common length in American nondisclosure agreements (although many companies insist on two or three years). In European nondisclosure agreements, it is not unusual for the period to be as long as ten years. Ultimately, the length you decide to use will depend on the relative bargaining power of the parties.

One factor in your determination may be the shelf life of your idea. Ask the following questions:

* How long will it be before others stumble upon the same innovation?
* If the product were licensed in the next year or two, how long would it be before the secret was reverse engineered? (See Chapter 2 for an explanation of reverse engineering.)

If the answer to these questions is a few years, then you are unlikely to be damaged by a shorter (two- to three-year) period.

f. Miscellaneous

Miscellaneous provisions (sometimes known as "boilerplate") are included at the end of every agreement. The miscellaneous provisions provided at the end of our sample agreement are standard. That is, they are used without question in most licensing agreements. Even though they are standard, however, each element is important. Before striking or adding language to the miscellaneous section, you should review the discussion on boilerplate provisions in Chapter 14.

g. Signing the Agreement

Each party must sign the agreement in relation to the business that is represented (for example, as a general partner representing the partnership), and each party must have the authority to sign the agreement. To further reinforce this, you will note the language in the sample agreement: "Each party has signed this Agreement through its authorized representative." Use the following rules when determining the proper signature line:

Sole Proprietorship. If you or the other party is a sole proprietorship, simply sign your own name. If you have a fictitious business name (sometimes known as a *dba*), then list the name of the business above the signature line. For example, Tom Stein is a sole proprietor calling his business Eine Stein Inventions. He would sign as follows:

Eine Stein Inventions

By: _____
     Tom Stein

Partnership. If you or the other party is a general or limited partnership, then the only person authorized to sign the agreement is a general partner or someone who has written authority from a general partner (usually in the form a partnership resolution). The name of the partnership must be mentioned above the signature line or the partnership will not be bound (only the person signing the agreement). Cindy Barrett is a general partner in Reality Manufacturing Partnership. She would sign as follows:

Reality Manufacturing Partnership

By: _____

      Cindy Barrett, a general partner

Corporation or LLC. If you or the other party is a corporation or limited liability company (LLC), then only a person authorized by the corporation can sign the agreement. The president or chief executive officer (CEO) usually has such power, but not every officer of a corporation has the authority to bind the corporation. If in doubt, ask for written proof of the authority. This proof is usually in the form of a corporate resolution. The name of the corporation should be mentioned above the signature line or the corporation may not be bound (only the person signing the agreement). For example, Marya DeRosa is CEO of Sincere Marketing. She would sign as follows:

Sincere Marketing, Inc., a New York corporation

By: _____

      Marya DeRosa, CEO

Note: If you have reason to question the credibility of the company representative, then investigate the company (see Chapter 6). If you have doubts about the person's authority, don't proceed until you are satisfied that the person has full authority to represent the company.

Can You Fax Your Signature?

A faxed signature is suitable assuming that both parties do not dispute the authenticity of the signature. If there is a dispute about the signature (that is, one party claims a forgery), then you will have difficulty proving the signature is authentic from a fax. If you sign the agreement by fax, follow up the fax by mailing or overnighting signed copies.

B. Proceeding Without an Agreement

We advise you to get a prospective licensee to sign a nondisclosure agreement, but we are also aware of business realities. Many prospective licensees refuse to sign an unknown inventor's nondisclosure agreement. If you disclose without the agreement, you risk losing the secret. That may have a devastating effect. If you don't disclose the information, you risk losing a business opportunity.

Probably the most important factor is the reputation of the prospective licensee. If the company has a poor reputation, the dangers of losing your secrets outweigh the business opportunity. You can research the company using techniques discussed in Chapter 6.

Although a nondisclosure agreement is the best form of protection, there are methods of guarding your rights in the absence of an agreement. We discuss some of these methods below.

Most Companies Will Not Steal Your Secret

One study of trade secret cases determined that trade secret owners prevailed in 75% of the cases—poor odds for parties planning to steal. Most companies don't want to risk a lawsuit when the trade secrets can be acquired through a license. Since royalties and advances amount to a small portion of the overall costs, it is less expensive to license the work legitimately than risk litigation. In addition, the company may want more golden eggs from the inventor. For these reasons, companies generally play fairly. Still, you must investigate a company's reputation before making a disclosure without an agreement.

1. The Limits of State Trade Secret Laws

Trade secrets are protected under state laws, many of which are adopted from the federal Uniform Trade Secrets Act. However, you should not rely on these laws to protect you. These state laws only protect against the misappropriation of a trade secret. Misappropriation is:

- the acquisition of a trade secret by a person who has reason to know that the trade secret was obtained by improper means
- the unauthorized disclosure or use of a trade secret by a person who had a duty to maintain secrecy, or
- the disclosure or use of a trade secret by a person who used improper means to acquire it.

"Improper means" refers to unethical methods such as deliberate theft, burglary, industrial espionage or knowingly obtaining the secret from someone who has a duty not to disclosure the information. If you voluntarily disclose your secrets to a prospective licensee, that would not be an improper means of acquiring the information, and state laws will not be helpful.

2. Disclosing "Around" the Secret

A licensee is primarily concerned with two questions about your invention: a) What does it do? and b) Is it profitable? Try to determine if there is a way to present your invention and an estimate of its costs without disclosing trade secrets. (As discussed in Chapter 1, this cost analysis is often more crucial to your licensing ability than the invention itself.) If you can provide the licensee with this information, it may be an incentive for them to enter into a nondisclosure agreement.

3. Confidential Relationships Without Written Agreements

A confidential relationship can, in some cases, be established without a signed agreement. An implied confidential relationship occurs when the conduct

of the parties indicates that they intended to create a confidential relationship. In an implied confidential relationship, you have legal rights similar to those created by a written agreement. A confidential relationship can be implied if certain factors are present:

- the prospective licensee solicited the idea from you—that is, you did not send the information without prompting
- you indicated that the invention was a business proposition—you hoped for payment
- at the time of disclosure, you requested that the information be kept secret, and
- the information is a trade secret—it has commercial value and is not known by competitors.

Although a confidential relationship can be implied, it is always more difficult to prove than a relationship based upon a written nondisclosure agreement. In one case, an inventor developed a ratchet by combining parts of two existing tools and brought it to the attention of an independent dealer for the Snap-On Tools company. Later, the inventor submitted a tool suggestion form to Snap-On's corporate headquarters. The inventor never requested confidentiality and never indicated that he expected compensation for his idea. Snap-On manufactured and sold the ratchet without paying the inventor. The inventor sued, but the court ruled against him because he disclosed the information without stating that it was a business proposition in which he hoped for payment.

C. Waiver Agreements

Some companies are wary of reviewing an unknown inventor's information. In addition to lawsuits, a company may also be concerned because it is developing a similar product. The confidential relationship could preclude them from proceeding with their own research and development. Not only won't they sign a nondisclosure agreement, but they may require the inventor to waive (give up) all claims of confidentiality before they even look at the invention. This waiver is accomplished by having the inventor sign a written waiver agreement.

These agreements, needless to say, can be dangerous. Since trade secret protection is based upon confidentiality, your waiver could result in the loss of trade secret rights, and you will have no legal recourse. This section offers advice on how to identify and deal with waiver agreements.

1. Identifying a Waiver Agreement

A waiver agreement usually contains the following language:

- "This agreement does not create a confidential relationship."
- "No confidential relationship is established or implied by the exchange (or disclosure) of information (or submission)."
- "The exchange (or disclosure) of information (or submission) is not made in confidence."
- "No obligation of any kind is created (or assumed or implied or imputed) by the receipt (or exchange or disclosure) of information (or submission)."

2. Waivers and Patentable Inventions

If the only secrets you had were in a pending patent application and you were certain that the patent would issue, then signing a waiver would not be as risky. Why? Because once the patent issues, your secrets would be public and protected under patent law. The fact that you waive confidentiality would not matter. However, there are still considerable risks to this approach:

- Even if a patent is issued, there may be additional aspects of your patented device or process that are protected by trade secrets.
- You may devise improvements which, until patented, would only be protected by trade secret law. In such cases, only a confidential relationship will protect your trade secrets.

- If the patent is pending (remember the patent application process can take 18 months to two years), you could face a trade secrecy problem if you sign a waiver and ultimately don't get the patent.
- Trademarks (names for your products) will have no effective protection until they are distributed to the public. Therefore, if you disclose a clever trademark name or logo, it would not be protected.

Although you can freely disclose information about your patented invention, a waiver of trade secret rights may still affect non-patented trade secrets such as improvements to your invention. The decision whether to sign a waiver agreement should be made using the risk analysis described above. You'll need to weigh the risk of losing the business opportunity against the risk of losing trade secret rights.

D. When You Have Sufficient Bargaining Power

Normally, an inventor has little bargaining power and cannot control whether a prospective licensee signs a nondisclosure agreement. The three scenarios described above (written agreement, no agreement and waiver agreement) reflect this lack of bargaining power. However, in some cases you may have sufficient bargaining power to control the content of the agreement. In that case, you can consider strengthening your confidentiality agreement with the following additional provisions.

1. Indemnification

Some inventors seek to add an additional obligation —that the receiving party will pay for all damages (lost profits, attorney's fees or other expenses) incurred as a result of the receiving party's breach of the nondisclosure agreement. This obligation is known as indemnification and is discussed in Chapter 12. Leaving out the indemnity provision does not prevent you from collecting damages for a breach (contract law holds the receiving party responsible for a breach); however, the clause makes it easier to claim damages. To include indemnity in your nondisclosure agreement, add the following language at the end of the obligations section:

> The receiving party shall take all necessary action to protect the confidentiality of the Confidential Information and agrees to indemnify the disclosing party against any and all losses, damages, claims or expenses incurred or suffered by the disclosing party as a result of the receiving party's breach of this Agreement.

2. Injunctions

An injunction is a court order directing a person to do (or stop doing) something. In the case of trade secrets, it would be a court order directing the company to stop using your secrets. Normally, the inventor seeking the injunction must be able to demonstrate that they have suffered or will suffer an irreparable harm as a result of a company's using their secrets.

Proving these issues in court is expensive and time-consuming. In order to cut through some of that legal work, some nondisclosure agreements include a provision similar to the one below. This provision is an admission by the receiving party that the harm caused by a breach is irreparable. With this provision, you will have less to prove if and when you seek the court order. This provision only enhances your ability to obtain an injunction; by itself, it will not compel a judge to order an injunction.

> **Injunctive Relief.** The receiving party understands and acknowledges that any disclosure or misappropriation of any of the Confidential Information in violation of this Agreement may cause the disclosing party irreparable harm, the amount of which may be difficult to ascertain. Therefore, the receiving party agrees that the disclosing party shall

have the right to apply to a court of competent jurisdiction for an order restraining and enjoining any such further disclosure or misappropriation and for such other relief as the disclosing party shall deem appropriate. Such right of the disclosing party is to be in addition to the remedies otherwise available to disclosing party at law or in equity.

3. Jurisdiction and Choice of Law

In Chapter 14, we provide background on jurisdiction and choice of law. As we explain in that chapter, choice of law refers to what law will be applied if the matter is litigated or arbitrated. For example, if the agreement states, "This Agreement shall be governed in accordance with the laws of the State of California," then California law will apply even if a lawsuit is filed in Virginia. Generally we recommend that the choice of law be the law of your state of residence.

Jurisdiction is different than the choice of law. Jurisdiction—also called forum or venue—refers to the place where you must go to argue the dispute. We advise against being dragged into a distant location to litigate or arbitrate disputes. If the location is far enough from where you live or do business, then it will most certainly keep you from bringing a legitimate lawsuit or greatly harm your ability to defend against a lawsuit. If your bargaining power permits it, you should seek to have choice of jurisdiction in your state and county of residence. Below is a sample provision.

> **Jurisdiction.** The parties consent to the exclusive jurisdiction of the state courts and federal courts insert your state located in _____ County, *insert your state of residence* , in any action arising out of or relating to this Agreement and waive any other venue to which they might be entitled by domicile or otherwise.

If there is no mention of jurisdiction in the nondisclosure agreement, then it will be determined by state laws. In such cases, the first person to file the lawsuit generally determines jurisdiction.

E. Disclosing to Employees and Contractors

If you are paying an employee or an independent contractor for services, you should be concerned about confidentiality and should sign nondisclosure agreements. If you fail to obtain a nondisclosure agreement with an employee, you still have substantial protection under state trade secret laws. These laws were drafted primarily to protect employers. On the other hand, you may not be as well protected with an independent contractor (for example, consultants, agents, vendors or manufacturers), so you should be sure to sign a nondisclosure agreement if you will disclose secrets to one. For more information about service agreements, see Chapter 15.

F. Disclosing to an Attorney

When you retain the services of an attorney, a privileged relationship is created. The attorney cannot divulge information given in confidence. The attorney can only disclose information you've shared with her if you give your consent or under special circumstances such as a court order. This confidential relationship (attorney/client privilege) also applies to employees and agents of the attorney. You should observe the following guidelines regarding attorney/client relationships:

- Disclosures to an attorney are only protected when made in confidence. For example, public disclosures (in a diner or a ballpark) that could be overheard might not be protected.
- The attorney/client privilege only applies to *your* attorney—the attorney you have retained. A casual discussion with an attorney (sometimes known as "street corner advice") will generally not set the privilege in motion (although in some states it may). ∎

The Key Elements of Your Agreement

nce you find a company interested in licensing your invention, you and the prospective licensee must agree on a number of essential business issues. This chapter (and the next) will walk you through the basic foundations of the contract. In this chapter, we will review issues about defining your invention and identifying the parties. We will help you decide how long the license should last, whether it should be exclusive, what territory it should cover and other key issues. (In the next chapter we discuss how much you should get paid.) You should read this chapter if you answer yes to any of the following questions:

- Do you need to better understand the difference between your invention and the licensed product?
- Do you need help determining the sort of license that best suits your invention?
- Do you need an explanation of the difference between an exclusive or nonexclusive license?
- Do you need help in deciding the territory or length of your license agreement?

At the end of this chapter is a worksheet that you can use to help you identify the basic facts to be used in your license agreement.

A. From Handshake to License

License agreements usually develop in two stages. First, the parties—the licensor and the licensee—negotiate the essential elements of the agreement (sometimes referred to as the "business terms"—see sidebar). These basic elements are the foundation of the license and they include:

- identification of the parties
- a description of the invention
- a description of the licensee's products containing the invention
- the rights granted by the license
- how long the license will last
- whether or not it will be exclusive

- what territory it will cover
- how much and at what intervals you will get paid, and
- provisions for dispute resolution.

After agreeing on these basic elements, the parties incorporate this information into a more detailed written agreement. A licensee may refer to this second stage as "turning it over to the lawyers," because the licensee's lawyer becomes involved in revising or drafting the agreement. During this second stage, the parties may negotiate over a wide range of contract provisions such as post-termination rights, warranties or indemnity (discussed in Chapter 12).

Both stages of contract negotiation are important. Don't assume that the deal is done just because you have agreed upon the essential business terms.

The Term, Business Terms & Term Sheets

Although we have tried to avoid confusion, you should be aware that the word "term" could have different meanings in a license agreement. The basic contract elements are often referred to as the "business terms", and the sheet that contains these business elements is sometimes referred to as a "Term Sheet." The length of the agreement is also referred to as the "term."

If We Don't Get It Right, Can We Change the Agreement Later?

We urge you to work towards creating a final licensing agreement. It's true that if both parties agree to do so, you can amend contract terms and definitions after the contract is signed. However, it's not always easy to agree on alterations once the product is licensed and sales have begun. In addition, amendments and modifications are time-consuming. Concentrate on getting the agreement right before you sign it and use amendments only if necessary.

In order to assist you in your negotiation, we have prepared a worksheet that includes each of the essential elements of your license agreement. It is located at the end of this chapter. This worksheet can be converted into an exhibit (a separate document attached to the agreement). For example, see the exhibit attached to the sample license agreement in Chapter 11.

B. Identifying the Parties

Perhaps the most basic element of your licensing agreement is identifying the people or businesses that are entering into the agreement, otherwise known as the parties. The parties are the people signing the agreement—you (the licensor), the licensee and an agent (if there is one)—who must abide by its terms. The parties should always be identified at the beginning of the agreement by name, the business form and the business address. If you are not sure of your business form (sole proprietor, partnership or corporation), you should review Chapter 4.

Check out the business cards you have received from the licensee. They should provide you with information about the entity that is licensing the invention. If you are licensing to a company that is owned by another, ask which party will sign the agreement. Sometimes the parent company—the company that owns the other—signs the licensing agreement. If the licensee is incorporated, find out in which state it incorporated.

It's fairly simple to determine the parties, so this essential element does not require much discussion. Because the license agreement refers to the parties many times, they are sometimes referred to as Licensee and Licensor or given abbreviated names. For example, you can refer to a licensee named Medco Affiliated Industries, Inc. as MEDCO. Like most defined elements of the license, these names are capitalized throughout the agreement for easy reference.

1. Statement of Parties

Information about the parties is usually incorporated into the first paragraph of the agreement. A sample is provided below.

> This License Agreement (the "Agreement") is made between Joe Smith, a sole proprietor, of 34 Westwood Ave., Rolling Brook, New Mexico (referred to as "Licensor") and Flameco International Products, Inc., a California corporation with its principal address at 4356 Industrial Drive, Collingswood, California (referred to as "Licensee"). Licensor and Licensee shall be collectively referred to as "the parties."

2. How to Include Agents in Your Agreement

If there is an agent, the agent may or may not be a party to the agreement. (A "party" is named in the first paragraph, signs the agreement and is bound by the provisions.) Many agents want to be a party in order to obtain their payments directly from the licensee. Generally, we recommend that the agent become a party, since the agent should be bound by the contract, particularly the dispute resolution procedures. In addition, if the agent signs as a party, then both you and the agent can sue for recovery of royalty payments. A sample provision to include an agent is provided below.

> This License Agreement (the "Agreement") is made among Joe Smith, a sole proprietor, of 34 Westwood Ave., Rolling Brook, New Mexico (referred to as "Licensor"); Licensor's agent, Frances Representatives, a New Jersey corporation with its principal place of business at 27 Lodisco Drive, Burlinghead, Nevada (referred to as "Licensor's Agent"); and Flameco International Products, Inc., a California corporation with its principal address at 4356 Industrial Drive, Collingswood, California (referred to as "Licensee"). Licensor and Licensee shall be collectively referred to as "the parties."

C. Describing Your Invention and the Licensed Products

Although it may seem obvious, two essential elements of your agreement are specifying exactly what invention you are licensing and defining the products or processes in which the licensee will use your invention. In other words, don't assume that there's anything self-evident about what the invention is or how the licensee will use it.

It is important that you understand the difference between your invention and the licensed products. As you discuss the product or process that is the basis for the licensing agreement, you and the licensor will refer to *two* versions of your invention. One is the invention as you created or patented it. The other is the invention as the licensee sells it, which is usually referred to as the licensed product. In other words, your invention goes in one door and a licensed product (or products) comes out the other. The licensed product is your invention as packaged or modified by the licensee. Both versions of the invention—as you created it and as it is sold —require separate names (for example, "Property" and "Licensed Products"), because your payments are based upon sales of the licensed product.

⚠ Do not underestimate the importance of these definitions. Both definitions will have an impact on the license agreement. The definition of your invention explains what the licensee is getting from you. The definition of licensed products describes what the licensee is doing with your invention and affects how you are paid.

1. Defining the Invention

As part of your agreement, you and the licensee will need to agree upon a definition of your invention. It may seem obvious—it's *your invention*. But you will need to write a succinct statement of what you are licensing and agree on that definition because it will be incorporated into the definition of

the licensed product. Definitions of inventions are usually labeled or abbreviated with a term such as "the Invention," "the Property," "the Licensed Patents," "the Process," "the Technical Information" or "the Intellectual Property."

Below are some suggestions for creating a definition of your invention. Use the suggestions that apply to your situation.

a. You Have a Patent or Pending Patent Application

If you have a patent or have applied for one, you should define your invention based upon your patent claims and include a copy of the patent (or the claims listed in your application) with the final agreement. For example, you could use one of the following clauses:

☐ *Patent Issued*

The "Property" refers to the invention(s) described in U.S. Patent No(s). _____ *[insert patent number]*.

☐ *Patent Not Yet Issued*

The "Property" refers to the invention(s) described in U.S. Patent Application No(s). _____ *[insert patent application number]*, a copy of which is attached to this agreement.

If the licensee wants to acquire more rights to your invention such as improvements on your patent or foreign patent rights, then the definition may be more detailed. For example:

☐ *Patents & Improvements*

The "Property" is defined as the invention(s) described in U.S. Patent No(s). _____ *[insert patent number]* and any improvements, reissues or extensions, as well as any continuations, divisions or substitute U.S. patent applications that shall be based on U.S. Patent No(s). _____ *[insert patent number(s) (same number as above)]*; and any patent applications corresponding to the above-described patents and patent applications that are issued, filed or to be filed in any and all foreign countries.

The term "Improvements" may need its own definition, since some inventors may not want to permit a licensee to use every improvement that results from a patent. For example, if you only wanted the licensee to obtain rights to improvements that reduced the production cost, you could state that an Improvement is defined as "any modification or method that reduces the production cost of the Licensed Product." By limiting the definition of improvements, the licensee only obtains rights to the improvements that fall within the definition. However, before you make a decision about improvements, read the section on "Improvements" and "Grant Backs" in Chapter 15. Remember, the definitions often define the scope of your license.

b. You Don't Have a Patent

In the case of a non-patented invention, the definition of the invention should describe the invention and indicate the proprietary rights that you have acquired. For an explanation of proprietary rights, review Chapter 2. The description of the invention should tell what it looks like, what it is and what it does. For example:

Copyrights, Trade Secrets and Trademarks: No Patents

The "Property" refers to all proprietary rights, including but not limited to copyrights, trade secrets, formulas, research data, know-how and specifications related to the invention commonly known as the _____ [name of invention], as well as any trademark rights and associated good will. A more complete description is provided in the attached Exhibit A.

c. You Have a Copyright Registration for Your Invention

If you have a copyright registration for some aspect of your invention, you should make reference to that registration by number and date. Chapter 2 provides information about copyrights. You can use

the same provision as for non-patent proprietary rights (in Section 1b above), with the following modification to the first sentence:

Copyright Issued

The "Property" refers to all proprietary rights, including but not limited to copyrights as embodied in Copyright Registration No. _____ dated _____, trade secrets formulas, research data....

d. Trademark Rights

If you have acquired trademark rights, the licensee would want the right to use the mark. If you have registered the trademark, you should make reference to the registration by number and date. All you need to do is modify the first portion of the non-patents proprietary rights provision in Section 1b as follows:

Trademark Rights Registered

The "Property" refers to all proprietary rights, including but not limited to copyrights, trade secrets, formulas, research data, know-how and specifications related to the invention commonly known as the _____ [name of invention], as well as all trademark rights and good will associated with the Federal Trademark Registration Number _____ dated _____. A more complete description is provided in the attached Exhibit A.

See Chapter 2 for more information about trademark rights.

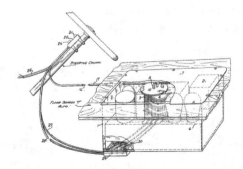

**Car Radio
No. 1,944,139**

e. Your Invention Has Patented and Non-Patented (but Protectible) Features

If you have a patent on some features of your invention and other features are protected by trade secret or copyright law, then your definition of your invention would be a combination of the two definitions above. For example:

Patents, Copyrights, Trade Secrets and Trademarks

The "Property" refers to all inventions described in U.S. Patent No._____ [insert patent number], and to all other proprietary rights, including but not limited to copyrights, trade secrets, formulas, research data, know-how and specifications related to the invention commonly known as _____ [name of invention], as well as any trademark rights and associated good will. A more complete description is provided in the attached Exhibit A.

2. Defining Licensed Products

The licensed products are the products sold by the licensee that incorporate your invention. For example, say you patented a device that can clean the submerged portion of a ship's hull. You license the invention to a swimming pool supply company. They sell your invention incorporated in a product called Aqua Buddy that can clean the bottom of swimming pools. Aqua Buddy would be the licensed product.

As we explained above, the definition of licensed products could affect how much money you make. Royalties are usually tied to the sales of licensed products. That is, you only receive payment for the sales of licensed products. For example, consider an agreement in which licensed products are defined as "any products in which the Property is the primary component." Your invention, a new type of hair comb, is incorporated into a three-way product that includes a brush, comb and curling iron. You may not receive a royalty for this because your invention is not the *primary component*.

How do you decide on a definition for licensed products? The simplest method is to state that a licensed product is "any product that incorporates the Property." If the licensee incorporates several inventions into one product, you can suggest creating a category of "Combination Products" with a separate royalty rate. In Chapter 9, we discuss how royalty rates can be set for different types of products.

When you define licensed products, you should refer to the invention as previously defined. For example,

Specific Listing of Licensed Products

Licensed Products are defined as those Licensee products incorporating the Property and more specifically described in Exhibit A (the "Licensed Products").

or

No Limitations on Licensed Products

Licensed Products are defined as any products sold by the licensee that incorporate the Property.

If you are licensing a process and not a product, you will need to determine which uses (rather than products) of your invention will be counted as licensed processes. As with products, you should refer to the invented process (normally called "Process") when defining the licensed processes. For example, say you are licensing a method of filtering gasoline. You can define licensed process as follows:

No Limitations on Licensed Process

A Licensed Process is any commercial application of the Process by Licensee. *[Change all references in the agreement to Licensed Process, rather than products.]*

Royalties can be tied to use of the process rather than the sale of products. See Chapter 9 for more information on use royalties.

D. Specifying Which Rights Are Granted

The heart of the license agreement—known as the grant—sets out the rights that you, as the licensor, are transferring to the licensee. This essential term of your licensing agreement conveys and sets limits on the licensee's right to make and sell your invention. A grant deals with the following:

- Grant of (Intellectual Property) Rights. The grant describes the intellectual property rights transferred to the licensee in the license, for example, the right to manufacture the patented invention. The grant also establishes whether the license is exclusive or nonexclusive. If it is exclusive, then only the licensee can have the rights conveyed in the grant provision.
- Reservation of Rights. The grant may also describe the intellectual property rights you are *not* giving, for example, you reserve all rights to license the invention to medical supply companies.
- Sublicense. The licensee can license its rights to other companies if it has a grant to sublicense.

Each aspect of the grant is discussed below.

1. Grant of (Intellectual Property) Rights

As we explained in Chapters 1 and 2, you don't license your invention *per se,* you license the intellectual property rights associated with your invention. It is in the grant section that these rights are conveyed or transferred. If your invention is patented, for example, you convey the right to make, sell or use the invention (the rights that come with a patent) as used and incorporated within the licensed products. If you have a copyright, you can convey the right to copy and sell your copyrighted material. You must also determine whether the license is exclusive or nonexclusive.

a. Exclusive or Nonexclusive?

Among the most important issues that a prospective licensor faces is whether to grant exclusive or nonexclusive rights. Exclusive means that only the licensee can have the rights granted in the agreement. A licensee often wants exclusive rights because that prevents a competitor from intruding on the licensee's market. More often than not, the licensor's decision on this issue will be based on:

- the willingness of a prospective licensee to take a nonexclusive license (many won't), and
- the amount that the licensee is willing to pay for an exclusive as opposed to a nonexclusive right.

As a general rule, when you grant exclusive rights, you are giving up your opportunity to license your invention to another company. Whenever you see (or use) the term exclusive, review the language carefully.

To make a license exclusive or nonexclusive, the magic words exclusive or nonexclusive are simply inserted within the grant. For example: "Licensor grants to Licensee an *[exclusive or nonexclusive]* license to make, use or sell the Property."

In the following sections, we will explain how you can limit exclusive licensing rights. That is, you can grant an exclusive right to license but can place some restrictions on the exclusivity. These limitations fall into four areas:

- time (length of the exclusive arrangement)
- scope (the right to make, use or sell)
- geographic area (the territory of exclusivity), or
- industry (exclusive only as to a particular industry).

For example, you want to enter into an exclusive license for one year for your brush product with a company in the "dental care products and supply industry." You want to limit this exclusive license to sales (not manufacturing) in North America. If you defined your grant accordingly, you would be free to: (1) license all rights to anyone after one year, (2) license the right to sell to any non-North American dental supply companies immediately, (3) license rights to any companies for non-dental supply uses immediately, or (4) license manufacturing rights (not sales) to any companies immediately.

b. What Rights Are Granted?

Usually the licensee wants every right you possess. For that reason, the licensee (or licensee's attorney) may propose a long list of rights, such as the right to sell, distribute, manufacture, modify, recast and revise, etc. You should only be concerned if this list of rights *also* conveys ownership. At that point, you may be moving away from a license (which allows you to retain ownership) and towards an assignment (which is an outright sale of all your rights). For example, giving a licensee the right to improve or revise the licensed products does not necessarily mean that the licensee will own the rights to the improvement. Ownership rights of improvements to your invention, particularly if the licensee makes the improvements, can be a tricky issue. Information about improvement ownership is provided in Chapter 15. Below is a sample grant provision.

> **Grant of Rights**. Licensor grants to Licensee a/an
> _____ *[exclusive or nonexclusive]*
> license to make, use or sell the Property solely in association with the manufacture, sale, use, promotion or distribution of the Licensed Products.

Below is an example of a grant that is too broad.

> **Grant of Rights**. Pursuant to the terms and conditions herein, Licensor conveys, grants and transfers to Licensee an exclusive license to manufacture, sell, copy, create derivatives, make improvements, transform, condense, lease, distribute, advertise, promote, market, edit, recast or revise the Property as incorporated and embodied in the Licensed Products.

Including, But Not Limited to...

You may see the phrase, "including, but not limited to..." used throughout a license agreement. This contract language is used to present an example without restricting rights to that example. For instance, a licensee may want to describe the term "licensed products as" "any hair care products that incorporate the Property, including but not limited to hair care products for pets." This way, licensed products includes hair care products for animals as well as humans. Since this phrase is often used to expand the licensee's rights, review carefully any use of "including, but not limited to...." If you think this phrase is being used to grant rights beyond what you feel comfortable with, negotiate to have it excluded from the contract.

2. Reservation of Rights

There is a legal presumption that if you have not expressly transferred a right, you have retained (or reserved) it. For example, if you do not convey the right to sell the licensed products in Thailand, then you have reserved that right for yourself—or for anyone to whom you wish to license it. So, technically, you don't have to make an express statement that you reserve a certain right.

Unfortunately, disputes can arise about this issue, so we recommend that you specifically reserve whatever rights you don't wish to transfer. The easiest method of reserving rights is to add a sentence in the grant that states:

> Licensor expressly reserves all rights other than those being conveyed or granted in this Agreement.

If you wish to be even more specific, you can do so. For example, if you want to make sure you preserve your right to license your invention for the computer game market:

Reservation of Rights Expressly Excluding a Particular Industry

Licensor expressly reserves all rights other than those being conveyed or granted in this agreement, including, but not limited to the right to license the Properties in _____

[list a particular market which you want to expressly exclude, for example, "the computer and video game market"].

If you have already licensed or plan to license to two parties (for example, Company A and Company B), it is wise to specifically reserve those rights you granted to Company A when licensing rights to Company B. For example, you invented a new type of brush bristle and first licensed it to a dental company. Now you are licensing the bristle to a vacuum cleaner company. Your grant to the vacuum cleaner company should specifically reserve "all rights to exploit the Properties within the dental care products and supply industry."

3. Sublicenses

A sublicense is like a sublease. A person acquires property rights and transfers the rights to someone else. Under a sublicense, the licensee can transfer its rights to a company who can make or sell your invention.

Licensees like to have the freedom to sublicense. For example, perhaps the licensee does not have a strong sales force in France, so it sublicenses the French rights to a strong French company (assuming the French rights were included in the original license). The French company then pays money to the licensee who then pays you a portion of the sublicensing revenue, often 50%.

You may not like the idea of sublicensing because a different company—perhaps a company with a philosophy or sales practices you don't agree

with—can sublicense and sell your invention. You can attempt to prohibit sublicensing altogether, but a better solution would be require the licensee to seek out your prior approval before granting a sublicense. The grant section can accomplish this limitation by using the following language:

Licensee may sublicense the rights granted pursuant to this agreement provided: Licensee obtains Licensor's prior written consent to such sublicense,and Licensor receives such revenue or royalty payment as provided in the Payment section below. Any sublicense granted in violation of this provision shall be void.

Under this provision, you can withhold your consent to a sublicense for any reason—no matter how arbitrary. Sometimes this is not suitable for a licensee who wants more predictability. You can satisfy the licensee's needs by adding the following language:

Consent to Sublicense Not Unreasonably Withheld

Licensee may sublicense the rights granted pursuant to this agreement provided: Licensee obtains Licensor's prior written consent to such sublicense and Licensor receives such revenue or royalty payment as provided in the Payment section below. Licensee's consent to any sublicense shall not be unreasonably withheld Any sublicense granted in violation of this provision shall be void.

Under this provision, you must have a good or "reasonable" motivation for rejecting the sublicense. That is, your decision must be based upon sound business reasons, such as proof that the licensee cannot adequately market the invention. Of course, such a provision has occasionally led to litigation as the parties attempt to determine the standards for what is a "good or reasonable motivation."

Assignments

If a licensee sublicenses its rights to manufacture or distribute the invention, the licensee is still responsible for overseeing production and sales and for paying you. However, if the licensee *assigns* its rights, it has permanently removed itself from its obligations and the new company (the assignee) has stepped into the licensee's shoes. This new company will market the invention and pay you royalties.

Most licenses are specifically made nonassignable because the licensor does not want to have another company replace the licensee. However, there are two occasions when an assignment may be necessary:

- the licensee might be purchased by another company and wants to reserve the freedom to transfer its rights to that company, or
- the licensee might create a subsidiary company and wants to be able to assign the agreement to its subsidiary.

A separate section in the Agreement, entitled "Assignment," will detail the conditions under which an assignment can be made. This provision may set the same standards ("cannot withhold consent unreasonably") as the right to sublicense, above. We provide samples of this Assignment section in Chapter 14. Sometimes, to make sure that the licensee can't escape its obligations to you, the words "nonassignable" and "nontransferable" are inserted in the grant. For example, "Licensor grants an exclusive, nonassignable license ..."

E. Defining the Territory

Where can the licensee sell the licensed products? The territory sets the geographical limits for sales. Generally, if you are licensing a patent, the choice of territory is limited to the country or countries where patent protection has been obtained. However, if you and the licensee agree to seek patent protection in foreign countries, then the Territory can go beyond the boundaries of the initial patent protection. If the license is worldwide, then establishing this is simple—the word "worldwide" is inserted in the grant. For example:

Licensor grants to Licensee an exclusive, worldwide license ...

If the territory is limited to a country or region, then that information is inserted in the territory section of the agreement, such as:

Territory. The rights granted to Licensee are limited to the United States and Canada (the "Territory").

In other words, if the license is worldwide you don't need a separate Territory section. But if the territory is limited to a certain area, then that needs to be stated in a separate Territory section.

What's the best approach for you as a prospective licensor? If the licensee has a history of worldwide sales and good sales connections throughout the world, then grant a worldwide license. But if the licensee appears to be familiar only with the U.S. market, it doesn't make sense to license rights to other areas. Doing so would restrict your ability to grant a license to another party for a foreign market.

If you have a difference of opinion with the licensee over the territorial scope of the license, one solution would be to initially grant worldwide rights but also provide that if the licensee has not exploited or sublicensed rights in an area after a certain period of time—say two years—then that area would be excluded from the territory. For example, if after three years the licensee has sold the licensed products everywhere but in France, the licensee would lose rights for France. Usually this type of provision is included in another portion of the license agreement, titled "Right to Terminate a Portion of the Agreement" (discussed in Chapter 13). The language would read as follows:

Licensor's Right to Terminate as to Territory Not Exploited

Licensor shall have the right to terminate the grant of license under this Agreement with respect to any country or region included in the Territory in which Licensee fails to offer the Licensed Products for sale or distribution or to secure a sublicensing agreement for the marketing, distribution and sale of the product within two years of the Effective Date.

(For an explanation of the "Effective Date," see Section F1).

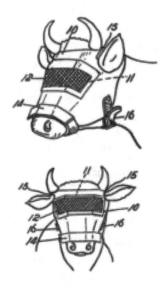

Face Fly Mask
No. 3,104,508

The Global Economy Makes Territory a Tricky Issue

This territory issue is not as simple as it may seem. In today's world of global shipping, there is a deceptive quality to territorial restrictions. You may want to enter three separate licenses: for North America, Europe and Asia. These are known as split territorial licenses. Each licensee is relying on your assurance that they will have exclusive rights to their respective territory. But what's to prevent someone from buying a lot of products in Asia at a low price and then shipping them to Europe to compete with your European licensee?

One suggestion for limiting this type of cross-territory activity is to add a provision such as the following:

Limiting Cross-Territory Sales

The rights granted to Licensee are limited to _____ [insert the territory] (the "Territory"). Licensee shall not make, use or sell the Licensed Products, or any products which are confusingly or substantially similar to the Licensed Products, in any country outside the Territory and will not knowingly sell the Licensed Products to persons who intend to resell them in a country outside the Territory.

Needless to say, this type of provision is not bulletproof. It's quite easy for companies to sell licensed products to distributors who then ship the licensed products to a country outside its territory (a procedure known as "gray marketing" products). For example, PhotoCo licenses its camera technology in Europe and Russia and uses a provision such as the one above. The European distributor sells the licensed products to a Central American company who then sells it to stores in the U.S. Because of this potential for abuse, split territorial licenses sometimes lead to litigation. For the same reasons, be aware that split territorial licenses may not work for products that are going to be sold and distributed over the Internet.

F. Setting the Length (Term) of the Agreement

The time that the license lasts is referred to as the "term." For how long should you license your invention? There are reasons for both long and short terms:

- A short term (two to five years) can be beneficial if the licensee is not doing a good job or if the product is a success, because you can terminate or renegotiate for a better license.
- A long term can be beneficial if you are happy with the licensee and want to make sure that you are locked in for a long period.

A licensee will usually want as long a term as possible because a long term guarantees a maximum period for exploitation of the invention. Sometimes, however, a product may have a limited life span and a licensee may want to limit the agreement to as long as the licensee sells the product. Sometimes the parties compromise on this issue by establishing renewal periods. For example, if certain conditions are met—sales or royalty payments at a certain level, for instance—the licensee will have the right to renew the agreement for a period of time, say one or two years.

In practical terms, you should be aware that if the invention is not profitable, the term makes little difference. It is difficult to force the licensee to keep selling the product if it is losing money. The licensee will either seek to amend the agreement to permit termination, or the agreement will end up terminating in litigation (a lawsuit).

With that in mind, you have three basic choices for determining the length of the term:

- The term can be for a fixed length (say, ten years).
- The term can be for a fixed length (say, two years) with a series of renewals. For example, at the end of two years, the licensee can renew the license, or the licensor may seek the right to renew.
- The term can be for as long as the licensee manufactures and sells the licensed products or until the agreement is terminated. The agreement could permit either party to terminate. For example, one party (or either party) could announce they want to end the agreement. The agreement would then terminate within a set period of 30 or 60 days.

Patents and License Length. Note that in the case of a patent license, the term cannot be for longer than the length of the patent (see below).

1. Commencement of Term

The date that a contract commences is usually referred to as the "date of execution" or the "effective date." This is the date when obligations begin—for example, the date when the licensee must pay an advance or when a licensor must deliver documentation.

The effective date is usually the date when you (the licensor) sign the license agreement. Sometimes it is the date when the licensee signs, when both of you have signed or the latter of the two. If the contract has a fixed date of termination, say ten years, then the contract would end ten years from the effective date.

Record the Effective Date. It's always wise to record the effective date and any subsequent termination or renewal dates in your calendar.

2. Right to Terminate a License

Even if your license has a fixed term, the agreement may be cut short for various reasons, including a failure to pay royalties or a failure to offer the licensed products for sale. These reasons are often listed in a contract section entitled "Termination Rights" or "Termination." These termination provisions work in conjunction with the Term section. For example, the licensor may have the right to terminate the agreement if the licensee fails to include the licensed products in its annual catalog.

Since the term and termination rights provisions are in different portions of the license agreement, the Term section usually includes a statement that the agreement can "be terminated pursuant to any provision of this agreement." We discuss the bases for termination in Chapter 13.

3. Licensing Terms for Patents

You cannot license a patent for longer than the length of the patent—20 years from the filing date for most patents. A longer patent license is a violation of federal antitrust laws (as explained in Chapter 17). If there are other aspects of your invention that are protected—by copyright or trademark, for instance—those elements can be licensed for a longer period. When drafting the term section, a licensee typically will seek language similar to the following:

Term for the Length of Patent Only

This Agreement shall commence upon the Effective Date and shall expire simultaneously with the expiration of the longest-living patent (or patents) or last-remaining patent application as listed in the definition of the Property, whichever occurs last, unless sooner terminated pursuant to a provision of this Agreement.

According to this provision, the patent license lasts as long as there is some form of patent protection or unless the agreement provides for termination for some other reason. Remember, this provision (and the one below) are based solely upon patent rights.

From the licensor's perspective, we recommend, if possible, a shorter period with renewal rights based upon sales or other criteria. For example:

Short Term With Renewal Rights Based Upon Sales

This Agreement shall commence upon the Effective Date and shall extend for a period of two years (the "Initial Term") and thereafter may be renewed by Licensee under the same terms and conditions for consecutive two-year periods (the "Renewal Terms"), provided that:

(a) Licensee provides written notice of its intention to renew this agreement within thirty days before the expiration of the current term,

(b) Licensee has met the sales requirements as established in Exhibit A, and

(c) in no event shall the Agreement extend longer than the date of expiration of the longest-living patent (or patents) or last-remaining patent application as listed in the definition of the Property.

What happens if you apply for a patent and a patent does not issue? In that case, the licensee may want the right to terminate the agreement. This right to terminate is discussed in Chapter 13.

If you do not have a patent but have a valuable trademark or trade secret, the license for trade secret and trademark rights can extend indefinitely. In this case, you may use language like the following:

No Patents; Indefinite Term

This Agreement shall commence upon the Effective Date and shall continue until terminated pursuant to a provision of this Agreement.

4. Fixed Terms and Renewals

You or the licensee may want to limit the license to a fixed period with no renewal rights. How long? That depends upon how long you and the licensee believe is necessary to exploit the invention. Usually, there is little danger in agreeing to a fixed term because both parties will be motivated to negotiate a new agreement if it's still working out for both of them. If it isn't working out for one of them, then the agreement probably isn't much good anyway. For example:

Fixed 10-Year Term

This Agreement shall commence upon the Effective Date and shall continue for ten years unless sooner terminated pursuant to a provision of this Agreement.

A right of renewal could be included as follows:

Initial Term With Renewals

This Agreement shall commence upon the latest signature date (the "Effective Date") and shall extend for a period of _____ *[insert number of years for initial term, for example, "two years"]* (the "Initial Term"). Following the Initial Term, this agreement may be renewed by Licensee under the same terms and conditions for _____ *[insert number of renewal terms]* consecutive _____ *[insert length of each renewal term, for example, "two-year"]* periods (the "Renewal Terms"), provided that Licensee provides written notice of its intention to renew this agreement within thirty days before the expiration of the current term. In no event shall the Agreement extend longer than the date of expiration of the patent listed in the definition of the Property.

As we explained, the renewal can be tied to some event, such as sales. For example, you could state that you must receive $100,000 in royalties in the preceding term in order for the Licensor to exercise a renewal right.

Short Term With Renewal Rights Based Upon Sales

This Agreement shall commence upon the Effective Date and shall extend for a period of _____ *[insert number of years]* years (the "Initial Term") and thereafter may be renewed by Licensee under the same terms and conditions for consecutive _____ *[insert number of years]* -year periods (the "Renewal Terms"), provided that:

(a) Licensee provides written notice of its intention to renew this agreement within thirty days before the expiration of the current term,

(b) Licensee has met the sales requirements as established in Exhibit A, and

(c) in no event shall the Agreement extend longer than the date of expiration of the longest-living patent (or patents) or last-remaining patent application as listed in the definition of the Property.

Finally, if you want to permit the term to extend for as long as the licensee sells the invention, you could draft a term provision as follows:

This Agreement shall commence upon the Effective Date as specified in Exhibit A and shall continue for as long as Licensee continues to offer the Licensed Products in commercially reasonable quantities or unless sooner terminated pursuant to a provision of this Agreement.

The worksheet below is intended to help you keep track of the essential business facts. (Information on royalties, audits and net sales is provided in the next chapter.)

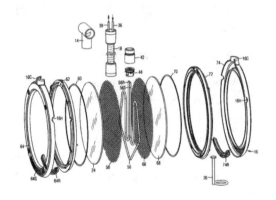

Non-Fogging Shower Mirror
No. 5,953,157

Contract Worksheet

Licensee

Name of Licensee Business _____

Licensee Address _____

_____

Licensee Business Form

☐ sole proprietorship   ☐ general partnership   ☐ limited partnership

☐ corporation   ☐ limited liability company

State of incorporation _____

Name, position and phone number of person signing for licensee _____

_____

Property Definition

Patent No. _____

Patent Application Serial No. _____

Copyrightable Features _____

_____

Copyright Registration No.(s) _____

Trade Secrets _____

_____

Trademarks _____

_____

Trademark Registration No.(s) _____

_____

Licensed Product Definition

Industry (Have you limited the license to a particular industry?) _____

_____

Product (Have you limited the license to a particular product or products?) _____

_____

Territory

☐ Worldwide ☐ Countries _____

☐ States _____

Rights Granted (check those rights granted to licensee)

☐ sell   ☐ make or manufacture   ☐ distribute

☐ use   ☐ revise   ☐ import

☐ lease   ☐ right to improvements   ☐ derivatives (copyright)

☐ copy (copyright)   ☐ advertise   ☐ promote

☐ other rights _____

☐ other rights _____

☐ other rights _____

Rights Reserved

☐ all rights reserved (except those granted in license)

☐ no rights reserved

☐ specific rights reserved _____

Have you signed any other licenses? If so, do you need to reserve specific rights? _____

_____

Term

Have you agreed upon:

☐ a fixed term (How long? _____) ☐ a term limited by patent length

☐ unlimited term until one party terminates ☐ an initial term with renewals (see below)

☐ other _____

Renewals

If you have agreed upon an initial term with renewals:

How many renewal periods? _____ How long is each renewal period? _____

What triggers renewal?

☐ Licensee must notify of intent to renew.

☐ Licensor must notify of intent to renew.

☐ Agreement renews automatically unless Licensee indicates it does not want to renew.

Net Sales Deductions

What is the licensee permitted to deduct when calculating net sales?

☐ quantity discounts   ☐ debts & uncollectibles   ☐ sales commissions

☐ promotion and marketing costs   ☐ fees   ☐ freight & shipping

☐ credits & returns   ☐ other _____

Is there a cap on the total amount of the deductions?   ☐ Yes   ☐ No

If so, how much? _____

Royalty Rates

Licensed Products _____%   Combination Products _____%

Accessory Products _____%

Per Use Royalty _____% or Usage Standard _____

Other Products _____%   Other Products _____%

Do you have any sliding royalty rates? _____

Advances and Lump Sum Payments

Advance $ _____   Date Due _____

Lump Sum Payment(s) $_____   Date Due _____

Guaranteed Minimum Annual Royalty (GMAR)

GMAR $ _____   Date Due _____

Does the GMAR carry forward credits?   ☐ Yes   ☐ No

Does the GMAR carry forward deficiencies?   ☐ Yes   ☐ No

Audit Rights

No. of audits permitted per year _____

No. of days notice _____

Money: It Matters

oney! It's the primary reason you are licensing your invention. But how much do you get and how do you get it? This chapter will provide information about royalties—what they are, how they're calculated and how they fit within the license agreement. You should read this chapter if you answer "yes" to any of the following questions:

- Would you like an explanation for basic royalty accounting principles?
- Would you like definitions for terms such as advances and net sales?
- Do you need an explanation of the methods you can use to audit a licensee's books?
- Do you need information about how your royalty income will be taxed?

In this chapter we will discuss the various ways that a licensor is paid, such as royalties, advances, guaranteed minimum payments, lump sum payments and use royalties. We will explore the difference between gross and net sales and review the types of deductions that are often claimed by licensees. We will also examine a few sample royalty and audit provisions. Finally, we will review how to anticipate payment predicaments such as late payments or a failure to pay.

Remember that the decisions you reach with a licensee may be binding and enforceable even without a written agreement. Therefore, keep notes of your conversations and close your discussions by reminding the licensee that any deal is subject to approval of the final contract. This reminder should be included on written correspondence as well.

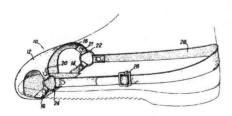

Shoe Protector
No. 4,780,970

Spreadsheets to the Rescue

When you work with royalties, you will want to be able to compute your potential earnings accurately and quickly. For this reason you should consider using a computer spreadsheet program such as *Microsoft Excel*. Spreadsheet programs are surprisingly easy to learn and use, and will prove invaluable when negotiating royalty payments.

A. Some Basic Royalty Definitions

Below are some simple royalty definitions. Don't worry if you don't fully grasp these concepts right away. A more complete explanation is offered in subsequent sections.

- gross sales—This is the total money received from the licensee's sale of the invention.
- net sales—This includes the gross sales (mentioned above) minus deductions such as shipping costs or returns (products returned by retailers.)

  EXAMPLE: A licensee receives $1,200,000 from gross sales and has shipping deductions and returns of $200,000. Net sales are $1,000,000.

- royalty—A royalty is a payment for licensing your invention. It is usually calculated as a percentage of the sales and is paid periodically. You may receive royalty checks once a year, twice a year or even four times a year. (A system of continuous royalty payments is sometimes referred to as a "running royalty.")
- net sales royalty—This is the most common form of royalty payment—a percentage of net sales. How do you compute your net sales royalty payment? Multiply the royalty rate against net sales.

EXAMPLE: A royalty rate of 5% times net sales of $1,000,000 equals a net sales royalty of $50,000. (Note: In some cases, royalties can be a percentage of unit sales or production. See below for an explanation.)

- per unit royalty—A per unit royalty is tied to the number of units sold, not the money earned by sales.

EXAMPLE: Under a per unit royalty, a licensor could receive $1 per each product sold.

- per use royalty—A per use royalty is based upon the number of times that the invention is used. This royalty is tied to production, not sales. A per use royalty is commonly chosen when the invention is a process, not a product, such as a method of sealing canned goods. The inventor receives a royalty based upon the amount of production (for example, the number of sealed cans produced).

EXAMPLE: Under a per use royalty, a licensor could receive ten cents for every 100 cans produced using his patented system.

- advances—This is an upfront payment to the licensor, usually made at the time the license is signed. An advance is almost always credited or "recouped" against future royalties unless the agreement provides otherwise. It's as if the licensee is saying, "I expect you will earn $10,000 in royalties so I am going to advance you that sum at the time we sign the agreement." When you do earn royalties, the first $10,000 will be kept by the licensee to repay the advance. If you don't earn the $10,000, then the licensee usually takes a loss and you do not have to return the advance. To assure that you do not have to return the advance, your agreement would state the advance is "nonrefundable" (see the sidebar).

- lump sum payments—Instead of receiving royalties, a licensor may prefer a one-time or lump sum payment for transfer of licensing rights.

EXAMPLE: The licensor receives a lump sum payment of $100,000. In return, the licensee has the exclusive right to sell the invention for five years. The licensor gets no other payments or royalties regardless of whether the invention sells millions of units.

- minimum annual royalty payments (sometimes referred to as guaranteed minimum annual royalty or GMAR)—A guarantee that you will receive a certain royalty payment each year. Think of a minimum annual payment as an advance that is paid every year of the agreement.

Nonrefundable and Nonrecoupable

The terms "nonrefundable" and "nonrecoupable" are sometimes used in license agreements. Nonrecoupable means that the payment cannot be credited against royalties. It is as if the licensee is saying, "Take this $10,000 payment and I won't deduct it from your future royalties." The term nonrefundable is often used to ensure that a licensor will not have to personally pay back an advance or minimum annual royalty payment. For example, you receive a $10,000 advance but the sales are dismal and the royalties never equal the advance. Although a licensor rarely has to return an advance, the use of the term "nonrefundable" is often added as reinforcement to guarantee that you don't have to write a check to the licensee.

B. Ways to Get Paid

Assuming you have a choice, how do you choose between the various payment methods? Your options are explained below.

1. Royalties Based on Net Sales

The payment of royalties based on net sales is the most common method of licensing payment. In business terminology, they are a direct cost that can be charged against the cost of goods. In other words, they are a predictable expense that is figured as part of the cost of selling the product. If the invention is not successful, there will be no royalties. Licensors prefer this system because if the invention is successful, the licensor will be richly rewarded over the life of the invention. We generally recommend choosing a royalty payment over a lump sum payment for invention licensing.

2. Per Unit Royalties

In some instances, an inventor may not want to use a royalty system based upon net sales. For example, computer hardware prices often drop radically. More units may be sold but the net sales revenue decreases because the price has dropped. If the wholesale price for your product drops, you may be better suited with royalties tied to unit sales. A payment of two dollars per unit may be more profitable than 5% of net sales. Unfortunately, licensees generally don't want to risk committing to unit royalties when the wholesale price can drop dramatically. If you have the bargaining power, look into a per unit royalty system.

3. Per Use Royalties

It's possible that you may have invented something that is used, rather than sold. For example, if you patented a method of coating glass for neon light, your process may be used in the manufacturing operation. That is, you are licensing a procedure that is used as part of a production process. Since the process may be used in a variety of ways, a royalty system based on net sales is difficult to justify and hard to audit. Under these circumstances, inventors choose a use royalty. This is a royalty applied to the number of units produced, or the number of times the method is used in manufacture.

> EXAMPLE: Fred has devised a method of compacting and sealing aluminum cans to produce building blocks. He licenses the method to RecyCo and receives a unit royalty of 15 cents for every cubic foot.

4. Lump Sum Payments

Lump sum payments are a gamble. Should you take one large payment or a royalty? If your invention is wildly successful, you may always regret the lump sum choice. If the invention is not successful, you won't see any royalties. You can attempt, if possible, to estimate potential sales over the period of the license. However, that is a speculative approach and the fact is, there is no proven method for successfully picking the form of payment.

There are two reasons that some licensors prefer a lump sum payment. First, the licensor doesn't have to be concerned with accounting or auditing records. Second, some licensors prefer lump sum payments for foreign licenses because of currency conversion rates. These rates—which measure the foreign currency against U.S. currency—may change dramatically, making your foreign royalty payments less valuable. If you are in doubt whether to choose a lump sum, you may wish to consult a patent attorney to evaluate your invention's commercial potential.

Note: A lump sum payment for a license is different from a lump sum payment for an assignment. A license may be limited in time, for example for two or three years. Under an assignment, however, you lose ownership of your invention (see Chapter 1).

5. Fluctuating Royalty Rates

A fluctuating royalty rate (sometimes referred to as a sliding royalty) is a rate that changes during the licensing period. The rate may change each year or it may change because of other circumstances, such as sales or inflation. For example, the royalty rate may go up if sales exceed a million units in one year. Similarly, a licensee may seek a decreasing royalty in the event that sales fall below a certain mark.

> EXAMPLE: Page has licensed a device to patch bicycle tubes. His royalty rate is 5% for net sales up to and including $100,000 and 6% for net sales above $100,000 in any one year. If net sales are $150,000 in one year, Page receives $8,000 [($100,000 x 5%) + ($50,000 x 6%)].

6. Hybrid License Royalties

If you are licensing a pending or issued patent and a trade secret, your arrangement is referred to as a "hybrid license." A hybrid license requires special attention because of antitrust laws (see Chapter 17). When you license a patent and some other intellectual property rights for an invention (such as a trademark or trade secret), courts presume that the patent is inherently more valuable than the other form of intellectual property. Therefore, if your pending patent does not issue or if your patent expires, it is unfair to require the licensee to pay the same royalty as if the patent existed.

Therefore we suggest a modification to your license agreement if you meet the following criteria:
1. you are licensing a patent or pending patent and some other form of intellectual property (such as a trademark or trade secret); and
2. your license agreement is expected to continue longer than the life of the patents.

If your license is longer than the life of the patents, you can continue to collect royalties provided that the royalty percentage decreases to reflect the value of the expired patents. We suggest allocating the royalty between the patent and the non-patented property. For example, 85% of the royalty can be attributable to the patent and 15% for a trademark. After the patent expires, the royalty rate would diminish by 85%. See the sample provision in Section E5, below.

You do not need a hybrid royalty provision if the term (that is, the length) of your agreement does not exceed the length of your patent protection. For example, if you licensed a patented invention and trade secrets and your license provided for termination "with the expiration of the patent," then you would not need to include the hybrid language.

7. Minimum Annual Royalty

The minimum annual royalty or guaranteed minimum royalty (we'll refer to it as a GMAR) is an annual payment. It's a guarantee that the licensor will receive a certain payment, regardless of how well the product sells in any year. How does a GMAR work? Each year, you receive your GMAR payment. At the end of each year, the earned royalties are totaled. (The earned royalties are the actual royalties that accumulated from net sales that year.) What happens next depends upon the agreement.

a. Credits—When Royalties Exceed the GMAR

The GMAR is a minimum payment to compensate you for royalties that are expected that year. But what happens if the royalties exceed the GMAR payment? In that situation, the licensee has paid less royalties to you through the GMAR than you actually earned. Depending upon how your agreement is negotiated, either: 1) you may receive a credit payment at the end of the year, or 2) the licensee may hold onto this money as a carry-forward credit, and then deduct it against your account in the following years if you have a loss.

We would recommend against the carry-forward credit because it prevents you from receiving earned royalties for another year. However, licensees prefer it because new product sales may be unpredictable. The first year may be booming, but sales may slow down the second year.

b. Deficiencies—When the GMAR Exceeds the Earned Royalties

What happens if the GMAR payment is more than the royalties that you actually earned in a year? For example, say you were paid a $10,000 GMAR but the royalties only totaled $9,000 that year. The licensee paid more royalties to you than you earned.

Depending upon how your agreement is negotiated: 1) the licensee may have to absorb the deficiency; or 2) the contract may permit the licensee to carry forward or cumulate royalty deficiencies, diminishing next year's GMAR payment accordingly; or 3) if there is a carry-forward credit provision (see above), then the deficiency is applied against a previous year's credit.

> EXAMPLE: Your license agreement provides for a GMAR of $10,000 to be paid on January 1 of each year. The first year's total royalty was only $6,000, which is $4,000 less than the GMAR, so there is a deficiency of $4,000. The second year's total royalty was $14,000. That's $4,000 more than the GMAR. So, for the second year, there is a credit of $4,000.
>
> If you had a "carry-forward" provision, you would have received a total of $20,000 for the two years because the first-year deficiency of $4,000 would have canceled out the second-year credit of $4,000. If you had no carry-forward provision, you would have received a total of $24,000. You would have received the $4,000 credit from the second year and the $4,000 first-year deficiency would have no effect on your payments.
>
> To sum up, if you are fortunate enough to negotiate a GMAR, your preference should be for a GMAR without a carry-forward (sometimes referred to as noncumulating) requirement. You should also be aware that GMARs can be suspended (that is, no payment is required) if certain things occur. Sometimes a contract will provide that no GMAR has to be paid if, through no fault of the licensee, it is impossible to manufacture the product or to obtain the raw materials for the product.

GMARs, Royalties and Diminished Profits

The licensee does not necessarily lose money just because there is a deficiency (that is, your royalties were less than the GMAR). It's possible that the licensee profited because the GMAR and royalties represent a fraction of the cost of the invention. All that can be definitely concluded in this case is that the profit margin for the invention has been diminished. That is, the licensee did not make as much money as it hoped.

C. The Mysteries of Net Sales and Deductions

Net sales are the most common measurement for royalty payments. In a net sales license, the royalty rate is multiplied against the net sales. There is no standard definition of net sales and it can change in every license agreement.

During negotiations, a licensee will attempt to define net sales in a very narrow way with many deductions. This way, the licensee can make a lower royalty payment. The licensor, on the other hand, wants a broad definition. The licensor would prefer if net sales were the same as gross sales.

The big issue when negotiating net sales is what deductions should be included in the definition of net sales. A net sales definition that favors a licensor would read as follows:

> "Net Sales" are defined as Licensee's gross sales minus returns that are actually credited. Gross sales are the total amount on invoices billed to customers.

Using this definition, a licensor would receive royalty payments based solely upon sales that had occurred. The only deduction is for products that are actually returned and credited, which are either defective or unsold merchandise.

License agreements often include many more deductions. In order for you to sort through these deductions, the common ones are explained below.

1. Quantity Discount Deduction

Sometimes a licensee may seek to increase sales by offering a discount on large quantity orders. The licensee then deducts this discount (also referred to as a volume discount) from net sales. This can be favorable to the licensor because it increases sales. If you choose to include it, you should qualify the discount by describing a quantity discount as "a discount made at the time of shipment" or a "discount actually shown on the invoice," since it is possible that an unscrupulous licensee may attempt to offer a discount after items are shipped, splitting the discount with the purchaser and diminishing your royalty payment.

2. Debts and Uncollectible Account Deductions

Sometimes a licensee may seek to deduct bad debts and uncollectible accounts. For example, say a third party orders products and then fails to pay. The licensee feels no royalty should be paid since no money was earned for these sales. On the other hand, you are not a collection agency and should not have to lose money because of the licensee's bad business dealings. Even though insolvency and uncollected debts are not especially common, it would be better for you to avoid this deduction.

3. Sales Commission Deductions

Sometimes a salesperson is paid a commission for each sale of the licensed product. The licensee may seek to deduct these commissions under the net sales definition. We would discourage the deduction of commissions because they are a cost of the licensee's business.

4. Promotion/Marketing/ Advertising Deduction

As we have stated, net sales are supposed to be total sales, not a collection of business deductions. For that reason we would discourage the use of promotional, marketing or advertising deductions in the definition of net sales. Marketing should be a cost of doing business, not a licensor expense.

5. Fee Deduction

This vague term includes a wide range of costs and business expenses. If the term "fees" can be made more specific, you may be more comfortable with the deduction. Otherwise we discourage the deduction of fees from net sales.

6. Freight/Shipping Deduction

Freight and shipping costs of the product, although a cost of doing business, are traditionally treated as a deduction against net sales. We recommend that you accept this as a deduction from net sales.

7. Credits and Returns Deduction

It is acceptable for a licensee to deduct credits and returns from the total net sales, since returns reflect merchandise which was not purchased or was defective. Some licensors prefer to qualify the definition to state "bona fide returns" or "returns actually made or allowed as supported by credit memoranda" in order to weed out returns which are part of some unscrupulous arrangement between distributors and retailers.

8. Tax Deductions

If a product is taxed locally, it is common to include this as a deduction against net sales.

Summing up, it is generally acceptable for net sales to include deductions for shipping, freight, taxes, credits, returns and discounts made at time of sale. It is less desirable—and we recommend against—deductions for sales commissions, debts, uncollectible accounts, promotions, marketing and advertising.

9. Putting a Cap on Net Sales Deductions

One way to limit net sales deductions is to place a limit on the amount to be deducted. For example, in your license agreement you could include a statement that reads as follows:

> In no event may the total amount deducted from net sales (for discounts, credits or returns) during any royalty period exceed ten percent of the gross sales of the products during that royalty period.

A provision such as this guarantees that the deductions will never be more than 10% of gross sales. Some license agreements forego a listing of the deductions and simply state that net sales are "gross sales minus ten percent for shipping, freight, taxes, returns and other deductions." This provision may not accurately reflect the actual deductions but it does remove any accounting issues. That is, you no longer have to wonder whether net sales deductions are accurate.

D. How Much Do You Get?

In an ideal world, there would be a chart describing the correct value and appropriate royalty payments for new inventions. You need only consult this chart and you would know how much your invention is worth. There would be no need for negotiation or discussion. Unfortunately, there is no such chart. Instead, the decisions about advances and royalties are often arbitrary. Sometimes they're based upon industry standards, and sometimes the licensee bases them on projections of savings or earnings.

Usually, a licensee makes an offer of an advance and a royalty. This offer is usually determined by one of three methods:

- The licensee offers royalty payments based upon the industry standard.
- The licensee offers royalty payments based upon financial analysis.
- The licensee offers royalty payments based upon a combination of industry standards and financial analysis.

1. Basing Royalty Rates Upon Industry Standards

A licensee may offer you a $10,000 advance and a 5% royalty, telling you that these numbers are "the industry standard." What she means is that the royalty rate is customary and every company within the industry uses these same numbers. Licensees can be stubborn about industry standards. As the licensee will explain, the company's projected sales are based upon these numbers and these rates have worked within the industry for other inventors and generated profits.

If there is an industry standard, you will probably be stuck with it. But your first objective should be to verify the rates. If you are working with a product rep or agent it's easy. They should have information about industry rates. Otherwise, it's tricky. Although invention licensing rates fluctuate between 3% and 10% of net sales, some dip to 1% or 2% and some rise higher than 10%.

If you're not working with a rep, or don't have experience in the industry, it can be very difficult to obtain information about standard rates. You will need help from fellow inventors or others familiar with the industry. A fellow inventor who has already licensed or a friendly executive within the trade will prove to be an invaluable colleague when determining industry standards. If such personal contacts are not available, you will have to dig into trade publications as discussed in Chapter 6 and attempt to discern the current rates. Even if you are not using a rep, you may be able to pay an hourly consulting fee to reps, agents or other industry consultants to obtain basic rate information.

2. Basing Royalty Rates Upon Financial Analysis

Sometimes a licensee calculates royalty payments and advances based upon the value of your invention. This calculation is established by facts, guesses and a little bit of financial voodoo. Often, the licensee predicts the cost of manufacturing and raw materials and then attempts to predict sales based upon history, politics or marketing trends. Sometimes the rates are also affected by whether the invention is a "pioneer," that is, a breakthrough invention such as the first instant camera or facsimile machine.

The 25/75 Split

In the case of an invention that is expected to sell well for a period of years, a common starting point for calculating a royalty rate is the 25/75 split. Under this split the licensor receives 25% of the profit. That is, for every four dollars of profit, the licensor receives one dollar. Note that this is not the same as a 25% royalty—royalties are a percentage of sales, not profits. But some licensees begin the royalty calculation process by estimating future profits, deducting 25% for the licensor and then recalculating this sum in the product pie (described below) to arrive at the licensor's royalty.

a. Earnings and Savings

Two common indicators are used to make financial determinations: an earnings analysis or a savings analysis. An earnings analysis determines how much the licensee will earn. If you have a new product, an earnings analysis would measure the costs of materials, production and advertising and subtract that from the potential sales. The result is the potential earnings or profit.

A savings analysis determines how much the licensee will save. If you have a method or invention that will save money, the licensee will determine the amount of the potential savings. For example,

you devised a more efficient method of manufacturing paper bags. The method will save a licensee several hundred thousand dollars each year.

If there is money to be made or saved by your invention, then the licensee will attempt to project those earnings or savings. Once the analysis is made, the licensee then determines royalty and advance payments that will coincide with the predictions. If predictions are high, for example, the advance payment may be high. If it is expected that the item will sell more in the second or third year, the royalty rate may increase over time.

b. The Product Pie

The licensee may make further financial calculations based upon a product pie. Each company sets aside a certain amount of money for a new product based upon forecasts of sales and expenses. For example, a company may allocate $200,000 for a new product: $5,000 for administrative costs and insurance, $70,000 for manufacturing, $100,000 for marketing. That leaves $25,000 which is earmarked to you as an advance. If you seek more money, the company either has to increase the total amount of the new product pie or subtract money from another portion. Most companies don't like to increase the total allocation, because that means a greater risk—more products will have to be sold. Cutting another portion, such as marketing, may impact potential sales.

The company may cook up a second product pie which details the costs and revenues once the product has been introduced. This pie is usually based upon revenue. For example, if the company sells the product for $20, then the pie would be divided as $5 for materials, $5 for manufacturing, $1 for royalties, $4 advertising and $5 profit. Your slice of royalties and advances is sometimes based upon the size of the product pie.

3. Basing Royalty Rates Upon Both Industry Standards and Financial Analysis

This may be the most common method of figuring how much you get for licensing your invention. A licensee will offer you the industry standard royalty rate but will give you an advance or a series of minimum annual payments based upon a financial analysis. For example, say that based upon market research, it looks like your invention will be very successful. The company may offer you the industry standard royalty rate—say 5%—but also offers you a guaranteed minimum royalty payment of $50,000 a year. In other words, the royalty rate may not fluctuate, but the company is flexible about advances or minimum annual payments.

4. If They're So Rich, How Come They Won't Give Me More Money?

You believe your invention will be very successful. However, the licensee is offering you what seems to be the minimum royalty rate and a relatively small advance. Having worked for years to perfect your invention, you feel that the proposed royalty and advance is too small. After all, the licensee is a successful company, so it should be able to pay more money.

First, you need to ask yourself whether you really should be seeking more money. Remember, the number one reason license negotiations fall apart is because the inventor wants more money than the licensee is willing to pay. Are you being unrealistic about how much the company can or will pay? Have you made any financial analysis of projected earnings or savings? Have you asked to see the licensee's projections?

There are usually two reasons why a licensee won't offer more money:

- offering more money means taking a bigger risk on the product and the company can't afford to take risks

- the company knows you have no other choices and has a take it or leave it attitude.

The first reason is valid. Your success is tied to the company's success, so you don't want them taking unnecessary risks. The second reason is more difficult to navigate. You may have to weigh the alternatives before rejecting an offer.

One possible solution may be to accept an offer but limit the time period for the agreement for as short as possible. That way, if the product is successful, you can renegotiate for a better arrangement. Another possible solution is to suggest a fluctuating or sliding royalty that increases as sales increase. For more information about limiting the time period of the agreement, see Chapters 8 and 13.

E. Royalty Provisions

You have reviewed a great deal of information about royalties. How do you incorporate it into your agreement? Below are sample provisions for royalties with some additional commentary.

1. Royalties

The first part of the royalty provision, below, states that the royalties accrue on a certain date. This means the date for recording sales—either the sale date, shipping date or payment date, whichever comes first. This guarantees that net sales are recorded on the earliest possible date. In other words, you don't have to wait for the following quarter before the transaction is considered a sale.

All royalties ("Royalties") provided for under this Agreement shall accrue when the respective items are sold, shipped, distributed, billed or paid for, whichever occurs first. Royalties shall also be paid by the Licensee to Licensor on all items, even if not billed (including, but not limited to introductory offers, samples, promotions or distributions) to individuals or companies which are affiliated with, associated with or subsidiaries of Licensee.

2. Net Sales

The net sales definition permits deduction for promotional items which are sold to companies "affiliated with, associated with or subsidiaries of" the licensee. What does this mean? Sometimes a company will give promotional items (not subject to royalties) to an affiliate or subsidiary who then sells them. The company makes money through its affiliate or subsidiary, but the transaction is not registered as a net sale. Although this practice is not common, this contract provision establishes that all transactions that earn money are net sales.

Note: A licensed product is usually defined in the license agreement as a product that is sold by the licensee that includes your licensed technology. It may be the invention as you created it or it may be your invention with some additions, such as packaging or other design features. See Chapter 8 for more information on the difference between your invention and licensed products.

> "Net Sales" are defined as Licensee's gross sales (i.e., the gross invoice amount billed customers) less quantity discounts and returns actually credited. A quantity discount is a discount made at the time of shipment. No deductions shall be made for cash or other discounts, for commissions, for uncollectible accounts or for fees or expenses of any kind which may be incurred by the Licensee in connection with the Royalty payments.

3. Advance Against Royalties

This provision establishes the amount of the advance payment. Execution refers to the date when you sign the agreement.

> As a nonrefundable advance against royalties (the "Advance"), Licensee agrees to pay to Licensor upon execution of this Agreement the sum of _____ [insert the amount of the advance, if any].

4. Royalty Rate

The provision below establishes the royalty rate.

Royalty for All Rights

> Licensee agrees to pay a Royalty of _____ [insert appropriate royalty percentage] % of all Net Sales revenue of the Licensed Products ("Licensed Product Royalty").

5. Hybrid Royalty Payments

As mentioned in Section B6, if you have a hybrid license that lasts longer than the length of your patents, we suggest allocating a value between the various forms of intellectual property. You can add the following language after the last sentence of the sample royalty provision in Section 4, above. Remember when making these allocations, the courts presume that a patent has inherently more value than other forms of intellectual property. For example, the patents might account for 80 per cent or more of the value of the license.

Hybrid Royalty; Patent and Non-Patented Rights

> Licensee agrees to pay a Royalty of _____ [insert appropriate royalty percentage] % of all Net Sales revenue of the Licensed Products ("Licensed Product Royalty"). The "Licensed Product Royalty" shall be allocated according to the percentages as provided in this Agreement. In the event that a patent does not issue or an issued patent expires or is otherwise terminated, the allocated percentage for such patent or pending patent shall be subtracted from the Licensed Product Royalty. The Licensed Product Royalty shall be adjusted accordingly.
> _____% of the royalty for the license of the patent No. _____.
> _____% of the royalty for the license of pending patent No. _____.
> _____% of the royalty for the license of trade secrets [or trademarks, copyrights or other intellectual property].

6. Guaranteed Minimum Annual Royalty Payments

The last sentence of this sample provision prohibits cumulating or carrying forward royalty deficiencies or credits, which we recommend.

> In addition to any other advances or fees, Licensee shall pay an annual guaranteed royalty (the "GMAR") as follows: _____ [insert the terms of your GMAR: for example, $10,000 per year]. The GMAR shall be paid to Licensor annually on _____ [insert the date when the GMAR should be paid each year]. The GMAR is an advance against royalties for the twelve-month period commencing upon payment. Royalty payments based on Net Sales made during any year of this Agreement shall be credited against the GMAR due for the year in which such Net Sales were made. In the event that annual royalties exceed the GMAR, Licensee shall pay the difference to Licensor. Any annual royalty payments in excess of the GMAR shall not be carried forward from previous years or applied against the GMAR.

7. Royalties on Spin-Offs

Sometimes an invention may lead to sales of related products or accessories. For example, say you invented a toy car. In addition to selling the car, the licensee may also sell t-shirts featuring pictures of your cars. This provision provides that you will be paid for these spin-offs. Normally, a spin-off royalty is smaller than a licensed product royalty.

> Licensee agrees to pay a Royalty ("Spin-Off Product Royalty") of _____ % [insert appropriate royalty percentage] for all Net Sales of "Spin-Off Products." A "Spin-Off Product" is any product derived from, based on or adapted from the Licensed Product.

8. Adjustment of Royalties for Third Party Licenses

Sometimes a licensee may wish to enhance sales of your product by including another company's trade-mark, such as Mickey Mouse. Mickey's owner, the Disney Company, will charge a royalty. The licensee is now faced with two royalties: yours and Disney's. Since Mickey will be increasing your sales, the licensee will ask you to take a reduced royalty known as a third party license royalty. For example, if your regular royalty rate is 5%, the third party license rate might be 3%.

> In the event that any Licensed Product (or other items for which Licensee pays Royalties to Licensor) incorporates third party character licenses, endorsements, or other proprietary licenses, Licensor agrees to adjust the Royalty rate to ____ % [insert appropriate royalty percentage] for such third party licenses. Licensee shall notify Licensor of any such third party licenses prior to manufacture. Third party licenses shall not include licenses accruing to an affiliate, associate or subsidiary of Licensee.

9. F.O.B. Royalties

Sometimes, the products are manufactured outside the United States (also referred to as offshore) and then sold to U.S. retailers through a "letter of credit" or F.O.B. system (the initials stand for "free on board"). F.O.B. sales are made at a much lower rate, sometimes one-third less than similar sales within the U.S. If a licensee uses F.O.B. sales, we recommend that you include an F.O.B. royalty rate (usually 2 to 4 points higher than the net sales rate). For example, if your net sales royalty is 5%, your F.O.B. royalty rate might be 7% or 8%.

> Licensee agrees to pay the Royalty ("F.O.B. Royalty") of _____ % [insert appropriate royalty percentage] for all F.O.B. sales of Licensed Products.

10. Sublicensing Revenues

Before agreeing to the sublicensing provision, below, you should review the section on sublicensing in Chapter 8. Fifty percent is the common rate for sublicensing payments. Note that this is not a royalty. You will receive 50% of all revenues from licensing. There is no need for a net sales formula or deductions. Why? Because there are no production, freight or other costs incurred by the licensee. All of this is being done by the sublicensee.

> In the event of any sublicense of the rights granted pursuant to this Agreement, Licensee shall pay to Licensor _____ % [*insert the amount of the sublicensing percentage*] percent of all sublicensing revenues.

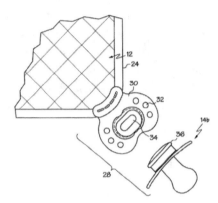

Infant Blanket with Teeth Pacifier
No. 6,292,962

11. Payments and Statements to Licensor

The sample payment provision below provides when payment shall be made ("within 30 days after the calendar quarter"). Sometimes licensees may want to pay 90 days after the end of the quarter. This is common, though undesirable—especially since, in reality, a licensee may take 30 days longer. This is because most agreements provide for a 30-day "cure" provision. This means that if anything goes wrong during the agreement, the licensee has 30 days to cure or fix the problem. So it may take 120 days from the end of the quarter before you get your payment. It is to your advantage to keep this period as short as possible.

The payment provision below also provides that "The acceptance by Licensor of any of the statements furnished or royalties paid shall not preclude Licensor from questioning the correctness at any time of any payments or statements." This protects you, establishing that your acceptance of a payment does not prevent you from later claiming that the payment was inaccurate. Finally, this provision provides that you get paid in U.S. currency. This guarantees that you will not have to deal with fluctuating currency conversion rates.

> Within thirty days after the end of each calendar quarter (the "Royalty Period"), an accurate statement of Net Sales of Licensed Products along with any royalty payments or sublicensing revenues due to Licensor shall be provided to Licensor, regardless of whether any Licensed Products were sold during the Royalty Period. All payments shall be paid in United States currency drawn on a United States bank. The acceptance by Licensor of any of the statements furnished or royalties paid shall not preclude Licensor questioning the correctness at any time of any payments or statements.

12. What's an Audit?

So you've negotiated a good royalty, but how do you know the payments you receive are accurate? Since sales figures and deductions are within the control of the licensee, you will want the right to audit, or review licensee records. This right can be provided in the license agreement and is traditionally referred to as an audit provision.

The audit provision generally provides:

- that the licensor (or the licensor's representative) shall have access to the licensee's books and records
- that the audit information will remain confidential, and
- a method for resolving any disputes over discrepancies.

a. Opening up the Books

An audit provision will provide who can audit the books and how often. Normally, a licensee will want to limit the frequency of audits. It is common for a licensee to limit the number of audits to once or twice a year. Also, the licensee will want several day's notice before the audit is to occur. Five days is common.

The licensee may also seek to limit who can audit the books. For example, a licensee may request that you hire a Certified Public Accountant (CPA) to perform the audit. It will be more expensive for you to hire a CPA, and therefore we would recommend that you avoid this requirement. It would be less expensive if any accountant can serve as your representative for an audit. It also would be helpful to obtain the licensee's cooperation by designating an individual at the licensee's company to be available to assist you or your representatives.

Contingency Auditors

Sometimes a licensee will attempt to prohibit a licensor from using an accounting firm that works on a contingency basis. Working on a contingency basis means that the company will not get paid unless it finds a discrepancy. Licensees are not comfortable with these firms because they believe that contingency accountants "manufacture" discrepancies in order to receive a bigger commission. As a general rule, we would recommend that you retain the right to use whomever you want as your representative for an audit.

Since you may not discover or suspect a discrepancy right away, you should negotiate an audit provision that requires the licensee to keep all books and records available for at least two years after the termination of the license agreement.

b. Keeping the Audit Confidential

Since the licensee's books may contain confidential information about sales and prices, your representative may be required to sign a confidentiality agreement. You may be requested to keep the information confidential. This is reasonable, although this confidentiality provision should not apply in the event of litigation about payments.

c. Settling Audit Disputes

In the case of an underpayment in which you receive less money than you should, the license agreement should provide for a method of settling the dispute. Usually, there are three parts to this dispute resolution.

First, the licensee must promptly pay you the money you should have received.

Second, you should seek an interest payment. If you had received the proper payment in the first place, you could have deposited it in a bank and earned interest on it.

Third, you may seek to have the licensee pay for the costs of your audit if there is an underpayment. A licensee will not want to pay for the audit for just any discrepancy, only substantial ones. What counts as substantial? Some agreements set a dollar amount, for example, $1,000. Other agreements set a percentage (for example, if any underpayment was more than 2% of the amount paid).

Interest Rates

You cannot arbitrarily choose an interest rate. State laws, known as usury laws, prohibit excessive interest rates. Some agreements provide for interest "at a rate of 1% or 1.5% per month, or the maximum rate permitted by law, whichever is less." This language prevents the interest rate from exceeding the limits of state usury laws. The interest rate provided in the sample agreement, below, is tied to the prime rate, a fluctuating national rate that is commonly used in business.

EXAMPLE: A licensor had received a $10,000 royalty payment. An audit determined that the licensee should have received $10,300. The underpayment was $300, or 3% of the amount actually paid. In the licensing agreement, the licensee had agreed to pay for the audit if any underpayment was more than 2% of the amount paid. The Licensee must pay the $300 plus interest, plus the costs of the audit.

Audit. Licensee shall keep accurate books of accounts and records covering all transactions relating to the license granted in this Agreement. Licensor or its duly authorized representatives shall have the right upon five days' prior written notice, and during normal business hours, to inspect and audit Licensee's records relating to the Property licensed under this Agreement. Licensor shall bear the cost of such inspection and audit, unless the results indicate an underpayment greater than _____ *[insert either amount of underpayment, for example, "$1,000," or percentage, such as "2% of the amount paid"]* for any six-month period. In that case, Licensee shall promptly reimburse Licensor for all costs of the audit along with the amount due with interest on such sums. Interest shall accrue from the date the payment was originally due and the interest rate shall be 1.5% per month, or the maximum rate permitted by law, whichever is less. All books of account and records shall be made available in the United States and kept available for at least two years after the termination of this Agreement.

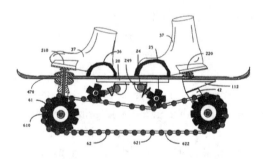

**Frictionless Noncontact Engaging
Drive Skate & Skateboard
No. 6,007,074**

13. How Do You Deal With Late Payments?

Late payments are similar to underpayments: you are losing money because you could have invested the payment earlier and earned interest. Therefore, a license agreement can require that the licensee pay interest from the date that the payment should have been made. The interest rate can be the prime rate (see the audit provision above) or it can be any legal rate. Monthly rates of 1% or 1.5% are common in audit and late payment provisions. The agreement below also includes the language, "time is of the essence," which is basically legal double-talk meaning that you and the licensee agree that it's a material aspect of the agreement for you to get paid on time.

> **Late Payment.** Time is of the essence with respect to all payments to be made by Licensee under this Agreement. If Licensee is late in any payment provided for in this Agreement, Licensee shall pay interest on the payment from the date due until paid at a rate of 1.5% per month, or the maximum rate permitted by law, whichever is less.

Taxation of License Income

Generally, licensing income is taxed as an ordinary gain, just like ordinary business income. You may claim certain deductions or credits where applicable, but you must pay taxes on all of the income you receive during each year. However, when you assign your invention and give up all of your rights to it, your income from the assignment can be taxed as capital gains. In other words, your tax treatment is different if you permanently transfer your rights in the invention. These rules may vary slightly depending upon whether patent, trademark, trade secret or copyright law protects the invention. You should also realize that the title of your agreement or the terms you use (that is, license, sale or assignment) are not what governs tax treatment. For tax purposes, these are only "transactional labels." The IRS examines the substance of the agreement to determine if it transfers all of the assets. If you are concerned about how your income will be taxed, you should consult with a tax attorney or financial adviser before entering into a license agreement.

Negotiating Your Agreement

n the previous two chapters we provided background on the essential business terms—such as territory, length of the agreement and amount of royalties. In this chapter we provide some negotiating tips and suggest some ways to incorporate the important contract elements into a formal document such as a license agreement, option agreement or letter of intent. You should read this chapter if you answer "yes" to any of these questions:

- Do you want suggestions about negotiating?
- Would you like to prepare a summary of the important contract elements?
- Would you like information about option agreements?
- Would you like to learn about letters of intent?

A. What, Me Negotiate?

It's not always possible to convince a licensee to give you more royalties or larger advances. It's often difficult to even get a licensee to budge on issues such as net sales or audit provisions. You may have to concede several issues in order to get something else you want.

Negotiation is like navigating a trip. You need to know where you're going and then decide the best route. We can't teach you how to negotiate—that's beyond the scope of this book—but we can give you some tips.

1. Negotiate in Person Whenever Possible

E-mail, faxes and phone work fine, but a personal meeting creates an atmosphere where solutions and compromises are more likely to result. Don't get upset if you are outnumbered at a business meeting. During the meeting you'll be able to see who the real decision maker is among the group and address your comments to him or her. Face each person you speak with, speak directly and make eye contact. Pay attention to responses and demonstrate your attention by nodding your head or stating your opinion. Avoid talking while another person is speaking or making gestures of disgust or disrespect such as rolling your eyes, snorting or sighing. And try not to crowd anyone—that is, don't sit or stand too close.

2. Ask Questions

Avoid confrontations by asking questions. For example, say the licensee is offering you less than the industry standard. Don't create a confrontation and demand a higher rate. Start by asking why. A question rather than a demand is more likely to result in a change because questions articulate the underlying issues without creating a conflict.

3. Things to Avoid

Negotiations can be stressful events. It may be easier to remember what not to do so you can avoid potentially costly mistakes. Below is a list of "don'ts" to help you in your negotiations.

- **Don't have unrealistic expectations.** According to the president of the Licensing Executives Society, the major reason licensing negotiations fall apart is unrealistic expectations. Know what you want. A good negotiator knows what he wants and has a range of "worst to best" alternatives. Create flexible expectations based upon the realities of the business.
- **Don't bluff.** The false display of confidence may work in a poker game, but it is not recommended in business negotiations. It may cause a licensee to walk out or to call your bluff. If your bluff is called, you will lose credibility when you accept less.
- **Don't keep negotiating after you've agreed on terms.** According to one consultant, inventors often talk themselves into a sale and then out of it again because they won't stop talking.

- **Don't ask for an exorbitant amount of money when you're willing to settle for a fraction of it.** In his book *Smart Negotiating: How to Make Good Deals in the Real World,* author James C. Freund suggests that your starting point for payments be no more than 15% to 25% away from your realistic expectation.
- **Don't reject an offer today if you can put it off till tomorrow.** Even if you're sure you won't accept an offer, it's usually better to delay so you can reflect on your decision.

4. Take It or Leave It

Sometimes a licensee may present you with a finalized agreement and ask you to sign it, explaining that you can take it or leave it. For example, say the president of a licensee company tells you, "You get a $10,000 advance and a 5% royalty and we get exclusive worldwide rights for the life of the patent. Take it or leave it." This type of offer really says, "We dictate the terms and we don't negotiate." If you have no other prospects and are afraid of losing an opportunity, then you must decide on their terms. Don't mistakenly assume the company is bluffing. They're probably not.

Review the elements of your deal according to principles provided in this chapter and the subsequent contract chapters. Review the licensee company to determine if it is strong within the industry. A good general rule is if the company is strong and the terms are standard (or close to standard), you should accept the offer. However, if the arrangement is inherently unfair and the licensee company's reputation is not good, you're better off rejecting the offer.

5. Negotiating Resources

If you'd like more background on negotiating, the bible is *Getting to Yes: Negotiating Agreement Without Giving In,* by Roger Fisher, William Ury and Bruce Patton (Penguin Books, 1991). Another good source is James Freund's *Smart Negotiating: How to Make Good Deals in the Real World* (Simon & Schuster, 1992). *Negotiator Pro* is a software program that takes you through the steps of a formal negotiation and provides advice from experts in the field. The program is available from Negotiator Pro (800-448-3308; www.negotiatorpro.com).

Be Careful How You Characterize Other Inventors

If the licensee has a business relationship with a competing inventor, be careful how you characterize the competition. If you make false statements about another inventor or invention, or about your own invention in order to induce the licensee to break a business relationship, you could be setting yourself up for several lawsuits including defamation, a claim known as "interference with a business (or contractual) relationship" or "interference with prospective economic advantage." Every state has laws prohibiting such behavior.

B. Documenting the Important Contract Elements

Once you have negotiated the essential business terms, we recommend that you prepare a one-page sheet that summarizes the results. This sheet is a simple way of memorializing the contract facts.

This sheet may be attached to your final license agreement or it may be attached to a pre-license document such as an option agreement or letter of intent (discussed below). That way, if you change the details later (for example, you extend the length of the agreement), you need only modify the sheet, not the whole agreement. If you include your sheet as an attachment to your agreement, be sure to give it a title such as Exhibit A and make reference to it in the main body of the agreement. (An exhibit is simply a document that is included with the main agreement and that becomes part of the agreement.)

For example, in the body of your agreement you could refer to the fact sheet with the following language: "Licensee agrees to pay to Licensor the sum specified in Exhibit A."

⚠ In the event that you fail to negotiate a written agreement, the fact sheet may also—although we do not recommend it—become a memorandum of an oral license. For example, you and the licensee sit down for lunch and work out the basic elements of the license. You and the licensee write down these elements on your fact sheet. The licensee is in a hurry and wants to begin manufacturing. He promises to send you a complete license agreement within a month. Six months later, you have not received the license agreement. You sue for royalties and argue that you had an oral agreement, based upon the fact sheet.

1. License Summary

The sheet below summarizes the basic contract elements between Joan Smith, an inventor (referred to as SMITH), and MEDCO, a medical supply company.

2. What Do You Do With the Fact Sheet?

What you do with your sheet summarizing the contract depends on the licensee's course of action. Below are the common scenarios.

- **Written license.** The licensee wants a written license agreement. The summary sheet can be used as a reference for filling out the agreement, or it can be used as an exhibit. That is, you would attach it to the license agreement and refer to it as Exhibit A. For example, "The Royalty shall be as defined in Exhibit A."
- **Letter of intent.** The licensee desires a written license agreement but since it may take several weeks or months to prepare the agreement, the licensee requests a letter of intent—a non-binding document that states the intentions of the parties. The summary sheet (or the substance of the sheet) is incorporated into the letter of intent. Review the section on letters of intent, below.
- **Option agreement.** The licensee is not sure if it will enter into a license agreement and wants more time before executing a license agreement—for example, to evaluate or test market the product. In that case, you can incorporate the summary sheet into an option agreement. An option agreement lets a licensee buy time (usually known as the option period) from the inventor—a few weeks, months or years. In return for receiving an option payment, the inventor agrees not to license the invention to anyone else during the option period. Review the section on option agreements, below.
- **Oral license.** The licensee doesn't care about a written license agreement and wants to start selling the product based solely on the basic contract facts. In other words, the licensee wants to operate on your oral license. We do not recommend that you proceed on the basis of an oral agreement. In the event, however, that you decide to disregard this advice, we suggest adding a dispute resolution provision to the sheet and having the licensee sign it. Review the section on oral licenses, below.

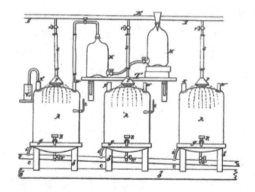

Brewing Beer and Ale
No. 135,245

Medco-Smith License

1. The Properties

US Patent Pending #09/998,944.

US Patent Application #09/023,484.

PCT Application #US92/15874.

Copyrighted Packaging Imagery.

All Patent Disclosures including #343561.

Certain SMITH proprietary information and trade secrets.

2. License

Exclusive. No assignment or sublicense without licensor's written consent.

3. Licensed Products

Medical supply products.

4. Term

17 years or life of any Patents on the Properties, whichever is longer.

5. Territory

World.

6. Advance

$25,000.

7. Minimum Annual Royalty

None.

8. Licensed Product Royalty Rate

Five percent (5%) of Net Sales (all revenues, less credited returns, from sale, distribution and transfer of any such products by MEDCO).

[Note: When licensing patents, pending patents and trade secrets (known as a hybrid license), you may choose to allocate the respective percentage values. See Chapter 9 for sample language.]

9. Date for Commencement of Sale

January 2003.

C. Letter of Intent

After agreeing to the essential business terms, a licensee may prepare and sign a letter of intent. The letter of intent sets forth the essential terms and establishes a date when the parties plan to enter into a license agreement.

A letter of intent is usually not a binding contract. That is, even if you sign it, you can still reject the deal for any reasonable basis. For example, you sign a letter of intent but then reject the final contract because you and the licensee disagree about provisions such as warranties or indemnity.

Most letters of intent specifically state they are not binding agreements. Why bother preparing and signing one? Licensees like the letter of intent because it serves as a guide for the final agreement, establishes that both parties are going to work in good faith to consummate the license and provides some comfort level to the parties as they progress through the contract negotiation.

The sample letter of intent below could have included the sheet summarizing the contract facts as an exhibit. Instead, in our sample the terms were written into the body of the letter. Sometimes a licensee prefers this format because it starts to flesh out language that may be used in the license agreement.

Letter of Intent. This introductory paragraph guarantees that the letter of intent is not intended to be a contract. Even though it does not impose any legal obligation, some courts have interpreted a letter of intent to require that the parties act in good faith. This means that the parties will deal fairly and reasonably. For example, a licensor would be acting unfairly if the sole purpose of obtaining the letter of intent was to get a better deal from a different company.

The Properties. Insert your name, business form and address. This introductory statement defines the invention or technology that is being licensed. You should have agreed upon a definition as part of your business negotiation. See Chapter 8 for information on defining the invention. You should

strike the patent references if you do not have a patent or pending application for patent.

The Grant. Insert the name, business form (for example, an Illinois corporation) and address of the prospective licensing company. This statement establishes the elements of the prospective license. See Chapter 8 for information on defining the license. If an agent is acting on behalf of the licensor, then the agent's name will be inserted into this statement. For example, "JONES is acting as Inventor's agent." You should also insert the territory (for example, "the world"). Insert the length of agreement (the term). See Chapter 8.

Operations. This Operations provision establishes the licensing company's obligations for manufacturing and accounting. This type of provision is not necessary, but is often included in a letter of intent. Operations provisions are often more detailed and more specific in the license agreement.

Royalties. This provision establishes the basic licensor payments, royalties and advance, and also incorporates the definition for "Net Sales." An explanation of these terms is provided in Chapter 9. The term "execution of the Agreement" refers to the signing of the contract. If royalties are to be paid directly to the agent, then that information would be included in this section.

License Agreement. This provision establishes that the parties will use "best efforts," which is similar to saying that the parties will act reasonably and not do anything unfair that would thwart the objective. For example, if the licensee refused to speak with the licensor, that would not be best efforts. The date for executing a written contract can be extended. Even if the date is not extended, both parties can still execute a license agreement at any time. The date is simply a guidepost.

1. What If the Letter of Intent Is Binding?

Most letters of intent are non-binding and they say so with explicit language. A non-binding letter is often preferred because both parties are free to get

Sample Letter of Intent

Dear _[insert name of contact person at company that wants to option invention]_ :

This letter reflects our discussions regarding the terms and conditions of the proposed licensing agreement for certain technologies, more specifically described below. Please review this letter of intent, and if it accurately reflects our discussions, return a copy with your signature. We will then proceed to a written draft of the licensing agreement. Thanks for your cooperation.

Letter of Intent. This document is a Letter of Intent only. It is not intended to be, and shall not constitute in any way, a binding or legal agreement, or impose any legal obligation or duty on Inventor and Company.

The Properties. _[insert your name]_ ("Inventor") is the owner of the certain proprietary and intellectual property rights collectively known as "the Properties." The Properties include: U.S. Patent Pending # _[insert patent number]_, U.S. Patent Application # _[insert patent application number]_ and certain Inventor proprietary information and trade secrets.

The Grant. _[insert name of company that wants to option your invention]_ ("Company") is a manufacturer and distributor who desires to enter into a Licensing Agreement (the "Agreement") for the purpose of _exclusively or nonexclusively_ exploiting the Properties in the form of products (the "Licensed Products") throughout _[insert countries or regions for the license]_ (the "Territory") for _[insert the length of the potential license, for example, "five years"]_ (the "Term"). The license shall not include the right to assign or sublicense such rights to other parties without the express written consent of Inventor.

Operations. Company will bear all responsibility for manufacturing, advertising, marketing, promotion and support of the Licensed Products. Company will keep accurate records of accounting, distribution and costs and will make these records available for inspection on a reasonable basis.

Royalties. Company shall pay to Inventor a royalty rate of _[insert appropriate royalty percentage]_ % of all "Net Sales" from the Licensed Products or any Licensed Products that use technology developed or derived from the Properties. "Net Sales" shall be all revenues (less credited returns) from the sale, distribution and transfer of any such products by Company.

☐ **Advance [Optional].** As an advance against future royalties, Company shall pay to Inventor $ _[insert amount of advance]_ upon execution of the Agreement.

License Agreement. In the event that the parties agree to proceed upon these terms, Inventor and Company agree to use their best efforts to execute a written contract incorporating the terms of this Letter of Intent on or before _[insert date when option must be exercised]_ .

If this accurately reflects your intention, please sign, date and return the enclosed copy of this Letter of Intent.

_____	_____
Inventor	Date
_____	_____
Company	Date

out of the agreement if they desire. However, if there is no mention of the word "non-binding" or if the letter of intent does not disclaim or deny that it is an enforceable agreement (by saying, for example, "this letter is not a contract"), then your signature will bind you. In other words, you will be signing a binding contract. Unlike a non-binding letter of intent, you (and the licensee) will not be able to terminate the arrangement at will. You're both locked in. If you don't meet the terms of the letter—for example, sign a written license on the date set in the agreement—your arrangement with the licensee will terminate unless you agree to extend the time to sign an agreement.

If you are happy with the basic contract elements, entering into a binding letter of intent with a potential licensee might work for you. An alternative, however, when a licensee wants a binding contractual commitment to enter into an license agreement by a certain date, is to execute an option agreement. In an option agreement, a licensee pays you for keeping the licensing deal open to them for a certain period of time. Options are discussed below.

D. Option Agreements

An option agreement is essentially a contract to make another contract, if certain conditions are met. A licensee who thinks it may want to enter into a license agreement with you pays you a fee to keep the offer open while it makes its decision. In exchange for the payment, you agree not to enter into a license agreement with anyone else for a period of time—perhaps six months or a year (sometimes referred to as the option period). If the licensee decides to proceed (sometimes referred to as "exercising its option"), you then sign a license agreement. If not, you can keep the option payment and are free to take the invention somewhere else after the option period expires.

Why does a licensee pay for the option? Because the company wants to be sure that you will not take the invention to anyone else during the option period. In other words, the company is paying you to keep the invention away from others for a specified period of time.

1. Attaching the License Agreement to the Option Agreement

If the licensee exercises the option, you are obligated to sign the license agreement. Shouldn't you see the whole license agreement before signing the option deal? Ideally, yes, you should see the complete license deal that you are expected to sign. It would be great (and we recommend) that the license agreement be attached to the option deal as an exhibit. That way, if the licensee later exercises the option, both of you will have already agreed on the provisions.

Unfortunately, many situations are not as neat and clean as this. The parties—you and the licensee—may be willing to agree on the business terms but not willing to discuss and negotiate all of the contract provisions at the time of the option agreement. Instead the parties may agree to use "good faith" or "best efforts" to agree upon contract provisions, basically a promise to use reasonable efforts and fair business judgment.

Since a disagreement is always possible, it is wise to use an arbitration or mediation provision in the option agreement. That way, a third party can be brought in to iron out or force a solution for contract provision disputes. For more information about arbitration and mediation, review Chapter 14.

2. Option Payments

Option payments are usually smaller than license payments. That is, don't expect to get rich off an option. As a general rule, the longer the option period, the more money you should seek for the option. For example, a six-week option payment may cost $1,000 while a three-month option may go for $5,000. Remember, the longer the option, the longer that your invention is out of the marketplace.

Option Agreement

Introduction

This Option Agreement (the "Agreement") is made between _____

_____

[insert your name, address and business form] (referred to as "Inventor") and _____

_____

[insert the company's name, address and business form] (referred to as "Company"). Inventor and Company shall be collectively referred to as "the parties." Inventor is the owner of certain proprietary rights to an invention tentatively referred to as the "_____

_____" *[insert the name of your invention]*.

Company desires to acquire an exclusive option to enter into a License Agreement for these ideas, processes and technologies. The parties agree as follows:

The Properties; Licensed Products

Inventor is the owner of licensing rights to all inventions embodied in U.S. Patent No. _____ *[insert patent number]*, a copy of which is attached as Attachment A, and to all other proprietary rights, including but not limited to copyrights, trade secrets, formulas, research data, know-how and specifications related to the invention presently known as

"_____" *[insert the name of your invention]* and referred to in this Option Agreement as "the Properties." Inventor has submitted the Properties to Company. Inventor represents that he has the authority to grant rights to Company for the Properties. Company desires an exclusive option to enter into a License Agreement to sell the Properties as incorporated in Company's products ("the Licensed Products").

Exclusive Option

For the consideration provided below, Inventor grants to Company the exclusive option to enter into a license agreement (the "License Agreement") for the Properties. The License Agreement shall be substantially similar to that attached to this Option Agreement as Attachment B and shall incorporate the License Terms as set forth below.

Terms & Conditions of Option

Company shall have six months from the date of execution of this Agreement (the "Option Period") to exercise its option for the Properties. During the Option Period, Inventor shall refrain from offering or granting any third party any rights to the Properties which will interfere with the exercise of the option granted to Company. In consideration for the option and rights granted in this Option Agreement, Company shall pay to Inventor the nonrefundable sum of $_____ *[insert amount of option payment]*. In the event that Company exercises its option, such payment shall be considered as an advance against future royalties.

License

In the event Company decides to enter into a License Agreement, such agreement shall contain the business terms as set forth below.

License Grant

Exclusive worldwide license of all rights to the Properties, including, but not limited to, any patent, copyright or similar rights, if applicable. No assignment or sublicensing of rights without written consent of Inventor.

Term

For the life of any patents obtained on the Properties or fifteen years, whichever is longer.

☐ Advances [Optional]

A nonrefundable advance against royalties of $_____ *[insert amount of advance]* to be paid as follows: _____% *[indicate when advance is to be paid]*.

Royalties; Net Sales

_____ *[insert royalty rate]* % of Net Sales of the Licensed Products. Net Sales are defined as Company's gross sales minus returns that are actually credited. Gross sales are the total amount on invoices billed to customers.

☐ Guaranteed Minimum Annual Royalty [Optional]

A Guaranteed Minimum Annual Royalty of $_____ *[insert amount of GMAR]* payable (in advance) at the beginning of each calendar year of the Licensing Agreement. Company may carry forward or cumulate royalty deficiencies for any year in which the minimum royalty guarantee did not exceed the actual royalties earned by Inventor.

Confidentiality

The parties acknowledge that each may be furnished or have access to confidential information that relates to each other's business (the "Information"). In the event that Information is in written form, the disclosing party shall label or stamp the materials with the word "Confidential" or some similar warning. In the event that Information is transmitted orally, the disclosing party shall promptly provide a writing indicating that such oral communication constituted Information. The parties agree to preserve and protect the confidentiality of the Information and no party shall disclose such Information to third parties without the prior written consent of the other.

Termination

Company shall have the right to terminate this Option Agreement at any time, upon written notice to Inventor. In the event: (a) Company elects to terminate this Option Agreement, or (b) Company has not exercised its option before the end of the Option Period, or (c) Company materially breaches this Agreement, Company agrees to promptly return to Inventor all rights, models and documentation in and to the Properties and not to use or disclose to any third parties information relating to the Properties. In such an event, Inventor shall be free to license the Properties to others with no further obligation to Company and Company shall have no further obligation to Inventor with the exception of any confidentiality agreements executed by the parties (the terms of which are incorporated in this Option Agreement) and which shall survive the termination of this Option Agreement.

General; Miscellaneous

Any material contained in an attachment, exhibit or addendum to this Option Agreement shall be incorporated by reference in this Option Agreement. Nothing contained in this Option Agreement shall be deemed to constitute either Inventor or Company a partner, joint venturer or employee of the other party for any purpose. This Option Agreement may not be amended except in a writing signed by both parties. No waiver by Inventor of any right shall be construed as a waiver of any other right. If a court finds any provision of this Option Agreement invalid or unenforceable as applied to any circumstance, the remainder of this Option Agreement shall be interpreted so as best to effect the intent of the parties. This Option Agreement shall be governed by and interpreted in accordance with the laws of the State of _____ _[insert your state of residence]._ Any controversy or claim arising out of or relating to this Option Agreement, or the breach of this Option Agreement shall be settled by arbitration in accordance with the rules of the American Arbitration Association and judgment upon the award rendered by the arbitrator(s) may be entered in any court having jurisdiction. The prevailing party shall have the right to collect from the other party its reasonable costs and attorney's fees incurred in enforcing this agreement. Any such arbitration hearing shall include a written transcript of the proceedings and a written explanation for any final determination. This Option Agreement expresses the complete understanding of the parties with respect to the subject matter and supersedes all prior proposals, agreements, representations and understandings.

If these terms and conditions are agreeable, please sign and execute both copies of this Option Agreement.

_____   _____
Inventor   Date

_____   _____
Company   Date

You may be losing opportunities and money if the option period is longer than a year.

If the option is ultimately exercised, the option payment is usually considered as part of the advance and later deducted against your royalties. This is a matter of negotiation. If you're in a strong bargaining position, you may be able to negotiate a payment that is not deductible.

If the potential licensee does not exercise the option, then you can keep the money without any obligation. To guarantee this result, you should explicitly state in your option agreement that the option payment is nonrefundable.

Introduction. This introductory paragraph establishes the purpose of the agreement and defines the parties. Note that the key terms for the parties are capitalized throughout the agreement for easy reference.

The Properties; Licensed Products. This section provides two definitions—for the invention and for the licensed products. The parties are using the term "Properties" to refer to the invention. As we explained in Chapter 8, many names can be used to signify the invention. If you are not familiar with the concepts of defining the invention or the licensed products, review Chapter 8.

Exclusive Option. This provision establishes that the option is exclusive, that is, the inventor cannot option rights to another company. We recommend attaching a copy of the license agreement (or a sample license agreement) to the option agreement. If that is not possible, then strike the last sentence and add a sentence that states: "The parties, acting in good faith, shall use best efforts to incorporate the terms set forth in this Option Agreement into the final License Agreement."

Terms & Conditions of Option. The option payment is nonrefundable, meaning the inventor does not have to return the money. However, the payment can be deducted against future royalties if the option is exercised. If you have the ability, you should negotiate an option payment that is non-refundable and nonrecoupable. Nonrecoupable means that the payment cannot be deducted against

royalties. In this agreement, the inventor expects to license all rights. He is not reserving any rights. If you do not intend to license all rights, you can option rights for specific licensed products or in certain territories.

License. This provision lists all the negotiated business elements (exclusive license, royalties, etc.). Your sheet summarizing the contract facts could have been used instead. In that case, you would state that the "License elements shall be as established in the attached exhibit entitled Exhibit A." For more information on determining these basic elements, review Chapters 8 and 9.

Confidentiality. In the event that the parties have not previously signed a confidentiality agreement, you should include a provision such as this requiring confidentiality (see Chapter 7).

Termination. This option agreement terminates if the company does not exercise the option. That is, if the company does not indicate that it wants to proceed, the parties walk away and the inventor keeps the option payment. However, option agreements can include renewals. For example, at the end of six months, the potential licensee can pay a certain sum for another six-month option period. This provision also establishes that the potential licensee must return all materials (prototypes and documentation, etc.) in the event of termination.

General; Miscellaneous. Each state has varying rules regarding contract interpretation, and this section provides which state's law will govern disputes. We recommend that you seek your state of residence, although the potential Company may insist on its home state. Usually, this is not a crucial point. However, beware if the potential Company wants to include a sentence in which you agree to the jurisdiction of another state. This means that you will have to travel to that state for any dispute arising from the agreement. Sometimes option agreements omit this miscellaneous section because the parties want a contract that does not appear "too legalistic." However, we recommend that you include these provisions because they are important for resolving disputes. This contract also provides for resolving disputes by a method known as arbitration, which is usually faster and less expensive than litigation. These provisions are explained in detail in Chapter 14. Be forewarned that many companies are reluctant to arbitrate and may ask you to strike that section.

E. What If the Licensee Wants to Proceed Without a Written License Agreement?

Although most licensees prefer a written license—it provides more security and may be required for patent rights—companies sometimes want to proceed without a written agreement. A licensee may want to begin manufacturing your invention based upon your oral agreement of the material terms. Although it's unlikely, it can happen.

If the licensee is adamant about moving ahead without a written agreement and does not want to execute a letter of intent or option agreement, then you have a difficult choice—to proceed without a written agreement or to terminate the arrangement.

We recommend against oral agreements. They are more difficult to prove and enforce and do not provide sufficient protection in the event of infringement or lawsuits. In addition, the law may set limits on oral agreements or interpret the agreements in a manner that does not adequately protect you.

You may be inclined to disregard this advice. In that case, we suggest that you take some precautions. First, ask the licensee whether they have proceeded with other inventors without written agreements. Ask to speak with the other inventors to determine if the relationship has been successful—for instance, whether they have been paid and are satisfied with the arrangement.

Second, if the licensee insists on moving ahead without a license agreement, use your summary sheet as a skeletal written agreement with the modifications provided below. Both you and the licensee should sign this document. These changes will never protect you as well as a complete written license, but they are better than relying solely upon a handshake and an oral agreement.

This sample document contains an abbreviated version of an insurance provision, discussed in more detail in Chapter 12. It requires that the licensee maintain product liability insurance—which pays for damages in the event a consumer of the product is injured. The document also contains a provision that establishes a method of resolving disputes. If the licensee balks at arbitration, consider other dispute resolution methods as discussed in Chapter 14. Because oral agreements are more difficult to interpret and enforce, we recommend that you find some method of dispute resolution if you insist on proceeding without a written agreement.

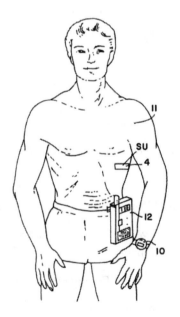

System for Long-Term Remote Medical Monitoring No. 6,315,719

Company/Inventor License Terms

1. **The Properties:**

    US Patent Pending #09/998,944

    US Patent Application #09/023,484

    PCT Application #US92/15874

    Copyrighted Packaging Imagery

    All Patent Disclosures including #343561

    Certain Inventor proprietary information and trade secrets

2. **License**

    Exclusive. No assignment or sublicense without licensor's written consent.

3. **Licensed Products**

    Medical supply products

4. **Term**

    17 years or life of any Patents on the Properties, whichever is longer

5. **Territory**

    World

6. **Advance**

    $25,000

7. **Minimum Annual Royalty**

    None

8. **Licensed Product Royalty Rate**

    Five percent (5%) of Net Sales (all revenues, less credited returns, from sale, distribution and transfer of any such products by Company)

9. **Date for Commencement Of Sale**

    January 2003

10. **Insurance**

    Licensee shall, throughout the Term obtain and maintain, at its own expense, standard product liability insurance coverage, naming Licensor as additional named insureds.

11. Dispute Resolution

This agreement shall be governed by and interpreted in accordance with the laws of the State of _____*[insert state of governing law. See Chapter 14 for more information about governing law provisions.]*_____. Any controversy or claim arising out of or relating to this agreement shall be settled by arbitration in accordance with the rules of the American Arbitration Association and judgment upon the award rendered by the arbitrator(s) may be entered in any court having jurisdiction. The prevailing party shall have the right to collect from the other party its reasonable costs and attorney's fees incurred in enforcing this agreement. Any such arbitration hearing shall include a written transcript of the proceedings and a written explanation for any final determination.

11

Sample Agreement

n this chapter we offer a sample agreement. If you're in a hurry you may have opened to this chapter without reviewing the rest of the book first. You'd like to use the form agreement, fill in the blank sections and get started. That's okay, but you should be prepared for the fact that this form agreement is not like an income tax form or a lease form. That is, the sample license agreement is not fixed—you may need to modify the content, reorder the sections or add or remove sections. We'll give you advice on how to do that later in this chapter.

You should take the time to review the other relevant chapters in this book if you run into any of the following problems:

- You don't understand why you need a particular provision.
- You don't know what information should be supplied in one of the blanks.
- You want to remove, alter or add a provision.

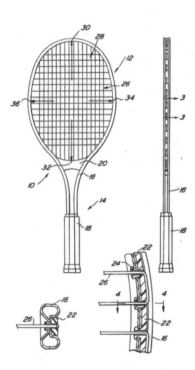

Tennis Racket
No. 3,999,756

Definitions Upfront

One common variation in a license agreement is to place a list of the contract definitions after the introductory paragraph. That is, to group terms such as "Net Sales" and "Licensed Products" at the top of the agreement. That way, you know where to look for a definition, rather than searching through the agreement to find where it was originally introduced and defined. This is mostly a matter of personal preference. If you'd prefer to have your definitions upfront, simply pull them out of the body of the agreement and alphabetize them, for example:

Definitions

"Effective Date" is defined as the date when the agreement commences and is established by the latest signature date.

"Information" is defined as any confidential information that relates to each Party's business.

"Net Sales" is defined as Licensee's gross sales (i.e., the gross invoice amount billed customers) less quantity discounts and returns actually credited.

"Property" is defined as all inventions described in U.S. Patent No. _____.

A. License Agreement

1. Introduction Provision

Insert your name, business form (if any) and address (for example, "Phil Patel, a sole proprietor, with his address at 5678 Hempstead Turnpike, Wantagh, NY 11793"). If you are unsure of your business form, review Chapter 4. Supply the same information for the Licensee (for example, "Medco, a California corporation, with its address at Pierpont Plaza, San Francisco, CA 94102"). The licensee will supply you with information about its business form.

You should also supply a name that you are using for your invention. If the item has been sold to the public already, you can use the trademark name. If it is a patented invention, use the title of the patent—for example, "Portable Popcorn Making Device." Otherwise, just insert whatever nickname you and the licensee have been using to refer to the invention.

The second half of the introductory paragraph starting with "Licensor is the owner of certain proprietary rights ..." replaces the "whereas" provisions that are common in many license agreements. The "whereas" provisions are a summary of what the parties intend to do. They usually begin with statements such as "Whereas the parties desire to enter into an agreement .... There is no need to use the "whereas" format. You can simply summarize the intentions of the parties as shown in the sample agreement. If the sample agreement does not accurately reflect your intentions, it should be modified accordingly. This portion of the agreement is not considered to be enforceable (that is, it's not legally binding) because it occurs before the statement, "therefore the parties agree ...." Regardless of its enforceability, this introductory paragraph should accurately summarize the intentions of the parties.

2. The Property

This provision defines your invention. You can use the term "the Property" (or Properties) or "the Invention." If you are licensing a method or procedure, you can use the term "the Process." Whatever term is used, it must be consistent throughout the agreement. There are many ways to write a Property definition.

If you have applied for a patent but it has not yet issued, you should define your invention based upon your patent claims and include a copy of the patent application (or the claims enunciated in your application) with the final agreement. (This will not work if you only have a Provisional Patent Application.) Simply label the application "Exhibit A" at the top and attach it to the end of the agreement. For an explanation of the difference between a provisional patent application and a pending patent application, review Chapter 2. For example, you could use the following alternative clause:

Patent Not Yet Issued

The "Property" refers to the invention(s) described in U.S. Patent Application No(s). _____ [insert patent application number], a copy of which is attached to this agreement.

If the licensee wants to acquire more than the present U.S. patent rights to your invention, such as derivative rights or improvements on your patent or foreign patent rights, then the definition may be more detailed. For example:

Patents & Improvements

The Property is defined as the invention(s) described in U.S. Patent No(s). _____ *[insert patent number]* and any improvements, reissues or extensions, as well as any continuations divisions, or substitute U.S. patent applications that shall be based on U.S. Patent No(s). _____ *[insert patent number(s) (same numbers as above)]*; and any patent applications corresponding to the above-described patents and patent applications that are issued, filed or to be filed in any and all foreign countries.

Note: The term "Improvements" may need its own definition, since some inventors may not want to permit a licensee to use every improvement that results from a patent. By limiting the definition (for example, "improvements related to the sports and recreation industry"), the licensee only obtains rights to the improvements that fall within the definition. Read Chapter 8 for information on defining the Property and read Chapter 15 regarding improvements to your invention.

License Agreement

Introduction

This License Agreement (the "Agreement") is made between _____ _____ (referred to as "Licensor") *[insert Licensor's name, business form and address]*, and _____ _____ (referred to as "Licensee") *[insert Licensee's name, business form and address]*.

Licensor and Licensee shall be collectively referred to as "the parties." Licensor is the owner of certain proprietary rights to an invention referred to as _____ _____ *[insert name of invention]*.

Licensee desires to license certain rights in the invention. Therefore the parties agree as follows:

The Property *[Select One]*

☐ **Patent Issued**

The "Property" refers to the invention(s) described in U.S. Patent No(s). _____ *[insert patent number(s)]*.

☐ **Patent Not Yet Issued**

The "Property" refers to the invention(s) described in U.S. Patent Application No(s). _____ *[insert patent application number]*, a copy of which is attached to this agreement.

☐ **Patents & Improvements**

The Property is defined as the invention(s) described in U.S. Patent No(s). _____ *[insert patent number]* and any improvements, reissues or extensions, as well as any continuations, divisions or substitute U.S. patent applications that shall be based on the patent(s); and any patent applications corresponding to the above-described patent(s) and patent applications that are issued, filed or to be filed in any and all foreign countries.

☐ **Copyright, Trade Secrets and Trademarks: No Patents**

The Property refers to all proprietary rights, including but not limited to copyrights, trade secrets, formulas, research data, know-how and specifications related to the invention commonly known as the _____ *[name of invention]* as well as any trademark rights and associated good will. A more complete description is provided in the attached Exhibit A.

☐ **Copyright or Trademark Registration**

The Property refers to all proprietary rights, including but not limited to copyrights as embodied in Copyright Registration No. _____ dated _____ (or Trademark Registration No. _____ dated _____ and associated goodwill).

☐ **Patents and Copyright, Trade Secrets and Trademarks**

The "Property" refers to all inventions described in U.S. Patent No. _____ *[insert patent number]* and to all other proprietary rights, including but not limited to copyrights, trade secrets, formulas, research data, know-how and specifications related to the invention commonly known as _____ *[name of invention]* as well as any trademark rights and associated good will. A more complete description is provided in the attached Exhibit A.

In the case of a non-patented invention, the definition of the invention should describe the invention and indicate the proprietary rights that you have acquired. The description of the invention should tell what it looks like, what it is and what it does. For example:

Copyright, Trade Secrets and Trademarks: No Patents

The Property refers to all proprietary rights, including, but not limited to, copyrights, trade secrets, formulas, research data, know-how and specifications related to the invention commonly known as the _____ [name of invention], as well as any trademark rights and associated good will. A more complete description is provided in the attached Exhibit A.

If you have a copyright or trademark registration for some feature of your invention that is being licensed, you should reference that registration by number and date.

Copyright or Trademark Registration

The Property refers to all proprietary rights, including but not limited to copyrights as embodied in Copyright Registration No. _____ dated _____ (or Trademark Registration No. _____ dated _____ and associated goodwill).

If you are licensing patent rights and other features protected by trademark, trade secret or copyright law, then your definition of your invention would be a combination of the two definitions above. For example:

Patents and Copyright, Trade Secrets and Trademarks

The "Property" refers to all inventions described in U.S. Patent No. _____ [insert patent number], and to all other proprietary rights, including, but not limited to, copyrights, trade secrets, formulas, research data, know-how and specifications related to the invention commonly known as _____ [name of invention], as well as any trademark rights and associated good will. A more complete description is provided in the attached Exhibit A.

3. Licensed Products

The definition of "licensed products" has a crucial impact on your license, because these are the types of products that the licensee can sell. That is, the licensee will package or modify your invention to sell to different markets. If you are unsure of how to define "licensed products," review Chapter 8. If you are licensing a process or method (not a product), you should review Chapter 8 and modify the grant provision accordingly. If there is no limitation on Licensed Products (that is, you have agreed that the licensee may put your invention in any of its products), you can simply state:

No Limitations on Licensed Products Definition

Licensed Products are defined as any products sold by the licensee that incorporate the Property.

If you want to use the same broad definition for a *process*, state:

No Limitations on Licensed Process

A Licensed Process is any commercial application of the Process by the licensee. *[Change all references in the agreement to Licensed Process, rather than Products.]*

4. Grant of Rights

The license is either exclusive or nonexclusive. If it is exclusive, only the licensee can have the rights conveyed in the grant provision. No one else, not even you, can exercise these rights.

5. Sublicense

Under this provision, the licensee can license its rights to another company, but only with your written consent. Usually, a licensee will sublicense rights to foreign companies. If the licensee finds this too rigid, you can agree not to withhold consent except for a valid business reason. For more information about sublicensing, see Chapter 8.

Licensed Products *[Select One]*

☐ *Licensed Products Specifically Defined*

Licensed Products are defined as the Licensee products incorporating the Property and specifically described in Exhibit A (the "Licensed Products").

☐ *No Limitations on Licensed Products Definition*

Licensed Products are defined as any products sold by the licensee that incorporate the Property.

☐ *No Limitations on Licensed Process Definition*

A Licensed Process is any commercial application of the Process by the licensee. *[Remember to change all references in the agreement to Licensed Process, rather than products.]*

Grant of Rights

Licensor grants to Licensee a/an_____ *[exclusive or nonexclusive]* license to make, use and sell the Property solely in association with the manufacture, sale, use, promotion or distribution of the Licensed Products.

Sublicense *[Select One]*

☐ *Consent to Sublicense Required*

Licensee may sublicense the rights granted pursuant to this agreement provided: Licensee obtains Licensor's prior written consent to such sublicense, and Licensor receives such revenue or royalty payment as provided in the Payment section below. Any sublicense granted in violation of this provision shall be void.

☐ *Consent to Sublicense Not Unreasonably Withheld*

Licensee may sublicense the rights granted pursuant to this agreement provided: Licensee obtains Licensor's prior written consent to such sublicense, Licensee's consent to any sublicense shall not be unreasonably withheld; and Licensor receives such revenue or royalty payment as provided in the Payment section below. Any sublicense granted in violation of this provision shall be void.

Reservation of Rights *[Select One]*

☐ *All Rights Reserved*

Licensor expressly reserves all rights other than those being conveyed or granted in this Agreement.

☐ *Reservation of Rights Expressly Excluding a Particular Industry*

Licensor expressly reserves all rights other than those being conveyed or granted in this agreement, including but not limited to the right to license the Properties in _____
_____ *[list a particular market which you want to expressly exclude, for example, "the computer and video game market"].*

Territory *[Select One]*

☐ *Statement of Territory*

The rights granted to Licensee are limited to _____
[insert the territory] (the "Territory").

Consent to Sublicense Not Unreasonably Withheld

Licensee may sublicense the rights granted pursuant to this agreement provided: Licensee obtains Licensor's prior written consent to such sublicense. Licensee's consent to any sublicense shall not be unreasonably withheld; and Licensor receives such revenue or royalty payment as provided in the Payment section below. Any sublicense granted in violation of this provision shall be void.

6. Reservation of Rights

This establishes the intellectual property rights that are *not* being given. Generally, you reserve all rights not granted in the Agreement. However, if you already have a license with someone in another industry, you may want to place your new licensee on alert and specifically mention that industry. For example, you could reserve all rights to license the invention to aquatic recreational companies.

Reservation of Rights Expressly Excluding a Particular Industry

Licensor expressly reserves all rights other than those being conveyed or granted in this agreement, including but not limited to the right to license the Properties in _____ *[list a particular market which you want to expressly exclude, for example, "the computer and video game market"].*

For more information, review Chapter 8.

7. Territory

Generally, if you are licensing a patent, the choice of territory is limited to the country or countries where patent protection has been obtained. However, if you and the licensee agree to seek patent protection in foreign countries, then the Territory can go beyond the boundaries of the initial patent protection. If the license is worldwide, for example, you can simply write "the world," but if the territory is limited to a certain area, then state it here (for

example, "United States and Canada"). We have provided an alternate provision if you are concerned about a licensee selling products in an area where you have another license (referred to as "cross-territory activity"). For a more detailed discussion of Territory issues, see Chapter 8.

Limiting Cross-Territory Sales

The rights granted to Licensee are limited to _____ _____ *[insert the territory]* (the "Territory"). Licensee shall not make, use or sell the Licensed Products or any products which are confusingly or substantially similar to the Licensed Products in any country outside the Territory and will not knowingly sell the Licensed Products to persons who intend to resell them in a country outside the Territory.

8. Term

As discussed in Chapter 8, there are three common ways to structure the term (or length) of your license agreement: (1) the term can be for a fixed length (say ten years, or alternatively, the length of your patent); (2) the term can be for a fixed length (say, two years) with a series of renewal periods; or (3) for as long as the licensee manufactures and sells the licensed products or until the agreement is terminated.

If you have negotiated a term for the length of the patents only, the provision should be as below.

Term for the Length of the Patents Only

This Agreement shall commence upon the Effective Date and shall expire simultaneously with the expiration of the longest-living patent (or patents) or last-remaining patent application as listed in the definition of the Property, whichever occurs last, unless sooner terminated pursuant to a provision of this Agreement.

If you want a short term with renewal rights based upon sales or other criteria, consider the sample provision below.

☐ *Limiting Cross-Territory Sales*

The rights granted to Licensee are limited to _____
[insert the territory] (the "Territory"). Licensee shall not make, use or sell the Licensed Products or any products which are confusingly or substantially similar to the Licensed Products in any country outside the Territory and will not knowingly sell the Licensed Products to persons who intend to resell them in a country outside the Territory.

Term *[Select One]*

☐ *Specified Term With Renewal Rights*

This Agreement shall commence upon the latest signature date, (the "Effective Date") and shall extend for a period of _____ years (the "Initial Term") *[insert number of years for initial term, for example, "two years"].*

    Following the Initial Term, this agreement may be renewed by Licensee under the same terms and conditions for _____ *[insert number of renewal terms]* consecutive _____
_____ *[insert length of each renewal term, for example, "two-year"]* periods (the "Renewal Terms"), provided that Licensee provides written notice of its intention to renew this agreement within 30 days before the expiration of the current term. In no event shall the Agreement extend longer than the date of expiration of the patent listed in the definition of the Property.

☐ *Term for the Length of Patent Only*

This Agreement shall commence upon the Effective Date and shall expire simultaneously with the expiration of the longest-living patent (or patents) or last-remaining patent application as listed in the definition of the Property, whichever occurs last, unless sooner terminated pursuant to a provision of this Agreement.

☐ *Short Term With Renewal Rights Based Upon Sales*

This Agreement shall commence upon the Effective Date and shall extend for a period of _____
[insert number of years] years (the "Initial Term") and thereafter may be renewed by Licensee under the same terms and conditions for consecutive _____ *[insert number of years]*-year periods (the "Renewal Terms"), provided that:

    (a) Licensee provides written notice of its intention to renew this agreement within 30 days before the expiration of the current term;

    (b) Licensee has met the sales requirements as established in Exhibit A *[if you choose this alternative be sure to include the sales requirements in Exhibit A]*; and

    (c) in no event shall the Agreement extend longer that the date of expiration of the longest-living patent (or patents) or last-remaining patent application as listed in the definition of the Property.

☐ *No Patents; Indefinite Term*

This Agreement shall commence upon the Effective Date and shall continue until terminated pursuant to a provision of this Agreement.

☐ *Fixed Yearly Term*

This Agreement shall commence upon the Effective Date and shall continue for _____
[insert number of years] unless sooner terminated pursuant to a provision of this Agreement.

☐ *Term for as Long as Licensee Sells Licensed Products*

This Agreement shall commence upon the Effective Date as specified in Exhibit A and shall continue for as long as Licensee continues to offer the Licensed Products in commercially reasonable quantities unless sooner terminated pursuant to a provision of this Agreement.

Short Term With Renewal Rights Based Upon Sales

This Agreement shall commence upon the Effective Date and shall extend for a period of two years (the "Initial Term") and thereafter may be renewed by Licensee under the same terms and conditions for consecutive two-year periods (the "Renewal Terms"), provided that:

(a) Licensee provides written notice of its intention to renew this agreement within 30 days before the expiration of the current term;

(b) Licensee has met the sales requirements as established in Exhibit A; and

(c) in no event shall the Agreement extend longer that the date of expiration of the longest-living patent (or patents) or last-remaining patent application as listed in the definition of the Property.

If you want an agreement that will continue indefinitely until terminated, use the provision below.

No Patents; Indefinite Term

This Agreement shall commence upon the Effective Date and shall continue until terminated pursuant to a provision of this Agreement.

If you want a fixed term with no renewal rights, consider the sample provision below.

Fixed Yearly Term

This Agreement shall commence upon the Effective Date and shall continue for ten years unless sooner terminated pursuant to a provision of this Agreement.

If you want to permit the term to extend for as long as the licensee sells the invention, you could draft a term provision as follows:

Term for as Long as Licensee Sells Licensed Products

This Agreement shall commence upon the Effective Date as specified in Exhibit A and shall continue for as long as Licensee continues to offer the Licensed Products in commercially reasonable quantities unless sooner terminated pursuant to a provision of this Agreement.

Review Chapter 8 for more information on Term provisions. Remember to keep track of your exhibits. If you are attaching a copy of your patent application as Exhibit A, then attach the sales requirements as Exhibit B.

9. Advance Against Royalties

A nonrefundable advance means that you will only have to pay it back by deductions from future royalties. If you are receiving a payment that you do not have to pay back from royalties (that is, no strings attached), substitute the following optional provision: As a nonrefundable, nonrecoupable fee for executing this license, Licensee agrees to pay to Licensor upon execution of this Agreement the sum of _____ *[insert amount of license fee].*

See Chapter 9 for more information.

10. Net Sales

The definition of net sales has a substantial impact on how much you will get paid. In Chapter 9 we explain and recommend certain limitations on net sales. Modify the sample accordingly.

11. Licensed Product Royalty

For an explanation of royalties, review Chapter 9. If you are licensing a combination of patents and other intellectual property, you should consider the alternate hybrid royalty provision and review hybrid licenses in Chapter 9.

Hybrid Royalty; Patent and Non Patented Rights

Licensee agrees to pay a Royalty of _____ % *[insert appropriate royalty percentage]* of all Net Sales revenue of the Licensed Products ("Licensed Product Royalty"). The "Licensed Product Royalty" shall be allocated according to the percentages as provided in this Agreement. In the event that a patent does not issue or an issued patent expires or is otherwise terminated, the allocated percentage for such patent or pending patent

Royalties

All royalties ("Royalties") provided for under this Agreement shall accrue when the respective items are sold, shipped, distributed, billed or paid for, whichever occurs first. Royalties shall also be paid by the Licensee to Licensor on all items, even if not billed (including, but not limited to introductory offers, samples, promotions or distributions) to individuals or companies which are affiliated with, associated with or subsidiaries of Licensee.

Net Sales

"Net Sales" are defined as Licensee's gross sales (i.e., the gross invoice amount billed customers) less quantity discounts and returns actually credited. A quantity discount is a discount made at the time of shipment. No deductions shall be made for cash or other discounts, for commissions, for uncollectible accounts or for fees or expenses of any kind which may be incurred by the Licensee in connection with the Royalty payments.

☐ Advance Against Royalties *[Optional]*

As a nonrefundable advance against royalties (the "Advance"), Licensee agrees to pay to Licensor upon execution of this Agreement the sum of $_____ *[insert the amount of the advance, if any]*.

Licensed Product Royalty *[Select One]*

☐ Royalty for All Rights

Licensee agrees to pay a Royalty of _____% *[insert amount of royalty]* of all Net Sales revenue of the Licensed Products ("Licensed Product Royalty").

☐ Hybrid Royalty; Patent and Non-Patented Rights

Licensee agrees to pay a Royalty of _____% *[insert amount of royalty]* of all Net Sales revenue of the Licensed Products ("Licensed Product Royalty"). The "Licensed Product Royalty" shall be allocated according to the percentages as provided in this Agreement. In the event that a patent does not issue or an issued patent expires or is otherwise terminated, the allocated percentage for such patent or pending patent shall be subtracted from the Licensed Product Royalty. The Licensed Product Royalty shall be adjusted accordingly.

_____% of the royalty for the license of the patent No. _____.
_____% of the royalty for the license of pending patent No. _____.
_____% of the royalty for the license of trade secrets [or trademarks, copyrights or other intellectual property].

☐ Guaranteed Minimum Annual Royalty Payment *[Optional]*

In addition to any other advances or fees, Licensee shall pay an annual guaranteed royalty (the "GMAR") as follows: _____ *[insert the terms of your GMAR: for example, $10,000 per year]*. The GMAR shall be paid to Licensor annually on _____ *[insert the date when the GMAR should be paid each year]*. The GMAR is an advance against royalties for the twelve-month period commencing upon payment. Royalty payments based on Net Sales made during any year of this Agreement shall be credited against the GMAR due for the year in which such Net Sales were made. In the event that annual royalties exceed the GMAR, Licensee shall pay the difference to Licensor. Any annual royalty payments in excess of the GMAR shall not be carried forward from previous years or applied against the GMAR.

shall be subtracted from the Licensed Product Royalty. The Licensed Product Royalty shall be adjusted accordingly.

_____ % of the royalty for the license of the patent No. _____.

_____ % of the royalty for the license of pending patent No. _____.

_____ % of the royalty for the license of trade secrets [or trademarks, copyrights or other intellectual property].

If you have negotiated a Spin-Off, Third Party or F.O.B. royalty, you can use the alternate provisions. An explanation is provided in Chapter 9.

Royalties on Spin-Offs *[Optional]*

Licensee agrees to pay a Royalty ("Spin-Off Product Royalty") of _____ % *[insert appropriate royalty percentage]* for all Net Sales of "Spin-Off Products." A "Spin-Off Product" is any product derived from, based on or adapted from the Licensed Product.

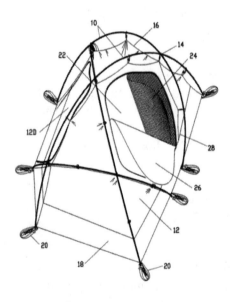

**Convertible Tent for Rain,
Cold and Hot Conditions
No. 6,216,715**

Adjustment of Royalties for Third Party Licenses
[Optional]

In the event that any Licensed Product (or other items for which Licensee pays Royalties to Licensor) incorporates third party character licenses, endorsements or other proprietary licenses, Licensor agrees to adjust the Royalty rate to _____ % *[insert appropriate royalty percentage]* for such third party licenses. Licensee shall notify Licensor of any such third party licenses prior to manufacture. Third party licenses shall not include licenses accruing to an affiliate, associate or subsidiary of Licensee.

F.O.B. Royalties *[Optional]*

Licensee agrees to pay the Royalty ("F.O.B. Royalty") of _____ % *[insert appropriate royalty percentage]* for all F.O.B. sales of Licensed Products.

12. Guaranteed Minimum Annual Royalty (GMAR)

If you have negotiated a GMAR, then you may need to modify this sample provision according to your conditions. See Chapter 9. Insert the amount of the annual GMAR.

13. Sublicensing

For more information on sublicensing, read Chapter 9.

14. Payment and Statements to Licensor

If you have an agent and your agent wants payments sent directly to him or her, add the following language:

Payments and Statements. All payments and statements made by Licensee pursuant to this Agreement shall be made and remitted to Agent at the following address: _____.

☐ **License Fee** *[Optional]*

As a nonrefundable, nonrecoupable fee for executing this license, Licensee agrees to pay to Licensor upon execution of this Agreement the sum of $_____.

☐ **Royalties on Spin-Offs** *[Optional]*

Licensee agrees to pay a Royalty ("Spin-Off Product Royalty") of _____% *[insert appropriate royalty percentage]* for all Net Sales of "Spin-Off Products." A "Spin-Off Product" is any product that is derived from, based on or adapted from the Licensed Product, provided that if the product uses the Property it shall be considered to be a Licensed Product and not a Spin-Off Product.

☐ **Adjustment of Royalties for Third Party Licenses** *[Optional]*

In the event that any Licensed Product (or other items for which Licensee pays Royalties to Licensor) incorporates third party character licenses, endorsements, or other proprietary licenses, Licensor agrees to adjust the Royalty rate to _____% *[insert appropriate royalty percentage]* for such third party licenses. Licensee shall notify Licensor of any such third party licenses prior to manufacture. Third party licenses shall not include licenses accruing to an affiliate, associate or subsidiary of Licensee.

☐ **F.O.B. Royalties** *[Optional]*

Licensee agrees to pay the Royalty ("F.O.B. Royalty") of _____% *[insert appropriate royalty percentage]* for all F.O.B. sales of Licensed Products.

☐ **Sublicensing Revenues** *[Optional]*

In the event of any sublicense of the rights granted pursuant to this Agreement, Licensee shall pay to Licensor _____% *[insert the amount of the sublicensing percentage]* of all sublicensing revenues.

Payments and Statements to Licensor

Within 30 days after the end of each calendar quarter (the "Royalty Period"), an accurate statement of Net Sales of Licensed Products along with any royalty payments or sublicensing revenues due to Licensor shall be provided to Licensor, regardless of whether any Licensed Products were sold during the Royalty Period. All payments shall be paid in United States currency drawn on a United States bank. The acceptance by Licensor of any of the statements furnished or royalties paid shall not preclude Licensor questioning the correctness at any time of any payments or statements.

Audit

Licensee shall keep accurate books of account and records covering all transactions relating to the license granted in this Agreement, and Licensor or its duly authorized representatives shall have the right upon five day's prior written notice, and during normal business hours, to inspect and audit Licensee's records relating to the Property licensed under this Agreement. Licensor shall bear the cost of such inspection and audit, unless the results indicate an underpayment greater than $_____ *[insert amount of underpayment, for example, "$1,000"]* for any six-month period. In that case, Licensee shall promptly reimburse Licensor for all costs of the audit along with the amount due with interest on such sums. Interest shall accrue from the date the payment was originally due and the interest rate shall be 1.5% per month, or the maximum rate permitted by law,

15. Audit

This provision establishes your rights to review the licensee's records. See Chapter 9.

16. Warranties and Indemnity

Warranties are promises upon which the other party can rely. For example, you may warrant that the invention does not infringe other inventions. (In other words, you are not trying to license an invention you don't actually own.) If the warranty is false, you receive financial punishment in the form of indemnity. When you provide indemnity (that is, you indemnify someone) you agree to pay for their damages if they are successfully sued. Such damages might include:

- consumer injuries from the product
- infringement by another company, or
- a challenge to your ownership.

Warranties and indemnity are often the most debated aspects of a license agreement. You should review Chapter 12 for an explanation of the provisions offered here. One alternate provision is the establishment of a royalty fund in the event of indemnity. When a third-party claim is made against the licensee, the licensee stops paying you royalties and instead puts the money into a fund. All or part of the fund is then used for indemnity. If anything is left after the case is resolved, it is returned to you. If you want to establish a fund, you can use the alternate provision.

17. Compliance With Intellectual Property Laws

This provision deals with the licensee's duty to obey intellectual property laws and to properly mark the licensed products with notices. (For example, if the licensed products are copyrightable, a notice such as *"Copyright 1997 Sally Smith"* should be included. Review Chapter 2.)

18. Infringement Lawsuits Against Third Parties

This provision deals with suing people or companies who infringe your patent rights. Who has the right to sue these people and how do you split any money you recover from infringers? For more information on suing infringers, review Chapters 2 and 17.

19. Exploitation

It's important to guarantee that your invention is offered for sale by a certain date. You may need to customize this provision to include reference to a specific trade show or a seasonal catalogue that you definitely want to be included in. For more information, read Chapter 12.

20. Samples & Quality Control

You (the licensor) will want this provision if it is important for you to review the product before it is offered for sale. If you would like more information about samples and quality control issues, review Chapter 12. If you are licensing a trademark (see Chapter 2), then you should insist on these quality controls. Failure to maintain quality over a trademark may result in loss of trademark rights.

21. Insurance

The amount of product liability insurance coverage is usually between one to ten million dollars, depending upon the product and the industry. The purpose of this provision is to protect you in the event a consumer is injured because of a defective licensed product. Insurance should be available so that you (and the licensee) can avoid the financial liability. For more information about insurance, review Chapter 12.

whichever is less. All books of account and records shall be made available in the United States and kept available for at least two years after the termination of this Agreement.

Late Payment

Time is of the essence with respect to all payments to be made by Licensee under this Agreement. If Licensee is late in any payment provided for in this Agreement, Licensee shall pay interest on the payment from the date due until paid at a rate of 1.5% per month, or the maximum rate permitted by law, whichever is less.

Licensor Warranties

Licensor warrants that it has the power and authority to enter into this Agreement and has no knowledge as to any third party claims regarding the proprietary rights in the Property which would interfere with the rights granted under this Agreement.

Indemnification by Licensor *[Select One]*

☐ ***Statement of Licensor Indemnification***
Licensor shall indemnify Licensee and hold Licensee harmless from any damages and liabilities (including reasonable attorneys' fees and costs) arising from any breach of Licensor's warranties as defined in Licensor's Warranties, above, provided: (a) such claim, if sustained, would prevent Licensee from marketing the Licensed Products or the Property; (b) such claim arises solely out of the Property as disclosed to the Licensee, and not out of any change in the Property made by Licensee or a vendor, or by reason of an off-the-shelf component or by reason of any claim for trademark infringement; (c) Licensee gives Licensor prompt written notice of any such claim; (d) such indemnity shall only be applicable in the event of a final decision by a court of competent jurisdiction from which no right to appeal exists; and (e) that the maximum amount due from Licensor to Licensee under this paragraph shall not exceed the amounts due to Licensor under the Payment Section from the date that Licensor notifies Licensee of the existence of such a claim.

☐ ***Licensor Indemnification With Fund***
Licensor shall indemnify Licensee and hold Licensee harmless from any damages and liabilities (including reasonable attorneys' fees and costs) arising from any breach of Licensor's warranties as defined in Licensor's Warranties, above, provided: (a) such claim, if sustained, would prevent Licensee from marketing the Licensed Products or the Property; (b) such claim arises solely out of the Property as disclosed to the Licensee, and not out of any change in the Property made by Licensee or a vendor, or by reason of an off-the-shelf component or by reason of any claim for trademark infringement; (c) Licensee gives Licensor prompt written notice of any such claim; (d) such indemnity shall only be applicable in the event of a final decision by a court of competent jurisdiction from which no right to appeal exists; and (e) that the maximum amount due from Licensor to Licensee under this paragraph shall not exceed the amounts due to Licensor under the Payment Section from the date that Licensor notifies Licensee of the existence of such a claim. The maximum amount due from Licensor to Licensee under this paragraph shall not exceed _____% *[50% to 100%]* of the amounts due to Licensor under the Payment Section *[if you have numbered the sections of your agreement, include the number of the payment section]* from the date that Licensor notifies Licensee of the existence of such a claim. After the commencement of a lawsuit against Licensee that comes within the scope of this paragraph, Licensee may place _____% *[same percentage as listed above]* of the royalties due to Licensor under the Payment Section in a separate interest-bearing fund which shall be called the "Legal Fund." Licensee may draw against such Legal Fund to satisfy all of the reasonable expenses

of defending the suit and of any judgment or settlement made in regard to this suit. In the event the Legal Fund is insufficient to pay the then-current defense obligations, Licensee may advance monies on behalf of the Legal Fund and shall be reimbursed as payments are credited to the Legal Fund. Licensor's liability to Licensee shall not extend beyond the loss of its royalty deposit in the Legal Fund. After the suit has been concluded, any balance remaining in the Legal Fund shall be paid to Licensor and all future royalties due to Licensor shall be paid to Licensor as they would otherwise become due. Licensee shall not permit the time for appeal from an adverse decision on a claim to expire.

Licensee Warranties

Licensee warrants that it will use its best commercial efforts to market the Licensed Products and that their sale and marketing shall be in conformance with all applicable laws and regulations, including but not limited to all intellectual property laws.

Indemnification by Licensee

Licensee shall indemnify Licensor and hold Licensor harmless from any damages and liabilities (including reasonable attorneys' fees and costs) (a) arising from any breach of Licensee's warranties and representation as defined in the Licensee Warranties, above; (b) arising out of any alleged defects or failures to perform of the Licensed Products or any product liability claims or use of the Licensed Products; and (c) any claims arising out of advertising, distribution or marketing of the Licensed Products.

☐ Limitation of Licensor Liability *[Optional]*

Licensor's maximum liability to Licensee under this agreement, regardless on what basis liability is asserted, shall in no event exceed the total amount paid to Licensor under this Agreement. Licensor shall not be liable to Licensee for any incidental, consequential, punitive or special damages.

Intellectual Property Protection

Licensor may, but is not obligated to seek, in its own name and at its own expense, appropriate patent, trademark or copyright protection for the Property. Licensor makes no warranty with respect to the validity of any patent, trademark or copyright which may be granted. Licensor grants to Licensee the right to apply for patents on the Property or Licensed Products provided that such patents shall be applied for in the name of Licensor and licensed to Licensee during the Term and according to the conditions of this Agreement. Licensee shall have the right to deduct its reasonable out-of-pocket expenses for the preparation, filing and prosecution of any such U.S. patent application (but in no event more than $5,000) from future royalties due to Licensor under this Agreement. Licensee shall obtain Licensor's prior written consent before incurring expenses for any foreign patent application.

Compliance With Intellectual Property Laws

The license granted in this Agreement is conditioned on Licensee's compliance with the provisions of the intellectual property laws of the United States and any foreign country in the Territory. All copies of the Licensed Product as well as all promotional material shall bear appropriate proprietary notices.

Infringement Against Third Parties

In the event that either party learns of imitations or infringements of the Property or Licensed Products, that party shall notify the other in writing of the infringements or imitations. Licensor shall have the right to commence lawsuits against third persons arising from infringement of the Property or Licensed Products. In the event that Licensor does not commence a lawsuit against an alleged infringer within 60 days of notification by Licensee, Licensee may commence a lawsuit against the third party. Before the filing suit, Licensee shall obtain the written consent of Licensor to do so and such consent shall not be unreasonably withheld. Licensor will cooperate fully and in good faith with Licensee for the purpose of securing and preserving Licensee's rights to the Property. Any recovery (including but not limited to a judgment, settlement or licensing agreement included as resolution of an infringement dispute) shall be divided equally between the parties after deduction and payment of reasonable attorneys' fees to the party bringing the lawsuit.

Exploitation

Licensee agrees to manufacture, distribute and sell the Licensed Products in commercially reasonable quantities during the term of this Agreement and to commence such manufacture, distribution and sale within the following time period: _____ [*insert time period, for example, "six months"*]. This is a material provision of this Agreement.

Samples & Quality Control

Licensee shall submit a reasonable number of production samples of the Licensed Product to Licensor to assure that the product meets Licensor's quality standards. In the event that Licensor fails to object in writing within ten business days after the date of receipt, the Licensed Product shall be deemed to be acceptable. At least once during each calendar year, Licensee shall submit two production samples of each Licensed Product for review. The quality standards applied by Licensor shall be no more rigorous than the quality standards applied by Licensee to similar products.

Insurance

Licensee shall, throughout the Term, obtain and maintain, at its own expense, standard product liability insurance coverage, naming Licensor as additional named insureds. Such policy shall: (a) be maintained with a carrier having a Moody's rating of at least B; and (b) provide protection against any claims, demands and causes of action arising out of any alleged defects or failure to perform of the Licensed Products or any use of the Licensed Products. The amount of coverage shall be a minimum of $_____ [*insert amount of insurance coverage*] with no deductible amount for each single occurrence for bodily injury or property damage. The policy shall provide for notice to the Agent and Licensor from the insurer by Registered or Certified Mail in the event of any modification or termination of insurance. Licensee shall furnish Licensor and Agent a certificate from its product liability insurance carrier evidencing insurance coverage in favor of Licensor, and in no event shall Licensee distribute the Licensed Products before the receipt by the Licensor of evidence of insurance. The provisions of this section shall survive termination for three years.

Confidentiality

The parties acknowledge that each may be furnished or have access to confidential information that relates to each other's business (the "Confidential Information"). In the event that Information is in written form, the disclosing party shall label or stamp the materials with the word "Confidential" or some similar warning. In the event that Confidential Information is transmitted orally, the disclosing party shall promptly provide a writing indicating that such oral communication constituted Information. The parties agree to maintain the Confidential Information in strictest confidence for the sole and exclusive benefit of the other party and to restrict access to such Confidential Information to persons

22. Confidentiality

Every license agreement contains some assurance of confidentiality. If you have signed a separate confidentiality agreement, then your license agreement may refer to that. For more information about confidentiality, review Chapter 7.

23. Termination

Have you and the licensee already agreed upon the length of time the license agreement will last? If you have provided for a fixed term in your term provision (see Chapter 8), then your agreement has a built-in ending—the conclusion (or expiration) of the term. Some license agreements don't include a term provision. Instead, the parties specify the date the contract will end in the termination provision. If you are using both a term and termination provision, make sure they conform (that is, they both provide for the same basis for termination and the same periods of time).

If you want the license to terminate after a period of years:

Fixed Term

This Agreement shall terminate at the end of ___ [insert number of years] years, unless terminated sooner under a provision of this Agreement.

If you are licensing a patent, the term should not extend beyond the length of the patent protection.

Term Based Upon Length of Patent Protection

This Agreement shall terminate with the expiration of the longest-living patent (or patents) or last-remaining patent application (as listed in the definition of the Property), whichever occurs last, unless terminated sooner under a provision of this Agreement.

If you have established a fixed term with renewal periods:

Initial Term With Renewals

This Agreement terminates at the end of two years (the "Initial Term") unless renewed by Licensee under the same terms and conditions for consecutive two-year periods (the "Renewal Terms") provided that Licensee provides written notice of its intention to renew this agreement within 30 days prior to expiration of the current term. In no event shall the Agreement extend longer than the date of expiration of the longest-living patent (or patents) or last-remaining patent application as listed in the definition of the Property.

Termination at will means that one party can end the agreement simply by notifying the other. In this type of termination, it's not necessary to provide an explanation or reason. The agreement ends simply because one party decides to terminate it. This provision does not have to be mutual. In fact, the licensee usually wants this ability, but does not want the licensor to have it. In other words, they can terminate at will but you can't. This is often true if the licensee is required to pay a minimum guaranteed royalty payment. The at-will provision lets the licensee bail out of the agreement (and royalty commitment) if the licensed products are not selling well. An example is below.

Termination at Will: Licensee's Option

Upon 90 days' notice, licensee may, at its sole discretion, terminate this agreement by providing notice to the licensor.

24. Effect of Termination

What happens when the agreement is over? There's usually still some clean-up work including sales of remaining products and payment of royalties. For more information about post-termination requirements, read Chapter 13.

bound by this Agreement, only on a need-to-know basis. Neither party, without prior written approval of the other, shall use or otherwise disclose to others, or permit the use by others of the Confidential Information.

Termination *[Select One]*

☐ *Initial Term With Renewals From the Term Section*

This Agreement terminates at the end of two years (the "Initial Term") unless renewed by Licensee under the terms and conditions as provided in the Term Section of this Agreement.

☐ *Fixed Term*

This Agreement shall terminate at the end of _____ *[insert number of years]* years unless terminated sooner under a provision of this Agreement.

☐ *Term Based Upon Length of Patent Protection*

This Agreement shall terminate with the expiration of the longest-living patent (or patents) or last-remaining patent application (as listed in the definition of the Property), whichever occurs last, unless terminated sooner under a provision of this Agreement.

☐ *Initial Term With Renewals*

This Agreement terminates at the end of two years (the "Initial Term") unless renewed by Licensee under the same terms and conditions for consecutive two-year periods (the "Renewal Terms") provided that Licensee provides written notice of its intention to renew this agreement within 30 days prior to expiration of the current term. In no event shall the Agreement extend longer than the date of expiration of the longest-living patent (or patents) or last-remaining patent application as listed in the definition of the Property.

☐ *Termination at Will: Licensee's Option*

Upon 90 days' notice, Licensee may, at its sole discretion, terminate this agreement by providing notice to the Licensor.

Licensor's Right to Terminate

Licensor shall have the right to terminate this Agreement for the following reasons:

a) Licensee fails to pay Royalties when due or fails to accurately report Net Sales, as defined in the Payment Section of this Agreement, and such failure is not cured within 30 days after written notice from the Licensor;

b) Licensee fails to introduce the product to market by _____ *[insert date by which Licensee must begin selling Licensed Products]* or to offer the Licensed Products in commercially reasonable quantities during any subsequent year;

c) Licensee fails to maintain confidentiality regarding Licensor's trade secrets and other Information;

d) Licensee assigns or sublicenses in violation of the Agreement; or

e) Licensee fails to maintain or obtain product liability insurance as required by the provisions of this Agreement.

☐ *Terminate as to Territory Not Exploited* *[Optional]*

Licensor shall have the right to terminate the grant of license under this Agreement with respect to any country or region included in the Territory in which Licensee fails to offer the Licensed Products for sale or distributions or to secure a sublicensing agreement for the marketing, distribution and sale of the product within two years of the Effective Date.

25. Survival

When the agreement is terminated, that doesn't mean that all of the obligations in the agreement should end. We recommend the following provisions survive the agreement:

- payment obligations
- warranties
- licensee indemnity
- confidentiality, and
- product liability insurance.

If you would like more information about survival, review Chapter 13.

26. Attorneys' Fees and Expenses

In the event of a legal dispute with the licensee, this provides that the prevailing party is entitled to payment for legal fees. If you would like more information about attorneys' fees, review Chapter 14.

27. Dispute Resolution

This provides a method of resolving disputes without resorting to litigation. Alternatives to litigation such as arbitration and mediation are sometimes unpopular with licensees (see Chapter 14).

In mediation, a neutral evaluator (the mediator) attempts to help the parties reach a resolution of their dispute. That is, the parties sit down with the mediator and tell their story. The mediator advises ways to resolve the dispute and the two parties try to agree (and sign an enforceable settlement). Because it is not binding and because it is less expensive than litigation or arbitration, some licensees prefer mediation.

Arbitration is like going to court with less formality and expense. Instead of filing a lawsuit, the parties hire one or more arbitrators to evaluate the dispute and make a determination. The arbitrators are trained to evaluate disputes, and many of them are retired judges.

If you want to use a mediation clause, we suggest a provision like the one below which progresses from informal meeting to mediation and then to arbitration.

Mediation and Arbitration

The Parties agree that every dispute or difference between them, arising under this Agreement, shall be settled first by a meeting of the Parties attempting to confer and resolve the dispute in a good faith manner. If the Parties cannot resolve their dispute after conferring, any Party may require the other Parties to submit the matter to non-binding mediation, utilizing the services of an impartial professional mediator approved by all Parties. If the Parties cannot come to an agreement following mediation, the Parties agree to submit the matter to binding arbitration at a location mutually agreeable to the Parties. The arbitration shall be conducted on a confidential basis pursuant to the Commercial Arbitration Rules of the American Arbitration Association. Any decision or award as a result of any such arbitration proceeding shall include the assessment of costs, expenses and reasonable attorney fees and shall include a written record of the proceedings and a written determination of the arbitrators. Absent an agreement to the contrary, any such arbitration shall be conducted by an arbitrator experienced in intellectual property law. The Parties reserve the right to object to any individual who shall be employed by or affiliated with a competing organization or entity. In the event of any such dispute or difference, either Party may give to the other notice requiring that the matter be settled by arbitration. An award of arbitration shall be final and binding on the Parties and may be confirmed in a court of competent jurisdiction.

If the licensee is opposed to arbitration (and many are), you can try a less formal approach to dispute resolution with the following mediation provision. It does not require that the parties commit to arbitration, but it allows for the parties to work out some method of alternative dispute resolution.

Effect of Termination

Upon termination of this Agreement, all Royalty obligations as established in the Payments Section shall immediately become due. After the termination of this license, all rights granted to Licensee under this Agreement shall terminate and revert to Licensor, and Licensee will refrain from further manufacturing, copying, marketing, distribution or use of any Licensed Product or other product which incorporates the Property. Within 30 days after termination, Licensee shall deliver to Licensor a statement indicating the number and description of the Licensed Products which it had on hand or is in the process of manufacturing as of the termination date. Licensee may dispose of the Licensed Products covered by this Agreement for a period of three months after termination or expiration except that Licensee shall have no such right in the event this agreement is terminated according to the Licensor's Right to Terminate, above. At the end of the post-termination sale period, Licensee shall furnish a royalty payment and statement as required under the Payment Section. Upon termination, Licensee shall deliver to Licensor all tooling and molds used in the manufacture of the Licensed Products. Licensor shall bear the costs of shipping for the tooling and molds.

Survival

The obligations of Sections _____ *[insert section names or numbers that will survive termination]* shall survive any termination of this Agreement.

Attorneys' Fees and Expenses

The prevailing party shall have the right to collect from the other party its reasonable costs and necessary disbursements and attorneys' fees incurred in enforcing this Agreement.

Dispute Resolution *[Select One]*

☐ *Arbitration*

If a dispute arises under or relating to this Agreement, the parties agree to submit such dispute to binding arbitration in the state of _____ *[insert state in which parties agree to arbitrate]* or another location mutually agreeable to the parties. The arbitration shall be conducted on a confidential basis pursuant to the Commercial Arbitration Rules of the American Arbitration Association. Any decision or award as a result of any such arbitration proceeding shall be in writing and shall provide an explanation for all conclusions of law and fact and shall include the assessment of costs, expenses and reasonable attorneys' fees. Any such arbitration shall be conducted by an arbitrator experienced in _____ *[insert industry experience required for arbitrator]* and in invention licensing law and shall include a written record of the arbitration hearing. The parties reserve the right to object to any individual who shall be employed by or affiliated with a competing organization or entity. An award of arbitration may be confirmed in a court of competent jurisdiction.

☐ *Mediation and Arbitration*

The Parties agree that every dispute or difference between them, arising under this Agreement, shall be settled first by a meeting of the Parties attempting to confer and resolve the dispute in a good faith manner. If the Parties cannot resolve their dispute after conferring, any Party may require the other Parties to submit the matter to non-binding mediation, utilizing the services of an impartial professional mediator approved by all Parties. If the Parties cannot come to an agreement following mediation, the Parties agree to submit the matter to binding arbitration at a location mutually agreeable to the Parties. The arbitration shall be conducted on a confidential basis pursuant to the Commercial

Alternative Dispute Resolution

If a dispute arises and cannot be resolved by the parties, either party may make a written demand for formal resolution of the dispute. The written request will specify the scope of the dispute. Within 30 days after such written notice, the parties agree to meet, for one day, with an impartial mediator and consider dispute resolution alternatives other than litigation. If an alternative method of dispute resolution is not agreed upon within 30 days of the one-day mediation, either side may start litigation proceedings.

28. Governing Law

In the event of a dispute, this clause establishes which state law will govern the arbitration or lawsuit. Generally, we suggest that this state (and the state listed in the next provision) be your state of residence. If you would like more information about governing law (sometimes referred to as choice of law), review Chapter 14.

29. Jurisdiction

In the event of a dispute, this establishes the state (and county) in which the lawsuit must be filed. In other words, this is the place where you will have to travel to fight the licensee. We recommend that you use your state of residence. If you would like more information about jurisdiction, review Chapter 14.

30. Waiver

This permits the parties to waive a portion of the agreement without establishing a precedent. For example, imagine that the licensee is several months late making a payment. You agree to accept the delay. The fact that you have "waived" the requirement for prompt payment *once* does not mean that you will always permit a late payment. If you would like more information about waiver, review Chapter 14.

31. Invalidity

Also referred to as severability, this permits a court to sever (take out) an invalid provision while keeping the rest of the agreement intact. If you would like more information about invalidity, review Chapter 14.

32. Entire Understanding

Also referred to as "integration," this provision establishes that the agreement is the final version and that any further modification must be in writing. For more information, review Chapter 14.

33. Attachments & Exhibits

This guarantees that attachments and exhibits will be included as an enforceable part of the agreement. If you would like more information, review Chapter 14.

34. Notices

This describes how each party must provide notice of disputes. For more information about the necessity for notice provisions, see Chapter 14.

35. No Joint Venture

This provision, sometimes referred to as relationships, prevents either party from claiming a certain relationship with the other, for example, stating that you are a partner or in a joint venture. If you would like more information, review Chapter 14.

Arbitration Rules of the American Arbitration Association. Any decision or award as a result of any such arbitration proceeding shall include the assessment of costs, expenses and reasonable attorney's fees and shall include a written record of the proceedings and a written determination of the arbitrators. Absent an agreement to the contrary, any such arbitration shall be conducted by an arbitrator experienced in intellectual property law. The Parties reserve the right to object to any individual who shall be employed by or affiliated with a competing organization or entity. In the event of any such dispute or difference, either Party may give to the other notice requiring that the matter be settled by arbitration. An award of arbitration shall be final and binding on the Parties and may be confirmed in a court of competent jurisdiction.

☐ *Alternative Dispute Resolution*

If a dispute arises and cannot be resolved by the parties, either party may make a written demand for formal resolution of the dispute. The written request will specify the scope of the dispute. Within 30 days after such written notice, the parties agree to meet, for one day, with an impartial mediator and consider dispute resolution alternatives other than litigation. If an alternative method of dispute resolution is not agreed upon within 30 days of the one-day mediation, either side may start litigation proceedings.

Governing Law

This Agreement shall be governed in accordance with the laws of the State of _____ *[insert the choice of state law]*.

Jurisdiction

The parties consent to the exclusive jurisdiction and venue of the federal and state courts located in _____ *[insert county and state in which parties agree to litigate]* in any action arising out of or relating to this Agreement. The parties waive any other venue to which either party might be entitled by domicile or otherwise.

Waiver

The failure to exercise any right provided in this Agreement shall not be a waiver of prior or subsequent rights.

Invalidity

If any provision of this Agreement is invalid under applicable statute or rule of law, it is to be considered omitted and the remaining provisions of this Agreement shall in no way be affected.

Entire Understanding

This Agreement expresses the complete understanding of the parties and supersedes all prior representations, agreements and understandings, whether written or oral. This Agreement may not be altered except by a written document signed by both parties.

Attachments & Exhibits

The parties agree and acknowledge that all attachments, exhibits and schedules referred to in this Agreement are incorporated in this Agreement by reference.

36. Assignability

There may be some instances where you don't want a company to acquire rights to your invention. The sample provision prohibits any assignment without your consent. If the licensee is afraid that you have too much control, you can soften the effect by withholding consent only if you have a valid business reason. What's a valid reason? Perhaps the company to whom your licensee wants to grant an assignment has a reputation for not paying royalties, or maybe it is in poor financial shape. You cannot, however, withhold consent for an arbitrary reason, such as someone from the company once treated you rudely. For more information about assignments, see Chapter 14.

Consent Not Unreasonably Withheld

Licensee may not assign or transfer its rights or obligations pursuant to this Agreement without the prior written consent of Licensor. Such consent shall not be unreasonably withheld. Any assignment or transfer in violation of this section shall be void.

If you don't have much bargaining power and the licensee wants freedom to transfer to affiliates or new owners (under the same terms as your license agreement), then you can use a provision such as the one below.

Consent Not Needed for Licensee Affiliates or New Owners

Licensee may not assign or transfer its rights or obligations pursuant to this Agreement without the prior written consent of Licensor. However, no consent is required for an assignment or transfer that occurs: (a) to an entity in which Licensee owns more than 50% of the assets, or (b) as part of a transfer of all or substantially all of the assets of Licensee to any party. Any assignment or transfer in violation of this section shall be void.

37. Signatures

Each party must sign the agreement in relation to the business that is represented (for example, as a general partner representing the partnership), and each party must have the authority to sign the agreement. To further reinforce this, you will note the language in the sample agreement: "Each party has signed this Agreement through its authorized representative." Use the following rules when determining the proper signature line.

Sole Proprietorship. If you or the licensee is a sole proprietor, simply sign your own name. If you have a fictitious business name (sometimes known as a dba), then list the name of the business above the signature line. For example, Tom Stein is a sole proprietor calling his invention business Eine Stein Inventions. He would sign as follows:

Eine Stein Inventions

By: _____

     Tom Stein

Partnership. If you or the licensee is a general or limited partnership, then the only person authorized to sign the agreement is a general partner or someone who has written authority (usually in the form of a partnership resolution) from a general partner. The name of the partnership must be mentioned above the signature line or the partnership will not be bound (only the person signing the agreement). Cindy Barrett is a general partner in Reality Manufacturing Partnership. She would sign as follows:

Reality Manufacturing Partnership

By: _____

     Cindy Barrett, a general partner

Corporation or LLC. If you or the licensee is a corporation or limited liability company (LLC), then only a person authorized by the corporation can sign the agreement. The president or chief executive officer (CEO) usually has such power, but not

Notices

Any notice or communication required or permitted to be given under this Agreement shall be sufficiently given when received by certified mail, or sent by facsimile transmission or overnight courier.

No Joint Venture

Nothing contained in this Agreement shall be construed to place the parties in the relationship of agent, employee, franchisee, officer, partners or joint ventures. Neither party may create or assume any obligation on behalf of the other.

Assignability *[Select One]*

☐ *Statement of Assignability*

Licensee may not assign or transfer its rights or obligations pursuant to this Agreement without the prior written consent of Licensor. Any assignment or transfer in violation of this section shall be void.

☐ *Consent Not Unreasonably Withheld*

Licensee may not assign or transfer its rights or obligations pursuant to this Agreement without the prior written consent of Licensor. Such consent shall not be unreasonably withheld. Any assignment or transfer in violation of this section shall be void.

☐ *Consent Not Needed for Licensee Affiliates or New Owners*

Licensee may not assign or transfer its rights or obligations pursuant to this Agreement without the prior written consent of Licensor. However, no consent is required for an assignment or transfer that occurs: (a) to an entity in which Licensee owns more than 50% of the assets, or (b) as part of a transfer of all or substantially all of the assets of Licensee to any party. Any assignment or transfer in violation of this Section shall be void.

Each party has signed this Agreement through its authorized representative. The parties, having read this Agreement, indicate their consent to the terms and conditions by their signature below.

LICENSOR: LICENSEE:

_____   _____
Signature   Signature

_____   _____
Name/Title   Name/Title

_____   _____
Company   Company

_____   _____
Date   Date

every officer of a corporation has the authority to bind the corporation. If in doubt, ask for written proof of the authority. This proof is usually in the form of a corporate resolution. The name of the corporation should be mentioned above the signature line or the corporation may not be bound (only the person signing the agreement). For example, Marya DeRosa is CEO of Sincere Marketing. She would sign as follows:

Sincere Marketing, Inc., a New York corporation

By: _____

     Marya DeRosa, CEO

Note: If you have reason to question the credibility of the licensee's representative, then investigate the company (see Chapter 6). If you have doubts about the person's authority, don't proceed until you are satisfied that the person has full authority to represent the company.

Can You Fax Your Signature?

A faxed signature is suitable assuming that both parties do not dispute the authenticity of the signature. If there is a dispute about the signature (that is, one party claims a forgery), then you will have difficulty proving the signature is authentic from a fax. If you execute the agreement by fax, follow up the fax by mailing or overnighting signed copies.

38. Exhibit A

As we explain in Chapters 8 through 10, your Exhibit A can include a list of important contract facts. In this sample, we have limited the Exhibit A only to the Properties and Licensed Products. It is quite common to provide a description of several paragraphs of the Property (or to include a copy of the patent or patent application).

You can also use Exhibit A to reference the territory, the length of the agreement, the royalty and advance payments, dates when the agreement is effective and when the product must be offered for sale. For example, instead of listing the amount of the royalty in the Payment section, you would state "see Exhibit A." Then you would place the royalty amount in the Exhibit. If you were entering into several similar nonexclusive licenses, this would work well because you would only need to modify the exhibit, introductory paragraph and signature lines each time you entered into a new agreement.

B. Optional License Agreement Provisions

The sample agreement contains the provisions most commonly used in license agreements. Several others can be included if appropriate. Below is a brief description of additional provisions.

1. Force Majeure (Pronounced Fors-Mazhoor')

The force majeure provision (sometimes referred to as "Acts of God") establishes that the Agreement will be suspended in the event of unforeseen natural disasters. For example, if there is a tornado that ruins the licensee's manufacturing plant for three months, the license agreement would be suspended for three months.

In the event of an act of God such as fire, riot, act of public enemy, war or similar cause not within the control of Licensee, the Licensee shall have the right to suspend the term of this Agreement. Licensee may suspend the term only for the duration of any such contingency. Licensee shall not suspend its obligation to make payments to Licensor if such payments are due and are not otherwise prevented. At the conclusion of the contingency, Licensee shall notify Licensor in writing and the Agreement shall be reinstated.

EXHIBIT A

THE PROPERTY
[insert description of the Property]

_____

_____

_____

_____

_____

_____

_____

_____

_____

_____

LICENSED PRODUCTS
[indicate type of products, for example "medical supply products"]

_____

_____

_____

_____

_____

_____

_____

_____

_____

_____

_____

_____

2. Escrow

If you execute an escrow agreement, it should be attached to your License Agreement and the following provision should be inserted:

Escrow Account. The parties have executed a separate Escrow Agreement (attached to this Agreement and incorporated by reference) for the deposit of escrow materials.

If you cannot execute an escrow agreement at the time of license, you can still express your intention to do so in the license agreement by including the following provision.

Establishment of Escrow Account. The parties shall execute a separate Escrow Agreement to establish an escrow account for the deposit of *[indicate what will be deposited]* ("Escrow Items"). The Escrow Items shall be released to _____ *[name of party (Licensor or Licensee)]* upon the following conditions: *[list reasons for release from escrow. For example, "The funds will be released to Licensor upon completion of the Services and furnishing of Deliverables."].*

In the event you need an escrow or want to learn more about the escrow process, review Chapter 14.

3. Grant Back of Improvements

Who owns the improvements that the licensee makes to your invention? A grant back provision transfers ownership to you. For more information, review Chapter 15.

4. Training

If you wish to include a training provision in your license agreement, below is a sample provision. As explained in Chapter 15, if the training is ongoing or more complex, you should use a separate

services agreement that will better define your obligations and protect your rights.

Licensor will provide _____ *[number of days and whether they are consecutive]* days of basic training for _____ *[names or number of Licensee employees to be trained]* Licensee employees at Licensee's facility in _____ *[location of Licensee's facility].* Training will be performed by _____ *[name of Licensor or person who will provide training].* Licensee shall bear all costs of travel and accommodations and shall pay Licensor on a direct cost basis computed on the number of hours worked and an hourly rate of _____ *[hourly rate]* for services. Licensee shall indemnify Licensor for any and all claims that may result from such training. All payments for services and other expenses shall be paid by Licensee within 30 days of receipt of Licensor's written invoice.

5. Installation

If you wish to include an installation services provision in your license agreement, a sample appears below.

Licensor shall supervise and assist in the installation of equipment as described in Exhibit __ *[whatever letter you have chosen for the service agreement exhibit, for example, Exhibit B].* Licensor's installation services will be performed by _____ *[name of Licensor or Licensor employee who will perform services].* Licensee shall bear all costs of travel and accommodations for Licensor and shall pay Licensor on a direct cost basis computed on the number of hours worked and an hourly rate of _____ *[hourly rate]* for services. Licensee shall indemnify Licensor for any and all claims that may result from such installation services. All payments for services and other expenses shall be paid by Licensee within 30 days of receipt of Licensor's written invoice.

For more on installation services, see Chapter 15.

6. Tech Support

For a tech support arrangement in which you assist the licensee's support staff, use a provision such as the sample below.

Licensor will provide reasonable telephone and e-mail assistance to Licensee's designated representatives for Licensee's technical support of licensed products.

If you are providing limited end user tech support, you will need a more detailed provision. The sample provision below should address most of your concerns.

Licensor shall, for a period of six months after introduction of the licensed products, provide reasonable ongoing _____ [describe the type of assistance, for example, "telephone"] assistance to Licensee. Such support shall relate only to troubleshooting and identification of reported problems relating to the use of the Licensed Products. Telephone technical support shall be provided by Licensor _____ [indicate what days and what times, for example "Monday through Friday 12:00 p.m. to 4:00 p.m. PST"] at a rate of _____ [indicate the hourly, weekly or monthly rate, for example "$2,000 per month"] and not to exceed _____ [indicate maximum amount of support hours per week, for example, "20 hours per week of Licensor's personnel time"]. In the event that Licensee needs technical support provided by a third party other than Licensor, such determination shall not affect any other provisions of this agreement.

For more on tech support and other service provisions, see Chapter 15.

7. Deliverables: Schedules & Development Services; Delivery & Approval

Below is a sample deliverables provision that can be inserted in your license agreement. The two parts of the provision ("Schedules & Development Services" and "Delivery & Approval") attempt to anticipate the problems that result when, for example,

the inventor believes the deliverable has been perfected and the licensee thinks the work is insufficient. For more information on deliverables, see Chapter 15.

Schedules & Development Services.

Licensor shall perform certain development services for Licensee. A description of such services, as well as the delivery schedule and the technology or invention to be delivered ("Deliverables"), is provided in Exhibit A. Payments for such services shall be as provided in Exhibit A. Any Deliverable listed in Exhibit A shall consist of three stages: (1) concept/planning, (2) design/prototype, and (3) development/test.

Licensor shall submit for Licensee's written approval a budget for each Deliverable. Any expenses or charges in excess of those budgeted must be pre-approved in writing by Licensee. If requested, Licensor shall, within 72 hours of notification, meet with Licensee and provide a status report on the schedule and budget for any Deliverable. Licensor shall invoice Licensee pursuant to the payment schedule set forth in the appropriate Exhibit A. [Or Exhibit B—Remember to attach the deliverables and schedule as an exhibit.]

Delivery & Approval

Licensee shall have five working days from receipt of any Deliverable in which to provide Licensor with written notice of its decision to either accept the Deliverable or to reject it because it fails to conform to the specifications in Exhibit A. If Licensee determines that any Deliverable does not substantially conform to the specifications, Licensee shall deliver to Licensor a written report describing each manner that the Deliverables fail to conform. Licensor shall, within five working days of receipt of Licensee's statement, correct such errors or failures and resubmit the Deliverables. After resubmission, Licensee shall have a second evaluation period of five working days to either accept the Deliverables or reject them because they still fail to conform to the original specifications. If Licensee again rejects the Deliverables, Licensee may pay a third party to correct such failures and deduct the cost either from

Licensor's next scheduled payment from Licensee or from Licensor's future royalties.

8. Right of First Refusal

If your license agreement includes a right of first refusal, you must give the licensee the first right to license any improvements. This provision is common in an exclusive license. For more information, see Chapter 15.

Licensor may identify and develop improvements for the Licensed Property ("Improvements"). Improvements may be patentable or unpatentable, and may also be protected under copyright, trade secret or other legal principles. Licensee shall have the first right to license such Improvements and the parties shall negotiate in good faith to reach agreement as to the terms and conditions for such license. In the event that the parties fail to reach agreement and Licensor receives an offer from a third party for the Improvements, Licensee shall have 30 days to notify Licensor whether Licensee desires to execute a license on similar terms and conditions. In the event that Licensee matches any third party terms and conditions, Licensor shall enter into a License Agreement with Licensee and terminate negotiations with any third parties.

9. Most Favored Nations Clause (Sometimes Referred to As a Most Favored Licensee Provision)

This provision is common in a nonexclusive arrangement and guarantees that the licensee won't be charged any more for the invention or improvements than any other licensee. See Chapter 15 for more information.

Licensor may identify and develop new features or improvements for the Licensed Property ("Improvements"). Improvements may be patentable or unpatentable, and may also be protected under copyright, trade secret or other legal principles. In the event that Licensee enters into a license agreement for these Improvements with a third party licensee ("Third Party License"), Licensor

agrees to offer Licensee terms and conditions which are as favorable as the third party licensee. Licensor shall promptly notify the Licensee of any Third Party License as well as any additional obligations or undertakings in the Third Party License. Licensee shall have 30 days to notify Licensor whether Licensee desires to execute a license on similar terms and conditions.

C. Modifying the Sample Agreement for Your Needs

You may think, "Since I'm not an expert, I'd better not change anything in the agreement." Surprisingly, lawyers often take a similar view and are equally paranoid about changing the form agreements found in their legal books. They blindly copy unnecessary legal language simply because "that's the way it's always been done."

Since each license agreement is unique, we recommend that you modify the agreement as necessary to suit your needs. Review the appropriate chapter and then make the changes. For example, if you must modify the payment section, first read Chapter 9 and then make your changes. If you use simple, unambiguous language and follow the rules established in each chapter, your agreement will be enforceable and understandable.

If you're unsure of how to write new language or a new section, just use clear language and avoid trying to sound like a lawyer. For instance, avoid using legal language such as "heretofore" and "therein." Review the appropriate chapter in this book to make sure your addition is legal and doesn't conflict with another provision.

1. Modifications With a Word Processor

We recommend that you use a word processor to modify your agreement. A word processor allows you to make many changes and still have a sharp-looking agreement. You can also save multiple drafts and keep a clean or unmodified copy of the agreement in a separate computer file. You can type the agreement into your word processor and modify it accordingly, or scan the agreement into your word processor. If you don't have a scanner, local computer service companies can perform the service and give you a disk containing the agreement. Modify the agreement according to your needs.

> EXAMPLE: You and the licensee have a unique element in your agreement—one of the licensed products will only be manufactured in a gold-plated limited edition run of 1,000 units and you will receive a special royalty rate. How do you add this to the form agreement? Simple! Give the product a name ("Gold Plated Products"), list it in Exhibit A under licensed products and add a new section under Payment, such as: "Gold Plated Special Edition Royalties—Licensee shall pay Licensor a royalty of _____% for Net Sales of Gold Plated Products," and indicate the royalty rate.

2. Modifications by Typewriter

For a minor modification, you can type it on the side margin or between the lines of a double-spaced agreement. If you want to strike out a section, you can use a typewriter to "XX" it out. However, as with handwritten modifications, every time you change something on the printed form agreement, *both you and the licensee (and any other parties to the agreement) must initial each modification.*

If you don't wish to type directly on the agreement, or if you want to add a new section, you can use a separate sheet of paper titled "Addendum" and type a list of the changes to the form agreement. For example: "In Section 5, add the word 'taxes' so that the deductions to Net Sales reads, 'less quantity discounts, taxes and returns actually credited.'" Then attach the addendum to the agreement and have both parties sign it.

3. Modifications by Hand

Although we don't recommend modifying your agreement by hand, it can be done for small changes. To strike certain words or phrases or to add words or phrases, you can write them in with a pen on the form agreement. Every time you write something on the printed form agreement, *both you and the licensee (and any other parties to the agreement) must initial each modification.*

4. Inserting New Sections

Where do you insert a new section? Wherever it makes sense. There is no legal requirement for the ordering of the paragraphs. That is, you can place them in any order, and as long as they come after the statement "Therefore, the parties agree," they will be legally enforceable. However, certain general principles are followed, such as placing the grant and royalty provisions near the front and the termination and miscellaneous provisions near the end. You may also group provisions together under one heading. For example, you can group all of the miscellaneous provisions under the heading "Miscellaneous." ■

12

Warranties, Indemnification and Proprietary Rights Provisions

In this chapter we discuss protective aspects of license agreements—legal provisions that protect your interests and the interests of the licensee. These provisions are not directly related to the marketing of your invention, and you may not have discussed them during your business negotiations. However, in the event of lawsuits, infringements or product injuries, these provisions can have an important impact. You should read this chapter if you answer "yes" to any of the following questions:

- Would you like a definition of warranties, representations and covenants?
- Are you concerned about making a promise that your invention will not infringe other inventions?
- Would you like indemnity explained?
- Are you concerned about whether the invention will include the proper copyright and patent notices?
- Would you like the right to approve a sample of your invention before it is offered to the public?
- Are you worried about lawsuits caused by a defective product?

In this chapter, we review provisions that protect the interests of the parties or guard against certain problems. For example, warranties provide assurances of the rights granted under the license agreement (for example, the right to license or the right of title to the invention). Indemnity is a method of backing up your contract promises in which you agree to pay for certain damages. (Indemnity is one of the most disputed issues in licensing agreements.) We also discuss provisions that protect your intellectual property rights during the license period (for example, requirements that the licensee use the proper legal notices).

A. Promises, Promises ... Warranties, Representations and Covenants

One of the most important and often overlooked sections of a license agreement deals with warranties, representations and covenants. These three terms are used collectively ("Licensor warrants, represents and covenants....") or separately "Licensor warrants that.... Licensor represents that.... Licensor covenants that...."). Although there are subtle distinctions between the terms (see sidebar), all three generally refer to a promise upon which the other party can rely.

For purposes of our discussion we will avoid using all three terms and refer to any such promise as a *warranty*. If a warranty proves false, it can be the basis for termination, or worse, it may cause you to be liable for financial damages.

EXAMPLE: Tommi licenses a film-editing invention to Filmco. In her license agreement she warrants she owns the rights to the invention. Filmco is later sued by Tommi's former employer, VideoCo. VideoCo claims it owns the rights to the invention. If VideoCo proves that it does in fact own the rights to the invention, Filmco can terminate its license with Tommi and sue her for damages because they relied on Tommi's warranty.

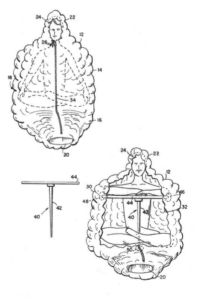

**Sleeping and Meditation Bag
No. 4,330,989**

The Difference Between Warranties, Representations and Covenants

Lawyers define a warranty as a guarantee, a representation as a statement of fact and a covenant as a contractual promise that legally must be kept. The historical basis for these distinctions is that each type of promise leads to a different legal claim. For example, if you made a false representation (an untruthful statement), you could be sued for misrepresentation. If you broke a covenant, you could be sued for a breach of covenant. If you made a false warranty, you could be sued for breach of warranty.

These distinctions don't matter as much in a licensing agreement today. If you sue the licensee, you will recover the same amount whether the broken promise is called a warranty, representation or covenant—as long as one of the terms is used. Although the term "warranty" is sufficient, lawyers, with their love of redundancy, continue to use all three terms.

1. Licensor Warranties

We recommend that you, as the licensor, include the following warranty provision in your agreements. The following sections will explain the provision in more detail.

Licensor Warranties

Licensor warrants that it has the power and authority to enter into this Agreement and has no knowledge as to any third party claims regarding the proprietary rights in the Property which would interfere with the rights granted under this Agreement.

a. Power and Authority—Warranting the Right to License

The first warranty in this provision—the *right* to license—is what one lawyer refers to as "the Brooklyn Bridge" issue. Many people can claim to sell you the Brooklyn Bridge, but only the person who actually has title will be able to legally sell it to you. As long as you have the "power and authority" to license your invention, you shouldn't have a problem making this warranty. If you are unsure, review ownership issues in Chapters 3 and 4.

b. Warranting That the Invention Does Not Infringe (With Qualification)

The second licensor warranty—that the invention does not infringe—requires your careful consideration. A licensee will want an assurance that the sale of the invention is not going to trigger infringement lawsuits. On its face, this seems like a reasonable request. After all, the licensee is investing a lot of money in your invention and doesn't want any surprises.

Unfortunately, no matter what precautions you take, there is always the possibility that your invention infringes upon some existing invention or patent. Therefore, we recommend that you qualify your warranty of non-infringement by stating that it is made "to the best of your knowledge." Another way to state it is that you "have no knowledge" of possible infringement. That way, you are qualifying your warranty based upon what you *know* (see sidebar) at the time of execution (signing) of the agreement. If you don't use this qualification, then you will be responsible for *any* infringement, whether or not you knew about it.

The "Best of Your Knowledge"

According to some court decisions, a warranty or representation as to your knowledge (that is, "to the best of my knowledge") refers not only to what you know, but also to what a reasonable person in your position *should* have known. For example, if you are an expert on radio-controlled devices, you would not be expected to know every patent in your field, but you would be expected to know about major developments.

c. Warranting That the Invention Does Not Infringe (Without Qualification)

What if the licensee demands a warranty of non-infringement without any qualification? In some cases, licensees want you to warrant that your invention does not infringe on another protected invention, period. Being unaware of an infringement would be no excuse. In that case, the licensee wants a provision such as the following:

Warranting Without Qualification

Licensor warrants that it has the power and authority to enter into this Agreement and that the Property does not infringe any valid rights of any third party. The provisions of this Section shall survive any termination.

Under this provision, it doesn't matter what you knew or should have known. If any infringement exists, you are responsible. If you are faced with an unqualified warranty like this, you should review your position. Has anyone done a patent search or a similar reliable analysis regarding your invention? If so, review it carefully, because your warranty is based upon this research. If no search has been done or if you are seeking a more thorough opinion, then you should consider obtaining a written

opinion from a patent attorney. The cost for this may range from $500 to several thousand dollars.

Sometimes a licensee may be willing to share the costs of this search. Why? A contract warranty only provides a means of going after the inventor *after* the agreement has been signed (and the product is for sale). Licensees usually prefer to know ahead of time if they are headed towards a potential infringement problem. Therefore, the search provides information that can benefit both parties. You should propose that the licensee pay for it and deduct half (or all) of the cost from future royalties. Explain that a written opinion is valuable because it may help the licensee head off any potential problem before manufacturing begins.

B. Indemnity—The "Hold Harmless" Provision

Warranties and indemnity work together. A licensee relies on your warranty. Indemnity is your financial punishment if the warranty is false. When you provide indemnity (that is, when you indemnify someone), you agree to pay for their damages for certain situations. For example, if you indemnify a licensee against infringement, then you will have to pay the licensee's damages (and legal fees) if the licensee is sued for infringement.

Indemnity acts like a powerful shield. The licensee can deflect a lawsuit and make you, the inventor, pay for the damages and legal fees. Indemnity provisions are also sometimes referred to as "hold harmless" provisions because the language for an indemnity provision often states that the "Licensor shall *hold* the Licensee *harmless* from any losses, etc."

As you can imagine, providing indemnity to a licensee can have a devastating effect. If there is a challenge to your invention, you may have to pay your own legal fees, as well as the legal fees and damages suffered by the licensee. For that reason, we recommend that you carefully review indemnity provisions and limit your indemnity obligations.

1. What Should You Indemnify?

There are four types of lawsuits that the licensee may become entangled in:

- lawsuits in which you sue the licensee
- lawsuits in which the licensee sues you
- lawsuits in which the licensee sues a third party (a third party is someone who is not a party to the agreement), or
- lawsuits in which a third party sues the licensee or licensor.

You should only indemnify the licensee against the last category—third party claims directed at the licensee—and you should only indemnify for claims that relate to your warranties—that is, a) your right to license the invention, and b) that the invention does not infringe upon any other inventions. These warranties—which should be in the "Licensor Warranties" section discussed above—should be referenced in the Indemnity section, as shown in the sample provision below.

Besides limiting indemnity to lawsuits in which a third party sues the licensee about ownership or infringement, we also believe that you should qualify the indemnification. Even if lawsuits over ownership or infringement are brought against the licensee, you should only have to pay the licensee's damages under the following circumstances:

- The claim prevents the licensee from selling the invention. In other words, it has to be a serious claim that keeps your invention off the market.
- The claim is not about something that the licensee did or added to your invention. That is, the third party lawsuit has to be about the invention as you furnished it to the licensee.
- The licensee has given you prompt written notice of the third party claim. The licensee cannot ignore the claim and cannot settle it secretly without your knowledge, then come after you for payment.
- The indemnity is only applicable in the event of a final decision by a court. You don't want

to have to pay for invalid claims or merely alleged defects that are not proven in court.

- The maximum amount you have to pay for indemnity will not exceed the total sum you were paid under the license agreement. This is usually a controversial issue, and we will provide more information below.

Following, is a suggested indemnity provision incorporating the above suggestions.

Indemnification by Licensor

Licensor shall indemnify Licensee and hold Licensee harmless from any damages and liabilities (including reasonable attorneys' fees and costs), arising from any breach of Licensor's warranties as defined in Licensor's Warranties, above, provided: (a) such claim, if sustained, would prevent Licensee from marketing the Licensed Products or the Property; (b) such claim arises solely out of the Property as disclosed to the Licensee, and not out of any change in the Property made by Licensee or a vendor, or by reason of an off-the-shelf component or by reason of any claim for trademark infringement; (c) Licensee gives Licensor prompt written notice of any such claim; (d) such indemnity shall only be applicable in the event of a final decision by a court of competent jurisdiction from which no right to appeal exists; and (e) that the maximum amount due from Licensor to Licensee under this paragraph shall not exceed the amounts due to Licensor under the Payment Section from the date that Licensor notifies Licensee of the existence of such a claim.

2. Indemnity—What to Avoid

A licensee may want you to indemnify *everything* in the agreement. Some licensor indemnification provisions are extremely broad and should be avoided. For example, the following is merely the first sentence of one large national licensing company's standard agreement:

Licensor agrees to indemnify, defend and hold harmless Licensee, its subsidiary, affiliated and/or controlled companies and all sublicensees, as well as their respective officers, directors, agents and employees, harmless from and against any and all damage, loss, expense, (including reasonable attorneys' fees and costs), award, settlement or other obligation arising out of any claims, demands, actions, suits or prosecutions that may be made or instituted against them or any of them by reason of any alleged breach of any representation, warranty or covenant in this Agreement, or from any injury or death arising from any defect in the Property, or from any other alleged claim or injury.

a. Avoid Indemnifying for All Warranties

You should avoid a provision that has language such as:

Not Recommended—Overbroad Indemnification Provision

Licensor shall indemnify Licensee and hold Licensee harmless from any damages (including reasonable attorneys' fees and costs), arising from any breach of any representation, warranty or covenant in this Agreement.

This statement is too broad. Many statements within the license agreement can be characterized as a representation, warranty or covenant. The indemnity provision should designate which warranties are indemnified. We recommend only two specific warranties (as explained above): (a) that you have the right to license the invention, and (b) that the invention does not infringe any other inventions. These specific warranties should be in a separate section titled "Licensor Warranties" and should be referenced directly in the Indemnity section, as shown in the sample provision above.

b. Avoid Indemnifying for Breaches of the License Agreement

You should avoid a provision that states:

Not Recommended—Overbroad Indemnification Provision

Licensor shall indemnify Licensee and hold Licensee harmless from any damages (including reasonable attorneys' fees and costs) arising from any breach of this License Agreement.

Indemnifying for a breach of the agreement is the ultimate in licensing masochism. Why? Because you are agreeing to punish yourself if you break the agreement. The license agreement can only be breached by the parties who signed it—the licensor and licensee. An indemnification for a breach means that if you do something wrong, you will pay the licensee legal fees when he sues you. That hurts! This provision is similar to the one-way attorneys' fees provision discussed in Chapter 14. Indemnification should *only* be provided for third party lawsuits. A third party lawsuit is a suit brought by someone who is not a party to the agreement. An example of a third party lawsuit would be someone other than the licensee who claims that your invention infringes.

c. Avoid Indemnifying for Damages or Injuries

You should avoid a provision that states:

Not Recommended—Overbroad Indemnification Provision

Licensor shall indemnify Licensee and hold Licensee harmless from any damages (including reasonable attorneys' fees and costs) from any injury or death arising from any defect in the Property.

By agreeing to this provision, you are effectively stepping into the insurance business. You should avoid it and, instead, insist that the licensee maintain adequate product liability insurance (as explained below).

d. Avoid Indemnifying for Alleged Claims

You should avoid a provision that states:

Not Recommended—Overbroad
Indemnification Provision

Licensor shall indemnify Licensee and hold Licensee harmless from any damages (including reasonable attorneys' fees and costs) from any alleged claim or injury arising from the Licensed Product.

Watch out for provisions that require you to indemnify for *alleged* breaches of warranties. These provisions require that you open your checkbook to defend against *any* claims, whether or not they are valid. Your indemnity provision should only require you to be obligated for actual infringement, not alleged infringement. That is why we recommend you include a qualification stating that you only have to pay indemnity if the claim results in a court verdict. Many people bring false lawsuits as a means of "shaking down" a licensee. You should only be responsible for allegations or claims if they result in a final judgment in a court of law.

3. Paying for Indemnity

All of this talk about indemnity is fine, but how are you going to pay for it? Chances are, the costs will be a massive burden. One successful toy licensor has a rule, "Never give back money." His indemnity provisions permit licensees to take money from royalties that accrue *after* the date of notification of the claim, but he does *not* have to pay any money that he has already received.

> EXAMPLE: Phil licenses an outdoor lighting invention to OutdoorsCo and indemnifies against infringement. When a rival company sues for infringement, OutdoorsCo notifies Phil and begins withholding royalty payments to pay for defending the lawsuit. Phil does not pay OutdoorsCo any money that he has already earned from them under the licensing agreement.

Get ready to negotiate, because the issue of how much to pay is a controversial topic. A licensee commonly wants you to pay all of the indemnity costs and doesn't want to limit it to future royalties. This is one area where it may be worthwhile to take a strong stand. Depending on your bargaining power, the following are the three most common choices:

- **Pay only from future royalties.** This is the "we don't give back money" approach which requires the licensee to withhold future royalties after the claim is filed for indemnity costs. You don't have to return advances or previously received royalties. Licensors with strong bargaining positions may even limit this further by requiring that only 50% or 75% of future royalties be deducted.
- **Pay only what you have earned.** The logic behind this is that you shouldn't have to pay the licensee more than what you earned. For example, if your total earnings from royalties is $50,000, then you would have to pay all or a portion of this sum back to the licensee. This is a burden, but at least there is a cap (or limit) on how much is to be paid.
- **Pay whatever it costs.** This is the worst case scenario where there is no limit and you have to pay all indemnity costs.

Naturally you should try to avoid paying for everything. If the licensee insists on it (and you lack the bargaining power to avoid it), then at least obtain an opinion from a patent attorney.

a. Paying From Future Royalties

If you can negotiate to have the indemnity paid from future royalties, then you should consider an indemnity provision such as the following:
The maximum amount due from Licensor to Licensee under this paragraph shall not exceed the amounts due to Licensor under the Payment Section from the date that Licensor notifies Licensee of the existence of such a claim.

b. Paying From Future Royalties— Establishing a Fund

A more sophisticated approach to the future royalties indemnity provision is to set up a fund. How does the fund work? When a third party claim is made against the licensee, the licensee stops paying you royalties and instead puts the money into a fund. All or part of the fund is then used for indemnity. If anything is left after the case is resolved, it is returned to you.

This is the ideal method, because you never have to reach into your own bank account and pay for indemnity. That is, you get to keep everything you earned until you were notified of the third party claim. After notification, royalties are deposited into the fund. A powerful licensor can even negotiate so that only half of the fund is used for indemnity. Some industries do not use indemnity funds, while in others (such as the toy business) it is common.

Sample Fund Provision

The maximum amount due from Licensor to Licensee under this paragraph shall not exceed _____ [50 to 100] % of the amounts due to Licensor under the Payment Section [if you have numbered the sections of your agreement, include the number of the payment section] from the date that Licensor notifies Licensee of the existence of such a claim. After the commencement of a lawsuit against Licensee that comes within the scope of this paragraph, Licensee may place _____ [same percentage as listed above] of the royalties due to Licensor under the Payment Section in a separate interest-bearing fund, which shall be referred to in this Agreement as the "Legal Fund." Licensee may draw against such Legal Fund to satisfy all of the reasonable expenses of defending the suit and of any judgment or settlement made in regard to this suit. In the event the Legal Fund is insufficient to pay the then-current defense obligations, Licensee may advance monies on

behalf of the Legal Fund and shall be reimbursed as payments are credited to the Legal Fund. Licensor's liability to Licensee shall not extend beyond the loss of its royalty deposit in the Legal Fund. After the suit has been concluded, any balance remaining in the Legal Fund shall be paid to Licensor, and all future royalties due to Licensor shall be paid to Licensor as they would otherwise become due. Licensee shall not permit the time for appeal from an adverse decision on a claim to expire.

c. Paying What You Earned

If you can't negotiate a future royalties indemnity provision, then attempt to cap it by limiting indemnity to what you earn under the agreement. A sample provision is as follows:

The maximum amount due from Licensor to Licensee under this paragraph shall not exceed the total sums paid to Licensor under this Agreement.

What If the Licensee's Agreement Doesn't Include Warranty or Indemnity Provisions?

In some instances, a licensee's agreement may not include warranties and indemnity. This may be a result of neglect or because the licensee prefers not to deal with these provisions. Even if warranties and indemnities are not written into the agreement, these legal principles can still be enforced under state court decisions and statutes such as the Uniform Commercial Code. Should you bring up the issue if the licensee leaves out these provisions? Probably not. As a general rule, licensors have a difficult time obtaining favorable indemnification provisions, and you will save negotiating time.

C. Licensee Warranties and Indemnity

You provide warranties and indemnity for the licensee, and it's logical to expect similar promises and assurances from the licensee. The licensee's warranties and the indemnity will differ, as described below.

1. Licensee Warranties

We recommend that you seek an assurance that the licensee will sell your invention as promised and obey laws regarding the manufacturing, marketing, sale or distribution of the final product. You should include a provision such as the following (which will be explained in more detail in the following sections):

Licensee Warranties

Licensee warrants that it will use its best commercial efforts to market the Licensed Products and that their sale and marketing shall be in conformance with all applicable laws and regulations, including but not limited to all intellectual property laws.

a. Warranting to Sell the Invention

The first warranty—that the licensee will sell the invention—is especially important. Some unscrupulous licensees may license your invention simply to keep it off the market. For example, a tire company might license a method of making indestructible tires and then keep it off the market in order to continue selling its inferior products. It is for this reason that you want the licensee to warrant that it will market the invention.

Exclusive Licensees and the Duty to Market

What if an exclusive licensee refuses to include a warranty that it will market the invention? Even without the provision, you may still have recourse under state laws, which have created a legal obligation for the licensee—known as an implied duty—to market or exploit the invention. For example, under many state laws, the company has a legal obligation (apart from the contract) to sell the product. This implied duty only applies to exclusive licensees. A nonexclusive licensee has *no* obligation by law to sell your invention—unless it has agreed to do so in your license agreement. These laws are usually referenced under your state's commercial or civil code. Review the index for these state codes in your local law library (or on the Internet if your state has posted its state laws).

b. Warranting to Obey the Laws

It may seem silly to require that the licensee obey all applicable laws. After all, why would the licensee want to risk violating laws? And even if the licensee violates the laws, what difference does it make to you, the inventor? We recommend this warranty because it allows you to hold the licensee responsible in the event there is a violation of these laws and it may provide a defense for you in case you are named in a lawsuit involving illegal practices.

2. Licensee Indemnity

We suggest that the licensee indemnify you for its warranties and representations and also indemnify you in the event of a product liability suit. A product liability suit occurs when someone is injured by a defective product. We discuss product liability later in this chapter in the section regarding insurance.

Indemnification by Licensee

Licensee shall indemnify Licensor and hold Licensor harmless from any damages and liabilities (including reasonable attorneys' fees and costs) (a) arising from any breach of Licensee's warranties and representation as defined in the Licensee Warranties, above; (b) arising out of any alleged defects or failures to perform of the Licensed Products or any product liability claims or use of the Licensed Products; and (c) any claims arising out of advertising, distribution or marketing of the Licensed Products.

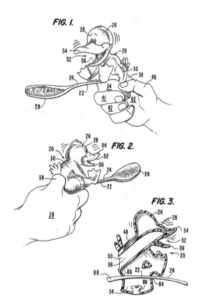

**Manipulatable Utensil Figure
N0. 4,779,344**

D. Proprietary Rights

The Proprietary Rights section of your licensing agreement usually deals with three "what if" issues:

- What if you or the licensee wants to register patent or copyright protection for the invention?
- What if the licensee fails to properly mark the products with the appropriate patent and copyright notices?
- What if someone infringes the invention?

The purpose of this provision is to protect intellectual property rights during the license agreement. This protection deals with registration of the intellectual property, marking the invention with the appropriate legal notices and suing anyone that infringes the rights licensed under the agreement.

1. Registering Patent, Trademark or Copyright Protection for the Invention

You may want to register for patent, trademark or copyright protection after the license is signed. The provision below grants you that right. Naturally, you can only register those elements that you created. That is, you can't register for trademarks, copyrighted works or inventions that the licensee has created or added to the licensed product.

If you have not registered your invention and don't plan to, the licensee may want to register for protection. There's nothing wrong with this, assuming you are named as the author or inventor and obtain the rights that go with the protection. But who pays for this registration? If you have the bargaining power to make the licensee pay, fine. But it is common for the licensee to deduct the costs of registration from future royalties. You will need to make sure that the expenses are reasonable and capped (limited). We recommend the provision below as a means to protect your interests while allowing for registration by the licensee.

Intellectual Property Protection

Licensor may, but is not obligated to seek, in its own name and at its own expense, appropriate patent, trademark or copyright protection for the Property. Licensor makes no warranty with respect to the validity of any patent, trademark or copyright which may be granted. Licensor grants to Licensee the right to apply for patents on the Property or Licensed Products provided that such patents shall be applied for in the name of Licensor and licensed to Licensee during the Term and according to the conditions of this Agreement. Licensee shall have the right to deduct its reasonable out-of-pocket expenses for the preparation, filing and prosecution of any such U.S. patent application (but in no event more than $5,000) from future royalties due to Licensor under this Agreement. Licensee shall obtain Licensor's prior written consent before incurring expenses for any foreign patent application.

When the Licensee Acquires Intellectual Property Registration in Its Name

It is often appropriate for the licensee to file a trademark or copyright registration under its own name. For example, if the licensee is the first to sell your invention, then the licensee acquires trademark rights for the licensed product. (If you don't understand the reasons for this, you should review the trademark section in Chapter 1.) If the invention has copyrightable features, the copyright act permits an exclusive licensee to register copyright. When the license terminates, the licensee's rights under copyright law will terminate. Copyright registration allows the licensee to go after copyright infringers without having you join in the lawsuit. Patent registrations, however, should only be done in the name of the inventor.

---

2. Marking Products With Appropriate Proprietary Notices

Different forms of intellectual property have different notice requirements. The failure to include a proprietary notice (for example, "Java Jacket®"—indicating it is a federally registered trademark) may affect your rights against infringers. The provision below requires that the licensee affix all of the required proprietary notices (copyright, patent, etc.) and obey the intellectual property laws.

Compliance With Intellectual Property Laws

The license granted in this Agreement is conditioned on Licensee's compliance with the provisions of the intellectual property laws of the United States and any foreign country in the Territory. All copies of the Licensed Product as well as all promotional material shall bear appropriate proprietary notices.

3. Dealing With Infringers

If your invention is successful, unethical competitors may create imitations. As we explained in Chapter 2, the government rarely gets involved in the prosecution of infringers. If you and the licensee do nothing, there is nothing to stop the infringement.

You may not have the financial resources to fight by yourself, so it's wise to include a provision that allows both you and the licensee to deal with infringers. The provision below provides for funding of a lawsuit and for determining how to divide any money that is recovered from the infringer. This provision establishes a 50/50 division of any award money after payment of attorneys' fees.

> EXAMPLE: Bob licenses his self-cleaning urinal invention to SaniCo. SaniCo sues an infringer and recovers $100,000. After deducting their attorneys' fees of $25,000, SaniCo splits the remaining $75,000 on a 50/50 basis with Bob.

Since there is some risk in bringing an infringement lawsuit (there's always the chance that you lose), it is common for a licensee to seek a provision that provides for the party bringing the lawsuit to get more than 50%. In many license agreements, the party bringing the lawsuit may obtain 75% of the payment or more.

You should also note that sometimes, instead of paying damages, an infringer is allowed to continue selling imitation products provided that an ongoing royalty is paid. This royalty would be divided according to the same percentage established for judgments or settlements.

Infringement Lawsuits Against Third Parties

In the event that either party learns of imitations or infringements of the Property or Licensed Products, that party shall notify the other in writing of the infringements or imitations. Licensor shall have the right to commence lawsuits against third persons arising from infringement of the Property or Licensed Products. In the event that Licensor does not commence a lawsuit against an alleged infringer within sixty days of notification by Licensee, Licensee may commence a lawsuit against the third party. Before filing suit, Licensee shall obtain the written consent of Licensor to do so and such consent shall not be unreasonably withheld. Licensor will cooperate fully and in good faith with Licensee for the purpose of securing and preserving Licensee's rights to the Property. Any recovery (including, but not limited to a judgment, settlement or licensing agreement included as resolution of an infringement dispute) shall be divided equally between the parties after deduction and payment of reasonable attorneys' fees to the party bringing the lawsuit.

Can't Afford to Sue? Help Is Available

There are two types of infringement lawsuits:
- lawsuits in which a third party sues you or the licensee (or both) for infringement, or
- lawsuits in which you or the licensee sue a third party for infringement.

There are two types of insurance available to cover these suits. One type of insurance is defensive and will provide coverage if you are sued for infringement. This insurance is offered by several large insurance companies, which you can find in the Yellow Pages.

Several companies now offer insurance for inventors who want to sue infringers. This is offensive, not defensive, insurance because it permits you to go after imitators. Assuming you can qualify for coverage, these companies will pay a percentage of your legal fees (usually 75%) and take a portion of any settlement. For more information about these policies, contact Lloyd's of London (www.lloyds.com) or Intellectual Property Insurance Services Corporation of Louisville, Kentucky (www.infringeins.com).

E. Commercialization and Exploitation

In Chapter 8, we recommended that you discuss the dates for commercialization and include those dates as material terms on your fact sheet. This provision expands on the commercialization requirements. In many industries, companies offer new products at certain times of the year. If a licensee fails to introduce the item at an appropriate trade show or in a seasonal catalogue, you may lose a full year of royalties. It is for this reason that this provision is defined as a "material" provision. In the event the licensee fails to commercialize the item, you can claim that there has been a "material breach," which is a basis for termination of your license agreement. We recommend a commercialization provision as follows:

Exploitation

Licensee agrees to manufacture, distribute and sell the Licensed Products in commercially reasonable quantities during the term of this Agreement and to commence such manufacture, distribution and sale within the following time period: _____[insert time period, for example "six months"]. This is a material provision of this Agreement.

The term "commercially reasonable quantities" requires that the licensee make a good faith effort to distribute more than a token amount of licensed products. In the event that there is a particular trade show or seasonal catalogue, you can add a sentence such as:

Licensee agrees to introduce the Licensed Product at the trade show or with the seasonal catalogue as specified in Exhibit A.

F. Samples and Quality Control

Imagine your disappointment if the licensee begins selling your invention and the product has defects or is inferior to competing products. The provision below permits you to review the quality standards of the licensee.

Samples and Quality Control

Licensee shall submit a reasonable number of production samples of the Licensed Product to Licensor to assure that the product meets Licensor's quality standards. In the event that Licensor fails to object in writing within ten business days after the date of receipt, the Licensed Product shall be deemed to be acceptable. At least once during each calendar year, Licensee shall submit two production samples of each Licensed Product for review. The quality standards applied by Licensor shall be no more rigorous than the quality standards applied by Licensee to similar products.

G. Insurance

What happens if a consumer is injured using your product and claims that it's defective? Perhaps the licensee has promised to indemnify you against such a disaster. Unfortunately, that's not enough. What's really needed is an insurance carrier with a solid rating—a Grade B or higher under the Moody Standard insurance rating system—who will cover both the licensee *and* you. If there is a licensing agent, the agent may also want to be named in the policy. If you are named in the policy, the insurance company will have a duty to defend you as well as the licensee in the event of product injuries. This insurance is intended to shield you from claims of product injuries, not infringement lawsuits. That is, it only covers you if consumers are hurt using the product.

It's possible that the licensee may already have a policy and that policy does not match the provisions below. You may have to be flexible and accept the licensee's policy. However, you should be aware of the difference between two types of policies. They are:

- **Occurrence Policies.** If the insurance was in place when the injury occurred, an occurrence policy will cover the suit, no matter when the claim is made or the lawsuit is filed. For

example, the policy covers 2002 and the injury occurs in 2002. The injured person files the lawsuit in 2003. There is coverage.

- **Claims Made Policies.** This type of insurance only covers claims if they are made during the policy period. For example, say the policy covers 2002 and the injury occurs in 2002. The injured person files the lawsuit in 2003. There is *no* coverage.

Since you may not be able to control whether the insurance is claims made or occurrence, we suggest that you include a statement that this provision shall survive for three years (this time period may be negotiable) after termination. That way you will still be protected in the event it is a claims made policy.

Insurance

Licensee shall, throughout the Term, obtain and maintain, at its own expense, standard product liability insurance coverage, naming Licensor as additional named insureds. Such policy shall: (a) be maintained with a carrier having a Moody's rating of at least B; and (b) provide protection against any claims, demands and causes of action arising out of any alleged defects or failure to perform of the Licensed Products or any use of the Licensed Products. The amount of coverage shall be a minimum of _____ *[insert amount of insurance coverage]* with no deductible amount for each single occurrence for bodily injury or property damage. The policy shall provide for notice to the Agent and Licensor from the insurer by Registered or Certified Mail in the event of any modification or termination of insurance. Licensee shall furnish Licensor and Agent a certificate from its product liability insurance carrier evidencing insurance coverage in favor of Licensor. In no event shall Licensee distribute the Licensed Products before the receipt by the Licensor of evidence of insurance. The provisions of this section shall survive termination for three years.

We do not provide you with the suggested amount of coverage, as that may differ from industry to industry. It is not unusual for product liability coverage to range between $1,000,000 and $5,000,000, or more. ■

Termination and Post-Termination

The conclusion of the license—known as termination—can occur for various reasons. Perhaps you agreed to end the license after a period of years or perhaps something has gone wrong, such as the licensee has stopped paying royalties. In this chapter, we discuss the ways by which a license agreement is terminated and what happens after termination. You should read this chapter if you answer "yes" to any of the following questions:

- Would you like to know the reasons a license agreement can be terminated?
- Does either party want the right to terminate without a reason?
- Would you like to know how bankruptcy will affect the license?
- Does the licensee want the ability to sell off inventory after the license is over?
- Would you like designs, plans, materials or molds returned after termination?

In the following sections, we discuss the various methods of ending a license agreement and provide sample provisions. For example, license agreements may terminate at the expiration of a time period or as a result of a dispute. We also discuss how disputes can be resolved (or "cured"). Bankruptcies can also affect the license agreement, and we explore the difference between a licensee and licensor bankruptcy. Finally, we provide you with advice on what to do *after* the license has terminated.

A. Termination and Post-Termination

When negotiating a license agreement, most people focus on the beginning of the relationship and don't think about the end. At some point, however, your license agreement will end, either peacefully or angrily. A well-drafted license agreement should deal with both types of situations. You don't have to include all the termination provisions provided below in your license. They're provided to make you aware of the different possibilities. Some common bases for termination are:

- termination based upon a deadline (sometimes referred to as a "fixed term" agreement)

  EXAMPLE: The agreement provides for termination after two years.

- termination at will

  EXAMPLE: One party terminates the agreement without providing a reason.

- termination based on a problem arising from the agreement

  EXAMPLE: You terminate because the licensee fails to pay royalties.

B. Termination Based Upon a Fixed Term

A fixed term means that the license agreement will end at a predetermined time. Some examples of a fixed term could be:

- a license that runs for three years
- a license that runs until the licensee fails to renew, or
- a license that runs until the patent expires.

Have you and the licensee already agreed upon the length of time the license agreement will last? If you have provided for a fixed term in your term provision (see Chapter 8 on establishing the basic elements of your licensing agreement), then your agreement has a built-in ending—the conclusion (or expiration) of the term. Some license agreements don't include a term provision. Instead, the parties express the contract length in the termination provision.

Note: If you are using both a term and a termination provision, make sure they conform (that is, that they both provide for the same fixed period of time).

- If you want the license to terminate after a period of years:

Fixed Term

This Agreement shall terminate at the end of _____ [insert number of years] years unless terminated sooner under a provision of this Agreement.

- If you have a patent, make sure to limit the term to the length of the patent:

This Agreement shall terminate with the expiration of the longest-living patent (or patents) or last-remaining patent application (as listed in the definition of the Property), whichever occurs last, unless terminated sooner under a provision of this Agreement.

- If you want to establish a fixed term with renewal periods:

This Agreement terminates at the end of two years (the "Initial Term") unless renewed by Licensee under the same terms and conditions for consecutive two-year periods (the "Renewal Terms") provided that Licensee provides written notice of its intention to renew this agreement within 30 days prior to expiration of the current term. In no event shall the Agreement extend longer than the date of expiration of the longest-living patent (or patents) or last-remaining patent application as listed in the definition of the Property.

If there is no patent, strike the last sentence at the end of the provision.

C. Termination at Will

Termination at will means that one party can end the agreement simply by notifying the other. In this type of termination, it's not necessary to provide an explanation or reason. The agreement ends simply because one party decides to terminate it. This provision does not have to be mutual. In fact, the licensee usually wants this ability, but does not want the licensor to have it. In other words, they can terminate at will but you can't. This is often true if the licensee is required to pay a minimum guaranteed royalty payment. The at-will provision lets the licensee bail out of the agreement (and royalty commitment) if the licensed products are not selling well.

A licensee's right to terminate at will may seem unfair, but it's just a business reality. If a licensee doesn't want to sell your product or is losing money, there is nothing you can do to change that position, no matter how the license is drafted. That's why termination at will is common. If you can avoid termination at will, fine. But if the licensee insists on it, accept it and try to negotiate a long notice period (perhaps 90 days), which will give you more time to find another licensee.

The following is a sample termination at will provision under which only the licensee can terminate:

Termination at Will: Licensee's Option

Upon 90 days notice, licensee may, at its sole discretion, terminate this agreement by providing notice to the licensor.

D. Termination Based on Contract Problems

What happens if the licensee fails to honor the agreement? If you sue, a court may award you damages, but the judge may not terminate the agreement. That is, you could be awarded a payment but the license agreement may continue.

A judge will only terminate an agreement if there is a material breach. Which breaches are "material"? That depends upon the contract, the events giving rise to the breach, the law governing the contract and the discretion of the judge. In some cases, for example, judges have determined that a failure to pay royalties is not a material breach.

1. Don't Rely on a Judge's Discretion

To you, a failure to pay royalties is a material breach. Rather than rely on a judge's discretion or interpretation of the law, you can write a provision stating that the agreement will terminate for specific types of breaches, such as a failure to pay royalties.

We recommend that you specify the particular problems that will be the basis for termination. In particular, we recommend that you consider termination for the reasons provided below:

- a failure to pay royalties (or make other payments as provided in the agreement)
- a failure to sell (or exploit) the invention
- a failure to maintain confidentiality as required under the confidentiality provision
- an assignment or sublicense of your rights in violation of the agreement, and
- a failure to maintain product liability insurance. (If your invention is the type of licensed product that requires product liability insurance, see Chapter 12.)

Not all of these reasons will fit within your agreement. For example, confidentiality, assignment or product liability may be irrelevant to your invention. Therefore, you should modify the provision accordingly.

All-Purpose Breach Provisions

Some license agreements state that, "In the event of a breach, either party can terminate this agreement." We do *not* recommend this type of provision because it is too broad and it will be left up to a judge to determine whether the activity—for example, failure to pay royalties—is a breach. In other words, this clause is still too discretionary. You will be better served by identifying the particular breaches that qualify for termination.

2. The Cure Period

Many companies run into temporary problems. For example, payments may be delayed because of computer snafus or cash shortages. For that reason, it is unfair to terminate the agreement until the licensee has had an opportunity to fix or cure the problem. Normally each side is given 30 or 60 days (the cure period) from the time of notification to cure the defect. For example, if you don't receive your royalty payment, you notify the licensee (see the Notice section in Chapter 14), and if you don't get paid within the cure period, then you can terminate the agreement. We recommend a 30-day cure period as a reasonable period to fix the problem.

Not every breach or problem is curable. A failure to obtain product liability insurance, for example, may not be curable because you're exposed to liability. The right to cure is usually included within the termination provision as shown below:

Licensor's Right to Terminate

Licensor shall have the right to terminate this Agreement for the following reasons:

a) Licensee fails to pay Royalties when due or fails to accurately report Net Sales, as defined in the Payment Section of this Agreement, and such failure is not cured within 30 days after written notice from the Licensor;

b) Licensee fails to introduce the product to market by _____ [insert date by which Licensee must begin selling Licensed Products] or to offer the Licensed Products in commercially reasonable quantities during any subsequent year;

c) Licensee fails to maintain confidentiality regarding Licensor's trade secrets and other Information;

d) Licensee assigns or sublicenses in violation of the Agreement; or

e) Licensee fails to maintain or obtain product liability insurance as required by the provisions of this Agreement.

Terminate as to Territory Not Exploited [Optional]

Licensor shall have the right to terminate the grant of license under this Agreement with respect to any country or region included in the Territory in which Licensee fails to offer the Licensed Products for sale or distribution or to secure a sublicensing agreement for the marketing, distribution and sale of the product within two years of the Effective Date.

E. Termination and Bankruptcy

What happens if the licensee goes bankrupt? Unfortunately, there is not much you can do to protect yourself against a licensee's bankruptcy. Many license agreements contain a provision stating that the licensor can terminate the agreement in the event of bankruptcy. Such provisions are unenforceable (with the exception of some trademark licenses). That is, you will *not* be able to terminate the license agreement if the licensee goes bankrupt. Once the licensee files for bankruptcy, only a federal bankruptcy court can determine your rights and obligations under a licensing agreement. The bankruptcy court can keep your invention rights tied up for months or years while a bankruptcy trustee attempts to sort out the financial mess. It's even possible that your license may be assigned to another company in order to pay off creditors of the licensee.

Seem unfair? Welcome to bankruptcy law, which, like tax law, relies on arcane rules and regulations that often defy logic. Oddly, if you (the licensor) become bankrupt, the licensee can elect to continue with the license or terminate it. That is, if the situation is reversed and you're insolvent, the licensee has the right to terminate or pay royalties to the trustee.

Summing up, you cannot claim bankruptcy or insolvency as a basis for termination. Although these termination provisions are often mistakenly included in license agreements, they are invalid and should not be used.

F. Post-Termination: What Happens Afterwards?

If a license ends bitterly, it will be very difficult to get the licensee to voluntarily return materials. That's why the contract must provide for various contingencies with a clause titled "Post-Termination" or "Effect of Termination." These post-termination provisions are like the conditions of a prenuptial agreement for newlyweds describing who gets what and how things should be divided after the split.

After termination, you should be concerned about three things:

- the licensee stops sales as soon as possible
- the licensee pays you all money that is due, and
- the licensee returns all designs, molds or other furnished materials.

1. Post-Termination Sales

At the time of termination, the licensee may have boxes of licensed products left in the warehouse. If you end the agreement amicably, then it seems reasonable to allow the licensee a period of time to sell off the remaining inventory. Naturally, you're entitled to royalties for these products. How long should the sell-off period be? If it's too short, the licensee will be unable to unload its inventory. If it's too long, it may conflict with another license. A period between three to six months is probably sufficient. In addition, the licensor should obtain an accounting of the remaining inventory.

Obviously, if the licensee is not paying royalties, it makes no sense to allow a sell-off of inventory. The same is true if there is no product liability insurance or if there has been a government recall of the invention. The provision provided below prevents sales unless all of these conditions have been met.

2. Return of Molds, Plans, Etc.

If your invention is a product—an item that was mass-produced—then one of the most expensive start-up costs is the preparation of molds or tooling for manufacture. Since the licensee will have no further use for them, you should request the tooling and molds. It is only fair that you should pay for the shipping of these items.

There are two important reasons to obtain the tooling and molds. First, it removes the materials from the licensee who no longer has the right to manufacture the invention, and second, in the event you can locate a new licensee, it will give you a head start for manufacturing.

3. Post-Termination Provision

Below is an example of a recommended post-termination provision.

Effect of Termination

Upon termination of this Agreement, all Royalty obligations as established in the Payments Section shall immediately become due. After the termination of this license, all rights granted to Licensee under this Agreement shall revert to Licensor, and Licensee will refrain from further manufacturing, copying, marketing, distribution or use of any Licensed Product or other product which incorporates the Property. Within 30 days after termination, Licensee shall deliver to Licensor a statement indicating the number and description of the Licensed Products which it had on hand or is in the process of manufacturing as of the termination date. Licensee may dispose of the Licensed Products covered by this Agreement for a period of three months after termination except that Licensee shall have no such right in the event this agreement is terminated according to the Licensor's Right to Terminate, above. At the end of the post-termination sale period, Licensee shall furnish a royalty payment and statement as required under the Payment Section. Upon termination, Licensee shall deliver to Licensor all tooling and molds used in the manufacture of the Licensed Products. Licensor shall bear the costs of shipping for the tooling and molds.

G. Survival of the Fittest

Just because the license terminates, it doesn't mean that all of the obligations in the agreement terminate. For example, it's important that the parties maintain confidential information after the agreement ends. It's also important that you receive any other payments that may accrue after termination. Therefore, the parties often designate that some obligations continue or survive the agreement. We recommend that the following sections survive termination:

- confidentiality
- warranties
- licensee indemnity
- product liability insurance, and
- payment obligations.

The licensee may insist that other provisions survive as well.

You indicate which provisions survive by adding a sentence at the end of the provision such as: "This obligation shall survive any termination of this Agreement." Some license agreements have a separate provision that says:

Survival

The obligations of Sections _____, _____ and _____ shall survive any termination of this Agreement.

It doesn't matter which method is used, but you should carefully review which sections survive termination. ■

Boilerplate and Standard Provisions

n this chapter we discuss contract provisions that are sometimes referred to as boilerplate, general, miscellaneous or standard provisions. These provisions are usually grouped at the end of an agreement and deal with a range of miscellaneous issues such as resolving disputes and interpreting the agreement. You should read this chapter if you answer "yes" to any of the following questions:

- Would you like an explanation of attorneys' fees provisions?
- Would you like information about the process of arbitration?
- Are you confused about issues such as choice of law or jurisdiction?
- Do you want a definition for "waiver," "integration," "force majeure," "invalidity" or "severability" ?
- Would you like to know what is meant when an attachment or exhibit is "incorporated" into an agreement?
- Are you concerned about whether the licensee can assign your invention to another company?

As you read through this chapter, you may wonder why these contract provisions are grouped together. Boilerplate provisions actually have little in common with one another except for the fact that they don't fit anywhere else in the agreement. For that reason, they are usually dumped at the end of the agreement and labeled with titles such as "Miscellaneous," "General" or "Standard."

Don't be misled by the fact that boilerplate is buried in the back of the agreement. These provisions are very important and can affect how disputes are resolved and how the contract is enforced by a court.

Below is a summary of the boilerplate provisions we will discuss in this chapter:

- **Attorneys' Fees.** In the event of a legal dispute, this provision determines if the winner receives payment for legal fees.
- **Arbitration.** This provision provides for a method of resolving disputes without resorting to a lawsuit.
- **Choice of Law.** In the event of a dispute, this provision determines which state law will govern the lawsuit.
- **Jurisdiction.** In the event of a dispute, this provision establishes in which state (and county) the lawsuit must be filed.
- **Waiver.** This provision permits the parties to waive (forgo or give up claim to) a portion of the agreement without establishing a precedent (without giving up future claims under the same portion).
- **Severability.** This provision permits a court to sever (or take out) an invalid provision and still keep the rest of the agreement intact.
- **Integration.** This provision establishes that the agreement is the final version and that any further modification must be in writing.
- **Attachments.** This provision guarantees that attachments and exhibits will be included as part of the agreement.
- **Notice Provisions.** This provision describes how each party must provide notice of disputes.
- **Relationships.** This provision prevents either party from claiming a business relationship with the other, for example, stating that you are a partner or in a joint venture.
- **Assignment.** This provision affects the ability of the parties to sell their rights under the agreement to another party.
- **Force Majeure (pronounced fors-mazhoor').** This provision establishes that the agreement will be suspended in the event of unforeseen disasters (such as earthquakes, hurricanes, floods, etc.).
- **Headings.** This provision provides that the headings used throughout the agreement have no special significance.
- **Escrow.** This provision allows you and the licensee to place trade secrets, payments or other information into a special account which will only be opened under certain conditions.

A. Paying the Lawyer's Bills

Hopefully, your relationship with the licensee will be prosperous and peaceable. But what if the licensee breaches the agreement and you are forced to sue? The hourly rate for business lawyers is between $200 and $400 an hour. The filing and initial stages of a lawsuit cost between $5,000 and $50,000 and can quickly escalate to more than $100,000 depending on the length of the suit and the subject matter. The amount you pay in attorneys' fees could quickly overshadow the amount you seek in damages.

Unfortunately, in the United States (unlike other countries), the winner of a lawsuit is not automatically awarded his or her attorneys' fees. In other words, each party has to pay its own lawyer, regardless of the outcome of the suit. This is known as the American Rule and there are two exceptions: 1) a court may award fees if a specific law permits it, and 2) a court must award attorneys' fees if a contract provides for it.

1. Laws That Allow Award of Attorneys' Fees

Federal statutes provide for the award of attorneys' fees in cases where intellectual property laws (laws involving copyrights, trademarks or patents, for example) have been violated. This is also true for certain state laws regarding trade secrets. In other words, if someone violates one of these laws and you sue them—say for infringement of a patent— the judge may award you attorneys' fees.

The judge *may* award attorneys' fees? That's right. Under these laws, the award of attorneys' fees is not mandatory, it's discretionary (it's up to the judge). In reality, attorneys' fees are usually not awarded unless one party's behavior is especially offensive—for example, a company knew they were infringing and proceeded despite your protests.

In addition, these laws do not cover all licensing lawsuits. Your lawsuit must arise from a violation of the patent, trademark, copyright or trade secret laws (all of which are geared towards protecting against infringement). Common license agreement problems, such as failure to pay royalties, are not a violation of these laws because such disputes are based on contract law, not intellectual property law.

In summary, don't count on these laws for getting attorneys' fees in a lawsuit against a licensee. Chances are your case will not qualify under the statutes, and even if it does, the discretionary aspect makes the award unpredictable. If you're seeking attorneys' fees, you are far better off using an attorneys' fees provision, as described below.

2. Attorneys' Fees and Expenses

You and the licensee can create a contract provision that provides for the award of attorneys' fees to the winner (also known as the prevailing party) of any lawsuit arising from the license agreement. However, don't be surprised if the licensee is opposed to the use of an attorneys' fees provision. Why? Because it is the licensee that is usually sued by the licensor, not vice-versa, and the licensee believes the provision will encourage the licensor to sue.

If you can get your licensee to agree to it, we recommend the following sample attorneys' fees provision:

The prevailing party shall have the right to collect from the other party its reasonable costs and necessary disbursements and attorneys' fees incurred in enforcing this Agreement.

Watch Out for One-Way Attorneys' Fees Provisions. We encourage the use of mutual attorneys' fees provisions, such as the one above. Under a mutual provision, the party that wins the lawsuit is the party that is awarded attorneys' fees. This is fair and encourages the quick resolution of lawsuits. We discourage a one-way provision that allows only the licensee to receive attorneys' fees. That is, if the licensee wins, you, the licensor, would pay the licensee's attorneys' fees, but if you win, you would get nothing to pay your lawyer.

One-way provisions, no matter which side they favor, create an uneven playing field for resolving disputes. Some states, such as California, have recognized this unfairness and automatically convert a one-way attorneys' fees contract provision into a mutual provision. We urge you to strike any one-way attorneys' fees provisions.

B. Dispute Resolution

Arbitration is like going to court with less formality and expense. Instead of filing a lawsuit, the parties hire one or more arbitrators to evaluate the dispute and make a determination. The arbitrators are trained to evaluate disputes, and many of them are retired judges. Mediation is similar to arbitration except that instead of making a determination, a neutral evaluator attempts to help the parties settle their dispute. That is, the mediator offers advice so that the parties reach a solution together.

1. Arbitration

The arbitration process can be relatively simple. Usually it involves some document preparation and a hearing. The arbitrator's determination may be advisory (a suggested resolution), or it may be binding and can be entered in a court. A binding arbitration cannot be overturned unless something especially unfair happened—for example, the arbitrator ruled against you and you later learned that the arbitrator owned stock in your opponent's company.

In order to arbitrate the dispute, both parties must consent. Unfortunately, when you are in the midst of a dispute, it's hard to get the parties to agree to anything. Therefore, the best method of guaranteeing arbitration is to include an arbitration provision in your license agreement.

Despite the advantages of arbitration, many licensees are opposed to the procedure. They may have recently lost an arbitration proceeding and refuse to participate in another one. They may be fearful that the dispute will be placed in the hands of an inappropriate arbitrator, or they may prefer the litigation process in order to intimidate the licensor. In addition, some arbitrations are expensive, require attorneys and end up being appealed in the court system.

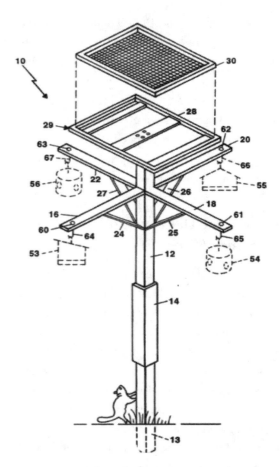

Multi-Station Bird Feeder with Squirrel Guard
No. 6,269,771

Summing up, below are the pros and cons for arbitration:

- Pros—Arbitration is usually less expensive and more efficient than litigation. If the subject of the dispute is technical—for example, about a patent—the parties can select an arbitrator who has technical knowledge.
- Cons—There is no right to discovery (the process by which the parties must disclose information about their cases). However, you can include a requirement for discovery in your arbitration provision. Unlike a court ruling, a binding arbitration ruling is not appealable. It can only be set aside if it can be demonstrated that the arbitrator was biased or that the ruling violated public policy. Arbitrators must be paid (unlike state and federal judges), and these fees can often run to $10,000 or more. And most participants hire attorneys, so you will still have attorneys' fees (although probably lower than in a lawsuit).

There are many associations and companies that offer private arbitration, the most well-known of which is the American Arbitration Association (AAA). The AAA also has special Patent Arbitration Rules and a national panel of patent arbitrators.

We recommend the following sample arbitration provision with your state of residence placed in the blank:

Arbitration

If a dispute arises under or relating to this Agreement, the parties agree to submit such dispute to binding arbitration in the state of _____ *[insert state in which parties agree to arbitrate]* or another location mutually agreeable to the parties. The arbitration shall be conducted on a confidential basis pursuant to the Commercial Arbitration Rules of the American Arbitration Association. Any decision or award as a result of any such arbitration proceeding shall be in writing and shall provide an explanation for all conclusions of law and fact and shall include the assessment of costs, expenses and reasonable attorneys' fees. Any such arbitration shall be conducted by an arbitrator experienced in _____ *[insert industry experience required for arbitrator]* and in invention licensing law and shall include a written record of the arbitration hearing. The parties reserve the right to object to any individual who shall be employed by or affiliated with a competing organization or entity. An award of arbitration may be confirmed in a court of competent jurisdiction.

2. Mediation

In mediation, a neutral evaluator (the mediator) attempts to help the parties reach a resolution of their dispute. That is, the parties sit down with the mediator and tell their story. The mediator advises ways to resolve the dispute, and the two parties try to agree (and sign an enforceable settlement). Because it is not binding and because it is less expensive than litigation or arbitration, some licensees prefer mediation.

- Pros—Mediation is the most "peaceable" method of solving your problem. You can arrive at a settlement rather than being told how to resolve the dispute by an arbitrator or judge.
- Cons—By itself, mediation is often not enough, because it doesn't force the parties to end the dispute. If the parties cannot resolve their dispute with mediation, they must find some binding method of ending the battle: either arbitration or litigation (a lawsuit). In addition, the licensee may elect mediation simply to buy more time. For example, if the licensee owes royalties, mediation will simply prolong the time period before the payment *must* be made.

If you want to use a mediation clause, we suggest a provision like the one below which progresses from informal meeting to mediation and then to arbitration.

Mediation & Arbitration

The Parties agree that every dispute or difference between them, arising under this Agreement, shall be settled first by a meeting of the Parties attempting to confer and resolve the dispute in a good faith manner. If the Parties cannot resolve their dispute after conferring, any Party may require the other Parties to submit the matter to non-binding mediation, utilizing the services of an impartial professional mediator approved by all Parties. If the Parties cannot come to an agreement following mediation, the Parties agree to submit the matter to binding arbitration at a location mutually agreeable to the Parties. The arbitration shall be conducted on a confidential basis pursuant to the Commercial Arbitration Rules of the American Arbitration Association. Any decision or award as a result of any such arbitration proceeding shall include the assessment of costs, expenses and reasonable attorneys' fees and shall include a written record of the proceedings and a written determination of the arbitrators.

Absent an agreement to the contrary, any such arbitration shall be conducted by an arbitrator experienced in intellectual property law. The Parties reserve the right to object to any individual who shall be employed by or affiliated with a competing organization or entity. In the event of any such dispute or difference, either Party may give to the other notice requiring that the matter be settled by arbitration. An award of arbitration shall be final and binding on the Parties and may be confirmed in a court of competent jurisdiction.

If the licensee is opposed to arbitration (and many are), you can try a less formal approach to dispute resolution with the following mediation provision. It does not require that the parties commit to arbitration, but it allows for the parties to work out some method of alternative dispute resolution.

Alternative Dispute Resolution

If a dispute arises and cannot be resolved by the parties, either party may make a written demand for formal resolution of the dispute. The written request will specify the scope of the dispute. Within 30 days after such written notice, the parties agree to meet, for one day, with an impartial mediator and consider dispute resolution alternatives other than litigation. If an alternative method of dispute resolution is not agreed upon within 30 days of the one-day mediation, either side may start litigation proceedings.

C. Governing Law

Every state has laws regarding contract interpretation. The parties can choose any state's laws to govern the agreement, regardless of where they live or where the agreement is signed. The licensee usually favors the state where its headquarters are located, often New York or California. Does it matter which state is chosen? Some states have a reputation as being favorable for certain kinds of disputes. That's usually because so many similar disputes have been brought in that state that a body of law has developed which makes the resulting decision more predictable. Generally, however, the differences in state law are not great enough to make this a major negotiating issue. Your choice of which state's law will govern your agreement can be stated in a clause such as the following:

This Agreement shall be governed in accordance with the laws of the State of _____.

Don't Confuse Jurisdiction and Governing Law. The selection of which state is used for governing law is not a crucial negotiating issue. But the selection of the state for jurisdiction, described below, is important. Sometimes these two provisions are grouped in one paragraph, so read them carefully.

D. Jurisdiction

Jurisdiction (sometimes referred to as personal jurisdiction) is the power of a court to bind you by its decision. If the court doesn't have authority over you, the judgment isn't worth anything. A court can get jurisdiction over you in three ways: 1) you are a resident of the state in which the court is located; 2) you have sufficient contacts in the state, such as selling a lot of merchandise there; or 3) you consent (or agree) to jurisdiction.

The purpose of the jurisdiction provision in a license agreement is to get you to consent in advance to jurisdiction in one state and to waive (give up) your right to sue or be sued anywhere else. For example, if you consent to jurisdiction in Alaska, then any lawsuits arising from your agreement will have to be filed in Alaska. This can have an important effect on your ability to enforce the agreement. You will have to hire attorneys in Alaska and, if the case proceeds to trial, you will have to travel there for the lawsuit.

Consider the couple who opened a Burger King franchise in Florida. In their agreement with Burger King, they consented to jurisdiction in Michigan. Later, when problems arose, the couple argued that it wasn't fair to have to travel to Michigan and that they were not aware of the meaning of this provision. The courts upheld the jurisdiction clause and the couple was forced to fight Burger King in Michigan.

This may seem like a trivial issue at the time you are negotiating an agreement, but it will be a major issue in the event of a dispute. In fact, knowing that they have to hire lawyers and travel to another state is often enough to dissuade many licensors from asserting their rights and pursuing a lawsuit. Therefore, we recommend the following strategies:

1. If you have sufficient bargaining power, obtain jurisdiction in your home county.
2. If you cannot obtain jurisdiction in your home county, don't include any reference to jurisdiction. If there is no reference to jurisdiction, then the location of the case is usually determined by whoever files the lawsuit.
3. If you *do* include a jurisdiction clause, then it may be helpful to have the choice of law (as discussed above) conform to the same state as that of the jurisdiction. It may prove simpler and more efficient to use the governing law of the state in which you are litigating.

In Some States, Jurisdiction Clauses Are Invalid

In the past, many courts believed that citizens should not be able to bargain for jurisdiction (sometimes referred to as forum shopping) and would not enforce jurisdiction provisions. Today, only three states—Idaho, Montana and Alabama —refuse to honor jurisdiction provisions in contracts. In those states if you use a jurisdiction provision, it will be invalid.

We recommend the following provision to establish jurisdiction for disputes arising out of your agreement. (Note: Sometimes this jurisdiction clause is included within the Governing Law provision.) The parties consent to the exclusive jurisdiction and venue of the federal and state courts located in _____ *[insert county and state in which parties agree to litigate]* in any action arising out of or relating to this Agreement. The parties waive any other venue to which either party might be entitled by domicile or otherwise.

E. Waiver

If you allow the licensee to do something that is prohibited under the agreement (that is, to breach the agreement), then you may have waived (given up) your right to complain about it later. For example, imagine that the licensee is several months late making a payment. You agree to accept the delay. Let's say that the following year, the licensee is again several months late paying royalties, and you again accept it without a dispute. In the third year, the licensee is again several months late, but you're tired of the late payments and you sue the licensee. The licensee successfully defends himself by claiming that since you allowed the late payments during the past two years, you waived your right to contest the late payment during the third year.

In order to prevent this result, you should include a waiver provision similar to the one below. This clause provides that if you don't contest a breach of the agreement, you are not waiving your right to contest such breaches in the future. The licensee cannot defend itself by claiming it relied on your past behavior of accepting its breaches. (Of course, the provision swings both ways. If you breach the agreement, you cannot rely on the licensee's past acceptance of *your* behavior.)

The failure to exercise any right provided in this Agreement shall not be a waiver of prior or subsequent rights.

F. Invalidity

The severability clause (sometimes referred to as the invalidity clause) provides that if one part of the agreement is invalid, it can be cut out (severed) and the rest of the agreement will remain valid. In other words, if something is wrong with part of the agreement, that portion will be cut out of the agreement without the rest of the agreement being affected. If you don't include a severability clause and some portion of your license agreement is deemed invalid, then the whole agreement may be canceled. To avoid this result, your agreement should include the following provision.

If any provision of this Agreement is invalid under applicable statute or rule of law, it is to be considered omitted and the remaining provisions of this Agreement shall in no way be affected.

G. Entire Understanding

In the process of negotiation and contract drafting, you and the licensee may make many oral or written statements. Some of these statements make it into the final agreement. Others don't. The integration provision verifies that the version you are signing is the final version and that neither you nor the licensee can rely on statements made in the past. *This is it!* Without an integration provision, it's possible that either party can claim rights based upon promises made before the deal was signed.

A second function of the integration provision (sometimes labeled as "Entire Understanding") is to establish that if any party makes promises after the agreement is signed, those promises will only be binding if they are done formally (that is, by a signed written amendment to the agreement).

This Agreement expresses the complete understanding of the parties and supersedes all prior representations, agreements and understandings, whether written or oral. This Agreement may not be altered except by a written document signed by both parties.

⚠ Watch Out for "We'll Fix It Later" Promises. The integration clause closes the door on any oral or written promises. Don't sign an agreement if something is missing, and don't accept an assurance that the licensee will do something later to correct it.

H. Attachments and Exhibits

Many agreements have attachments and exhibits—separate documents that are stapled or clipped to the agreement. For example, in Chapter 11, we suggested that you summarize the essential business elements on a sheet that could be attached. These additional pages are attached to the agreement and there is special language that guarantees that they are considered as part of the agreement—the "exhibit is incorporated by reference."

Below is an example of a provision that incorporates all attachments or exhibits. If there are no attachments or exhibits, you don't need it.

The parties agree and acknowledge that all attachments, exhibits and schedules referred to in this Agreement are incorporated in this Agreement by reference.

I. Notices

If a dispute arises, each party is entitled to be notified of the problem. The purpose of the notice provision is to establish the method of notification. Sometimes, a licensee may make the procedure more difficult than necessary. For example, the licensee may require notification by certified mail with return receipt and that the licensee's lawyers are notified in the same manner. There's really not much point arguing over notice provisions. However, you should remember that if you don't follow the notice procedures, your claim against the licensee might be delayed until you provide proper notification. The following sample provision establishes a reasonable notice method:

Any notice or communication required or allowed under this Agreement shall be sufficiently given when received by certified mail or sent by facsimile transmission or overnight courier.

J. No Joint Venture

Your relationship with the licensee is defined by the agreement. But to an outsider, it may appear that you have a different relationship, such as a partnership or joint venture. It's possible that an unscrupulous licensee will try to capitalize on this appearance and make a third party deal. That is, a licensee may claim to be your partner and obtain a benefit from a distributor or sublicensee. In order to avoid liability for such a situation, most agreements include a provision (sometimes referred to as "No Joint Venture") disclaiming any relationship other than licensee/licensor. We recommend that you include such a provision.

Nothing contained in this Agreement shall be construed to place the parties in the relationship of agent, employee, franchisee, officer, partners or joint ventures. Neither party may create or assume any obligation on behalf of the other.

K. Assignments

When the licensee assigns an agreement, a new company will sell your product and pay you royalties. This new company steps into the shoes of the original licensee. Assignments occur for a number of reasons: 1) a licensee needs money and is willing to sell its rights to your invention to another company, 2) a licensee creates an affiliate or subsidiary and assigns the licensing business to its affiliate or subsidiary, or 3) a licensee company is acquired by another company.

For example, if you licensed your invention to PCMac, a software company that was acquired by Microsoft, then Microsoft would become your new licensee. Microsoft, even though it didn't negotiate with you, would have to abide by all the provisions of the license agreement and pay you royalties.

There may be some instances where you don't want a company to acquire rights to your invention. For example, perhaps you had a bad experience with a company and now they're in line to become your new licensee. Maybe the new licensee is a competitor of yours. Or perhaps the new licensee plans to sell off your invention as a business maneuver. In today's world of acquisitions and mergers, most companies want some freedom to assign agreements and will oppose a complete prohibition on assignments.

Some suggested strategies:

1. If you have the bargaining power, it's best to prohibit any assignment of your contract unless you give written consent.

Statement of Assignability

Licensee may not assign or transfer its rights or obligations pursuant to this Agreement without the prior written consent of Licensor. Any assignment or transfer in violation of this section shall be void.

2. If the licensee is afraid that you have too much control, you can soften the effect by withholding consent only if you have a valid business reason. What's a valid reason? Perhaps the company to

which your licensee wants to grant an assignment has a reputation for not paying royalties, or maybe it is in poor financial shape. You cannot, however, withhold consent for an arbitrary reason, such as someone from the company once treated you rudely.

Consent Not Unreasonably Withheld

Licensee may not assign or transfer its rights or obligations pursuant to this Agreement without the prior written consent of Licensor. Such consent shall not be unreasonably withheld. Any assignment or transfer in violation of this section shall be void.

3. If you don't have much bargaining power and the licensee wants freedom to transfer to affiliates or new owners (under the same terms as your license agreement), then you can use a provision such as the one below.

Consent Not Needed for Licensee Affiliates or New Owners

Licensee may not assign or transfer its rights or obligations pursuant to this Agreement without the prior written consent of Licensor. However, no consent is required for an assignment or transfer that occurs: (a) to an entity in which Licensee owns more than 50% of the assets, or (b) as part of a transfer of all or substantially all of the assets of Licensee to any party. Any assignment or transfer in violation of this Section shall be void.

4. If you don't have any bargaining power and the licensee wants absolute freedom to assign, then you will have to take out this provision.

L. Force Majeure

The force majeure provision (sometimes referred to as "Acts of God") establishes that the Agreement will be suspended in the event of unforeseen natural disasters. For example, if a tornado ruins the licensee's manufacturing plant for three months, the license agreement would be suspended for three months.

How does this delay affect your license? If you had a fixed term license (say for three years) and the disaster resulted in a six-month delay, then the licensee would have a license for three years and six months. Similarly, the payment schedule would also be altered and the licensee would have a six-month grace period before the first post-disaster payment is due.

You will notice that we have not included a force majeure provision in the model agreement. That's because a force majeure provision is not essential and you need not include it unless the licensee insists. This provision is intended to deal with unpredictable disasters that are out of the control of the licensee, not business contingencies such as union disputes. If possible, remove references to things such as "failure of technical facilities," "failure or delay of transportation facilities," "strike" or "shortage of raw materials."

In the event of an act of God such as fire, riot, act of public enemy, war or similar cause not within the control of Licensee, the Licensee shall have the right to suspend the term of this Agreement. Licensee may suspend the term only for the duration of any such contingency. Licensee shall not suspend its obligation to make payments to Licensor if such payments are due and are not otherwise prevented. At the conclusion of the contingency, Licensee shall notify Licensor in writing and the Agreement shall be reinstated.

M. Headings

Although it's not really necessary, some licensees like to include a provision that states that the headings used throughout the agreement have no special significance. The headings are the titles of each provision, usually in bold type. It's not necessary, but if requested, it won't hurt to include it.

Headings of the sections of this Agreement are included for reference only and are not intended to affect the interpretation of the Agreement.

N. Establishing Escrow Accounts

An escrow is like a safety deposit box. You and the licensee place something (for example, trade secrets or money) in an account controlled by an escrow agent, and only under certain conditions will it be released. Escrow accounts are normally used to maintain secret information that has not been licensed but is necessary for maintenance or repair of the invention. For example, you modify your invention to meet the licensee's specifications and the modifications are done using your secret software code. You did not license this code, but there may be circumstances when the licensee will need access to it (for example the invention has to be modified and you are unavailable to make the modification).

Instead of giving the trade secrets to the licensee, you can place them in a special account, monitored by an escrow agent. The contents of the account (the escrow items) will be available to the licensee *only* under certain conditions, for example, if you, the licensor, are unable to repair the invention.

Escrow arrangements are also used to hold money, stock or documents transferring ownership of inventions. This is similar to a traditional escrow account used for selling a house. The title (for example, the assignment of your invention) is placed in escrow. When the other party makes the proper payment, the title is released.

The rules regarding the release of the escrow items are established in an escrow agreement that is signed by you, the licensee and the escrow agent. Lawyers or banks often act as escrow agents. If you use an escrow agreement, the following provision should be inserted in your license agreement and you should attach a copy of your escrow agreement to the license agreement.

Established Escrow Account

The parties have executed a separate Escrow Agreement (attached to this Agreement and incorporated by reference) for the deposit of escrow materials.

If you cannot execute an escrow agreement at the time of license, you can still express your intention to do so in the license agreement by including the following provision.

Future Establishment of Escrow Account

The parties shall execute a separate Escrow Agreement to establish an escrow account for the deposit of _____ [indicate what will be deposited] ("Escrow Items"). The Escrow Items shall be released to _____ [name of party—Licensor or Licensee] upon the following conditions: [list reasons for release from escrow. For example, "The funds will be released to Licensor upon completion of the Services and furnishing of Deliverables."].

As explained, above, the escrow agent often prepares the escrow agreement. Below is a sample escrow agreement for release of trade secrets upon certain conditions.

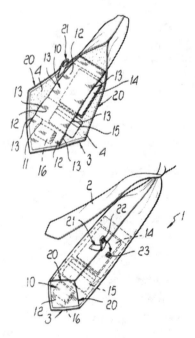

Tie with Concealed Pockets
No. 6,266,823

Escrow Agreement

This escrow agreement (the "Escrow Agreement") is made between _____ _____ _____

[insert your name, address and business form] ("Inventor"), and _____ _____ _____

[insert licensee's name, address and business form] ("Company") and _____ _____ _____ *[insert escrow agent's name and address]* ("Escrow Agent"). Company is a licensee of Inventor's invention (the "Properties") indicated on Exhibit A and pursuant to the agreement dated _____ *[insert date of license agreement]* between Inventor and Company (the "License Agreement"). The parties desire to place trade secrets and related materials with the Escrow Agent. Therefore, Inventor, Company and the Escrow Agent agree as follows:

1. Escrow Items

Inventor will promptly place copies of _____ _____ *[indicate what will be placed into escrow]* (collectively the "Escrow Items") under the control of the Escrow Agent.

2. Release Conditions

Company may submit a request for release of the Escrow Items to the Escrow Agent (the "Company's Release Request") upon the occurrence of one of the following release conditions during the term of the License Agreement:

(a) Inventor's filing of a petition under any chapter of the federal bankruptcy laws; or

(b) the failure by Inventor, within 30 days after Company's request to Inventor, to perform any of Inventor's obligations under the License Agreement.

3. Duties of Escrow Agent

The Escrow Agent's duties are limited to:

(a) safeguarding the Escrow Items against access or disclosure by any person or entity except as expressly provided in this Agreement, and

(b) notifying Inventor and Company that it has received the Escrow Items.

The Escrow Agent is not responsible for verifying the accuracy or completeness of the Escrow Items. The Escrow Agent's performance under this Escrow Agreement is excused when it is prevented by acts of God and other causes beyond its reasonable control.

4. Release of Escrow Item

The Escrow Agent shall, subject to the conditions below, deliver all of the Escrow Items to Company upon receipt of Company's Release Request, signed by an Officer of Company stating that Company has the right to receive all of the Escrow Items.

Company shall deliver its Release Request to the Escrow Agent and, at the same time, deliver a duplicate copy of its Release Request to Inventor. Within 30 days after the receipt of such Release Request, the Inventor shall either (a) submit a written authorization to the Escrow Agent to make the delivery, or (b) submit a written objection to the Escrow Agent and to Company.

If the Inventor authorizes the delivery or does not respond within 30 days, the Escrow Agent shall deliver the Escrow Items. If Inventor objects to the delivery of the Escrow Items in writing, Company and Inventor shall attempt in good faith to agree upon their respective rights to the Escrow Items. If Company and Inventor do so agree, an agreement shall be prepared and signed by both Company and Inventor and delivered to the Escrow Agent. The Escrow Agent shall be entitled to rely on the agreement and shall distribute the Escrow Items. If no such agreement can be reached after good faith negotiation, either Company or Inventor may demand arbitration of the matter. In such an event, the American Arbitration Association shall be asked to appoint one arbitrator, familiar with the subject matter of the license in the United States, to rule on the matter. Such appointment is to be in accordance with the then-current Commercial Arbitration Rules of the American Arbitration Association. The decision of the arbitrator shall be binding and conclusive upon Company and Inventor, and the Escrow Agent shall be entitled to act in accordance with such decision. Any such arbitration shall be held in _____ [indicate county and state for arbitration]. The prevailing party in any such arbitration shall be entitled to receive payments of its attorneys' fees and costs.

The Escrow Agent's duties may be altered, amended, modified or revoked only by a writing signed by officers of Company and Inventor.

The Escrow Agent shall not be personally liable for any act the Escrow Agent may do or omit to do under this Agreement while acting in good faith and in the exercise of its own good judgment.

The Escrow Agent is authorized to comply with orders, judgments or decrees of any court and of the arbitrator provided for above. If the Escrow Agent obeys or complies with any such order, judgment or decree, the Escrow Agent shall not be liable to any of the parties or to any other person, firm or corporation by reason of such compliance. The Escrow Agent shall not be liable even if such order, judgment or decree is subsequently reversed, modified, annulled, set aside, vacated or found to have been entered without jurisdiction.

The Escrow Agent shall be entitled to employ legal counsel and other experts as the Escrow Agent may deem necessary to advise it in connection with its obligations under this Escrow Agreement, and may rely upon the advice of such counsel and pay such counsel reasonable compensation.

The responsibilities of the Escrow Agent shall terminate if the Escrow Agent resigns by written notice to Company and Inventor. In that event, Inventor shall promptly appoint a successor Escrow Agent, subject to the approval of Company. Company's approval will not be unreasonably withheld.

It is understood and agreed that should any dispute arise with respect to the delivery, ownership or right of possession of any part of the Escrow Items held by the Escrow Agent, the Escrow Agent is directed to retain the Escrow Items in its possession, without liability to anyone, until such dispute is settled either by: 1) mutual written agreement, as provided above; or by 2) final order, decree or judgment of the arbitrator provided for above; or by 3) a court of competent jurisdiction after the time for appeal has expired and no appeal has been perfected. The Escrow Agent shall be under no duty to institute or defend any such proceedings.

5. Miscellaneous

Any notice or communication required or permitted to be given under this Escrow Agreement shall be sufficiently given when received by certified mail, or sent by facsimile transmission or overnight courier. If any term, provision, covenant or condition of this Agreement is held to be illegal or invalid for any reason whatsoever, such illegality or invalidity shall not affect the validity of the remainder of this Agreement. This Escrow Agreement and the License Agreement constitute the entire understanding between the Parties and can only be modified by written agreement. No party may assign or transfer its rights under this Escrow Agreement without the prior written consent of the other parties. This Agreement shall be binding upon the parties and their respective successors and assigns.

LICENSEE:

_____   _____
Signature   Date

LICENSOR:

_____   _____
Signature   Date

ESCROW AGENT:

_____   _____
Signature   Date

Service Provisions

In this chapter we discuss and examine service provisions. These provisions define jobs you agree to perform for the licensee (for example, the licensee wants you to offer technical assistance). You should read this chapter if you answer "yes" to any of the following questions:

- Does the licensee want you to train personnel in the production or use of your invention?
- Does the licensee want your services for the installation of machinery or technology needed to make your invention?
- Has the licensee asked you to provide technical assistance?
- Does the licensee want you to develop improvements to your invention?
- Are you expected to deliver improvements according to an established schedule?
- Are you concerned about who owns rights to improvements?

In some situations, the work that you agree to do for a licensee is so substantial that a separate services agreement is necessary. In those cases, the service provisions discussed in this chapter will not be sufficient. In Section A below, however, we will briefly explain when a separate service agreement may be necessary and how to include such an agreement with the rest of your licensing agreement. We also provide information (and sample provisions) for service-related activities, such as employee training, installation of equipment, technical support, improvements and providing and scheduling deliverables. We will also discuss the right of first refusal and a provision known as "most favored nation."

A. Service Provisions vs. Separate Service Agreements

The service provisions discussed in this chapter are limited in scope. They are geared toward simple, short-term services that you perform for a licensee. These provisions are *not* suitable for larger projects, which may require many employees or contractors. For this reason, we suggest that if services are substantial, you should prepare a separate services agreement, which is beyond the scope of this book. That is, you should execute two agreements: a licensing agreement (as explained in this book) and a services agreement.

How do you know if you will need a separate services agreement? You may need one if you answer "yes" to one or more of the following questions:

- Are the services open-ended with no fixed termination? Will the services last longer than the length of the license agreement?
- Do you have to hire or use employees or contractors?
- Do you have to obtain a separate work space?
- Do you have to create a separate company to perform the services?
- Do the payments for services exceed the amount of money you are receiving for your license?

In the event that you need a separate services agreement, we recommend that you read *Working for Yourself,* by Attorney Stephen Fishman (Nolo), which contains various sample service agreements. If the services are substantial, you may also need additional financial advice. For example, there may be tax issues if revenue from services is subject to different taxes than licensing revenue. However, if the services are limited to work that you can perform without employees or contractors and it is incidental to your licensing, the provisions below should be suitable.

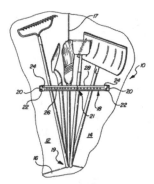

Method of Storing Elongated Implements Between Corner Side Walls No. 6,142,320

B. Training the Licensee's Personnel

If you possess knowledge that can assist in the manufacturing, selling or pre-production process (sometimes referred to as know-how), the licensee may want you to pass that information to its employees. This is sometimes referred to as training. If you are asked to do it, you should consider the following issues:

- How much will you be paid for the services?
- Where will you do the training?
- If you have to travel, how will you be reimbursed for travel, housing, etc.?
- What will the extent of the training be (how long, how many people, etc.)?
- Whom from the licensee's company will you work with?
- What if you are injured or the licensee's personnel are injured during the training period?

Sometimes, as a goodwill gesture, inventors perform training services for free (particularly if there is no travel involved). However, training provisions usually provide for compensation. You should be able to determine your own hourly rate. (An hourly rate between $50 to $150 per hour is common.) You'll also want reasonable expenses for travel and lodging. It's likely that you'll have to travel to the licensee's headquarters or plant to train personnel, and the costs of travel can really add up.

You should also define the extent of the training. Try to summarize what type of training you will perform and, if possible, how many people you will train and the length of time that you expect the training will take. You may want your fee to increase if any of the training exceeds what was agreed upon. For example, say you agreed to train two employees for 40 hours at $75 per hour. In the event that you had to train for 50 hours, your hourly rate might go up for the time over 40 hours. It is also helpful to list the names or titles of the persons you will train. This sets parameters on the training and helps both parties prepare for the session.

If you wish to include a training provision in your license agreement, a sample provision would look like the following:

Training

Licensor will provide _____ [number of days and whether they are consecutive] days of basic training for _____ [names or number of Licensee employees to be trained] Licensee employees at Licensee's facility in _____ [location of Licensee's facility]. Training will be performed by [name of Licensor or person who will provide train-ing]. Licensee shall bear all costs of travel and accom-modations and shall pay Licensor on a direct cost basis computed on the number of hours worked and an hourly rate of _____ [hourly rate] for services. Licensee shall indemnify Licensor for any and all claims that may result from such training. All payments for services and other expenses shall be paid by Licensee within 30 days of receipt of Licensor's written invoice.

As noted above, if the training is ongoing (such as regular training during the term of the license agreement) or more complex (for example, training employees around the world), you should use a separate services agreement that will better define your obligations and protect your rights. See Section A above on separate services agreements.

C. Installation of Equipment

A licensee may require that you (the licensor) supervise the installation of equipment related to your invention or process. This type of service raises similar issues to the training of personnel (discussed above): Where is the work done? How much is paid for time, travel, lodgings, etc., and what happens in the event of injuries? What will the installation entail? We recommend that you summa-rize the work to be done in one or two paragraphs (perhaps in the form of a job summary or invoice) and attach this information as an exhibit to the agreement. If you wish to include an installation services provision in your license agreement, a sample appears below.

Licensor shall supervise and assist in the installation of equipment as described in Exhibit _____ [whatever letter you have chosen for the service agreement exhibit, for example, Exhibit B]. Licensor's installation services will be performed by _____ [name of Licensor or Licensor's employee who will perform services]. Licensee shall bear all costs of travel and accommodations for Licensor and shall pay Licensor on a direct cost basis computed on the number of hours worked and an hourly rate of _____ [hourly rate] for services. Licensee shall indemnify Licensor for any and all claims that may result from such installation services. All payments for services and other expenses shall be paid by Licensee within 30 days of receipt of Licensor's written invoice.

D. Technical Support for the Licensee or for End Users

It's possible that either the licensee or buyers of the products (sometimes referred to as end users) will need technical assistance for your invention. This is particularly common in software licensing where the purchaser of the program needs help using the product. Normally, the licensee will provide this technical assistance to consumers of the licensed products. However, in some cases the licensee may ask you to provide technical assistance, either to its tech people (similar to personnel training) or to consumers of the product.

If you are willing to provide tech support, the major issues are:

- What are the hours for tech support?
- If it is phone support, who pays for the phone services?
- If it is via e-mail or the Web, who pays for the computer equipment and services?
- How are you compensated for tech service—that is, by the number of phone calls or e-mail responses, length of phone calls or the total hourly services rendered?

We do not recommend that you get into the tech support business. Tech support is a major commit-ment of time and usually requires hiring contractors or employees. These types of services usually require a separate services agreement detailing tech support responsibilities (discussed above in Section A). How-ever, if you have a limited tech support arrangement or you are simply assisting the licensee's tech support people, the following provisions are suit-able for insertion in your licensing agreement.

For a tech support arrangement in which you assist the licensee's support staff, use a provision such as the sample below.

Technical Support

Licensor will provide reasonable telephone and e-mail assistance to Licensee's designated representatives for Licensee's technical support of licensed products.

If you are providing limited end user tech support, you will need a more detailed provision. The sample provision below should address most of your concerns.

Limited End User Technical Support

Licensor shall, for a period of six months after introduction of the licensed products, provide reasonable ongoing _____ [describe the type of assistance, for example "telephone"] assistance to Licensee. Such support shall relate only to troubleshooting and identification of reported problems relating to the use of the Licensed Products. Telephone technical support shall be provided by Licensor _____ [indicate what days and what times, for example, "Monday through Friday, 12:00 p.m. to 4:00 p.m. PST"] at a rate of [indicate the hourly, weekly or monthly rate, for example "$2,000 per month"] and not to exceed _____ [indicate maximum amount of support hours per week, for example, "20 hours per week of Licensor personnel time"]. In the event that Licensee needs technical support provided by a third party other than Licensor, such determination shall not affect any other provisions of this agreement.

E. Improving, Modifying and Delivering the Invention

The licensee may want you to modify or develop improvements to your invention. For example, say you've invented a gyroscopic device that, when inserted inside a toy, spins the toy. The licensee wants you to modify your invention to fit into different sized toys. Or perhaps the licensee wants you to develop a series of gyroscopic toy ideas based around cartoon characters. These types of services have three major components: defining the services, scheduling delivery of the work and establishing standards for acceptance of the work.

1. What Are Deliverables?

The term deliverables is commonly used to refer to work that you must deliver to the licensee. That is, if you were obligated to modify your invention or make a specific improvement, that would be a deliverable. These deliverables, which are variations on your invention, must be defined in the license agreement, usually in a separate exhibit to the agreement. For example, your services provision would state that the "Licensor shall provide the Deliverables, as defined in Exhibit A."

Define the deliverables with care and be specific as to what you intend to produce for the licensee. How can you be specific? Here are some tips on what to cover:

- **Functionality.** Describe specifically what the deliverable will do, for example: "It is a flashlight that emits light at both ends."
- **Dimensions.** Describe the size or shape, for example: "It is a mini-flashlight, no longer than 6 inches, no wider than 1 square inch and weighing no more than 8 ounces."
- **Materials.** Describe the materials used in manufacturing or use, for example: "It is a mini-flashlight made of case-hardened steel and using two AA batteries."

2. Scheduling and Approving Deliverables

A licensee will want to establish deadlines for the deliverables. These deadlines will probably be tied to payments. For example, you must deliver an improvement within 90 days, at which point you will receive a payment.

An acceptance provision defines the standards that the licensee uses for accepting or rejecting your deliveries. The licensee does not have to accept your deliverable. However, the acceptance provision should establish the criteria used in accepting or rejecting your deliverables and should provide a means for you to correct any errors.

Below is a sample deliverables provision that can be inserted in your license agreement. The two parts of the provision ("Schedules & Development Services" and "Delivery & Approval") attempt to anticipate the problems that result when, for example, the inventor believes the deliverable has been perfected and the licensee thinks the work is insufficient.

Schedules & Development Services

Licensor shall perform certain development services for Licensee. A description of such services, as well as the delivery schedule and the technology or invention to be delivered ("Deliverables"), is provided in Exhibit A. Payments for such services shall be as provided in Exhibit A. Any Deliverable listed in Exhibit A will consist of three stages: (1) concept/planning, (2) design/prototype, and (3) development/test.

Licensor will submit for Licensee's written approval, a budget for each Deliverable. Any expenses or charges in excess of those budgeted must be pre-approved in writing by Licensee. If requested, Licensor will, within 72 hours of notification, meet with Licensee and provide a status report on the schedule and budget for any Deliverable. Licensor will invoice Licensee pursuant to the payment schedule set forth in the appropriate Exhibit A.

Delivery & Approval

Licensee will have five working days from receipt of any Deliverable within which to provide Licensor with written notice of its decision to either accept the Deliverable or to reject it because it fails to conform to the specifications in Exhibit A. If Licensee determines that any Deliverable does not substantially conform to the specifications, Licensee will deliver to Licensor a written report describing each manner that the

Deliverables fail to conform. Licensor will, within five working days of receipt of Licensee's statement, correct such errors or failures and resubmit the Deliverables. After resubmission, Licensee will have a second evaluation period of five working days to either accept the Deliverables or reject them because they still fail to conform to the original specifications. If Licensee again rejects the Deliverables, Licensee may pay a third party to correct such failures and deduct the cost either from Licensor's next scheduled payment from Licensee or from Licensor's future royalties.

Make Sure Deliverables Are Included as Part of Your Invention. The reason you are preparing modifications or improvements or developing related inventions is so that they will become licensed products and you will receive royalties. If you are providing deliverables, your grant or definition of the invention should state that it includes "all Deliverables required under this agreement." (The grant provision, discussed in Chapter 8, defines what rights you have transferred. If you are unsure as to what a grant provision or definition of the invention is, refer to Chapter 8.)

In some cases your modifications or improvements may result in something that goes beyond the rights you granted under the license agreement. For example, say you licensed an invention for controlling stage lighting. The licensee asks you to improve the design of the switch box, and in the process you devise a unique anti-shock safety feature. This is an improvement, but it may also be a separately patentable invention that has implications beyond your invention. Who owns it? That depends on the wording of your license agreement, specifically the definition of the licensed property and the grant provision. Often, the licensee acquires these rights but they revert to the inventor at the end of the license. Sometimes these rights are acquired under a right of first refusal, as explained below. However, absent such provisions, some inventions (particularly if they are independently patentable) may fall outside the license agreement and require a separate licensing agreement. These issues—determining if the licensee can acquire new invention rights—are often complex and require the advice of an intellectual property attorney. See Chapter 18, Help Beyond This Book, for information on how to find an attorney.

3. Independently Created Improvements

It's possible that you may design new features or improvements to your invention without being required to do so by the licensee. That is, they are not categorized as deliverables under your services arrangement. You may have already agreed to license such features or improvements to the licensee. Any such agreement should be included in the grant or invention definition portion of your license—be sure to review it carefully.

Even if it is not included in the grant provision, the licensee may seek a provision asking for the right to license these improvements at competitive license rates. This request to acquire improvements can be phrased in two ways: a right of first refusal or most favored nations clause.

a. Right of First Refusal

If your license agreement includes a right of first refusal, you must give the licensee the first right to license any improvements. This provision is common in an exclusive license. For example, say you license a place-kicking invention to SportsCo, including a right of first refusal to any major improvements or new inventions stemming from the place-kicking invention. You later modify the invention for use as a baseball batting tee. You must show the new invention to SportsCo first, who may then license it. If they reject it and you get a better offer from GameCo, SportsCo will also have a limited period of time to match the GameCo offer. Licensor may identify and develop improvements for the Licensed Property ("Improvements"). Improvements may be patentable or unpatentable, and may also be protected under copyright, trade secret or other legal principles. Licensee shall have the first right to license such Improvements, and the parties shall negotiate in

good faith to reach agreement as to the terms and conditions for such license. In the event that the parties fail to reach agreement and Licensor receives an offer from a third party for the Improvements, Licensee shall have 30 days to notify Licensor whether Licensee desires to execute a license on similar terms and conditions. In the event that Licensee matches any third party terms and conditions, Licensor shall enter into a License Agreement with Licensee and terminate negotiations with any third parties.

New Inventions: Licensing the Unknown. A right of first refusal can also be used for new inventions, not just improvements. For example, the licensee obtains a right of first refusal to license any new inventions you create in the sporting goods field. In that situation, you are tying up rights to an invention that does not yet exist. Whether or not you are willing to make such a commitment as to new inventions depends upon your bargaining power and your trust in the licensee. As a general rule, we recommend against committing inventions that you have not yet created.

b. Most Favored Nations (Most Favored Licensee)

A most favored nations clause (sometimes referred to as a most favored licensee provision) is common in a nonexclusive arrangement and guarantees that a licensee won't be charged any more for the invention or improvements than any other licensee. For example, say you have a nonexclusive license agreement with SportsCo for your place-kicking invention and any improvements. Your SportCo agreement pays you 10% and includes a most favored nations clause. You subsequently improve your invention you execute a nonexclusive license with GameCo with a royalty rate of 9% for the improved place kicker. Under the most favored nation provision, you couldn't enter into this agreement unless you lowered your royalty rate with SportsCo to 9% for the same invention.

Most Favored Nations

Licensor may identify and develop new features or improvements for the Licensed Property ("Improvements"). Improvements may be patentable or unpatentable, and may also be protected under copyright, trade secret or other legal principles. In the event that Licensee enters into a license agreement for these Improvements with a third party licensee ("Third Party License"), Licensor agrees to offer Licensee terms and conditions which are as favorable as those offered to the third party licensee. Licensor shall promptly notify the Licensee of any Third Party License as well as any additional obligations or undertakings in the Third Party License. Licensee shall have 30 days to notify Licensor whether Licensee desires to execute a license on similar terms and conditions.

Most Favored Nations and Confidentiality

Try not to sign a confidentiality agreement that prohibits you from discussing a licensing agreement with anyone. If you are prohibited from discussing an agreement, that can prevent you from fulfilling your obligations under a most favored nations clause. For example, you sign a nonexclusive license with GameCo that prohibits you from discussing the terms with anyone. But you had another license agreement with a most favored nations provision with SportsCo. You're supposed to tell SportsCo about the GameCo terms, but you're prohibited by the confidentiality agreement. What do you do? You, as the licensor, have an obligation to get permission from GameCo to discuss the confidential agreement (known as a waiver), or you must draft the agreement so that you can discuss the third party agreement with any other licensee who has licensed the same invention.

4. Improvements by the Licensee: Grant Backs

It's possible that, in the process of preparing licensed products, the licensee may improve your invention by adding new features or functions that help sell the product. The licensee owns these improvements because it has paid for and supervised the work. That does not mean that the licensee can freely copy your invention when using the improvements. It only means that in the event your patent expires, the licensee will own the right to use the improvements with the invention—which is now in the public domain.

If you are dealing with trade secrets, trademarks or copyrightable works, you can control the right to modifications to your work by including a grant back provision in your license agreement. A grant back provision allows you to reclaim rights to any licensee improvements. For example, if you have a trade secret or create a copyrightable computer program and the licensee wants to modify it, you can insist: a) that you will own all such modifications after the license expires, or b) that the licensee will grant you the nonexclusive right to use the improvements without having to pay royalties.

It's not quite as simple with a patented invention. Although grant back provisions for patentable improvements are usually upheld by the courts, there are cases where they are declared invalid. Generally, a grant back will not be upheld if a court determines that it is anti-competitive. What's anti-competitive? It would be anti-competitive if you are demanding an exclusive grant back as a condition of the license for a patented invention, and as a result the licensee was discouraged from making any innovations (knowing it would later have to give them up). Normally, invalid grant backs occur when large companies stifle competition, for example, in cases where the grant back is linked to illegal price fixing. For more information on these anti-competitive rules (referred to as patent misuse), see Chapter 17. ■

16

Handling the Licensee's Agreement

What happens if the licensee wants to make substantial changes to your license agreement or, instead, wants to furnish you with its own license agreement? How do you use the information in this book to interpret other agreements? In this chapter we show you how to analyze modifications or agreements prepared by the licensee. You should read this chapter if you answer "yes" to either of the following questions:

- Has the licensee furnished you with a list of requested changes to your license agreement?
- Has the licensee furnished you with its own license agreement?

In this chapter we offer advice on how to deal with modifications to a license agreement. We provide tips on dealing with a licensee's suggested changes to your agreement, and we also provide a system that should enable you to identify and modify important provisions in a licensee's agreement.

A. Dealing With Suggested Changes

It is rare for a licensee to accept a license agreement without requesting at least some modifications. You should expect to receive a list of suggested changes, which may be several pages long. The company may have even retyped your entire agreement in a redline/strikeout version (see sidebar) that indicates new additions and material to be stricken.

Some of the requested changes will be stylistic. That is, the licensee may want you to move provisions, use different terminology or place all of the definitions at the front of the agreement. You should feel comfortable making stylistic changes. The bulk of the changes, however, will be substantive. These are changes that affect the rights or obligations of each party. As for substantive changes, be prepared to spend several hours reviewing the requests and comparing them to the material in this book.

1. You Can't Always Get What You Want

As we have explained in other portions of this book, you may not always be able to obtain the ideal provision. Your ability to respond to requested modifications is a reflection of your bargaining power. Very often you, the licensor, have little bargaining power, and you will be forced to accept a modification. There's nothing wrong with giving in on contract issues provided that you understand what you are giving up and that you are not giving up something that will substantially impair your ability to profit from the license.

EXAMPLE: The licensee requests a change to your jurisdiction provision (the provision that states where litigation or arbitration must be filed). The licensee is adamant about using its home state, Michigan. You have offered a compromise—each party can file a respective lawsuit in its home state—and that's been rejected by the licensee. You weigh the consequences and although it's not your first choice, you decide you are willing to accept the risk of traveling to Michigan for the lawsuit.

**Interactive Toy
No. 6,253,058**

A Brief Excursion Into Legalese

Throughout this book, we have tried to shield you from unnecessary legalese—the contrived language commonly used in contracts. However, you may encounter such language in license provisions presented to you or in proposed modifications to your agreement. Below are some common examples and translations. For other terms or phrases, consult a legal dictionary or an unabridged English dictionary.

As provided herein .... As provided in this agreement

Hereinafter referred to ..... Referred to in this agreement

Heretofore granted .... Previously granted

Notwithstanding .... In spite of

Foregoing .... Previous

Deemed .... Considered

2. Review, Evaluate and Negotiate Modifications

When you receive requested changes to your agreement, evaluate each request by comparing it to the information in this book. For instance, if there is a requested change to the indemnity section, review indemnity in Chapter 12 and evaluate what is at issue. Then comes the hard part—deciding whether you want to make the change.

Below are two common methods of handling requested changes:

- **The "Yes, No, Maybe" approach.** Make three lists: "Yes" (the changes you will make), "No" (the changes you won't make) and "Maybe" (the changes about which you are undecided or upon which you are willing to negotiate). When negotiating with the licensee, use your "Maybe" list for bargaining purposes. For example, if the licensee won't agree to one of your "Yes" or "No" items, offer to give in on a "Maybe."

- **The "Most Important" approach.** Make a list of the things that are most important to you in a license agreement and list them in order of importance. For example:
  - size of the advance
  - size of the royalty
  - location for lawsuits
  - arbitration as method for resolving disputes.

Review the licensee's suggested changes and categorize them according to your list. This helps to sort the modifications in order of importance to you. Negotiate accordingly. Fight hardest for those items that are highest on your list, and be more flexible on items that are not as important.

What Is Redline/Strikeout?

Redline/strikeout refers to a method commonly used by attorneys to revise agreements. Before word processors were commonly used, contracts went through several drafts and new sections that were to be added to a contract were underlined in red ink. A dark line striking out text signified that this material was to be removed. Word processors are now used to draft and modify agreements, and most popular word processing programs include redline/strikeout features. In the most recent versions of *Microsoft Word*, for example, under the Tools menu you can choose the color and type of marking you want to use for revisions. If you wish, the computer will merge these revisions into a clean (or unmarked) draft.

B. Evaluating an Agreement Presented to You

What do you do if the licensee insists that you use its license agreement? Deciphering a company's contract is a challenge, even for experienced attorneys.

If you have turned directly to this chapter without reviewing any other material in this book, you may have some difficulty. In order to evaluate the agreement, you will need some familiarity with common licensing provisions. We suggest you review the sample agreement in Chapter 8 before you begin.

In order to analyze a new agreement, we suggest the following strategies:

- *Don't freak out!* Be prepared to spend several hours making your analysis.
- Make a photocopy of the agreement.
- Locate the major provisions (as discussed below) and label them in the margin.
- Compare each provision with the language suggested in this book.
- Underline everything you don't like or don't understand.
- Prepare a chart, listing the number of the provision and your concerns about that section.
- Convert the chart into a response letter detailing your requested changes for the licensee.

Ready to begin? You'll need a clean (unmarked) photocopy of the license agreement, a pen and a ruler (for underlining). Your job, should you choose to accept it, is to untangle the provisions and locate the key ones. Unfortunately, there are no rules for the ordering and placement of provisions in a license agreement. Many agreements seem haphazardly organized. That is, the order doesn't make any sense. The following checklist offers a methodology for scrutinizing the licensee's proposed license agreement.

Have You Got a Scanner?

If you have a scanner (or access to a scanner), consider scanning the licensee's agreement into your computer's word processing program. It is much easier to search for keywords and terms using your computer. In addition, it's a lot easier to request changes. Instead of having to retype sections, you can copy the appropriate provision and use redline/strikeout to add or take out language.

Below is a list of the provisions you should be looking for as well as keywords that often identify the provisions. The list also includes some tips for evaluating the provisions once you've found them, though analyzing the provisions is more fully discussed in Chapters 8, 9, 11, 12, 13, 14 and 15. Trying to locate phrases within a mass of legal verbiage can be a tedious job, but it will get easier as you go along. The procedure is a little bit like putting together a jigsaw puzzle; once you find a few key parts, the rest fall into place.

C. Evaluating the Provisions and Suggesting Changes

Once you have identified the key provisions, you must evaluate each section and decide if the language should be modified. This task requires a lot of intellectual labor. In fact, the work may seem incredibly daunting. After all, you're an inventor, not a lawyer. If you are becoming tense, confused and frustrated, then consider hiring an attorney.

If, however, you decide to proceed, you will need to analyze each provision and decide if it adequately protects your interests. If it does not, you'll need to decide what language should be added or stricken in order to bring the agreement in line with your standards.

There's no limit to the number of modifications you can request, but you'll probably have more success if you limit your requests to the most important revisions (that is, those changes which directly affect your rights or finances).

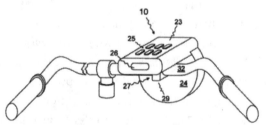

Voice Alert System for Use on Bicycles
No. 6,317,036

Checklist for Reviewing a License Agreement

Contract Provision & Comments	What to Look For
1. Introductory Statement	Keywords: Whereas, Introduction This is usually the first few paragraphs of the agreement and often includes the term "Whereas" (as in, "Whereas the parties agree to enter into a license agreement"). This statement should accurately indicate the intentions, names and addresses of the parties. See Chapter 8 for more information.
2. The Property	Keywords: Property, Invention, Concept, Know-How, Technology Locate the word or phrase used to define your invention ("Invention," "Property" or similar names). This term should accurately describe your invention. See Chapter 8 for more information.
3. Licensed Products	Keywords: Licensed Product, Licensed Goods, Products, Licensed Property Locate the word or phrase defining the products the licensee will sell ("Licensed Products" or similar phrase). This term should accurately describe what will be sold. It's possible that a licensee may use the same term for the invention as for the licensed products. See Chapter 8 for more information.
4. The Grant of Rights	Keywords: Grant, License, Exclusive, Nontransferable, Nonassignable, Perpetual Find the grant language. It should be somewhere on the first page. You're looking for terms such as "exclusive," "perpetual" or "worldwide." This language should reflect the boundaries of your grant and may include information about the territory. See Chapter 8 for more information.
5. Sublicense	Keyword: Sublicense There may or may not be a reference to sublicensing. Often sublicensing references are found in the grant section, although sometimes they are located in the payment section or even in the section regarding assignments. If there is no provision, make a note to include one. See Chapter 8 for more information.

Checklist for Reviewing a License Agreement (continued)	
Contract Provision & Comments	**What to Look For**
6. Reservation of Rights	Keywords: Reserve, Reservation There may or may not be a reference to "reservation of rights." If there is no reference, make a note to add it. For more information, review Chapter 8.
7. Territory	Keywords: Territory, Region, Area, Worldwide It's not unusual for the territorial restrictions to be included in the grant section rather than in a separate territory section. You're looking for any reference to the geographic location of the grant (words such as "world-wide" or "North America"). For more information, review Chapter 8.
8. Term	Keywords: Term, Length, Duration, Renew, Initial Term Term refers to the length of the agreement; it's not unusual for this information to be found in the grant or termination section. You're looking for any reference to the length or renewability of the agreement. For more information, review Chapter 8.
9. Payment	Keywords: Payment, Royalty, Advance, Consideration, Guaranteed Minimum Annual Royalty, Lump Sum, Nonrecoupable, Net Sales, Per Use The payment section is usually in the first half of the agreement. You need to isolate information about advances and royalties. If applicable, look for guaranteed minimum annual royalty payments and sublicensing revenues. If you are selling a product (and not a technology licensed per use), then you will need to find the definition of net sales. If you are licensing technology based upon usage, then there should be a method for tracking usage. For more information, review Chapter 9.
10. Payment Statements	Keywords: Statement, Accounting, Quarterly, Annually You are looking for a provision that details the contents of the payment statement and when it will be mailed. This information is usually incorporated in or near the payment section. For more information, review Chapter 9.

Checklist for Reviewing a License Agreement (continued)

Contract Provision & Comments	What to Look For
11. Late Payments and Audit Rights	Keywords: Audit, Late Payment, Accounting, Inspect If it's not in the payment section, then somewhere nearby should be a section explaining what happens when payments are late and what your rights are in the event you need to audit the licensee's records. If you can't find it, it's possible that the licensee may have deliberately left this information out of the agreement. Make a note to request a modification to include audits and late payments. For more information, review Chapter 9.
12. Warranties and Indemnification	Keywords: Warrant, Warranty, Represent, Covenant, Indemnify, Indemnification The warranties (or contractual promises) may be in one section, or they may be spread throughout the agreement. You are looking for statements that start with "Licensor warrants..." or "Licensee warrants and represents..." or some similar variation. If they are spread throughout the agreement, you'll need to index them for your own reference so you will have a list of all the warranties that you are making. Indemnifications, which are your promises to defend lawsuits, are usually grouped together and always use the word "indemnify." For example, "Licensee indemnifies for any and all claims..." You should list all of your indemnification obligations. You should be searching for language describing who pays for these defensive lawsuits and how the payments are calculated. Compare the provisions to those in Chapter 12.
13. Intellectual Property Protection	Kewords: Registration, Intellectual Property, Patent, Copyright, Trademark, Notice, Infringement Somewhere in the license agreement you should be able to find references to the following: • Registration of patents, copyrights or trademarks (U.S. or foreign). Who has the right to register, and who pays for the registration? For more information, review Chapter 12.

Checklist for Reviewing a License Agreement (continued)

Contract Provision & Comments	What to Look For
13. Intellectual Property Protection (continued)	• Infringement against third parties. What happens when someone copies your invention? There should be a section discussing who pays for offensive lawsuits against infringers of your invention. (Note: this is different from a defensive lawsuit when someone claims your invention is infringing. That would be covered in indemnification.) For more information, review Chapter 12.
	• Compliance with laws. Look for a provision stating that the licensee will comply with intellectual property laws. If it's missing, make a note to add it. For more information, review Chapter 12.
14. Exploitation	Keywords: Exploit, Commence, Offer for Sale, Anti-Shelving
	There should be some reference as to when the licensee must commence sales and that the licensee must continue to sell the invention. If not, make a note to include this provision. For more information, review Chapter 12.
15. Samples and Quality Control	Keywords: Samples, Examples, Prototypes, Quality
	Have you agreed upon a samples or quality control provision? Locate the reference to production samples. If not, make a note to include this provision. For more information, review Chapter 12.
16. Insurance	Keywords: Insurance, Coverage, Claims, Product Liability
	The licensee should maintain adequate insurance. This requirement may be in its own section, or it may be located in a provision such as licensee obligations. For more information, review Chapter 12.
17. Confidentiality	Keywords: Confidentiality, Nondisclosure, Trade Secrets, Information
	Confidentiality provisions are usually labeled with obvious titles such as "Confidentiality," Nondisclosure" or "Trade Secrets." For more information, review Chapter 7.

Checklist for Reviewing a License Agreement (continued)

Contract Provision & Comments	What to Look For
18. Termination	Keywords: Terminate, Termination, Breach, Default, Insolvency Information about termination is usually either in the front of the agreement in the term section, or it is near the back in a separate termination section. You are looking for language describing the conditions for termination. In particular, look for language describing each party's right to terminate. Compare this language with our suggested grounds for termination in Chapter 13.
19. Post-Termination	Keywords: Sell-Off, Return, Molds, Models After the license ends, each party may have additional obligations. The licensor may want a sell-off period (a limited time to sell remaining products), and you may want materials returned. Look for a section that details these and other post-termination rights. For more information, review Chapter 13.
20. Survival	Keywords: Survive, Survival As you read through the agreement, various provisions may include a statement such as: "The obligations of this section shall survive any termination of this Agreement." Make a list of these surviving provisions. It's also possible that there may be a separate section entitled "Survival." Compare the list of surviving provisions with our recommendations in Chapter 13.
21. Attorneys' Fees	Keywords: Arising, Attorney, Fees It's very possible that there is no attorneys' fees provision in your agreement. Many licensees do not use them in standard agreements. The term "attorneys' fees" may appear in various sections, such as indemnity or offensive litigation sections. However, what you are looking for is a section which states something to the effect that in the event of a lawsuit arising from the agreement, the prevailing party is entitled to attorneys' fees. For more information, review Chapter 14.
22. Arbitration or Mediation	Keywords: Arbitrate, Arbitration, Arbitrator, Mediation It's possible that there is no arbitration or mediation provision. For more information, review Chapter 14.

Checklist for Reviewing a License Agreement (continued)	
Contract Provision & Comments	**What to Look For**
23. Governing Law	Keywords: Govern, State, Controlling Law This is usually one sentence near the end of the agreement and includes language such as: "This agreement will be governed by the law of the state of ___." For more information, review Chapter 14.
24. Jurisdiction	Keywords: Consent, Bound, Jurisdiction, State It's possible that there is no jurisdiction provision. If there is one, it will be near the end of the agreement (usually near the governing law provision) and will include language such as: "The parties consent to the exclusive jurisdiction of the courts located in ___." This provision indicates where you have to file or defend lawsuits. For more information, review Chapter 14.
25. Assignability	Keywords: Assign, Assignment Look for any references to the licensee's ability to assign the agreement. This language may be in the back of the agreement near the general contract provisions, or it may be in the grant section (usually near the front). (Note: the word "assign" may appear in other contexts—for example, an assignment of patent rights—however, you are looking for references to assignment of the agreement.) Compare the contract language with our recommendations in Chapters 8 and 14.
26. New Inventions	Keywords: Most Favored Nation, Right of First Refusal, Improvement Sometimes a licensee wants to claim a right to your next invention or to improvements you make on your invention. An arrangement can be established giving the licensee the first right to review and license these new inventions. This right is sometimes referenced by the use of language such as "favored nation" or "right of first refusal." Look for similar language. For more information, review Chapter 15.
27. Grant Back of Improvements	Keywords: Grant Back, Improvement Who owns the improvements that the licensee makes to your invention? A grant back provision transfers ownership to you. It's possible that there is no such provision in the agreement. Since there are important legal issues tied to such provisions, you should review Chapter 15.

Checklist for Reviewing a License Agreement (continued)	
Contract Provision & Comments	**What to Look For**
28. Escrow Provisions	Keywords: Escrow, Deposit Although it's not a common provision, it's possible that you and the licensee need an escrow provision. An escrow account is a secure location where trade secrets or payments are stored until certain conditions are met for their release. Escrow provisions are easily identifiable by the use of the word "escrow." For more information, review Chapter 14.
29. Exhibits and Attachments	Keywords: Exhibit, Attachment, Reference Every attachment or exhibit is an enforceable part of the agreement. As you read through the agreement, underline every reference to an exhibit or attachment. Make a list of these references and make sure that the appropriate exhibit is included. For example, if the agreement states that a definition is included in Exhibit B, verify that this is correct. You'll be surprised at how often the information is incorrect.
30. Miscellaneous Provisions	Keywords: General, Miscellaneous (or any of the individual headings provided below) As we explained in Chapter 14, the following are a group of contract provisions that are usually included near the end of every agreement. Sometimes they are grouped in one section titled "General Provisions" or "Miscellaneous Provisions," and sometimes they are listed separately.
a. **Waiver**	Keywords: Waiver, Failure This provision protects your contract rights. For more information, review Chapter 14.
b. **Invalidity**	Keywords: Invalid, Effect, Sever, Omit, Affect This provision allows you to preserve your agreement even if there is an unenforceable section. For more information, review Chapter 14.
c. **Entire Understanding**	Keywords: Complete, Entire, Full, Oral This establishes that this agreement is the complete understanding between the parties. For more information, review Chapter 14.

Checklist for Reviewing a License Agreement (continued)

Contract Provision & Comments	What to Look For
d. Attachments & Exhibits	Keywords: Attachment, Exhibit, Incorporated, Reference This guarantees that exhibits and attachments are an enforceable part of the agreement. For more information, review Chapter 14.
e. Notices	Keywords: Notice, Mailed, Sufficient This provides a method for sending and getting notices about the agreement. For more information, review Chapter 14.
f. No Joint Venture	Keywords: Joint Venture, Agent, Partner This confirms that you and the licensee are not partners or joint venturers. For more information, review Chapter 14.
31. Service Provisions	The following provisions are not in every license agreement. Their presence depends upon the nature of the technology or services provided. (Service provisions and service agreements are explained in detail in Chapter 15.) Many of these provisions may be grouped together under one heading, such as "Licensor Services." If you are performing services for the licensee, look for the following, if applicable.
a. Installation	Keywords: Install, Installation Look for language describing your obligations and payment for installing equipment. For more information, review Chapter 15.
b. Technical Assistance	Keywords: Technical, Support, Assistance Look for language defining technical assistance obligations and payments, if any. For more information, review Chapter 15.
c. Training	Keywords: Train, Teach, Instruct Look for language discussing training obligations and payments. For more information, review Chapter 15.
d. Development	Keywords: Develop, Improve, Modify Look for language dealing with converting your invention into a form that is sold to consumers. Review Chapter 15.
e. Acceptance Provisions	Keywords: Approve, Approval, Accept Look for language that defines the standards that the licensee uses for accepting or rejecting your deliveries. For more information, review Chapter 15.

1. The Modification Chart

We suggest that you prepare a chart like the one below to outline your proposed changes. You'll submit the chart with a short cover letter, which is discussed below. On the left side of the chart are the section numbers and titles of the provisions you're concerned with, and on the right side, a space for comments, questions or modifications. The tone should be civil, not demanding. Refer to yourself as the Licensor, not as "I."

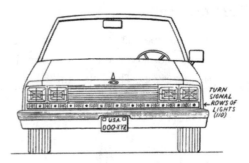

**Vehicle Direction Signal
No. 4,556,862**

Section		Comment
	Introduction	Please strike the address for the Licensor. It is incorrect. The correct address is 14 Lincoln Road, Salmagundo, California 94366.
2	(Term)	Please modify the Term section to state "This Agreement shall commence as of the effective date and shall continue for the life of any patent (and extensions), if any, issued on the Invention, or until terminated in accordance with the provisions of this Agreement."
6.5	(Patents)	Can this section be modified so that the Licensor approves costs for foreign patents?
8	(Late Payments)	Please modify the second line so that it reads, "If Licensee is late in any payment provided for in this Agreement, Licensee shall be liable to Licensor for the sum of the payment plus interest from due date at a rate of 1.5% per month or the maximum rate permitted by law."
10	(Indemnification)	It seems unfair that the Licensor should have to absorb 100% of the indemnification costs. Could we at least limit indemnification to sums that have been paid under the agreement?
11.2	(Termination)	Please strike Section 11.2. It was my understanding that the Licensor had the right to terminate during any year if: (1) Licensee halts sales of the Licensed Products for a period of six continuous months, or (2) annual royalties from sales of the Licensed Products during the preceding year do not exceed $10,000.
11.4	(Termination)	Could you please revise Section 11.4 as follows: "In the event of termination of Agreement, pursuant to this Section 11, no advances shall be repayable to Licensee."
14	(Jurisdiction)	The Licensor should not have to travel to New York for litigation. Either strike the jurisdiction section or provide for jurisdiction in both New York and California.

2. The Cover Letter

You should submit the chart with a short cover letter. Don't use your cover letter for a long dissertation on contract rights. The letter and chart are basically a guide for a meeting or phone conversation in the future.

Dear Mr. Smith:

I've reviewed the license agreement. Attached is a list of comments and proposed modifications. I think we are close to a final agreement and I look forward to discussing it with you. Please call after you have an opportunity to review this letter.

Sincerely,

Licensor

After You've Signed the Agreement

Congratulations! You've signed a license agreement and are ready to sit back and collect royalty checks. Not so fast. The signing of the license agreement creates some new responsibilities. How do you review royalty statements? What does it mean to monitor product quality? How do you schedule due dates? What if things begin to break down between you and the licensee? There are a whole host of business and legal issues that will arise once your license agreement has taken effect.

You will find that the suggestions and advice in this chapter are a mixture of law and common sense. If you are an experienced business person, you are probably familiar with most of this material. However, you should read this chapter if you answer "yes" to any of the following questions:

- Would you like advice on how to schedule contract due dates and intellectual property obligations?
- Will this be the first royalty check you have ever received?
- Would you like advice on how to handle a royalty dispute with the licensee?
- Are you concerned about tax issues regarding income from your license agreement?
- Are you concerned about the licensee's possible breach of the agreement?
- Would you like information about patent misuse?

In this chapter we provide you with information about monitoring your license arrangement after the agreement has been signed. We advise you to create a calendar that indicates the important dates in your license agreement (such as royalty payments and termination), and we help you interpret your royalty statements. We also suggest some strategies if you believe that the royalty reporting is inaccurate (that is, you think you're being ripped off). Finally, we provide some advice on a subject called "patent misuse," which refers to situations in which a patent owner uses a valuable patent to coerce a licensee.

Treat Yourself!

One inventor told us that whenever he licenses a new invention, he uses some portion of the advance to buy something memorable for himself—a piece of artwork or some other special purchase. That way, long after the deal has come and gone (as well as the income) he still has the purchase to remind him that he successfully licensed an invention.

A. Create Your Contract Calendar

After you've celebrated the signing of your licensing agreement, you should take the following steps:

- Make sure you have filed a clean copy of your license agreement (without any marks or scribbles) in your business file.
- Make a list of all relevant due dates as established by the final, signed license agreement (explained below).
- Make a list of relevant dates for intellectual property protection (explained below).

Your license agreement contains many dates and time periods. For example, the licensee must introduce the product to the market by a certain date. Or, perhaps you have a certain time period to review samples and approve them. You may want to summarize these dates and time periods. Below is a chart with the common contract dates. Write the appropriate date on the left side.

Your Licensing Calendar. We suggest that you calendar (that is, write these dates on a calendar) or prepare a chronological list of these dates and keep it in your business file. A computer can also be helpful because most of the popular applications, such as *Quicken* or *Microsoft Office*, include methods of calendaring dates and offer pop-up reminders. You'll find these particularly handy in dealing with contract and intellectual property dates.

License Dates

1. Effective date	This is the date that the license agreement goes into effect. This date is in either the introductory paragraph, the term section or the exhibit attached to your agreement (which contains the essential business terms). Sometimes, the date is on the signature page.
2. Renewal dates	If you have an agreement that is renewable, then the dates for renewal should be listed. These dates would be in either the term section, the termination section or the exhibit attached to your agreement. Locate and chart these dates. For example, if you signed the agreement on September 10, 1998, and the agreement could be renewed in two years, the renewal date would be September 10, 2000.
3. Renewal notice date	A renewal usually occurs when one side notifies the other of its intention to renew (or not to renew), depending on the agreement. Most often, the licensee has the choice to renew. This notice of renewal usually has to be sent to the other side by a certain date, for example, 60 days prior to the renewal date. If the renewal date is September 10, then 60 days prior would be July 11 (counting backwards on a calendar and not counting the date of renewal). That's the date when you must be notified of the renewal decision. This information would be listed in either the term section, the termination section or the exhibit attached to your agreement.
4. Delivery dates	These are dates you have established for deliverables, that is, items you must create and deliver to the licensee. (See Chapter 15 for more information on deliverables.) These dates would be in either the deliverables section, the services section or the exhibit attached to your agreement.
5. Service dates	These are dates you have established for performance of services (see Chapter 15 regarding service provisions). These dates would be listed in either the deliverables section, the services section or the exhibit attached to your agreement.
6. Advance or lump sum payment dates	Make a list of all dates when advances or lump sum payments are due. These dates are in either the payment section or the exhibit attached to your agreement.
7. Royalty payment dates	Royalty payments are commonly made 30, 60 or 90 days after the end of a calendar quarter. For example, if a calendar quarter ended March 31, 1998, and the licensee had 60 days to send you the payment, then the statement and payment would be due on May 30, 1998. These dates are in the payment section or the exhibit attached to your agreement.
8. Dates to complain about royalty statements	Generally, a licensor has a limited time to complain about the accuracy of a royalty statement. For example, if you establish a complaint time limit of one year, then you cannot complain after that date. Calculate the period of time based upon when you should receive each statement. The time period is usually in the audit or the payment section of the agreement.
9. Date for introduction of licensed products	This would be the date that the licensee has agreed to offer the licensed product for sale. This may also be the date that the licensee has agreed to show the licensed product at a certain trade show or exhibition. This date is usually found in the exploitation section or in the exhibit attached to your agreement.
10. Termination date	If there is a fixed termination date, calendar it. This date would be in either the term section, the termination section or the exhibit attached to your agreement.
11. Delivery of insurance information	If applicable, this would be the date by which the licensee must give you proof of insurance. This date would be in the insurance section.

Intellectual Property Protection Dates

As a diligent protector of your patents, trademarks and copyrights, remember to stay on top of important dates such as filing deadlines, patent expiration deadlines and dates when you should pay maintenance fees. Since it is possible to search the patent office abstracts for free, you may also want to calendar periodic searches to check for new inventions that are similar to your own. If you have a federal trademark registration, remember to calendar filing dates for trademark renewal and incontestability. For more information on patent deadlines, review Nolo's *Patent It Yourself,* by attorney David Pressman. For information on trademark deadlines, review Nolo's *Trademark: Legal Care for Your Business and Product Name,* by Stephen Elias.

B. Dealing With Royalty Statements

Your first experience with a royalty statement may not be as you imagined. For example, you rip open the envelope, toss aside the statement and look at the check. *$687.00???* How can it be so small? You find the statement and pore over the columns trying to decipher the codes and numbers. If they make you feel dizzy, you're not alone. Royalty statements can be a confusing experience. This section offers some advice on how to handle them.

Here are some general tips that should help you stay on top of your royalty statements.

- First, save the envelope in which the statement was mailed and staple it to the document. This will verify the date of your receipt.
- Second, examine the statement date and statement period for the payments. (The statement date is the date the royalty statement was completed—not necessarily the date it was mailed.) The statement period is the period covered by the statement, for example, 4th Quarter 1998. There may also be a period end date which indicates the final date of the period for which the statement is issued. Review your agreement to make sure that you are receiving a statement for the appropriate period. For example, if your quarterly report includes six months of activity, then there is a mistake.
- Third, compare the royalty rates in the statement with the rates that are established in your contract to make sure they are accurate.
- Fourth, look at the deductions and credits and compare them to what is permitted under the agreement. If you are confused about the size of a deduction, particularly if there is no explanation, request an itemized accounting for it.
- Fifth, find the sales figures (often titled "Units Sold"), or if you are paid per use, then look for the appropriate number (sometimes titled "Usage"). Locate the sublicensing revenue, if any.
- Finally, do the math. Prepare your own spreadsheet and verify that the statement is correct.

1. Common Royalty Problems

Most royalty statement errors are the results of negligence, not intentional acts of wrongdoing. The following are the types of errors that are commonly blamed on computer problems:

- incorrect royalty rates
- incorrect listing of deductions
- indecipherable statements.

If you have one of these problems or if you just don't understand the structure of the statement, call the licensee and ask for an explanation. Someone in the accounting department should be able to provide the information. If no one does, don't get mad. Ask for the supervisor or manager of the department. Keep trying to move up the chain of command. When you can't go any farther and if you still aren't satisfied, get the name and position of the final person you have spoken with and confirm your conversation with a letter. Keep a copy. We don't advise using a strident or angry tone in your confirming letter. For what to do next, review the section below on resolving disputes.

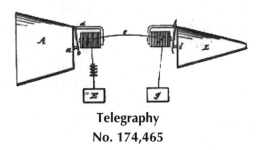

**Telegraphy
No. 174,465**

2. What If the Sales Figures Appear Inaccurate?

If you believe the licensee is misstating sales figures, you can begin your inquiry informally, for example, with a phone conversation. Tell the licensee or your contact at the licensee company that the sales figures seem low. Is there any way to verify the numbers? You should avoid accusing the licensee of wrongdoing. First, you may be wrong. Second, the misstatement may be a result of negligence or a technical problem such as a computer error, not intentional wrongdoing.

If this does not satisfy you and you still want to pursue the matter, you should have more than a hunch before proceeding. Do you have any other means of determining sales? Some trade magazines publish sales figures and charts. Some research companies can also obtain this information for you. It may also be available through company reports on online services such as Lexis/Nexis (see Chapter 6 for information on business research). You may want to consult with an accountant or lawyer familiar with invention licensing. (For more information on attorneys, see Chapter 18, Help Beyond This Book.)

You Have a Limited Period of Time to Complain

Most audit provisions establish a limited time period to challenge the accuracy of a royalty statement. Usually, this period is 12 or 24 months. Although we do not urge you to rush into a royalty dispute, you should be aware of these time limitations and make any necessary challenge in a timely manner. Otherwise, you may lose the right to question the statement.

3. Bringing in the Auditors

If you have exhausted every other method of obtaining accurate information regarding your suspicions, you may have to audit the licensee. An audit should be performed *only* as a last resort. It is fairly expensive (you're paying an accountant's hourly rate), and it is likely to generate considerable ill will. Since an audit can be expensive, you shouldn't begin it unless you have good reason to believe you'll recoup your expenses. Consult with an attorney or accountant knowledgeable in invention licensing and get an opinion as to the reasonableness of an audit (see Chapter 18, Help Beyond This Book).

In the event that you do hire an auditor, you should cap the costs. That is, you and the auditor should agree on the maximum to be spent on the audit. Under the model audit provision we provided in Chapter 9, the licensee pays your auditor's expenses in the event of a substantial discrepancy. In the model agreement, we suggested that the licensee pay expenses if the audit uncovers a difference of $1,000.

You will need to send an audit letter to the licensee as notification that you are seeking an audit. Below is an example.

Sample Audit Request Letter

Dear _____:

I have received your royalty statement dated _____ *[date of statement].* The amount of that statement, _____ *[indicate amount if any],* does not seem to reflect the sales success attributed to the licensed products. Since our previous attempts at resolving this issue have failed, I have no other choice but to exercise my rights under the audit provision of our license agreement, dated _____ *[date of agreement].*

I have contacted _____ *[name of CPA or accountant who will perform the audit]* to perform the audit. My auditor will be in contact with you shortly, and I hope that you will provide all of the information requested and permitted under our agreement.

My auditor will need access to all company books and records which relate to the agreement and to sales of the licensed products, including work sheets, foreign and domestic ledgers, calculations and statements and any other documents accessible to outside auditors of your company operating in accordance with the Generally Accepted Audit Standards (GAAS). In addition, the auditor will need access to company personnel who maintain the financial records and can answer questions that may arise.

Sincerely,

Licensor

C. Resolving Licensing Disputes

Licensing is not always a smooth experience, and you may have disputes with your licensee. The key to resolving disputes is negotiation—the same type of negotiation you used to work out your license in the first place. (Review Chapter 10 for suggestions on negotiation.)

1. Creating a Paper Trail

Always start with informal attempts at resolving disputes. Use the telephone or meet in person. If these attempts fail, you need to create a paper trail. That is, you need to build a series of documents that demonstrate that you have made every reasonable attempt to resolve your dispute.

Below is an example of a letter that could be used after informal methods to resolve the dispute have failed. Always set a date by which you would like to resolve the matter. You will also note that the letter does not threaten litigation. The letter writer states he will "consider exercising rights" and hopes to resolve the dispute "amicably." The reason for this is explained in the section on declaratory actions, described below.

Dear Tom:

In recent conversations with Jim Smith at SportCo, I have been unable to resolve a dispute arising from our licensing agreement dated February 1, 2002. According to the agreement, I was to receive an advance payment of $10,000 on March 1, 2002. That payment was not made.

I have suggested several solutions to resolve this problem, including a series of payments spread over three months. However, none of these suggestions have been accepted. As a result, we seem to have a serious problem affecting the license. I am hopeful that we can resolve this amicably within the next month. Unless we can resolve it, I must consider exercising my rights under the dispute resolution procedures in the agreement. Please contact me after you have reviewed this letter.

Sincerely,
Licensor

2. Avoiding Declaratory Actions

Normally, the party that is wronged or injured brings the lawsuit in their state of residence (unless the jurisdiction provision in your agreement provides otherwise). However, sometimes the other party, anticipating the lawsuit, files what is known as a declaratory action in their state of residence. A declaratory action is when one party goes to court claiming there is a dispute and asks for a declaration of each party's rights.

In order to bring a declaratory action, there must be proof of an actual controversy. An actual controversy exists when there is an explicit threat of a lawsuit or, to use legal lingo, when one party has a "reasonable apprehension of litigation."

This brings us back to your letter to the licensee. If the letter threatens legal action—for example, "If you do not pay the money next week, I will sue you in federal court"—then the licensee may file a declaratory action in its state of residence claiming there is an actual controversy. That is, even though you're the one who has suffered, you will have to go to the licensee's home state to fight. To avoid this possibility, we suggest that you do not threaten litigation in your letter and always leave open an option to resolve the dispute amicably.

If your agreement has a mandatory arbitration clause then you *can't* threaten litigation. You must proceed to arbitration. See Chapter 14 for more on arbitration provisions.

3. When Letters Fail

If letters have failed to resolve the problem, it's probably time to consult with an attorney knowledgeable in licensing inventions. A lawyer will be able to help you determine whether you should exercise your dispute resolution rights under the agreement. That is, will you file a lawsuit? Or, if your license agreement includes an arbitration provision, will you instigate arbitration? It can be very difficult to judge the merits of your case and the likelihood of winning in litigation or arbitration.

An experienced lawyer's advice is as important in deciding whether to sue as in representing you during the suit. If you need assistance in locating an attorney, see Chapter 18, Help Beyond This Book.

One issue that may be important is attorneys' fees. If you have an attorneys' fees provision in your agreement, you'll recover fees if you prevail. However, if you lose the dispute, you may be obligated to pay the licensee's attorneys' fees. Review these provisions in your agreement.

No matter how strongly you believe that you are in the right and should win a lawsuit, it is possible that an attorney will disagree with your assessment. If that is the case and you still feel strongly, get a second opinion. If two attorneys disagree with your assessment of the problem, you may have to face the fact that you should drop the dispute.

D. Avoiding Patent Misuse and Illegal Agreements

Sometimes the parties to a license agreement may unintentionally create an agreement that is illegal. In cases where the license agreement contains an illegal provision, a court may void the license agreement or terminate patent rights. For example, a grant back provision, as discussed in Chapter 15, may violate the law and may create an illegal license agreement. Illegal grant backs, tying agreements and similar problems are known as patent misuse. Below we discuss misuse and related issues and how to avoid these problems.

Antitrust Laws and Patent Misuse

Patent misuse is a subcategory of the antitrust laws. Antitrust laws prevent powerful companies from using their market strength to stifle competition. For example, if all of the manufacturers of cold remedies joined together and conspired to fix prices, this would be unfair to consumers and would violate antitrust laws.

1. Tying Arrangements

Patent misuse occurs when a patent holder coerces a licensee into an unfair or unethical business arrangement. How can a patent owner coerce a licensee? The most common example is called tying. Under an illegal tying arrangement, a licensee of a patented device is forced to purchase an additional unpatented product. For example, the licensee is told that if it wants the patented donut-making machine, it must also buy the licensor's donut dough.

Since misuse laws are aimed at patent bullies, you may not feel they have much importance to you. After all, you haven't coerced anyone to license your invention. Unfortunately, even if you have acted properly, you may still be subject to these issues because a licensee may claim patent misuse as a basis to cancel the license agreement. Patent misuse is commonly pleaded as a defense to breach of a patent license agreement. So if you sued your licensee for breaching your agreement—say for non-payment of royalties—you might suddenly find yourself in the position of having to prove that you did not misuse your patent.

For example, say you licensed a method for measuring blood pressure that uses a patented monitor and an unpatented wristband. After two years, the licensee stops making payments. You sue, but the licensee defends itself claiming patent misuse. The licensee argues that you engaged in an unfair tying arrangement because you forced it to use your wristband when it could have bought a cheaper imitation from a competitor. You are suddenly on the defensive—forced to prove that the wristbands are protectible and that the law permits you to jointly license both these items.

Fortunately, in 1988, after lobbying by patent owners, Congress enacted the Patent Misuse Amendments, which helped patent owners by giving the courts more leeway in determining if an arrangement is fair. In April 1995, the Federal Trade Commission and the Justice Department also announced new antitrust licensing guidelines that establish a safety zone for intellectual property licensing arrangements for licensors whose inventions account for less than 20% of a relevant market. For example, if your licensed product accounts for less than 20% of the market, there is a presumption that your tying arrangement is legal and not anti-competitive. This is only a presumption, not a hard-and-fast rule, but it helps to make litigation more predictable for smaller companies owning patents.

In addition, the Supreme Court has determined that it is permissible to require a licensee to purchase non-staple goods from a patent holder. Non-staple goods are goods designed to carry out the patented processes, with little or no use outside of the patented processes. For example, it was legal for the patent owners of a glucose-measuring device to require licensees to purchase its blood glucose test strips. The strips were separately patented and were non-staple items in that they had little use outside of the glucose-measuring process.

In summary, if you are licensing a patented invention and you are linking the license to the sale or license of another device, you should be aware of rules regarding tying arrangements. Your agreement will be legal and enforceable if you can demonstrate any of the following:

- you did not coerce the arrangement based upon your marketing power
- you offered the licensee reasonable alternative options to obtain the tied product, or
- the tied product is a non-staple—a product designed to carry out the patented processes that has little or no use outside of the patented process.

Tie-Ins and Tie-Outs

There are two types of tying arrangements. A tie-in requires that the licensee buy a separate product from the licensor. A tie-out prevents the licensee from purchasing or using a separate product made by a different company.

2. Illegal License Length and Hybrid Licenses

Throughout this book, we have advised against creating a license that lasts longer than the term of your patent. For example, if there are 15 years remaining on your patent, you should not negotiate for a license of 20 years. Why not? Because after the patent expires, the licensee should no longer have to pay you for the invention, which will then be in the public domain, free for all to make, use and sell. Therefore, you are misusing your patent when you demand a term that is longer than the length of the patent.

If you are not licensing a patent, this is not an issue. That is, for copyrights, trademarks and trade secrets, the license can extend for decades.

There are, however, two situations in which the license can last longer than the length of a particular patent. The first situation occurs if your license includes *all* patents that may issue during the term. As we explained in Chapter 13, this type of grant is terminated "upon the expiration of the last remaining patent."

The second situation occurs if you are licensing both patents *and* trade secrets, trademarks or copyrights (known as a hybrid license). If you are licensing a package of intellectual property rights, the license can continue for as long as protection exists for any one of the properties. In the case of trade secrets and trademarks, that can be perpetual (forever). However, in a hybrid license, it may be patent misuse to continue to receive the same royalty rate *after* the expiration of the patent. That is unfair because you are requiring the licensee to pay for a patent that is now in the public domain. The royalty rate must decrease in relation to the value of the expired patent. This is done by allocating varying values for each item (such as patents and trademarks) licensed.

For example, say you created a peel-off formula for nail polish and sold it under the trademark *Striptease*. The formula is patented and the trademark is federally registered. You license the patent and

trademark to a major cosmetic firm and your agreement contains two royalty rates: a) a fixed rate for licensed products, and b) a second rate in the event that the patent expires or is determined invalid. This second rate would apply only to use of the trademark *Striptease*. A sample hybrid royalty provision is provided in Chapter 9.

3. Preventing Development of Competitive Products

We advise against including a provision that bars the licensee from developing a similar invention. In other words, you should not forbid the licensee from independently creating a competing invention or technology. You can prohibit the licensee from any unauthorized use of your intellectual property rights in creating a competitive device. But you should not prohibit independent invention activity. A provision that bars development of competing products is likely to be challenged as patent misuse (or copyright misuse—see below).

E. The Taxman Cometh

You may have already received tax advice regarding license payments. If not, you should consult with an accountant or tax expert. Although detailed tax advice is beyond the scope of this book, below are some general tax concepts and principles.

1. Ordinary Income vs. Capital Gains

As we explained in Chapter 1, your licensing income will probably be taxed as an ordinary gain, that is, treated like ordinary business income. You may claim deductions or credits where applicable, but you must pay taxes on all income you receive in each year. Capital gains treatment—which offers some tax benefits—is only available when you sell "all substantial rights" to your patent. This would occur in a sale or an exclusive license in which you retain no rights. A typical license agreement, because it allows you to retain rights, would not qualify for capital gains treatment. To obtain capital gains benefit you would need to assign (or sell) all substantial rights.

2. Deductions

You should keep track of deductions to offset licensing income. An accountant or tax guide can advise you as to types of deductions available. For example, materials used for creating prototypes, phone, fax and travel, to the extent that they are part of your inventing business, are all deductions. Most of these can be deducted in the year in which they were incurred. However, large expenses must be depreciated. This means that the expense is spread out over several years—sometimes, the life of the patent—with a portion of it being deducted each year.

Double Taxation and Foreign Licensing

In the event that you entered into a licensing agreement with a company in another country, you will want to avoid double taxation. What is double taxation? Let's say you had a licensing deal with a British company. The British government would withhold a portion of your British royalty check for British taxes. The U.S. government would also tax your income. As a result, you would have paid income tax both to Britain and the U.S.

There are two ways that you can avoid double taxation. One way is to claim the foreign taxes paid as a deduction or credit against your U.S. taxes. A second method is sometimes available. A foreign tax authority may agree to refund taxes provided that U.S. tax authorities are notified of your income and of the tax payments to the foreign authority. The foreign tax authority will usually have a special tax form that you must complete in order to qualify for this refund.

F. Quality Control

We advise you to review samples of the licensed product periodically. Your samples or quality control provision will explain the number of samples you can obtain and the period of time in which you may complain about licensee quality. See Chapter 12 for an explanation of samples and quality control.

Your product review should help you determine if your invention is being utilized properly and if something has been done to your invention that is not permitted under the agreement. For example, say you believe that additions made to your invention may infringe another invention. Notify the licensee in writing of your approval or disapproval, and keep a copy of the letter. Make sure that your letter is received within the time required under your samples or quality control provision and that it is sent in accordance with the notice provision. ■

Help Beyond This Book

For many of you, this book provides all the information you will need to license your invention. However, you may find yourself in a complicated situation that will require additional research or professional advice from an attorney or other expert. If you do have to get outside help, don't fall into the trap of simply letting someone else control all the details of your situation. By educating yourself with this book and the other resources listed in this chapter, you'll be able to work with professionals more efficiently, keep your costs down and be in a better position to evaluate their services.

In Section A we direct you to sources of more information on the licensing process, and in Section B we offer guidance on working with attorneys.

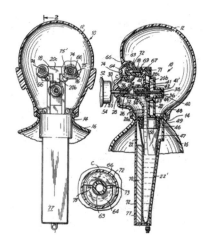

Doll Tearing Mechanism
No. 3,789,539

A. Licensing and Intellectual Property Resources

If you're looking for more information on the licensing process, you may want to review some of the resources and publications listed below. We've grouped background materials into the following categories:

- Licensing and Inventor Organizations
- Trade Show Directories
- Books, Publications and Software on Intellectual Property and Licensing
- Other Intellectual Property Resources.

Legal Research and Law Libraries

For the nitty gritty details of licensing and intellectual property law, you can conduct your own legal research. Especially if you find yourself in a dispute over your invention or if a lawsuit is threatened, you may want to find out exactly what the law says about your particular situation. Finding an answer to a specific legal question generally involves reading treatises for a general understanding of a particular legal area, finding applicable statutes and reading the cases in which judges have interpreted these statutes. (See sidebar in Section A3, below, on treatises.)

Conducting legal research is not as difficult as it may seem. Nolo publishes a basic legal research guide, *Legal Research: How to Find and Understand the Law,* by attorneys Stephen Elias and Susan Levinkind. It walks you through the various sources of law, explains how they fit together and shows you how to use them to answer your legal question. Some legal research can be performed on the Internet. Two good places to start your Internet research are Nolo (www.nolo.com) and Findlaw (www.findlaw.com).

For detailed legal research, however, you will probably have to visit a local law library. If there's a public law school in your area, it probably has a law library that's open to the public. Other public law libraries are often run by local bar associations or as an adjunct to the local courts. Law libraries associated with private law schools often allow only limited public access. Call to speak with the law librarian to determine your right to access. You can always call your local bar association to find out what public law libraries are in your area.

1. Licensing and Inventor Organizations

There is a network of inventor organizations throughout the United States. Through these organizations you can obtain a wealth of information about the licensing process, including legal and business advice and referrals to prototype makers, product agents and other professional contacts.

- Inventors Awareness Group (IAG) (www.inventorworld.com/IAG/index.html) is a watchdog group looking out for the rights of independent inventors. Contact them at 1533 East Mountain Road, Suite B, Westfield, MA 01085-1458. Phone: 413-568-5561, Fax: 413-568-5325, email: iagbob@aol.com. The IAG publishes *The Inventor's Resource Directory*, which includes advice on marketing plus contact information for state inventor organizations, prototype service companies (who will construct working models of your ideas), patent services, evaluation companies (who will evaluate your product idea) and legitimate invention marketing firms. The IAG maintains a database of scam marketing complaints, and its ads have been screened to exclude scam invention marketers.

- PTO Independent Inventor Resources (www.uspto.gov/web/offices/com/iip/indextxt.htm). In 1999, the PTO established a new office aimed at providing services and support to independent inventors. The office is expected to eventually offer seminars and expanded educational opportunities for inventors.

- United Inventors Association (UIA) (www.uiausa.org) is a national inventor's organization. For information, write to P.O. Box 23447, Rochester, NY 14692-3347, 716-359-9310, Fax: 716-359-1132, email: UIAUSA@aol.com.

- The Patent Café (www.patentcafe.com) is an excellent inventor resource maintained by inventor and entrepreneur Andy Gibbs. It contains the most thorough listing of inventor or-

ganizations and related links and provides information on starting an inventor organization.

- Invention Convention (www.inventionconvention.com). The National Congress of Inventor Organizations (NCIO) and its executive director, Stephen Paul Gnass, maintain this invention website that includes links, trade show information and advice for inventors. National Congress of Inventor Organizations, 727 North 600 West, Logan, UT 84321. Phone: 801-753-0888.

- *Inventors' Digest* and its accompanying website (www.inventorsdigest.com) publish information for independent inventors ($27/ year for six issues). Includes helpful articles on new inventions, licensing and marketing and advertisements from reputable inventor promotion companies.

- Venture Capital Resource Library (www.vfinance.com) provides information on venture capital firms, investment banks, accountants, attorneys, financial printers, advisors, public relations firms and related financing organizations.

- Ronald J. Riley's Inventor Resources (www.inventored.org/index.html). Links and advice for inventors.

- Licensing Executives Society (U.S.A. and Canada) (www.usa-canada.les.org). An organization for attorneys and licensing executives from the U.S. and Canada. The organization publishes a directory listing specialties for licensing attorneys throughout the U.S. and Canada. 1800 Diagonal Road, Suite 280, Alexandria, VA 22314-2840, Phone: 703-836-3106, Fax: 703-836-3107.

- National Technology Transfer Center (NTTC) (www.nttc.edu) at Wheeling Jesuit University helps entrepreneurs and companies looking to access federally funded research and development activity at U.S. universities. Write to 316 Washington Avenue, Wheeling, WV 26003, Phone: 800-678-6882, Fax: 304-243-4388, email: technology@nttc.edu.

- Arthur D. Little Enterprises (ADLE) (www.adlenterprises.com/default.htm) is the invention management subsidiary of Arthur D. Little, Inc., an invention consulting firm that licenses inventions for a percentage of the income.
- Intellectual Property Owners (IPO) (www.ipo.org) is an association that serves owners of patents, trademarks, copyrights and trade secrets. It is the sponsor of the National Inventor of the Year Award. Write to them at Intellectual Property Owners, 1255 23rd St. NW, Suite 850, Washington, DC 20037. Phone: 202-466-2396; Fax: 202-466-2893, email: info@ipo.org.
- Inventor's Bookstore (www.inventorhelp.com) offers condensed reports and other guidance for inventors. The site is maintained by inventor Jack Lander.
- *Idea Marketplace* is a semi-monthly magazine covering issues of interest to inventors. P.O. Box 131758, Staten Island, NY 10313, Phone: 800-IDEA-MRK ($14.95/year/6 issues).
- *Eureka!* The Invention and Innovation Newsletter is a quarterly inventor publication primarily for Canadian inventors. Write to 156 Columbia Street West, Waterloo, Ontario N2L 3L3.
- Patent License Exchanges such as Yet2.com (www.yet2.com), the Patent and License Exchange (www.pl-x.com), 2XFR.com (www.2xfr.com) and NewIdeaTrade.com (www.newideatrade.com) offer—for a fee— the ability to post information about patented inventions for would-be licensees.
- Knowledge Express Data Systems (www.KnowledgeExpress.com) is a private online service provider that charges fees for providing company and marketing research.

2. Trade Show Directories

The best source of trade show information is through a trade association in your particular industry. Many trade associations also publish newsletters or other publications that contain trade show information (see Chapter 6).

- There are also two directories that provide general information about trade shows: *Trade Shows Worldwide: An International Directory of Events; Facilities, and Supplies,* published annually by the Gale Group (www.gale.com); and *Directory of Conventions,* an annual directory published by Successful Meeting Magazines (www.successmtgs.com). Both of these should be available at your local library.
- Another resource is the Center for Exhibition Industry Research (www.ceir.org), 1660 Lincoln Street, Suite 2080, Denver, CO 80264. Phone: 303-860-7626, Fax: 303-860-7479.

3. Books, Publications and Software on Intellectual Property and Licensing

There are a number of other sources of information on intellectual property and licensing issues, including the business aspects of exploiting your invention. Many of the following titles provide background information that may be of help to you before you use this book to license your invention.

Can't find a book? If you can't find a book in your law library or local bookstore, try Internet bookstores such as Amazon (www.amazon. com) or Nolo (www.nolo.com).

a. Nolo Books on Intellectual Property

Before you start the licensing process, it's important that you understand the principles of intellectual property that apply to your invention. Nolo, the publisher of this book, also publishes a number of other titles on intellectual property, including:

- *The Copyright Handbook,* by attorney Stephen Fishman.
- *Copyright Your Software,* by attorney Stephen Fishman.

- *The Inventor's Notebook,* by Fred Grissom and attorney David Pressman.
- *Patent It Yourself,* by attorney David Pressman.
- *Patents for Beginners,* by attorneys David Pressman and Richard Stim.
- *Patent, Copyright and Trademark: A Desk Reference to Intellectual Property Law,* by attorney Stephen Elias.
- *Web and Software Development: A Legal Guide,* by attorney Stephen Fishman.
- *Trademark: Legal Care for Your Business & Product Name,* by attorney Stephen Elias.
- *Nondisclosure Agreements: Protect Your Trade Secrets and More,* by attorneys Richard Stim and Stephen Fishman.
- *The Public Domain: How to Find and Use Copyright-Free Writings, Music, Art & More,* by attorney Stephen Fishman.
- *Patent Pending in 24 Hours,* by attorneys Richard Stim and David Pressman.

b. Other Books and Treatises

There are a number of textbook-style books on the subject of licensing and intellectual property law. While these books aren't exactly "how-to" books that walk you through the process, they do provide extensive background information that you may find helpful.

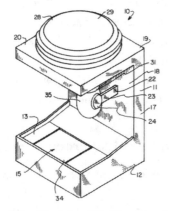

Hard-Boiled Egg Shelling Device
No. 6,314,872

> ### What's a Treatise?
>
> Treatises are often quite lengthy, academic-style books that discuss a certain area of law in depth. Many treatises are multi-volume sets, similar to encyclopedias. Not exactly user-friendly, these books are usually used by attorneys and law students who need detailed legal information about a certain subject, such as bankruptcy or patent law. Most treatises cost $100 or more and require frequent updating. When using a treatise, check to see that it has been updated within the past year or two. Treatises are commonly found in law libraries. Most public libraries usually don't stock them.

- *Milgrim on Licensing,* by Roger M. Milgrim (Matthew Bender). This two-volume treatise (see sidebar) is probably the leading authority on licensing law.
- *A Primer on Technology Licensing,* by Gregory J. Battersby and Charles W. Grimes (Kent Press). This is an easy-to-read paperback detailing many aspects of the invention licensing process. This book (as well as the Battersby and Grimes journal, *The Licensing Journal*) includes lists of reputable licensing agents and service organizations who will appraise new inventions.
- *Drafting License Agreements: User's Guide,* edited by Michael Epstein and Frank Politano (Aspen Law & Business). This one-volume treatise provides sections written by experts in various fields. The treatise is especially strong on tax and bankruptcy law issues.
- *How to License Technology,* by Robert C. Megantz (John Wiley & Sons). This practical handbook offers inventors and organizations a detailed guide to the licensing process and shows them how to maximize licensing arrangements.

- *Licensing of Intellectual Property,* by Jay Dratler, Jr. (Law Journal Seminars Press). This is a detailed one-volume treatise that covers all the bases on patent, software and trade secret licensing.
- The leading legal texts on trade secrets are *Trade Secrets,* by Roger Milgrim (Matthew Bender), and *Trade Secrets Law,* by Melvin F. Jager (Clark Boardman Callaghan).

c. Business Books and Publications

Nolo offers a series of books on small business issues, including:

- *Working for Yourself,* by attorney Stephen Fishman.
- *Hiring Independent Contractors: The Employer's Legal Guide,* by attorney Stephen Fishman.
- *The Employer's Legal Handbook,* by attorney Fred S. Steingold.
- *Tax Savvy for Small Business,* by attorney Fred W. Daily.
- *The Partnership Book,* by attorneys Denis Clifford and Ralph Warner.
- *Form Your Own Limited Liability Company,* by attorney Anthony Mancuso.
- *How to Form Your Own Corporation,* available for California, Florida, New York and Texas, by attorney Anthony Mancuso.
- Additional business information can be obtained from the U.S. Government Printing Office by writing to Superintendent of Documents, Government Printing Office, Washington, DC 20402 (on the Web at www.access.gpo.gov). There are also government bookstores located in many U.S. cities. To find one in your city, check the government section of your local white or Yellow Pages.
- The Small Business Administration (SBA) offers information and assistance to small businesses. Contact them at P.O. Box 30, Denver, CO

80201-0300. Phone: 800-368-5855. Among their publications is *Can You Make Money With Your Idea or Invention?* (Pub #2.013).

d. Negotiating Books and Software

If you're looking for more information on negotiating, consider the following resources:

- *Getting to Yes: Negotiating Agreement Without Giving In,* by Roger Fisher and William Ury (Penguin Books).
- *Smart Negotiating: How to Make Good Deals in The Real World,* by James Freund (Simon & Schuster).
- *Negotiator Pro* is a software program that takes you through the steps of a formal negotiation and provides advice from experts in the field. The program is available from Negotiator Pro, 800-448-3308 (www.negotiatorpro.com).

e. Books Offering Alternatives to Licensing

If, after reading this book, you decide you can't (or don't want to) license your invention and you'd rather manufacture and sell your product yourself, the following three books may help you:

- *Stand Alone, Inventor! And Make Money With Your New Product Ideas!* by Robert Merrick (Lee Publishing).
- *Success Leaves Clues: Practical Tools for Successful Sales and Marketing,* by John Stanton and Richard George (Merritt Publishing).
- *How to Market a Product for Under $500,* by Jeffrey Dobkin (Danielle Adams Publishing).

4. Other Intellectual Property Resources

Provided below are some additional sources of information on the various forms of intellectual property law. Many of these sources are accessible through the Internet.

Nolo's Legal Encyclopedia

Nolo's website (www.nolo.com) also offers an extensive Legal Encyclopedia which includes a section on intellectual property. You'll find answers to frequently asked questions about patents, copyrights, trademarks and other related topics, as well as sample chapters of Nolo books and a wide range of articles. Simply click on "Legal Encyclopedia" and then on "Patent, Copyright & Trademark."

a. Patents

The U.S. Patent & Trademark Office (PTO) offers a number of informational pamphlets, including an introduction to patents ("General Information About Patents") and an alphabetical and geographical listing of patent attorneys and agents registered to practice before the PTO ("Directory of Registered Patent Attorneys and Agents Arranged by States and Countries"). In addition, the PTO has established PTO Independent Inventor Resources (www.uspto.gov/web/offices/com/iip/indextxt.htm) that provides services and support to independent inventors. The PTO also has an online searchable database of patent abstracts (short summaries of patents). For purposes of patent searching, this database is an excellent and inexpensive first step in the searching procedure.

To visit the PTO's website—where you'll also find its searchable database—go to www.uspto.gov. Most patent forms can be downloaded from the PTO website, as well as many important publications including the Manual of Patent Examining Procedures, Examination Guidelines for Computer-Related Inventions and Disclosure Document Program.

You can order a copy of a patent by:

- writing a letter listing the number of the patent to "Commissioner of Patents and Trademarks, Washington, DC 20231" with a check for the price per patent (see Fee Schedule at the USPTO website) times the total number of patents you've ordered; or
- clicking on "Order Copy" at the "Manual Search" page at the PTO website; or
- conducting a computer patent search. See a description of computer patent searching, below.

Computer Patent Searching. Computer searching is ideal for locating a specific patent and performing preliminary research but, by itself, is not suitable for proving patentability or validity. The main reason for this is that the patents in most computer search data banks usually go back only to 1971 and it is possible that a patent issued before that date might demonstrate the obviousness or lack of novelty for a new invention. (For most high-tech inventions, this is not a problem since the relevant prior art is post-60s.)

Computer searching has some obvious advantages such as cost and ease of use. In order to perform computer searching, the searcher must have access to certain databases. This is done either with a personal computer with a modem or via an existing terminal that is dedicated to patent searching, such as at a PTDL, large company or law firm, or in the PTO. The following free databases are available:

- **The U.S. Patent & Trademark Office** (www.uspto.gov)—An online searchable database of patents and drawings that cover the period from January 1976 to the most recent weekly issue date (usually each Tuesday). In order to view drawings, your computer must be able to view TIFF drawings. For faster searching, there is also a Bibliographic Database that contains only the first page (title, inventor, abstract, etc.) of each patent.
- **Delphion** (www.delphion.com)—Delphion's free basic bibliographic and patentability search services has several advantages over the PTO. Delphion's database goes back to 1971 for U.S. patents and contains the front pages of Europatents and PCT published patent applications. However, Delphion requires a signup and charges for more ad-

vanced services such as full-text search patent or foreign patent searches. Delphion also charges for downloading patent images.

- **Micropatent** (www.micropatent.com)—a fee-based commercial database of U.S. patents searchable from 1836 to the present. It also includes Japanese and International PCT patent applications from 1983, European patents from 1988 and the Official Gazette (Patents). The U.S. patents before 1971 have been entered into the database by optical character recognition, so expect some errors.
- **Patent Miner** (www.patentminer.com)—a fee-based database of U.S. patents searchable from 1970 to the present. Copies of any patent dating from 1790 can be acquired.
- **LexPat** (www.lexis-nexis.com)—a fee-based database of U.S. patents searchable from 1971 to the present. In addition, the LEXPAT library offers extensive prior-art searching capability of technical journals and magazines.
- **QPAT** (www.qpat.com); **Questel/Orbit** (www.questel.orbit.com)—both commercial services access the QPAT database that includes U.S. patents searchable from 1974 to the present and full-text European A (1987-present) and B (1991-present) patents.

b. Copyright

The Copyright Office has numerous circulars, kits and other publications that can help you, including one on searching copyright records. These publications and application forms can be obtained by writing to the Copyright Office at Publications Sections, LM-455, Copyright Office, Library of Congress, Washington, DC 20559. Most Copyright Office publications can be downloaded directly from the World Wide Web at www.loc.gov/copyright. Frequently requested Copyright Office circulars and announcements are also available via the Copyright Office's fax-on-demand telephone line at 202-707-9100.

c. Trademarks

The Trademark Office is a division of the PTO. An introductory pamphlet about trademarks ("General Information About Trademarks") and information about the operations of the Patent and Trademark Office are available from the Superintendent of Documents, Government Printing Office, Washington, DC 20402, or from the PTO's website at www.uspto.gov. This site includes the relevant applications and trademark office forms. You can write to the Assistant Commissioner Of Trademarks, Washington, DC 20231.

d. Additional Intellectual Property Resources

- **Yahoo Intellectual Property Directory** (www.yahoo.com/Government/Law/Intellectual_Property) is a thorough listing of intellectual property resources on the Internet.
- **Nolo.com Self-Help Law** (www.nolo.com) provides definitions and explanations for patent, trademark, copyright and trade secret principles.
- **Legal Information Institute** (www.law.cornell.edu) offers intellectual property links and downloadable copies of statutes and cases.

B. Working With an Attorney

A number of situations may lead you to seek an attorney's advice: a complex license negotiation, a dispute over your invention or a simple need for guidance. Attorneys have various specialties, and you will need to select a lawyer who is qualified to provide the advice you need.

1. Intellectual Property Attorneys

First, you should make sure your attorney is knowledgeable about intellectual property law. Most intellectual property attorneys are familiar with licensing and can negotiate a deal or prepare a license agreement. Don't make the mistake of hiring a lawyer whom you trust but who works in a different field—such as the lawyer who masterfully handled your friend's personal injury case. Intellectual property law should be handled by a specialist.

Second, you should find an attorney that has expertise in the particular type of intellectual property that applies to your invention. Some intellectual property attorneys specialize in one type of intellectual property, either copyrights, trademarks or patents. If, for example, you are concerned about ownership or licensing of a patented invention, you should seek an intellectual property attorney who specializes in patents.

The American Intellectual Property Law Association (AIPLA) may be able to assist you in locating attorneys in your area. Contact it at 2001 Jefferson Davis Highway, Suite 203, Arlington, VA 22202, 703-415-0780. The Intellectual Property Law Association of the American Bar Association also has a listing of intellectual property attorneys. You can reach it at 312-988-5000.

2. Other Legal Specialties

For certain tasks, you will need an attorney who specializes in a particular area other than intellectual property. If you have concerns about taxes or an IRS dispute, you will need a tax attorney; if you are overwhelmed by debt, you will need a bankruptcy attorney; if you are sorting out your business form (for example, forming a corporation), you will need a business attorney.

In addition to all these specialties, some lawyers focus on litigation. Not all intellectual property attorneys are litigators. If you have a license dispute and want to sue someone (or someone has threatened to sue you) you will need an intellectual property attorney who specializes in litigation. Litigators usually bill on an hourly basis, though sometimes they may take a case on contingency. Under this arrangement, if you win, the attorney receives a percentage—usually one-third to one-half—of any money recovered in the lawsuit. If you lose, the attorney receives nothing.

3. Finding an Attorney

The best way to locate an attorney is by referrals through friends or other inventors. It is also possible to locate an attorney through a state bar association or through a local county or city bar association. Check your local Yellow Pages and ask the bar association if they have a lawyer referral service. When interviewing an attorney, ask questions about clientele, work performed, rates and experience. If you speak with one of the attorney's clients (for example, another inventor), ask questions about the attorney's response time, billing practices and temperament.

4. How to Keep Your Fees Down

Most attorneys bill on an hourly basis ($150 to $300 an hour) and send a bill at the end of each month. Some attorneys bill on a fixed fee basis. That is, you pay a set fee for certain services—for example, $5,000 for a license negotiation.

Here are some tips to reduce the size of your bills:

Keep it Short. If your attorney is being paid on an hourly basis, then keep your conversations short (the meter is always running) and avoid making several calls a day. Consolidate your questions so that you can ask them all in one conversation.

Get a Fee Agreement. We recommend that you get a written fee agreement when dealing with an attorney. The fee agreement is a negotiated arrangement establishing fixed fees for certain work rather than hourly billings. Read it and understand your rights as a client. Make sure that your fee agreement includes provisions that require an itemized statement along with the bill detailing the work done and time spent, and that allow you to drop the attorney at any time. If you can't get fixed billings, ask your attorney to estimate fees for work and ask for an explanation if the bill exceeds the estimates.

Mad at Your Lawyer?

In many states, such as California, a client always has the right to fire their attorney (although this does not terminate the obligation to pay the attorney). If you don't respect and trust your attorney's professional abilities you should switch and find a new attorney. Beware, though, switching attorneys is a nuisance and you may lose time and money. For more information on how to handle a dispute with your lawyer, see Nolo's book *Mad at Your Lawyer,* by attorney Tanya Starnes.

Review Billings Carefully. Your legal bill should be prompt and clear. Do not accept summary billings such as the single phrase "litigation work" used to explain a block of time for which you are billed a great deal of money. Every item should be explained with the rate and hours billed. Late billings are not acceptable, especially in litigation. When you get bills you don't understand, ask the attorney for an explanation—and ask the attorney not to bill you for the explanation.

Be Careful If You Engage a Law Firm. If you sign a fee agreement with a law firm (rather than a single attorney), be careful to avoid a particular billing problem sometimes referred to as multiple or "bounced" billings. This occurs when the same work is performed by several attorneys. For example, two attorneys at the firm have a 15-minute discussion about your case. You are billed by both attorneys. To avoid this, make sure that your fee agreement does not bind you to this type of arrangement. If

you are billed for these conferences, send a letter to your attorney at the firm explaining that you only want that attorney to work on your case and that you should be contacted before work is assigned to another attorney at the firm.

Watch Out for Hidden Expenses. Find out what expenses you must cover. Watch out if your attorney wants to bill for services such as word processing or administrative services. This means you will be paying the secretary's salary. Also beware of fax and copying charges. Some firms charge clients per page for incoming and outgoing faxes. Other firms charge a per page copy fee which surpasses any commercial copy center. Look out for these hidden expenses in your fee agreement.

What Is a Retainer?

A retainer is an advance payment to an attorney. The attorney places the retainer in a bank account (in some states, this must be an interest-bearing account), and the attorney deducts money from the retainer at the end of each month to pay your bill. When the retainer is depleted, the attorney may ask for a new retainer. If the retainer is not used up at the end of the services, the attorney must return what's left. The amount of the retainer usually depends on the project. Retainers for litigation, for instance, are often between $2,000 and $5,000.

Do Your Best to Limit the Attorney's Services. It is common for a license to take one to two months or more to negotiate. These agreements go through many drafts. You can help to limit the number of drafts by reaching a clear agreement with your attorney as to the goals of the negotiation. For example, if getting a $10,000 advance is most important, tell your lawyer that is your number one priority. Once you have achieved most or all of your goals, then be flexible on remaining issues so that you can save time.

Don't Take Litigation Lightly. As a general rule, beware of litigation! If you are involved in a lawsuit, it may take months or years to resolve. Some go on for decades. It often costs $10,000 or more, and the only ones who profit are usually the lawyers. If you're in a dispute, ask your attorney about dispute resolution methods such as arbitration and mediation. Often these procedures can save money, and they're faster than litigation. If those methods don't work or aren't available, ask your attorney for an assessment of your odds and the potential costs before filing a lawsuit. The assessment and underlying reasoning should be in plain English. If a lawyer can't explain your situation clearly to you, he probably won't be able to explain it clearly to a judge or jury.

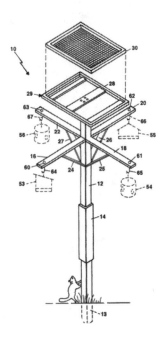

Multi-Station Bird Feeder with Squirrel Guard
No. 6,269,771

What's a Conflict of Interest?

Lawyers are bound by ethical rules to disclose if there is a potential conflict of interest. A conflict of interest occurs whenever the lawyer represents adverse interests, for example, if your attorney also represents the licensee. When there is a conflict of interest, there is the potential that your attorney may not battle as forcefully for your position. For example, if the attorney represents you and a licensee, it is possible that the attorney will be apprehensive of endangering a lucrative relationship with the licensee for the sake of you. Another danger is that the attorney may use confidential information obtained from one party against the other party.

Always ask your attorney if there is a potential conflict. The attorney should disclose a conflict without being asked, but some attorneys do not. Although we recommend against retaining a lawyer with a potential conflict of interest, it is possible, in some cases, that an attorney can vigorously represent your interests nonetheless. This is a judgment call that should be made based upon your feeling for the attorney and any other information you have obtained, such as references from other clients. If you want to proceed, you can sign a waiver in which you relinquish any right to complain about the situation later. If you do not want to proceed, do not sign a waiver and find a different attorney.

How to Use the CD-ROM

The tear-out forms in Appendix B are included on a CD-ROM in the back of the book. This CD-ROM, which can be used with Windows computers, installs files that can be opened, printed and edited using a word processor or other software. It is *not* a stand-alone software program. Please read this Appendix and the README.TXT file included on the CD-ROM for instructions on using the Forms CD.

Note to Mac users: This CD-ROM and its files should also work on Macintosh computers. Please note, however, that Nolo cannot provide technical support for non-Windows users.

How to View the README File

If you do not know how to view the file README.TXT, insert the Forms CD-ROM into your computer's CD-ROM drive and follow these instructions:

- Windows 9x, 2000, Me and XP: (1) On your PC's desktop, double-click the My Computer icon; (2) double-click the icon for the CD-ROM drive into which the Forms CD-ROM was inserted; (3) double-click the file README.TXT.
- Macintosh: (1) On your Mac desktop, double-click the icon for the CD-ROM that you inserted; (2) double-click on the file README.TXT.

While the README file is open, print it out by using the Print command in the File menu.

A. Installing the Form Files Onto Your Computer

Word processing forms that you can open, complete, print and save with your word processing program (see Section B, below) are contained on

the CD-ROM. Before you can do anything with the files on the CD-ROM, you need to install them onto your hard disk. In accordance with U.S. copyright laws, remember that copies of the CD-ROM and its files are for your personal use only.

Insert the Forms CD and do the following:

1. Windows 9x, 2000, Me and XP Users

Follow the instructions that appear on the screen. (If nothing happens when you insert the Forms CD-ROM, then (1) double-click the My Computer icon; (2) double-click the icon for the CD-ROM drive into which the Forms CD-ROM was inserted; and (3) double-click the file WELCOME.EXE.)

By default, all the files are installed to the \Licensing Forms folder in the \Program Files folder of your computer. A folder called "Licensing Forms" is added to the "Programs" folder of the Start menu.

2. Macintosh Users

Step 1: If the "Licensing Forms CD" window is not open, open it by double-clicking the "Licensing Forms CD" icon.

Step 2: Select the "Licensing Forms" folder icon.

Step 3: Drag and drop the folder icon onto the icon of your hard disk.

B. Using the Word Processing Files to Create Documents

This section concerns the files for forms that can be opened and edited with your word processing program.

All word processing forms come in rich text format. These files have the extension ".RTF." For example, the form for the Joint Ownership Agreement discussed in Chapter 4 is on the file

JOINTOWN.RTF. All forms and their filenames are listed at the beginning of Appendix B.

RTF files can be read by most recent word processing programs, including all versions of MS Word for Windows and Macintosh, WordPad for Windows, and recent versions of WordPerfect for Windows and Macintosh.

To use a form from the CD to create your documents you must: (1) open a file in your word processor or text editor; (2) edit the form by filling in the required information; (3) print it out; (4) rename and save your revised file.

The following are general instructions on how to do this. However, each word processor uses different commands to open, format, save and print documents. Please read your word processor's manual for specific instructions on performing these tasks.

Do not call Nolo's technical support if you have questions on how to use your word processor.

Step 1: Opening a File

There are three ways to open the word processing files included on the CD-ROM after you have installed them onto your computer.

- Windows users can open a file by selecting its "shortcut" as follows: (1) Click the Windows "Start" button; (2) open the "Programs" folder; (3) open the "Licensing Forms" subfolder; and (4) click on the shortcut to the form you want to work with.
- Both Windows and Macintosh users can open a file directly by double-clicking on it. Use My Computer or Windows Explorer (Windows 9x, 2000, Me or XP) or the Finder (Macintosh) to go to the folder you installed or copied the CD-ROM's files to. Then, double-click on the specific file you want to open.

- You can also open a file from within your word processor. To do this, you must first start your word processor. Then, go to the File menu and choose the Open command. This opens a dialog box where you will tell the program (1) the type of file you want to open (*.RTF); and (2) the location and name of the file (you will need to navigate through the directory tree to get to the folder on your hard disk where the CD's files have been installed). If these directions are unclear, you will need to look through the manual for your word processing program—Nolo's technical support department will *not* be able to help you with the use of your word processing program.

Where Are the Files Installed?

Windows Users
- RTF files are installed by default to a folder named \Licensing Forms in the \Program Files folder of your computer.

Macintosh Users
- RTF files are located in the "Licensing Forms" folder.

Step 2: Editing Your Document

Fill in the appropriate information according to the instructions and sample agreements in the book. Underlines are used to indicate where you need to enter your information, frequently followed by instructions in brackets. *Be sure to delete the underlines and instructions from your edited document.* If you do not know how to use your word processor to edit a document, you will need to look through the manual for your word processing program— Nolo's technical support department will *not* be able to help you with the use of your word processing program.

Editing Forms That Have Optional or Alternative Text

Some of the forms have check boxes before text. The check boxes indicate:

- Optional text, where you choose whether to include or exclude the given text.
- Alternative text, where you select one alternative to include and exclude the other alternatives.

If you are using the tear-out forms in Appendix B, you simply mark the appropriate box to make your choice.

If you are using the Forms CD, however, we recommend that instead of marking the check boxes, you do the following:

Optional text

If you **don't want** to include optional text, just delete it from your document.

If you **do want** to include optional text, just leave it in your document.

In either case, delete the check box itself as well as the italicized instructions that the text is optional.

NOTE: if you choose not to include an optional numbered clause, be sure to renumber all the subsequent clauses after you delete it.

Alternative text

First delete all the alternatives that you do not want to include.

Then delete the remaining check boxes, as well as the italicized instructions that you need to select one of the alternatives provided.

Step 3: Printing Out the Document

Use your word processor's or text editor's "Print" command to print out your document. If you do not know how to use your word processor to print a document, you will need to look through the manual for your word processing program—Nolo's technical support department will *not* be able to help you with the use of your word processing program.

Step 4: Saving Your Document

After filling in the form, use the "Save As" command to save and rename the file. Because all the files are "read-only" and you will not be able to use the "Save" command. This is for your protection. *If you save the file without renaming it, the underlines that indicate where you need to enter your information will be lost and you will not be able to create a new document with this file without recopying the original file from the CD-ROM.*

If you do not know how to use your word processor to save a document, you will need to look through the manual for your word processing program—Nolo's technical support department will *not* be able to help you with the use of your word processing program. ■

B

Forms

All of the following forms are on the disk which accompanies this book. All of the forms except for those preceded by an asterisk are provided as tear-out forms in this Appendix.

Chapter	Section	Form	File Name
1	D2	Agreement Worksheet	AGTWKSHT
3	E	Letter Confirming Employee's Ownership of Copyright	EMPLOWNR
4	A2	Joint Ownership Agreement	JOINTOWN
4	C6	Assignment of Rights: Patent	ASTPAT
4	C6	Assignment of Rights: Patent Application	ASTPATAP
4	C6	Assignment of Rights: No Patent Issued or Application Filed	ASTNOPAT
5	B	Agent Letter Agreement	AGENTAGT
7	A1	One-Way Nondisclosure Agreement	DISCLAGT
7	A1	Mutual Nondisclosure Agreement	MUTDISCL
8	End	Contract Worksheet	CONWKSHT
10	C1	*Letter of Intent	LTRINTNT
10	D2	Option Agreement	OPTAGT
10	E	*Terms Sheet	TERMSHET
11	A	License Agreement	LICENAGT
14	N	Escrow Agreement	ESCROAGT
16	B	Checklist for Reviewing a License Agreement	REVWAGT
17	A	License Dates Chart	LICEDATE
17	B3	*Audit Request Letter	AUDITREQ

Agreement Worksheet

Title of Agreement:_____

Category (circle one):

co-ownership   corporate   employment   nondisclosure   evaluation

option   outsourcing   loan or financial   representation   partnership

other: _____

Date of Agreement: _____

Parties to Agreement: _____

_____

Is there a Termination Date?   Yes ____   No ____   If yes, list date: _____

Is there a Renewal Date?   Yes ____   No ____   If yes, list date: _____

Where is the agreement located or filed? _____

Ownership Notes: _____

_____

_____

_____

_____

_____

_____

_____

_____

_____

_____

_____

_____

_____

_____

_____

_____

_____

_____

Letter Confirming Employee's Ownership of Copyright

Dear Employer:

This confirms the agreement between _____

_____ [name of company] and myself that I shall own exclusive rights

to the invention known as _____

_____ [name of invention] which is more specifically described below.

Although I created _____ [name

of invention] within the scope of my employment, _____

_____ [name of company] now agrees that I shall be the owner of all rights,

under patent, trademark, trade secret and copyright law to _____

_____ [name of invention], as well as to any derivative versions

under copyright law or improvements under patent law. You represent and warrant that you have the

power to grant these rights on behalf of _____

[name of company] and that if required, a representative of [name of company] will furnish any other

necessary documents that are required to demonstrate my ownership.

Description of Invention

_____ [name of invention]

comprises _____

_____

_____

_____

_____

_____

[Describe invention in detail. If there is a patent application, use the claims section to describe it. If a patent has already been issued to the company, you will need a patent assignment and the assignment will have to be recorded with the PTO.]

If this letter accurately reflects our agreement, please sign and return one copy to me.

Yours truly,

_____   _____
Inventor   Dated

Acknowledged and Agreed to:

_____   _____
Name of company   Dated

Joint Ownership Agreement

Introduction

This agreement is made between _____
_____ *[insert name, address and business form of owner #1]*
and _____
[insert name, address and business form of owner #2] (the "Parties") as of _____
[insert date agreement is to be effective]. The Parties wish to set forth their respective rights to and
obligations for the invention tentatively named _____
_____ *[insert the name of invention]* (the "Invention") and more
accurately described below. The ownership rights to the Invention include all patent rights, copyrights, trade secrets and trademark rights comprising, associated with or derived from the Invention.

The Invention *[Select One]*

☐ *Patent Issued*
The Invention is described in the United States patent number _____, dated
_____.

☐ *Patent Application Pending*
The Invention is described in the application for United States patent (U.S. Patent Office Application
Serial No. _____).

☐ *No Patent*
Description of Invention: _____
_____
_____

Therefore, the Parties agree as follows:

Ownership Percentage Interests

The Parties to this agreement are the owners of all legal rights in the Invention described above. The
percentage ownership interests of the Parties are as set forth below. Unless otherwise agreed: (a) all
income derived from exploiting the Invention shall be apportioned according to the percentage
interests set forth below; and (b) any costs, expenses or liabilities relating to the Invention and agreed
to by the Parties under this agreement, shall also be apportioned by the same percentage interests. In
the event any Party is unable to contribute a proportionate share for any cost or expense, the other
Parties may contribute the non-contributing Party's share and shall be reimbursed from subsequent
revenues related to the cost or expense. Reimbursement shall include interest at 1.5% per month, or
the maximum rate permitted by law, whichever is less.

Name	Percentage Interest
_____	_____
_____	_____
_____	_____
_____	_____
_____	_____

Decision Making

Each Party shall have the right to participate in the decisions regarding the Invention, including decisions regarding exploitation, protection and enforcement of legal rights associated with Invention. All decisions require a majority vote except for an assignment of all rights to the Invention. In the event there are equal votes in a case where a majority decision is required, the issue shall be resolved through the procedures set forth in the Dispute Resolution section, below.

Decision-Making Process/Time Limits

All decisions shall be made promptly and with the cooperation of all Parties, acting fairly and in good faith. If a decision requires some time to contemplate (for example, an offer to license, a decision by one Party to manufacture), the Parties may agree to postpone a decision for a period of up to 30 days.

Rights to Manufacture and Sell

Any Party may make, sell or use any product embodying the Invention (or any portion of the Invention) providing that the Parties have approved such action by a vote required under this agreement. In the event that any Party desires and is approved to license, manufacture, sell or distribute the Invention, the terms of such arrangement shall be the same as those available to third parties in similar transactions. That is, a Party to this agreement will have to pay a competitive royalty to the joint owners after deduction of reasonable manufacturing and overhead expenses.

Improvements, Revisions

Each Party to this agreement shall share, according to the proportions set forth in this Agreement, in any revenue derived from improvements or revisions of this Invention provided that each Party shall have made a good faith attempt to consult, contribute or otherwise make themselves available for services on such improvements or revisions of the Invention. In the event that any Party refuses to participate in any work resulting in an improvement or revision of the Invention, revenues derived from such improvements or revisions shall be distributed on a pro rata basis among the contributing Parties.

Disputes

The Parties agree that every dispute or difference between them arising under this Agreement, including a failure to reach a decision as described in this Agreement, shall be settled first by a meeting of the Parties attempting to confer and resolve the dispute in a good faith manner. If the Parties cannot resolve their dispute after conferring, any Party may require the other Parties to submit the matter to non-binding mediation, utilizing the services of an impartial professional mediator approved by all Parties. If the Parties cannot come to an agreement following mediation, the Parties agree to submit the matter to binding arbitration at a location mutually agreeable to the Parties. The arbitration shall be conducted on a confidential basis pursuant to the Commercial Arbitration Rules of the American Arbitration Association. Any decision or award as a result of any such arbitration proceeding shall include the assessment of costs, expenses and reasonable attorney's fees and shall include a written record of the proceedings and a written determination of the arbitrators. Absent an agreement to the contrary, any such arbitration shall be conducted by an arbitrator experienced in intellectual property law. The Parties reserve the right to object to any individual who shall be employed by or affiliated with a competing organization or entity. In the event of any such dispute or difference, either Party may give to the other notice requiring that the matter be settled by arbitration. An award of arbitration shall be final and binding on the Parties and may be confirmed in a court of competent jurisdiction.

Miscellaneous

Each Party shall act in good faith and not take any action which hinders the rights of the other parties. The provisions of this Agreement shall be binding upon the heirs, executors, administrators, successors and assigns of the Parties. If any term, provision, covenant or condition of this Agreement is held to be illegal or invalid for any reason whatsoever, such illegality or invalidity shall not affect the validity of the remainder of this Agreement. This Agreement constitutes the entire understanding between the Parties and can only be modified by written agreement. This Agreement shall be governed by the laws of the state of _____ *[insert choice of state law]*. In the event of any dispute arising under this agreement, the prevailing Party shall be entitled to its reasonable attorney's fees.

MY SIGNATURE BELOW INDICATES THAT I HAVE READ AND UNDERSTOOD THIS AGREEMENT.

_____   _____
Signature   Date

_____   _____
Signature   Date

_____   _____
Signature   Date

Assignment of Rights: Patent

_____

[insert name of person or company assigning rights] ("Assignor") is owner of U.S. Patent Number:

_____, dated _____, and titled

_____ _[insert name of invention]_ (the "Patent").

_____

[insert name of person or company to whom rights will be assigned] ("Assignee") desires to acquire rights in and to the Patent.

Therefore, for valuable consideration, the receipt of which is acknowledged, Assignor assigns to Assignee _____% _[insert percentage of interest that is being assigned—it can be less than 100%, but it cannot be more than 100%]_ of his right, title and interest in the invention and Patent to Assignee for the entire term of the Patent and any reissues or extensions and for the entire terms of any patents, reissues or extensions that may issue from foreign applications, divisions, continuations in whole or part or substitute applications filed claiming the benefit of the Patent as well as any priority rights resulting from patent application filings. The right, title and interest conveyed in this Assignment is to be held and enjoyed by Assignee and Assignee's successors as fully and exclusively as it would have been held and enjoyed by Assignor had this assignment not been made.

Assignor further agrees to: (a) cooperate with Assignee in the protection of the patent rights and prosecution and protection of foreign counterparts; (b) execute, verify, acknowledge and deliver all such further papers, including patent applications and instruments of transfer; and (c) perform such other acts as Assignee lawfully may request to obtain or maintain the Patent and any and all applications and registrations for the invention in any and all countries.

_____   _____
Assignor   Date

[To be completed by notary public]

On this _____ day of _____, before me, _____

_____, the undersigned Notary Public, personally appeared

_____, ASSIGNOR,

personally known to me (or proved to me on the basis of satisfactory evidence) to be the person whose name is subscribed to the within instrument, and acknowledged to me that he executed the same. WITNESS my hand and official seal in _____ County of

_____ on the date set forth in this certificate.

_____
Notary Public

Assignment of Rights: Patent Application

[insert name of person or company assigning rights] ("Assignor") is owner of _____
_____ *[insert name of invention]*
as described in the U.S. Patent Application signed by Assignor on _____ *[insert
date application was signed]*, U.S. Patent and Trademark office Serial Number:_____,
filed _____ *[insert filing date]*, (the "Patent Application"). _____
_____ *[insert name of person or company to whom rights
will be assigned]* ("Assignee") desires to acquire all rights in and to the Patent Application and the
patent (and any reissues or extensions) that may be granted.

Therefore, for valuable consideration, the receipt of which is acknowledged, Assignor assigns to
Assignee _____% *[insert percentage of interest that is being assigned—it can be less
than 100%, but it cannot be more than 100%]* of his right, title and interest in the invention and Patent
Application (as well as such rights in any divisions, continuations in whole or part or substitute applications) to Assignee for the entire term of the issued Patent and any reissues or extensions that may be
granted and for the entire terms of any and all foreign patents that may issue from foreign applications
(as well as divisions, continuations in whole or part or substitute applications) filed claiming the benefit of the Patent Application and any priority rights resulting from Patent Application.

Assignor authorizes the United States Patent and Trademark Office to issue any Patents resulting
from the Patent Application to Assignee according to the percentage interest indicated in this assignment. The right, title and interest is to be held and enjoyed by Assignee and Assignee's successors
and assigns as fully and exclusively as it would have been held and enjoyed by Assignor had this
assignment not been made.

Assignor further agrees to: (a) cooperate with Assignee in the prosecution of the Application and
foreign counterparts; (b) execute, verify, acknowledge and deliver all such further papers, including
patent applications and instruments of transfer; and (c) perform such other acts as Assignee lawfully
may request to obtain or maintain the Patent for the invention in any and all countries.

_____   _____
Assignor   Date

[To be completed by notary public]

On this _____ day of _____, before me, _____
_____, the undersigned Notary Public, personally appeared
_____, ASSIGNOR,
personally known to me (or proved to me on the basis of satisfactory evidence) to be the person
whose name is subscribed to the within instrument, and acknowledged to me that he executed the
same. WITNESS my hand and official seal in _____ County of
_____ on the date set forth in this certificate.

_____
Notary Public

Assignment of Rights:
No Patent Issued or Application Filed

[insert name of person or company assigning rights] ("Assignor") is the owner of all proprietary and intellectual property rights, including copyrights and patents, in the concepts and technologies known as _____

_____ *[insert name of invention]* and more specifically described in Attachment A *[attach a description of the invention to the Assignment and label it "Attachment A"]* to this Assignment (and referred to collectively as the "Invention") and the right to registrations to the Invention; and

[insert name of person or company to whom rights will be assigned] ("Assignee") desires to acquire the ownership of all proprietary rights, including, but not limited to, the copyrights, trade secrets, trademarks and associated good will and patent rights in the Invention and the registrations to the Invention.

Therefore, for valuable consideration, the receipt of which is acknowledged, Assignor hereby assigns to Assignee _____% *[insert percentage of interest that is being assigned—it can be less than 100%, but it cannot be more than 100%]* of all right, title and interest in the Invention, including:

(1) all copyrights, trade secrets, trademarks and associated good will and all patents which may be granted on the Invention;

(2) all applications for patents (including divisions, continuations in whole or part or substitute applications) in the United States or any foreign countries whose duty it is to issue such patents;

(3) any reissues and extensions of such patents; and

(4) all priority rights under the International Convention for the Protection of Industrial Property for every member country.

Assignor warrants that: (1) Assignor is the legal owner of all right, title and interest in the Invention; (2) that such rights have not been previously licensed, pledged, assigned or encumbered; and (3) that this assignment does not infringe on the rights of any person. Assignor agrees to cooperate with Assignee and to execute and deliver all papers, instruments and assignments as may be necessary to vest all right, title and interest in and to the intellectual property rights to the Invention in Assignee. Assignor further agrees to testify in any legal proceeding, sign all lawful papers and applications and make all rightful oaths and generally do everything possible to aid Assignee to obtain and enforce proper protection for the Invention in all countries.

_____   _____
Assignor   Date

[To be completed by notary public]

On this _____ day of _____, before me, _____

_____, the undersigned Notary Public, personally appeared

_____, ASSIGNOR,

personally known to me (or proved to me on the basis of satisfactory evidence) to be the person whose name is subscribed to the within instrument, and acknowledged to me that he executed the same. WITNESS my hand and official seal in _____ County of

_____ on the date set forth in this certificate.

_____
Notary Public

The sample agent agreement set out below is created in a letter format. Although a letter agreement is less formal, the agreement is as enforceable as a non-letter contract. If you don't want to use the letter format, simply remove the date and salutation at the top of letter.

Agent Letter Agreement

Date: _____

Dear _____ *[insert name of agent]:*

Introduction

This agreement sets forth the terms and conditions of this agreement (the "Agreement") between
_____ *[insert*
your name, business form and address] ("Inventor") and _____
_____
[insert Agent's name, business form and address ("Agent"). Inventor is the owner of licensing rights to various processes and technologies, referred to in this Agreement as the "Properties" and described more fully in Attachment A *[attach a description of the invention to the Assignment and label it "Attachment A"]* to this Agreement. Inventor agrees to have Agent serve as an exclusive representative and agent for the Properties within the _____
[indicate the industries in which the agent will represent your invention] industry (the "Industry").

Obligations of Agent

Agent shall perform the following services:

- Evaluation and Consultation. Agent will identify potential licensees for the Properties within the Industry.
- Sales Representation. Agent shall serve as Inventor's exclusive agent for the exploitation of the Properties within the Industry. As Inventor's agent, Agent shall contact and solicit potential licensees or purchasers and present and communicate potential license information between the parties.
- Negotiation of Agreements. Agent shall work in association with Inventor in the negotiation of sales, licensing, option or other agreements transferring licensing rights to the Properties.

Obligations of Inventor

Inventor shall perform the following services:

- Technical Assistance and Support. Inventor will consult with licensees of the Properties and provide technical assistance and support for the Properties.

Payments

Inventor agrees that all income paid as a result of any agreement, solicited or negotiated by Agent for the Properties (the "Properties Income") shall be paid directly to Agent and that Agent shall issue payments to Inventor within ten (10) days of Agent's receipt of any Properties Income along with any client accountings as provided by the licensee. As compensation for the services provided above,

Agent shall receive _____% [indicate percentage of income paid to Agent] of any Properties Income, including, but not limited to, any advances, guarantees or license fees. The provisions of this Payments Section shall survive any termination of this Agreement.

Proprietary Rights; Indemnity

Inventor represents and warrants that it has the power and authority to enter into this Agreement and that it is the owner of all proprietary rights, whether they are patent, copyright or otherwise and that the Properties are not in any way based upon any confidential or proprietary information derived from any source other than Inventor. Because Agent is relying on these representations, Inventor agrees to indemnify Agent and its assignees and hold them harmless from any losses or damages resulting from third party claims arising from a breach of these representations. Inventor's indemnification of Agent shall survive any termination of this Agreement.

Disclaimer

Nothing in this Agreement shall be interpreted by Inventor as a promise or guarantee as to the outcome of any solicitation or negotiation by Agent on behalf of Inventor or the Properties.

Confidentiality

The parties acknowledge that each may be furnished or may otherwise receive or have access to information that relates to each other's business and the affairs of the respective clients (the "Information"). The parties agree to preserve and protect the confidentiality of the Information and all physical forms. Information relating to the terms, provisions and substance of this Agreement shall remain within the strictest confidence of both parties, and neither party shall disclose such information to third parties without the prior written consent of the other.

Termination

This Agreement may be terminated at any time at the discretion of either Inventor or Agent, provided that written notice of such termination is furnished to the other party thirty (30) days prior to such termination. If this Agreement is terminated by Inventor, and within _____ [number of months] months of termination, Inventor enters into an agreement to option, license, sell or otherwise exploit the Properties with any company solicited or contacted by Agent on Inventor's behalf, Inventor agrees to pay the fees established in the Payments Section.

General

Nothing contained in this Agreement shall be deemed to constitute either Agent or Inventor a partner, joint venturer or employee of the other party for any purpose. Any material contained in an attachment, exhibit or addendum to this Agreement shall be incorporated in this Agreement. From time to time, the parties may revise the information specified in the attachments or exhibits. Such revisions, if executed by both parties, shall be incorporated in this Agreement and shall be binding on the parties. This Agreement may not be amended except in writing signed by both parties. Each and all of the rights and remedies provided for in this Agreement shall be cumulative. No waiver by either party of any right shall be construed as a waiver of any other right. If a court finds any provision of this Agreement invalid or unenforceable as applied to any circumstance, the remainder of this Agreement shall be interpreted so as best to effect the intent of the parties. This Agreement shall be governed by

and interpreted in accordance with the laws of the State of _____
[insert state law that shall govern the agreement]. Any controversy or claim arising out of or relating to this Agreement, or the breach of this Agreement shall be settled by arbitration in accordance with the rules of the American Arbitration Association and judgment upon the award rendered by the arbitrator(s) may be entered in any court having jurisdiction. The prevailing party shall have the right to collect from the other party its reasonable costs and attorney's fees incurred in enforcing this agreement. Any such arbitration hearing shall include a written transcript of the proceedings and a written explanation for any final determination. This Agreement expresses the complete understanding of the parties with respect to the subject matter and supersedes all prior proposals, agreements, representations and understandings.

If these terms and conditions are agreeable, please sign and execute both copies of this Agreement and return one copy to Agent.

INVENTOR: AGENT:

_____   _____
Signature   Signature

_____   _____
Name/Title   Name/Title

_____   _____
Company   Company

_____   _____
Date   Date

One-Way Nondisclosure Agreement

Parties

This Nondisclosure agreement (the "Agreement") is entered into by and between _____
_____
_____ *[insert your name, business form and address]*
("disclosing party") and _____
_____ *[insert name, business form*
and address of person or company to whom you will disclose information] ("receiving party") for the
purpose of preventing the unauthorized disclosure of Confidential Information (as defined below).

Summary

Disclosing party may disclose confidential and proprietary trade secret information to receiving
party. The parties mutually agree to enter into a confidential relationship with respect to the
disclosure of certain proprietary and confidential information (the "Confidential Information").

Definition of Confidential Information (Written or Oral)

For purposes of this Agreement, "Confidential Information" shall include all information or material
that has or could have commercial value or other utility in the business in which disclosing party is
engaged. In the event that Confidential Information is in written form, the disclosing party shall label
or stamp the materials with the word "Confidential" or some similar warning. In the event that
Confidential Material is transmitted orally, the disclosing party shall promptly provide a writing
indicating that such oral communication constituted Confidential Information.

Exclusions From Confidential Information

Receiving party's obligations under this Agreement shall not extend to information that is: (a) publicly
known at the time of disclosure under this Agreement or subsequently becomes publicly known
through no fault of the receiving party, (b) discovered or created by the receiving party prior to the
time of disclosure by disclosing party or (c) otherwise learned by the receiving party through
legitimate means other than from the disclosing party or anyone connected with the disclosing party.

Obligations of Receiving Party

The receiving party shall hold and maintain the Confidential Information of the other party in strictest
confidence for the sole and exclusive benefit of the disclosing party. The receiving party shall
carefully restrict access to any such Confidential Information to persons bound by this Agreement,
only on a need-to-know basis. The receiving party shall not, without prior written approval of the
disclosing party, use for the receiving party's own benefit, publish, copy or otherwise disclose to others, or permit the use by others for their benefit or to the detriment of the disclosing party, any of the
Confidential Information. The receiving party shall return to disclosing party any and all records,
notes, and other written, printed or tangible materials in its possession pertaining to the Confidential
Information immediately on the written request of disclosing party.

Time Periods

The nondisclosure and confidentiality provisions of this Agreement shall survive the termination of any relationship between the disclosing party and the receiving party.

Miscellaneous

Nothing contained in this Agreement shall be deemed to constitute either party a partner, joint venturer or employee of the other party for any purpose. This Agreement may not be amended except in a writing signed by both parties. If a court finds any provision of this Agreement invalid or unenforceable as applied to any circumstance, the remainder of this Agreement shall be interpreted so as best to effect the intent of the parties. This Agreement shall be governed by and interpreted in accordance with the laws of the State of _____ *[insert your state of residence]*. Any controversy or claim arising out of or relating to this Agreement, or the breach of this Agreement, shall be settled by arbitration in accordance with the rules of the American Arbitration Association and judgment upon the award rendered by the arbitrator(s) may be entered in any court having jurisdiction. The prevailing party shall have the right to collect from the other party its reasonable costs and attorney's fees incurred in enforcing this agreement. Any such arbitration hearing shall include a written transcript of the proceedings and a written explanation for any final determination. This Agreement expresses the complete understanding of the parties with respect to the subject matter and supersedes all prior proposals, agreements, representations and understandings. This Agreement and each party's obligations shall be binding on the representatives, assigns and successors of such party. Each party has signed this Agreement through its authorized representative.

DISCLOSING PARTY:

_____   _____
Disclosing Party's Name   Date

RECEIVING PARTY:

_____   _____
Receiving Party's Name/Title   Date

Mutual Nondisclosure Agreement

Parties

This Nondisclosure agreement (the "Agreement") is entered into by and between _____

_____

_____

_____

[insert your name, business form and address] and _____

_____

[insert name, business form and address of other person or company with whom you are exchanging information] (collectively referred to as the "parties") for the purpose of preventing the unauthorized disclosure of Confidential Information (as defined below).

Summary

The parties may disclose confidential and proprietary trade secret information to each other for the purpose of exploring a possible business relationship. The parties mutually agree to enter into a confidential relationship with respect to the disclosure by one or each (the "disclosing party") to the other (the "receiving party") of certain proprietary and confidential information (the "Confidential Information").

Definition of Confidential Information (Written or Oral)

For purposes of this Agreement, "Confidential Information" shall include all information or material that has or could have commercial value or other utility in the business in which disclosing party is engaged. In the event that Confidential Information is in written form, the disclosing party shall label or stamp the materials with the word "Confidential" or some similar warning. In the event that Confidential Material is transmitted orally, the disclosing party shall promptly provide a writing indicating that such oral communication constituted Confidential Information.

Exclusions From Confidential Information

Receiving party's obligations under this Agreement shall not extend to information that is: (a) publicly known at the time of disclosure under this Agreement or subsequently becomes publicly known through no fault of the receiving party, (b) discovered or created by the receiving party prior to the time of disclosure by disclosing party or (c) otherwise learned by the receiving party through legitimate means other than from the disclosing party or anyone connected with the disclosing party.

Obligations of Receiving Party

The receiving party shall hold and maintain the Confidential Information of the other party in strictest confidence for the sole and exclusive benefit of the disclosing party. The receiving party shall carefully restrict access to any such Confidential Information to persons bound by this Agreement, only on a need-to-know basis. The receiving party shall not, without prior written approval of the disclosing party, use for the receiving party's own benefit, publish, copy or otherwise disclose to others, or permit the use by others for their benefit or to the detriment of the disclosing party, any of the Confidential Information. The receiving party shall return to disclosing party any and all records, notes and other written, printed or tangible materials in its possession pertaining to the Confidential Information immediately on the written request of disclosing party.

Time Periods

The nondisclosure and confidentiality provisions of this Agreement shall survive the termination of any relationship between the disclosing party and the receiving party.

Miscellaneous

Nothing contained in this Agreement shall be deemed to constitute either party a partner, joint venturer or employee of the other party for any purpose. This Agreement may not be amended except in a writing signed by both parties. If a court finds any provision of this Agreement invalid or unenforceable as applied to any circumstance, the remainder of this Agreement shall be interpreted so as best to effect the intent of the parties. This Agreement shall be governed by and interpreted in accordance with the laws of the State of _____ *[insert your state of residence]*. Any controversy or claim arising out of or relating to this Agreement, or the breach of this Agreement, shall be settled by arbitration in accordance with the rules of the American Arbitration Association and judgment upon the award rendered by the arbitrator(s) may be entered in any court having jurisdiction. The prevailing party shall have the right to collect from the other party its reasonable costs and attorney's fees incurred in enforcing this agreement. Any such arbitration hearing shall include a written transcript of the proceedings and a written explanation for any final determination. This Agreement expresses the complete understanding of the parties with respect to the subject matter and supersedes all prior proposals, agreements, representations and understandings. This Agreement and each party's obligations shall be binding on the representatives, assigns and successors of such party. Each party has signed this Agreement through its authorized representative.

DISCLOSING PARTY:

_____   _____
Disclosing Party's Name   Date

RECEIVING PARTY:

_____   _____
Receiving Party's Name/Title   Date

Contract Worksheet

Licensee

Name of Licensee Business _____

Licensee Address _____

_____

Licensee Business Form

☐ sole proprietorship ☐ general partnership ☐ limited partnership

☐ corporation ☐ limited liability company

State of incorporation _____

Name, position and phone number of person signing for licensee: _____

_____

Property Definition

Patent No. _____

Patent Application Serial No. _____

Copyrightable Features _____

_____

Copyright Registration No(s). _____

Trade Secrets _____

_____

Trademarks _____

_____

Trademark Registration No(s). _____

_____

Licensed Product Definition

Industry (Have you limited the license to a particular industry?) _____

_____

Product (Have you limited the license to a particular product or products?) _____

_____

Territory

☐ Worldwide   ☐ Countries _____

☐ States _____

Rights Granted (check those rights granted to licensee)

☐ sell   ☐ make or manufacture   ☐ distribute

☐ use   ☐ revise   ☐ import

☐ lease   ☐ right to improvements   ☐ derivatives (copyright)

☐ copy (copyright) ☐ advertise   ☐ promote

☐ other rights _____

☐ other rights _____

☐ other rights _____

Rights Reserved

☐ all rights reserved (except those granted in license)

☐ no rights reserved

☐ specific rights reserved _____

Have you signed any other licenses? If so, do you need to reserve specific rights? _____

_____

Term

Have you agreed upon:

☐ a fixed term (How long? _____)   ☐ a term limited by patent length

☐ unlimited term until one party terminates   ☐ an initial term with renewals (see below)

☐ other _____

Renewals

If you have agreed upon an initial term with renewals:

How many renewal periods? _____ How long is each renewal period? _____

What triggers renewal?

☐ Licensee must notify of intent to renew.

☐ Licensor must notify of intent to renew.

☐ Agreement renews automatically unless Licensee indicates it does not want to renew.

Net Sales Deductions

What is the licensee permitted to deduct when calculating net sales?

☐ quantity discounts   ☐ debts & uncollectibles   ☐ sales commissions

☐ promotion and marketing costs   ☐ fees   ☐ freight & shipping

☐ credits & returns   ☐ other _____

Is there a cap on the total amount of the deductions?   ☐ Yes   ☐ No

If so, how much? _____

Royalty Rates

Licensed Products _____%   Combination Products _____%

Accessory Products _____%

Per Use Royalty _____% or Usage Standard _____

Other Products _____%   Other Products _____%

Do you have any sliding royalty rates? _____

Advances and Lump Sum Payments

Advance $ _____   Date Due _____

Lump Sum Payment(s) $_____   Date Due _____

Guaranteed Minimum Annual Royalty (GMAR)

GMAR $ _____   Date Due _____

Does the GMAR carry forward credits?   ☐ Yes   ☐ No

Does the GMAR carry forward deficiencies?   ☐ Yes   ☐ No

Audit Rights

No. of audits permitted per year _____

No. of days notice _____

Option Agreement

Introduction

This Option Agreement (the "Agreement") is made between _____

_____

[insert your name, address and business form] (referred to as "Inventor") and _____

_____

[insert the company's name, address and business form] (referred to as "Company"). Inventor and Company shall be collectively referred to as "the parties." Inventor is the owner of certain proprietary rights to an invention tentatively referred to as the "_____

_____" *[insert the name of your invention].*

Company desires to acquire an exclusive option to enter into a License Agreement for these ideas, processes and technologies. The parties agree as follows:

The Properties; Licensed Products

Inventor is the owner of licensing rights to all inventions embodied in U.S. Patent No.

_____ *[insert patent number],* a copy of which is attached as Attachment A, and to all other proprietary rights, including but not limited to copyrights, trade secrets, formulas, research data, know-how and specifications related to the invention presently known as

"_____" *[insert the*

name of your invention] and referred to in this Option Agreement as "the Properties." Inventor has submitted the Properties to Company. Inventor represents that he has the authority to grant rights to Company for the Properties. Company desires an exclusive option to enter into a License Agreement to sell the Properties as incorporated in Company's products ("the Licensed Products").

Exclusive Option

For the consideration provided below, Inventor grants to Company the exclusive option to enter into a license agreement (the "License Agreement") for the Properties. The License Agreement shall be substantially similar to that attached to this Option Agreement as Attachment B and shall incorporate the License Terms as set forth below.

Terms & Conditions of Option

Company shall have six months from the date of execution of this Agreement (the "Option Period") to exercise its option for the Properties. During the Option Period, Inventor shall refrain from offering or granting any third party any rights to the Properties which will interfere with the exercise of the option granted to Company. In consideration for the option and rights granted in this Option Agreement, Company shall pay to Inventor the nonrefundable sum of $_____ *[insert amount of option payment].* In the event that Company exercises its option, such payment shall be considered as an advance against future royalties.

License

In the event Company decides to enter into a License Agreement, such agreement shall contain the business terms as set forth below.

License Grant

Exclusive worldwide license of all rights to the Properties, including, but not limited to, any patent, copyright or similar rights, if applicable. No assignment or sublicensing of rights without written consent of Inventor.

Term

For the life of any patents obtained on the Properties or fifteen years, whichever is longer.

☐ **Advances** *[Optional]*

A nonrefundable advance against royalties of $_____ *[insert amount of advance]* to be paid as follows: _____% *[indicate when advance is to be paid]*.

Royalties; Net Sales

_____ *[insert royalty rate]* % of Net Sales of the Licensed Products. Net Sales are defined as Company's gross sales minus returns that are actually credited. Gross sales are the total amount on invoices billed to customers.

☐ **Guaranteed Minimum Annual Royalty** *[Optional]*

A Guaranteed Minimum Annual Royalty of $_____ *[insert amount of GMAR]* payable (in advance) at the beginning of each calendar year of the Licensing Agreement. Company may carry forward or cumulate royalty deficiencies for any year in which the minimum royalty guarantee did not exceed the actual royalties earned by Inventor.

Confidentiality

The parties acknowledge that each may be furnished or have access to confidential information that relates to each other's business (the "Information"). In the event that Information is in written form, the disclosing party shall label or stamp the materials with the word "Confidential" or some similar warning. In the event that Information is transmitted orally, the disclosing party shall promptly provide a writing indicating that such oral communication constituted Information. The parties agree to preserve and protect the confidentiality of the Information and no party shall disclose such Information to third parties without the prior written consent of the other.

Termination

Company shall have the right to terminate this Option Agreement at any time, upon written notice to Inventor. In the event: (a) Company elects to terminate this Option Agreement, or (b) Company has not exercised its option before the end of the Option Period, or (c) Company materially breaches this Agreement, Company agrees to promptly return to Inventor all rights, models and documentation in and to the Properties and not to use or disclose to any third parties, information relating to the Properties. In such an event, Inventor shall be free to license the Properties to others with no further obligation to Company and Company shall have no further obligation to Inventor with the exception of any confidentiality agreements executed by the parties (the terms of which are incorporated in this Option Agreement) and which shall survive the termination of this Option Agreement.

General; Miscellaneous

Any material contained in an attachment, exhibit or addendum to this Option Agreement shall be incorporated by reference in this Option Agreement. Nothing contained in this Option Agreement shall be deemed to constitute either Inventor or Company a partner, joint venturer or employee of the other party for any purpose. This Option Agreement may not be amended except in a writing signed by both parties. No waiver by Inventor of any right shall be construed as a waiver of any other right. If a court finds any provision of this Option Agreement invalid or unenforceable as applied to any circumstance, the remainder of this Option Agreement shall be interpreted so as best to effect the intent of the parties. This Option Agreement shall be governed by and interpreted in accordance with the laws of the State of _____ *[insert your state of residence].* Any controversy or claim arising out of or relating to this Option Agreement, or the breach of this Option Agreement shall be settled by arbitration in accordance with the rules of the American Arbitration Association and judgment upon the award rendered by the arbitrator(s) may be entered in any court having jurisdiction. The prevailing party shall have the right to collect from the other party its reasonable costs and attorney's fees incurred in enforcing this agreement. Any such arbitration hearing shall include a written transcript of the proceedings and a written explanation for any final determination. This Option Agreement expresses the complete understanding of the parties with respect to the subject matter and supersedes all prior proposals, agreements, representations and understandings.

If these terms and conditions are agreeable, please sign and execute both copies of this Option Agreement.

_____   _____
Inventor   Date

_____   _____
Company   Date

License Agreement

Introduction

This License Agreement (the "Agreement") is made between _____ _____ (referred to as "Licensor")
[insert Licensor's name, business form and address], and _____ _____ (referred to as "Licensee")
[insert Licensee's name, business form and address].

   Licensor and Licensee shall be collectively referred to as "the parties." Licensor is the owner of certain proprietary rights to an invention referred to as _____ _____ *[insert name of invention]*.
Licensee desires to license certain rights in the invention. Therefore the parties agree as follows:

The Property *[Select One]*

☐ **Patent Issued**
The "Property" refers to the invention(s) described in U.S. Patent No(s). _____
Insert patent number(s)] .

☐ **Patent Not Yet Issued**
The "Property" refers to the invention(s) described in U.S. Patent Application No(s). _____
Insert patent application number], a copy of which is attached to this agreement.

☐ **Patent & Improvements**
The property is defined as the invention(s) described in U.S. Patent No(s). _____
[Insert patent number] and any improvements, reissues or extensions, as well as any continuations, divisions or substitute U.S. patent applications that shall be based on the patent(s); and any patent applications corresponding to the above-described patent(s) and patent applications that are issued, filed or to be filed in any and all foreign countries.

☐ **Copyright, Trade Secrets and Trademarks: No Patents**
The Property refers to all proprietary rights, including but not limited to copyrights, trade secrets, formulas, research data, know-how and specifications related to the invention commonly known as the _____ *[name of invention]* as well as any trademark rights and associated good will. A more complete description is provided in the attached Exhibit A.

☐ **Copyright or Trademark Registration**
The Property refers to all proprietary rights, including but not limited to copyrights as embodied in Copyright Registration No. _____ dated _____
(or Trademark Registration No. _____ dated _____
and associated good will).

☐ **Patents and Copyright, Trade Secrets and Trademarks**
The "Property" refers to all inventions described in U.S. Patent No. _____
[insert patent number] and to all other proprietary rights, including but not limited to copyrights, trade secrets, formulas, research data, know-how and specifications related to the invention commonly known as _____
[name of invention] as well as any trademark rights and associated good will. A more complete description is provided in the attached Exhibit A.

Licensed Products *[Select One]*

☐ *Licensed Products Specifically Defined*

Licensed Products are defined as the Licensee products incorporating the Property and specifically described in Exhibit A (the "Licensed Products").

☐ *No Limitations on Licensed Products Definition*

Licensed Products are defined as any products sold by the Licensee that incorporate the Property.

☐ *No Limitations on Licensed Process Definition*

A Licensed Process is any commercial application of the Process by the Licensee. *[Remember to change all references in the agreement to Licensed Process, rather than products.]*

Grant of Rights

Licensor grants to Licensee a/an_____ *[exclusive or nonexclusive]* license to make, use and sell the Property solely in association with the manufacture, sale, use, promotion or distribution of the Licensed Products.

Sublicense *[Select One]*

☐ *Consent to Sublicense Required*

Licensee may sublicense the rights granted pursuant to this agreement provided: Licensee obtains Licensor's prior written consent to such sublicense, and Licensor receives such revenue or royalty payment as provided in the Payment section below. Any sublicense granted in violation of this provision shall be void.

☐ *Consent to Sublicense Not Unreasonably Withheld*

Licensee may sublicense the rights granted pursuant to this agreement provided: Licensee obtains Licensor's prior written consent to such sublicense. Licensee's consent to any sublicense shall not be unreasonably withheld; and Licensor receives such revenue or royalty payment as provided in the Payment section below. Any sublicense granted in violation of this provision shall be void.

Reservation of Rights *[Select One]*

☐ *All Rights Reserved*

Licensor expressly reserves all rights other than those being conveyed or granted in this Agreement.

☐ *Reservation of Rights Expressly Excluding a Particular Industry*

Licensor expressly reserves all rights other than those being conveyed or granted in this agreement, including but not limited to the right to license the Properties in _____
_____ *[list a particular market which you want to expressly exclude, for example, "the computer and video game market"].*

Territory *[Select One]*

☐ *Statement of Territory*

The rights granted to Licensee are limited to _____
[insert the territory] (the "Territory").

☐ *Limiting Cross-Territory Sales*

The rights granted to Licensee are limited to _____
[insert the territory] (the "Territory"). Licensee shall not make, use or sell the Licensed Products or any products which are confusingly or substantially similar to the Licensed Products in any country outside the Territory and will not knowingly sell the Licensed Products to persons who intend to resell them in a country outside the Territory.

Term *[Select One]*

☐ *Specified Term With Renewal Rights*

This Agreement shall commence upon the latest signature date, (the "Effective Date") and shall extend for a period of _____ years (the "Initial Term") *[insert number of years for initial term, for example, "two years"].*

Following the Initial Term, this agreement may be renewed by Licensee under the same terms and conditions for _____ *[insert number of renewal terms]* consecutive _____ _____ *[insert length of each renewal term, for example, "two-year"]* periods (the "Renewal Terms"), provided that Licensee provides written notice of its intention to renew this agreement within 30 days before the expiration of the current term. In no event shall the Agreement extend longer than the date of expiration of the patent listed in the definition of the Property.

☐ *Term for the Length of Patent Only*

This Agreement shall commence upon the Effective Date and shall expire simultaneously with the expiration of the longest-living patent (or patents) or last-remaining patent application as listed in the definition of the Property, whichever occurs last, unless sooner terminated pursuant to a provision of this Agreement.

☐ *Short Term With Renewal Rights Based Upon Sales*

This Agreement shall commence upon the Effective Date and shall extend for a period of _____ *[insert number of years]* years (the "Initial Term") and thereafter may be renewed by Licensee under the same terms and conditions for consecutive _____ *[insert number of years]*-year periods (the "Renewal Terms"), provided that:

(a) Licensee provides written notice of its intention to renew this agreement within 30 days before the expiration of the current term,

(b) Licensee has met the sales requirements as established in Exhibit A *[if you choose this alternative be sure to include the sales requirements in Exhibit A]*, and

(c) in no event shall the Agreement extend longer that the date of expiration of the longest-living patent (or patents) or last-remaining patent application as listed in the definition of the Property.

☐ *No Patents; Indefinite Term*

This Agreement shall commence upon the Effective Date and shall continue until terminated pursuant to a provision of this Agreement.

☐ *Fixed Yearly Term*

This Agreement shall commence upon the Effective Date and shall continue for _____ *[insert number of years]* unless sooner terminated pursuant to a provision of this Agreement.

☐ *Term for as Long as Licensee Sells Licensed Products*

This Agreement shall commence upon the Effective Date as specified in Exhibit A and shall continue for as long as Licensee continues to offer the Licensed Products in commercially reasonable quantities unless sooner terminated pursuant to a provision of this Agreement.

Royalties

All royalties ("Royalties") provided for under this Agreement shall accrue when the respective items are sold, shipped, distributed, billed or paid for, whichever occurs first. Royalties shall also be paid by the Licensee to Licensor on all items, even if not billed (including, but not limited to introductory offers, samples, promotions or distributions) to individuals or companies which are affiliated with, associated with or subsidiaries of Licensee.

Net Sales

"Net Sales" are defined as Licensee's gross sales (i.e., the gross invoice amount billed customers) less quantity discounts and returns actually credited. A quantity discount is a discount made at the time of shipment. No deductions shall be made for cash or other discounts, for commissions, for uncollectible accounts or for fees or expenses of any kind which may be incurred by the Licensee in connection with the Royalty payments.

☐ Advance Against Royalties *[Optional]*

As a nonrefundable advance against Royalties (the "Advance"), Licensee agrees to pay to Licensor upon execution of this Agreement the sum of $_____ *[insert the amount of the advance, if any]*.

Licensed Product Royalty *[Select One]*

☐ *Royalty for All Rights*

Licensee agrees to pay a Royalty of _____% *[insert amount of royalty]* of all Net Sales revenue of the Licensed Products ("Licensed Product Royalty").

☐ *Hybrid Royalty; Patent and Non-Patented Rights*

Licensee agrees to pay a Royalty of _____% *[insert amount of royalty]* of all Net Sales revenue of the Licensed Products ("Licensed Product Royalty"). The "Licensed Product Royalty" shall be allocated according to the percentages as provided in this Agreement. In the event that a patent does not issue or an issued patent expires or is otherwise terminated, the allocated percentage for such patent or pending patent shall be subtracted from the Licensed Product Royalty. The Licensed Product Royalty shall be adjusted accordingly.

_____% of the royalty for the license of the patent No. _____.

_____% of the royalty for the license of pending patent No. _____.

_____% of the royalty for the license of trade secrets [or trademarks, copyrights or other intellectual property].

☐ Guaranteed Minimum Annual Royalty Payment [Optional]

In addition to any other advances or fees, Licensee shall pay an annual guaranteed royalty (the "GMAR") as follows: _____ *[insert the terms of your GMAR: for example, $10,000 per year]*. The GMAR shall be paid to Licensor annually on _____ *[insert the date when the GMAR should be paid each year]*. The GMAR is an advance against royalties for the twelve-month period commencing upon payment. Royalty payments based on Net Sales made during any year of this Agreement shall be credited against the GMAR due for the year in which such Net Sales were made. In the event that annual royalties exceed the GMAR, Licensee shall pay the difference to Licensor. Any annual royalty payments in excess of the GMAR shall not be carried forward from previous years or applied against the GMAR.

☐ License Fee [Optional]

As a nonrefundable, nonrecoupable fee for executing this license, Licensee agrees to pay to Licensor upon execution of this Agreement the sum of $_____.

☐ Royalties on Spin-Offs [Optional]

Licensee agrees to pay a Royalty ("Spin-Off Product Royalty") of _____% [insert appropriate royalty percentage] for all Net Sales of "Spin-Off Products." A "Spin-Off Product" is any product that is derived from, based on or adapted from the Licensed Product, provided that if the product uses the Property it shall be considered to be a Licensed Product and not a Spin-Off Product.

☐ Adjustment of Royalties for Third Party Licenses [Optional]

In the event that any Licensed Product (or other items for which Licensee pays Royalties to Licensor) incorporates third party character licenses, endorsements or other proprietary licenses, Licensor agrees to adjust the Royalty rate to _____% [insert appropriate royalty percentage] for such third party licenses. Licensee shall notify Licensor of any such third party licenses prior to manufacture. Third party licenses shall not include licenses accruing to an affiliate, associate or subsidiary of Licensee.

☐ F.O.B. Royalties [Optional]

Licensee agrees to pay the Royalty ("F.O.B. Royalty") of _____% [insert appropriate royalty percentage] for all F.O.B. sales of Licensed Products.

☐ Sublicensing Revenues [Optional]

In the event of any sublicense of the rights granted pursuant to this Agreement, Licensee shall pay to Licensor _____% [insert the amount of the sublicensing percentage] of all sublicensing revenues.

Payments and Statements to Licensor

Within 30 days after the end of each calendar quarter (the "Royalty Period"), an accurate statement of Net Sales of Licensed Products along with any Royalty payments or sublicensing revenues due to Licensor shall be provided to Licensor, regardless of whether any Licensed Products were sold during the Royalty Period. All payments shall be paid in United States currency drawn on a United States bank. The acceptance by Licensor of any of the statements furnished or Royalties paid shall not preclude Licensor questioning the correctness at any time of any payments or statements.

Audit

Licensee shall keep accurate books of account and records covering all transactions relating to the license granted in this Agreement, and Licensor or its duly authorized representatives shall have the right upon five days' prior written notice, and during normal business hours, to inspect and audit Licensee's records relating to the Property licensed under this Agreement. Licensor shall bear the cost of such inspection and audit, unless the results indicate an underpayment greater than $_____ [insert amount of underpayment, for example, "$1,000"] for any six-month period. In that case, Licensee shall promptly reimburse Licensor for all costs of the audit along with the amount due with interest on such sums. Interest shall accrue from the date the payment was originally due and the interest rate shall be 1.5% per month, or the maximum rate permitted by law, whichever is less. All books of account and records shall be made available in the United States and kept available for at least two years after the termination of this Agreement.

Late Payment

Time is of the essence with respect to all payments to be made by Licensee under this Agreement. If Licensee is late in any payment provided for in this Agreement, Licensee shall pay interest on the payment from the date due until paid at a rate of 1.5% per month, or the maximum rate permitted by law, whichever is less.

Licensor Warranties

Licensor warrants that it has the power and authority to enter into this Agreement and has no knowledge as to any third party claims regarding the proprietary rights in the Property which would interfere with the rights granted under this Agreement.

Indemnification by Licensor *[Select One]*

☐ *Statement of Licensor Indemnification*
Licensor shall indemnify Licensee and hold Licensee harmless from any damages and liabilities (including reasonable attorneys' fees and costs) arising from any breach of Licensor's warranties as defined in Licensor's Warranties, above, provided: (a) such claim, if sustained, would prevent Licensee from marketing the Licensed Products or the Property; (b) such claim arises solely out of the Property as disclosed to the Licensee, and not out of any change in the Property made by Licensee or a vendor, or by reason of an off-the-shelf component or by reason of any claim for trademark infringement; (c) Licensee gives Licensor prompt written notice of any such claim; (d) such indemnity shall only be applicable in the event of a final decision by a court of competent jurisdiction from which no right to appeal exists; and (e) the maximum amount due from Licensor to Licensee under this paragraph shall not exceed the amounts due to Licensor under the Payment Section from the date that Licensor notifies Licensee of the existence of such a claim.

☐ *Licensor Indemnification With Fund*
Licensor shall indemnify Licensee and hold Licensee harmless from any damages and liabilities (including reasonable attorneys' fees and costs) arising from any breach of Licensor's warranties as defined in Licensor's Warranties, above, provided: (a) such claim, if sustained, would prevent Licensee from marketing the Licensed Products or the Property; (b) such claim arises solely out of the Property as disclosed to the Licensee, and not out of any change in the Property made by Licensee or a vendor, or by reason of an off-the-shelf component or by reason of any claim for trademark infringement; (c) Licensee gives Licensor prompt written notice of any such claim; (d) such indemnity shall only be applicable in the event of a final decision by a court of competent jurisdiction from which no right to appeal exists; and (e) the maximum amount due from Licensor to Licensee under this paragraph shall not exceed the amounts due to Licensor under the Payment Section from the date that Licensor notifies Licensee of the existence of such a claim. The maximum amount due from Licensor to Licensee under this paragraph shall not exceed _____% *[50% to 100%]* of the amounts due to Licensor under the Payment Section *[if you have numbered the sections of your agreement, include the number of the payment section]* from the date that Licensor notifies Licensee of the existence of such a claim. After the commencement of a lawsuit against Licensee that comes within the scope of this paragraph, Licensee may place _____% *[same percentage as listed above]* of the royalties due to Licensor under the Payment Section in a separate interest-bearing fund which shall be called the "Legal Fund." Licensee may draw against such Legal Fund to satisfy all of the reasonable expenses

of defending the suit and of any judgment or settlement made in regard to this suit. In the event the Legal Fund is insufficient to pay the then-current defense obligations, Licensee may advance monies on behalf of the Legal Fund and shall be reimbursed as payments are credited to the Legal Fund. Licensor's liability to Licensee shall not extend beyond the loss of its royalty deposit in the Legal Fund. After the suit has been concluded, any balance remaining in the Legal Fund shall be paid to Licensor and all future royalties due to Licensor shall be paid to Licensor as they would otherwise become due. Licensee shall not permit the time for appeal from an adverse decision on a claim to expire.

Licensee Warranties

Licensee warrants that it will use its best commercial efforts to market the Licensed Products and that their sale and marketing shall be in conformance with all applicable laws and regulations, including but not limited to all intellectual property laws.

Indemnification by Licensee

Licensee shall indemnify Licensor and hold Licensor harmless from any damages and liabilities (including reasonable attorneys' fees and costs) (a) arising from any breach of Licensee's warranties and representation as defined in the Licensee Warranties, above; (b) arising out of any alleged defects or failures to perform of the Licensed Products or any product liability claims or use of the Licensed Products; and (c) arising out of advertising, distribution or marketing of the Licensed Products.

☐ Limitation of Licensor Liability *[Optional]*

Licensor's maximum liability to Licensee under this agreement, regardless on what basis liability is asserted, shall in no event exceed the total amount paid to Licensor under this Agreement. Licensor shall not be liable to Licensee for any incidental, consequential, punitive or special damages.

Intellectual Property Protection

Licensor may, but is not obligated to seek, in its own name and at its own expense, appropriate patent, trademark or copyright protection for the Property. Licensor makes no warranty with respect to the validity of any patent, trademark or copyright which may be granted. Licensor grants to Licensee the right to apply for patents on the Property or Licensed Products provided that such patents shall be applied for in the name of Licensor and licensed to Licensee during the Term and according to the conditions of this Agreement. Licensee shall have the right to deduct its reasonable out-of-pocket expenses for the preparation, filing and prosecution of any such U.S. patent application (but in no event more than $5,000) from future royalties due to Licensor under this Agreement. Licensee shall obtain Licensor's prior written consent before incurring expenses for any foreign patent application.

Compliance With Intellectual Property Laws

The license granted in this Agreement is conditioned on Licensee's compliance with the provisions of the intellectual property laws of the United States and any foreign country in the Territory. All copies of the Licensed Product as well as all promotional material shall bear appropriate proprietary notices.

Infringement Against Third Parties

In the event that either party learns of imitations or infringements of the Property or Licensed Products, that party shall notify the other in writing of the infringements or imitations. Licensor shall have the right to commence lawsuits against third persons arising from infringement of the Property or

Licensed Products. In the event that Licensor does not commence a lawsuit against an alleged infringer within 60 days of notification by Licensee, Licensee may commence a lawsuit against the third party. Before the filing suit, Licensee shall obtain the written consent of Licensor to do so, and such consent shall not be unreasonably withheld. Licensor will cooperate fully and in good faith with Licensee for the purpose of securing and preserving Licensee's rights to the Property. Any recovery (including, but not limited to, a judgment, settlement or licensing agreement included as resolution of an infringement dispute) shall be divided equally between the parties after deduction and payment of reasonable attorneys' fees to the party bringing the lawsuit.

Exploitation

Licensee agrees to manufacture, distribute and sell the Licensed Products in commercially reasonable quantities during the term of this Agreement and to commence such manufacture, distribution and sale within the following time period: _____ *[insert time period, for example "six months"]*. This is a material provision of this Agreement.

Samples & Quality Control

Licensee shall submit a reasonable number of production samples of the Licensed Product to Licensor to assure that the product meets Licensor's quality standards. In the event that Licensor fails to object in writing within ten business days after the date of receipt, the Licensed Product shall be deemed to be acceptable. At least once during each calendar year, Licensee shall submit two production samples of each Licensed Product for review. The quality standards applied by Licensor shall be no more rigorous than the quality standards applied by Licensee to similar products.

Insurance

Licensee shall, throughout the Term, obtain and maintain, at its own expense, standard product liability insurance coverage, naming Licensor as additional named insureds. Such policy shall: (a) be maintained with a carrier having a Moody's rating of at least B; and (b) provide protection against any claims, demands and causes of action arising out of any alleged defects or failure to perform of the Licensed Products or any use of the Licensed Products. The amount of coverage shall be a minimum of $_____ *[insert amount of insurance coverage]* with no deductible amount for each single occurrence for bodily injury or property damage. The policy shall provide for notice to the Agent and Licensor from the insurer by Registered or Certified Mail in the event of any modification or termination of insurance. Licensee shall furnish Licensor and Agent a certificate from its product liability insurance carrier evidencing insurance coverage in favor of Licensor, and in no event shall Licensee distribute the Licensed Products before the receipt by the Licensor of evidence of insurance. The provisions of this section shall survive termination for three years.

Confidentiality

The parties acknowledge that each may be furnished or have access to confidential information that relates to each other's business (the "Confidential Information"). In the event that Information is in written form, the disclosing party shall label or stamp the materials with the word "Confidential" or some similar warning. In the event that Confidential Information is transmitted orally, the disclosing party shall promptly provide a writing indicating that such oral communication constituted Information. The parties agree to maintain the Confidential Information in strictest confidence for the sole and exclusive benefit of the other party and to restrict access to such Confidential Information to persons bound by this Agreement, only on a need-to-know basis. Neither party, without prior written approval of the other, shall use or otherwise disclose to others, or permit the use by others of the Confidential Information.

Termination *[Select One]*

☐ *Initial Term With Renewals From the Term Section*
This Agreement terminates at the end of two years (the "Initial Term") unless renewed by Licensee under the terms and conditions as provided in the Term Section of this Agreement.

☐ *Fixed Term*
This Agreement shall terminate at the end of _____ *[insert number of years]* years unless terminated sooner under a provision of this Agreement.

☐ *Term Based Upon Length of Patent Protection*
This Agreement shall terminate with the expiration of the longest-living patent (or patents) or last-remaining patent application (as listed in the definition of the Property), whichever occurs last, unless terminated sooner under a provision of this Agreement.

☐ *Initial Term With Renewals*
This Agreement terminates at the end of two years (the "Initial Term") unless renewed by Licensee under the same terms and conditions for consecutive two-year periods (the "Renewal Terms") provided that Licensee provides written notice of its intention to renew this agreement within 30 days prior to expiration of the current term. In no event shall the Agreement extend longer than the date of expiration of the longest-living patent (or patents) or last-remaining patent application as listed in the definition of the Property.

☐ *Termination at Will: Licensee's Option*
Upon 90 days' notice, Licensee may, at its sole discretion, terminate this agreement by providing notice to the Licensor.

Licensor's Right to Terminate

Licensor shall have the right to terminate this Agreement for the following reasons:

   a) Licensee fails to pay Royalties when due or fails to accurately report Net Sales, as defined in the Payment Section of this Agreement, and such failure is not cured within 30 days after written notice from the Licensor;

   b) Licensee fails to introduce the product to market by _____ *[insert date by which Licensee must begin selling Licensed Products]* or to offer the Licensed Products in commercially reasonable quantities during any subsequent year;

   c) Licensee fails to maintain confidentiality regarding Licensor's trade secrets and other Information;

   d) Licensee assigns or sublicenses in violation of the Agreement; or

   e) Licensee fails to maintain or obtain product liability insurance as required by the provisions of this Agreement.

☐ *Terminate as to Territory Not Exploited [Optional]*
Licensor shall have the right to terminate the grant of license under this Agreement with respect to any country or region included in the Territory in which Licensee fails to offer the Licensed Products for sale or distributions or to secure a sublicensing agreement for the marketing, distribution and sale of the product within two years of the Effective Date.

Effect of Termination

Upon termination of this Agreement, all Royalty obligations as established in the Payments Section shall immediately become due. After the termination of this license, all rights granted to Licensee under this Agreement shall terminate and revert to Licensor, and Licensee will refrain from further manufacturing, copying, marketing, distribution or use of any Licensed Product or other product which incorporates the Property. Within 30 days after termination, Licensee shall deliver to Licensor a statement indicating the number and description of the Licensed Products which it had on hand or is in the process of manufacturing as of the termination date. Licensee may dispose of the Licensed Products covered by this Agreement for a period of three months after termination or expiration, except that Licensee shall have no such right in the event this agreement is terminated according to the Licensor's Right to Terminate, above. At the end of the post-termination sale period, Licensee shall furnish a royalty payment and statement as required under the Payment Section. Upon termination, Licensee shall deliver to Licensor all tooling and molds used in the manufacture of the Licensed Products. Licensor shall bear the costs of shipping for the tooling and molds.

Survival

The obligations of Sections _____ *[insert section names or numbers that will survive termination]* shall survive any termination of this Agreement.

Attorneys' Fees and Expenses

The prevailing party shall have the right to collect from the other party its reasonable costs and necessary disbursements and attorneys' fees incurred in enforcing this Agreement.

Dispute Resolution *[Select One]*

☐ *Arbitration*

If a dispute arises under or relating to this Agreement, the parties agree to submit such dispute to binding arbitration in the state of _____ *[insert state in which parties agree to arbitrate]* or another location mutually agreeable to the parties. The arbitration shall be conducted on a confidential basis pursuant to the Commercial Arbitration Rules of the American Arbitration Association. Any decision or award as a result of any such arbitration proceeding shall be in writing and shall provide an explanation for all conclusions of law and fact and shall include the assessment of costs, expenses and reasonable attorneys' fees. Any such arbitration shall be conducted by an arbitrator experienced in _____
[insert industry experience required for arbitrator] and in invention licensing law and shall include a written record of the arbitration hearing. The parties reserve the right to object to any individual who shall be employed by or affiliated with a competing organization or entity. An award of arbitration may be confirmed in a court of competent jurisdiction.

☐ *Mediation and Arbitration*

The Parties agree that every dispute or difference between them, arising under this Agreement, shall be settled first by a meeting of the Parties attempting to confer and resolve the dispute in a good faith manner. If the Parties cannot resolve their dispute after conferring, any Party may require the other Parties to submit the matter to non-binding mediation, utilizing the services of an impartial professional mediator approved by all Parties. If the Parties cannot come to an agreement following mediation, the Parties agree to submit the matter to binding arbitration at a location mutually agreeable to the Parties. The arbitration shall be conducted on a confidential basis pursuant to the Commercial

Arbitration Rules of the American Arbitration Association. Any decision or award as a result of any such arbitration proceeding shall include the assessment of costs, expenses and reasonable attorney's fees and shall include a written record of the proceedings and a written determination of the arbitrators. Absent an agreement to the contrary, any such arbitration shall be conducted by an arbitrator experienced in intellectual property law. The Parties reserve the right to object to any individual who shall be employed by or affiliated with a competing organization or entity. In the event of any such dispute or difference, either Party may give to the other notice requiring that the matter be settled by arbitration. An award of arbitration shall be final and binding on the Parties and may be confirmed in a court of competent jurisdiction.

☐ *Alternative Dispute Resolution*

If a dispute arises and cannot be resolved by the parties, either party may make a written demand for formal resolution of the dispute. The written request will specify the scope of the dispute. Within 30 days after such written notice, the parties agree to meet, for one day, with an impartial mediator and consider dispute resolution alternatives other than litigation. If an alternative method of dispute resolution is not agreed upon within 30 days of the one-day mediation, either side may start litigation proceedings.

Governing Law

This Agreement shall be governed in accordance with the laws of the State of _____ *[insert the choice of state law]*.

Jurisdiction

The parties consent to the exclusive jurisdiction and venue of the federal and state courts located in _____ *[insert county and state in which parties agree to litigate]* in any action arising out of or relating to this Agreement. The parties waive any other venue to which either party might be entitled by domicile or otherwise.

Waiver

The failure to exercise any right provided in this Agreement shall not be a waiver of prior or subsequent rights.

Invalidity

If any provision of this Agreement is invalid under applicable statute or rule of law, it is to be considered omitted and the remaining provisions of this Agreement shall in no way be affected.

Entire Understanding

This Agreement expresses the complete understanding of the parties and supersedes all prior representations, agreements and understandings, whether written or oral. This Agreement may not be altered except by a written document signed by both parties.

Attachments & Exhibits

The parties agree and acknowledge that all attachments, exhibits and schedules referred to in this Agreement are incorporated in this Agreement by reference.

Notices

Any notice or communication required or permitted to be given under this Agreement shall be sufficiently given when received by certified mail, or sent by facsimile transmission or overnight courier.

No Joint Venture

Nothing contained in this Agreement shall be construed to place the parties in the relationship of agent, employee, franchisee, officer, partners or joint ventures. Neither party may create or assume any obligation on behalf of the other.

Assignability *[Select One]*

☐ *Statement of Assignability*

Licensee may not assign or transfer its rights or obligations pursuant to this Agreement without the prior written consent of Licensor. Any assignment or transfer in violation of this section shall be void.

☐ *Consent Not Unreasonably Withheld*

Licensee may not assign or transfer its rights or obligations pursuant to this Agreement without the prior written consent of Licensor. Such consent shall not be unreasonably withheld. Any assignment or transfer in violation of this section shall be void.

☐ *Consent Not Needed for Licensee Affiliates or New Owners*

Licensee may not assign or transfer its rights or obligations pursuant to this Agreement without the prior written consent of Licensor. However, no consent is required for an assignment or transfer that occurs: (a) to an entity in which Licensee owns more than 50% of the assets, or (b) as part of a transfer of all or substantially all of the assets of Licensee to any party. Any assignment or transfer in violation of this Section shall be void.

Each party has signed this Agreement through its authorized representative. The parties, having read this Agreement, indicate their consent to the terms and conditions by their signature below.

LICENSOR: LICENSEE:

_____   _____
Signature   Signature

_____   _____
Name/Title   Name/Title

_____   _____
Company   Company

_____   _____
Date   Date

EXHIBIT A

THE PROPERTY
[insert description of the Property]

_____

_____

_____

_____

_____

_____

_____

_____

_____

_____

LICENSED PRODUCTS
[indicate type of products, for example "medical supply products"]

_____

_____

_____

_____

_____

_____

_____

_____

_____

_____

_____

Escrow Agreement

This escrow agreement (the "Escrow Agreement") is made between _____
_____
_____

[insert your name, address and business form] ("Inventor"), and _____
_____
_____

[insert licensee's name, address and business form] ("Company") and _____
_____
_____ *[insert escrow
agent's name and address]* ("Escrow Agent"). Company is a licensee of Inventor's invention (the
"Properties") indicated on Exhibit A and pursuant to the agreement dated _____
[insert date of license agreement] between Inventor and Company (the "License Agreement"). The
parties desire to place trade secrets and related materials with the Escrow Agent. Therefore, Inventor,
Company and the Escrow Agent agree as follows:

1. Escrow Items

Inventor will promptly place copies of _____
_____ *[indicate what
will be placed into escrow]* (collectively the "Escrow Items") under the control of the Escrow Agent.

2. Release Conditions

Company may submit a request for release of the Escrow Items to the Escrow Agent (the "Company's
Release Request") upon the occurrence of one of the following release conditions during the term of
the License Agreement:

    (a) Inventor's filing of a petition under any chapter of the federal bankruptcy laws; or

    (b) the failure by Inventor, within 30 days after Company's request to Inventor, to perform any of
Inventor's obligations under the License Agreement.

3. Duties of Escrow Agent

The Escrow Agent's duties are limited to:

    (a) Safeguarding the Escrow Items against access or disclosure by any person or entity except as
expressly provided in this Agreement; and

    (b) Notifying Inventor and Company that it has received the Escrow Items.

The Escrow Agent is not responsible for verifying the accuracy or completeness of the Escrow Items.
The Escrow Agent's performance under this Escrow Agreement is excused when it is prevented by
acts of God and other causes beyond its reasonable control.

4. Release of Escrow Item

The Escrow Agent shall, subject to the conditions below, deliver all of the Escrow Items to Company
upon receipt of Company's Release Request, signed by an Officer of Company stating that Company
has the right to receive all of the Escrow Items.

Company shall deliver its Release Request to the Escrow Agent and, at the same time, deliver a duplicate copy of its Release Request to Inventor. Within 30 days after the receipt of such Release Request, the Inventor shall either (a) submit a written authorization to the Escrow Agent to make the delivery, or (b) submit a written objection to the Escrow Agent and to Company.

If the Inventor authorizes the delivery or does not respond within 30 days, the Escrow Agent shall deliver the Escrow Items. If Inventor objects to the delivery of the Escrow Items in writing, Company and Inventor shall attempt in good faith to agree upon their respective rights to the Escrow Items. If Company and Inventor do so agree, an agreement shall be prepared and signed by both Company and Inventor and delivered to the Escrow Agent. The Escrow Agent shall be entitled to rely on the agreement and shall distribute the Escrow Items. If no such agreement can be reached after good faith negotiation, either Company or Inventor may demand arbitration of the matter. In such an event, the American Arbitration Association shall be asked to appoint one arbitrator, familiar with the subject matter of the license in the United States, to rule on the matter. Such appointment is to be in accordance with the then-current Commercial Arbitration Rules of the American Arbitration Association. The decision of the arbitrator shall be binding and conclusive upon Company and Inventor, and the Escrow Agent shall be entitled to act in accordance with such decision. Any such arbitration shall be held in _____ *[indicate county and state for arbitration]*. The prevailing party in any such arbitration shall be entitled to receive payments of its attorneys' fees and costs.

The Escrow Agent's duties may be altered, amended, modified or revoked only by a writing signed by officers of Company and Inventor.

The Escrow Agent shall not be personally liable for any act the Escrow Agent may do or omit to do under this Agreement while acting in good faith and in the exercise of its own good judgment.

The Escrow Agent is authorized to comply with orders, judgments or decrees of any court and of the arbitrator provided for above. If the Escrow Agent obeys or complies with any such order, judgment or decree, the Escrow Agent shall not be liable to any of the parties or to any other person, firm or corporation by reason of such compliance. The Escrow Agent shall not be liable even if such order, judgment or decree is subsequently reversed, modified, annulled, set aside, vacated or found to have been entered without jurisdiction.

The Escrow Agent shall be entitled to employ legal counsel and other experts as the Escrow Agent may deem necessary to advise it in connection with its obligations under this Escrow Agreement, and may rely upon the advice of such counsel and pay such counsel reasonable compensation.

The responsibilities of the Escrow Agent shall terminate if the Escrow Agent resigns by written notice to Company and Inventor. In that event, Inventor shall promptly appoint a successor Escrow Agent, subject to the approval of Company. Company's approval will not be unreasonably withheld.

It is understood and agreed that should any dispute arise with respect to the delivery, ownership or right of possession of any part of the Escrow Items held by the Escrow Agent, the Escrow Agent is directed to retain the Escrow Items in its possession, without liability to anyone, until such dispute is settled either by: 1) mutual written agreement, as provided above; or by 2) final order, decree or judgment of the arbitrator provided for above; or by 3) a court of competent jurisdiction after the time for appeal has expired and no appeal has been perfected. The Escrow Agent shall be under no duty to institute or defend any such proceedings.

5. Miscellaneous

Any notice or communication required or permitted to be given under this Escrow Agreement shall be sufficiently given when received by certified mail, or sent by facsimile transmission or overnight courier. If any term, provision, covenant or condition of this Agreement is held to be illegal or invalid for any reason whatsoever, such illegality or invalidity shall not affect the validity of the remainder of this Agreement. This Escrow Agreement and the License Agreement constitute the entire understanding between the Parties and can only be modified by written agreement. No party may assign or transfer its rights under this Escrow Agreement without the prior written consent of the other parties This Agreement shall be binding upon the parties and their respective successors and assigns.

LICENSEE:

_____   _____
Signature   Date

LICENSOR:

_____   _____
Signature   Date

ESCROW AGENT:

_____   _____
Signature   Date

Checklist for Reviewing a License Agreement

1. Introductory Statement

   _____
   _____
   _____

2. The Property

   _____
   _____
   _____

3. Licensed Products

   _____
   _____
   _____

4. The Grant of Rights

   _____
   _____
   _____

5. Sublicense

   _____
   _____
   _____

6. Reservation of Rights

   _____
   _____
   _____

7. Territory

   _____
   _____
   _____

8. Term

   _____
   _____
   _____

9. Payment

   _____
   _____
   _____

10. Payment Statements

   _____
   _____

11. Late Payments and Audit Rights

   _____
   _____
   _____

12. Warranties and Indemnification

   _____
   _____
   _____

13. Intellectual Property Protection

   _____
   _____
   _____

14. Exploitation

   _____
   _____
   _____

15. Samples and Quality Control

   _____
   _____
   _____

16. Insurance

   _____
   _____
   _____

17. Confidentiality

   _____
   _____
   _____

18. Termination

   _____
   _____
   _____

19. Post-Termination

   _____
   _____
   _____

20. Survival

   _____
   _____

21. Attorneys' Fees

_____

_____

_____

22. Arbitration or Mediation

_____

_____

_____

23. Governing Law

_____

_____

_____

24. Jurisdiction

_____

_____

_____

25. Assignability

_____

_____

_____

26. New Inventions

_____

_____

_____

27. Grant Back of Improvements

_____

_____

_____

28. Escrow Provisions

_____

_____

_____

29. Exhibits and Attachments

_____

_____

_____

30. Miscellaneous Provisions
   a. Waiver

_____

_____

_____

b. Invalidity

_____

_____

_____

c. Entire Understanding

_____

_____

_____

d. Attachments & Exhibits

_____

_____

_____

e. Notices

_____

_____

_____

f. No Joint Venture

_____

_____

_____

31. Service Provisions
   a. Installation

_____

_____

_____

b. Technical Assistance

_____

_____

_____

c. Training

_____

_____

_____

d. Development

_____

_____

_____

e. Acceptance Provisions

_____

_____

_____

License Dates

1. Effective date　　　　　　　　　　　————————————————

2. Renewal dates　　　　　　　　　　　————————————————

3. Renewal notice date　　　　　　　　————————————————

4. Delivery dates　　　　　　　　　　　————————————————

5. Service dates　　　　　　　　　　　————————————————

6. Advance or lump sum payment dates　————————————————

7. Royalty payment dates　　　　　　　————————————————

8. Dates to complain about royalty statements　————————————————

9. Date for introduction of licensed products　————————————————

10. Termination date　　　　　　　　　————————————————

11. Delivery of insurance information　————————————————

Index